How Muftis Think

Studies in Islamic Law and Society

VOLUME 44

The titles published in this series are listed at *brill.com/sils*

How Muftis Think

Islamic Legal Thought and Muslim Women in Western Europe

By

Lena Larsen

BRILL

LEIDEN | BOSTON

The Library of Congress Cataloging-in-Publication Data

Names: Larsen, Lena, author. | Moe, Christian, translator.
Title: How muftis think : Islamic legal thought and Muslim women in Western Europe / by Lena Larsen.
Description: Leiden ; Boston : Brill, [2018] | Series: Studies in islamic law and society ; v. 44 | Includes bibliographical references and index.
Identifiers: LCCN 2018012757 (print) | LCCN 2018013523 (ebook) | ISBN 9789004367852 (E-book) | ISBN 9789004367791 (hardback : alk. paper)
Subjects: LCSH: Women (Islamic law)–Europe, Western. | Muftis (Muslim officials)–Europe, Western. | Fatwas–Europe, Western. | Islamic law–Interpretation and construction.
Classification: LCC KBP526.32.L37 (ebook) | LCC KBP526.32.L37 A34 2018 (print) | DDC 297.082/094–dc23
LC record available at https://lccn.loc.gov/2018012757

Translated by Christian Moe

Typeface for the Latin, Greek, and Cyrillic scripts: "Brill". See and download: brill.com/brill-typeface.

ISSN 1384-1130
ISBN 978-90-04-36779-1 (hardback)
ISBN 978-90-04-36785-2 (e-book)

This book is printed on acid-free paper and produced in a sustainable manner.

Printed by Printforce, the Netherlands

Contents

Acknowledgements

I am grateful to everyone who has given me academic advice, made comments, and discussed the topic with me through the many years I was devoted to the research which resulted in this book. First of all, a warm thanks to my mentors: Kari Vogt (University of Oslo) has followed my project from idea to book manuscript. I have benefited from her extensive knowledge and sober judgment, both in conversations and comments on texts. Jakob Skovgaard Petersen (University of Copenhagen) encouraged me to write, and gave me precise and helpful feedback on texts. Tore Lindholm (University of Oslo) introduced me to Tranøy's theory of moden common morality, and supported me throughout the project.

Many thanks to Alexandre Caeiro for sharing his reflections with me in fruitful conversations on our common field of research; to Ziba Mir-Hosseini for her encouragement, for shaping me intellectually, and for opening her house for me to stay during fieldwork in London; and to Muhammad Khalid Masud for his wise reflections on fatwa-giving and his interpretation of the objectives of Sharia, on which I draw in my discussion. Thanks also to numerous colleagues and friends whom I met during my fieldwork.

And not least many thanks to the muftis and other actors in the field who, with their kindness and patience, made it possible to gather the material on which this book is based. A special thanks to Mohammed al-Mansoori for conversations that opened my eyes to the world of muftis, and gave me a sense of its complexity.

The project started in 2001 with the idea of looking at fatwas for women in Western Europe. Thanks to a Ph.D. grant from the research programme "Cultural Complexity in the multicultural Norway" (Culcom), led by Thomas Hylland Eriksen at the University of Oslo, I was able to be a full-time research fellow from 2006 to 2010. Hylland Eriksen poured from his cornucopia of knowledge and inspired me with his ability to see opportunities and spread enthusiasm. He and the other research fellows made Culcom a special place.

The Norwegian Center for Human Rights at the University of Oslo provided me with office space and facilities, as well as financial support for translating the amended manuscript for publication. Thanks to Martha Herkenhoff, who provided excellent library services with unforgettable grace and kindness.

Jørgen Nielsen (then at the University of Copenhagen) was in my Ph.D committee and encouraged me to publish the dissertation as a book.

Many thanks to the anonymous reviewer at Brill Publishers, whose comments helped me to improve the manuscript and turn a thesis into a book.

A big thanks to Christian Moe. He translated the manuscript, and has commented throughout the process. His kind, but critical questions have helped me immensely to formulate my ideas in a way that communicates with a reader. The manuscript would not have reached publication without his support and patience.

A warm thanks to my husband Basim Ghozlan. Not only has he been at hand to discuss the meanings of Arabic words and sentences, he has also patiently tolerated hearing about new discoveries, enthusiasms and frustrations—and put up with the egoism that may be necessary for completing an academic work, included spending part of our vacations working on the text.

I want to share the joy of having this book published with my children Mounir, Karim and Dina. They have often made it clear that they are proud of my academic achievements, even when the topic is far outside their field of interest.

Last, but not least: I am solely responsible for the text. All errors and weaknesses are my own.

A Note on Transliteration

Transliteration of Arabic words in this book follows the example of the *International Journal of Middle East Studies*, with diacritics indicating long vowels (*ā*, *ī*, *ū*) and emphatic consonants (*ḍ*, *ḥ*, *ṣ*, *ṭ*, *ẓ*), half circles for *ayn* and *hamza*, and commonly used English digraphs. A simplified transliteration without diacritics is used for names, and words such as mufti, fatwa, Sharia and Quran are treated as common English words. Please note that quotations will differ, as the source transliteration has been preserved.

Introduction

"I urge you women to revolt!" said the late Dr. Zaki Badawi, head of the Muslim College and the Muslim Sharia Court, during a conference lecture in 2000.[1]

The suggestion was very well received by the women, but it caused much consternation among the men in the audience. Those who clearly did not accept this challenge argued that it clashed with the Islamic feminine ideal of the good wife and mother. Furthermore, a woman's place was in the home. When all was said and done, a revolt would be a threat to the family. Some of the women in the room strongly objected that the traditional feminine ideal did not accord with the lived reality of Muslim women in Europe, particularly the fact that many women worked a "double shift," and that their jobs outside the home were poorly paid. The audience only calmed down when Badawi ended the discussion by stating: "I urge you women to revolt, in order to be treated according to Islamic standards". What is it that makes "Islamic standards" soothing? Clearly, the lofty ideals perceived by the men did not accord with the experiences of the women. While the women wanted change, with a focus on rights, the men took up a defensive position on behalf of a patriarchal ideal of femininity.

The status of women is intensely debated among Muslims in Western Europe, both as part of a global debate, and as a central issue in the encounter of Islamic identity and Western societies. Muslim women are being drawn between two competing sets of norms: on the one hand, the traditional Islamic view of unequal gender rights, with an emphasis on women's submission and obedience; on the other, equal rights, with an emphasis on women's rights and equality before the law. Women's challenge is to find "Islamic" solutions to this dilemma. They search for "Islamic standards" in answers to the questions they have, rooted in their own experiences.

In this book, I examine fatwas given from 1992 onwards[2] as proposed solutions for the challenges faced by Muslim women in Western Europe, and ask whether Islamic scholars contribute, through their fatwas, to reconciling adherence to

1 Dr. Badawi (1922–2006) was lecturing on Islamic legal thought for minorities at the conference *Muslims in the New Millennium: Multiculturalism, Identity and Citizenship*, held in London in September 2000.

2 The institutionalization of fatwa-giving for Muslims in Western Europe started with the international conference that resulted in the report *Muslims in the West: A Fiqh Seminar in France* (1992).

 | DOI: 10.1163/9789004367852_002

the Islamic tradition with the Western European ideal of equality. I also tell the story of the muftis behind the fatwas. They represent a trend that understands the situation of women as a problem in the modern age, and sees its solution as lying in Islam. They devote particular attention to the local context, and to what they perceive as the reality in which the women who ask the questions live their lives.[3] In this way, the fatwas may be seen as supportive of the call for women to revolt in in order to be treated according to "Islamic standards."

This way of framing the question is at odds with with a common Western view of fatwas as the very embodiment of a clash between Islamic values and the modern common morality[4] and sense of justice. That perception is not least due to the so-called Rushdie fatwa issued by Khomeini, which has led the Western public to understand fatwa as "death sentence".

A fatwa, in Islamic legal thought, is a normative legal statement[5] made in answer to a question.[6] The institution is traditionally justified with reference to the Quran: The underlying formulation is "They ask thee ... Say ...," which is a minimal definition, as it only indicates form and not substance.[7] The Quran also uses various verb forms of the root *f-t-y* for question-and-answer activities: (i) "asking for guidance" (*istiftāʾ*) and (ii) "giving guidance" (*aftāʾ*).[8] The terminology for the fatwa institution in Islamic legal thought is derived from

---

3 This refers to actors within the modern Islamic revival movement, initiated by Jamal al-Din al-Afghani (d. 1897) and Muhammad Abduh (d. 1905). Islam was argued to be the solution for the problem of backwardness and stagnation compared with Europe (Abukhalil 2009). A line may be traced from the establishment of this movement in Egypt to Western Europe. In order to understand the argument that "Islam is the solution", it is important to understand the "Islamic Awakening" (*al-sahwa al-islamiyya*) that has taken hold since the 1960s. In the Arab world, it was tied to Islamist movement, particularly the Muslim Brotherhood (see Lacroix 2011, 51–52). Central concerns of the movement have been the focus of the scholars on a renewal of Islamic jurisprudence, and what Lacroix calls a claim of monopoly over *fiqh al-waqiʿ* ("the understanding of reality").

4 The Norwegian philosopher Knut Erik Tranøy (d. 2012) defines common morality (*allmennmoralen*) as "... the moral ideas and concepts held by most people, whatever their sources, of what is morally good and evil, of moral virtues and vices, of right and wrong in practical life." Tranøy 2001, 104.

5 Eggen 2001, 94.

6 I use the terms "law," "legal thought" and "legal" in a broader sense, and not exclusively about the positive law of states or international legal orders.

7 Quran 2:189.

8 Quran 4:127, 176.

the same root: *muftī*, the fatwa-giver; *mustaftī*, the questioner; *futyā* or *iftāʾ*, fatwa-giving; and *istiftāʾ*, request for a fatwa.

The best way to understand the specific nature of a fatwa is to compare it with a judgment, *qaḍāʾ*. A fatwa is information about a *ḥukm sharʿī*, an Islamic norm, whereas a *qaḍāʾ* is handed down to the parties in the judicial system. A fatwa does not imply any command addressed to the questioner or anyone else. The questioner (*al-mustaftī*) may hold that the fatwa is correct, and follow it; or reject it, and turn to a different mufti. A *ḥukm qaḍāʾī*, a judgment, is tied to a sanctioning authority. A mufti renders a fatwa as "God's judgment," that is, concerning the inner aspects of the case, whereas a judge renders judgment based on the external aspects. A judgment concerns a specific case, whereas a fatwa has general validity, both for the questioner and for others.[9] Furthermore, a judgment concerns only "this world" (*dunya*), whereas a fatwa has a view to both this world and the other world (*al-ākhira*).[10]

Fatwas are expressions of the encounter between text and experienced reality, and have played a key role for believers throughout history. Jakob Skovgaard-Petersen writes: "… fatwas not only helped regulate and islamize people's conduct, but also brought all sorts of human action into the sphere of *fiqh*. The fatwa and the mufti, then, are situated at the interface between worldly dealings and theorizing about them."[11]

By studying fatwas, I seek to answer: What are the questions asked? What answers are given, and how are they argued? What image of women is drawn in the fatwas? How and to what extent do the muftis argue that their answers are appropriate for women in Western Europe? From where do the fatwas draw their authority? And is there a dialectics that reconciles these sets of norms, or defers the conflict between them?

Muftis and Fatwas in Europe

Muslims in the West are a heterogeneous group with regard to nationality, language, and religious tradition, and this is reflected in the institutionalization of Islam, which bears the mark of the different backgrounds of immigrant Muslims. Islamic institutions in Western Europe are often extended branches of the corresponding institutions in the countries of origin, each with their religious

9 For the difference between judgment and fatwa, see *Mawsūʿat al-fiqhiyya* (Mawsuʿa 2003, 32:31).

10 Masud, Messick, and Powers 1996, 19.

11 Skovgaard-Petersen 1997, 2.

authorities. In the West, consequently, we witness a great diversity of fatwas, often with mutually contradictory contents.

During the 1990s there crystallized four categories of fatwa-giving in Europe:

1. *The local community scholar* often offers religious advice to members of his own community, and represents the community in the country of origin.
2. *Sharia councils* in European countries have been founded to assist Muslims in need of Sharia legal solutions; in a local setting, this especially means assisting women in family conflicts.[12] Of these, the one best known in the literature is the Islamic Sharia Council in England.
3. *Nation-wide organizations* like the French Union des Organisations Islamiques de France (UOIF), through the Dar al-Fatwa (House of Fatwa), give directions in *fiqh* matters. It is not least in France that we find a debate on the challenges that Muslims face in a European context, including women's issues.[13]
4. *Transnational* fatwa bodies like The European Council for Fatwa and Research, based in Ireland and founded in 1997. The Council's aim is to attempt to unify the jurisprudential views of different scholars with regard to the main *fiqh* issues, give collective answers (fatwas) to satisfy the needs of Muslims in Europe, publish legal studies dealing with new issues in the European arena, and guide Muslims in general and Muslim youth in particular by spreading an "authentic Islam".[14]

In this book, I examine the interplay between legal argument and social and cultural reality, as perceived by Muslims. I therefore choose to follow Talal Asad in his description of Islam as a "discursive tradition". Asad elaborates:

> Islam is neither a distinctive social structure nor a heterogeneous collection of beliefs, artifacts, customs, and morals. It is a tradition. [...] A tradition consists essentially of discourses that seek to instruct practitioners regarding the correct form and purpose of a given practice that,

12 Vogt 1995; King 1995; conversation with S.M. Darsh in November 1993. Darsh headed the Islamic Sharia Council until his death in 1997.

13 The difference between the Sharia-council category and the UOIF's Dar al-Fatwa is that members of the latter mainly give fatwas individually, whereas the decisions of the Islamic Sharia Council appear as collective fatwas.

14 From the Council's presentation of itself in ECFR 2002a.

> precisely because it is established, has a history. These discourses relate conceptually to a *past* (when the practice was instituted, and from which the knowledge of its point and proper performance has been transmitted) and a *future* (how the point of that practice can best be secured in the short or the long term, or why it should be modified or abandoned), through a *present* (how it links to other practices, institutions, and social conditions).[15]

Since the Muslim presence in Western Europe is of relatively recent date, it implies a new social reality, and a concomitant need for new *ijtihād* (independent reasoning) in the giving of fatwas. It might be fruitful to stress fatwas that imply a new *ijtihād*, especially since the fatwas are given for the European context. This led me to Syed Darsh (d. 1997), who in the 1990s answered questions in his column in the Islamic magazine *Q-News*. He has been described as "the first mufti of Western Europe," and was known for taking local conditions into account when answering questions.[16]

Darsh was also involved in cooperation with other scholars on religio-legal questions of Muslim life and conduct. This kind of cooperation led *inter alia* to the founding of the European Council for Fatwa and Research (ECFR, in Arabic *al-Majlis al-ūrūbī lil-iftāʾ wal-buḥūth*) in 1997. The Union des Organisations Islamiques de France (UOIF) was central to the establishment of the Council. Subsequently, the UOIF has been responsible for a local branch of the ECFR, and has established the Dar al-Fatwa in Paris. The fatwas given by this body follow the same method as those of the ECFR.

These three actors—two local ones (one in England, one in France) and one transnational—thus represent one trend among several within Sunni Islam in Europe. Most often, this trend is tied to the Muslim Brotherhood (*al-Ikhwān al-muslimūn*), which was founded in Egypt in 1928.[17] It is helpful here to distinguish between the Brotherhood's organization (*tanẓīm*) and their thought (*fikr*). It is in terms of their ties to Muslim Brotherhood thought that these actors may be described as an Ikhwan trend, and distinguished from other broad trends, such as the Salafi and madhhab ones.[18]

---

15 Asad 1986, 14.

16 Conversation with Fuad Nahdi, editor of *Q-News*, Istanbul, July 2006.

17 See Ternisien 2005; Roald 2001a.

18 The Salafi trend stresses an interpretation of the Sharia as unchangeable. This trend is described e.g. in Roald 2001a, 50–54. The madhhab trend stresses affiliation with a school of law and seeking answers to questions within the traditional teaching of the school.

A number of actors have contributed to their thought, not least Yusuf al-Qaradawi (b. 1926), whom many consider one of the leading scholars in Sunni Islam.[19] When giving fatwas, Qaradawi employs a certain conceptual and methodological apparatus in his *ijtihād*. This apparatus originates with Muhammad Abduh (d. 1905), a scholar and state Mufti of Egypt. Abduh was one of the architects of Islamic modernism, based on renewal (*tajdīd*) of Islamic thought. He placed emphasis on *ijtihād*, and by distinguishing between *ʿibādāt* (ritual actions) and *muʿāmalāt* (social transactions), he made space for norms to change in a new context.

The heritage of Abduh branches widely.[20] The fatwa-givers I have selected represent one branch. A line may be drawn from Abduh via Muhammad Rashid Rida (d. 1935) and Muhammad al-Ghazali (d. 1996) to Yusuf al-Qaradawi, who is a central actor in Europe. Not least, Qaradawi advocates establishing a particular jurisprudence for minorities (*fiqh al-aqalliyyāt*). All of these are known for taking social and cultural context into consideration when giving fatwas. It is a relevant question, then, whether muftis from other trends do not consider such factors, and whether the actors mentioned are isolated in their use of concepts and methods.

One opportunity to investigate this question was the Model Muslim Marriage Contract, launched in 2008, which provoked some strong and contradictory reactions. The many points raised in this document are all based on fatwas given by mufti Barkatullah Abdulkadir, who is of Indian origin. He was educated at the conservative Dar al-Uloom in Deoband, which follows the Hanafi school. My talks with Abdulkadir revealed his long experience and commitment in the British context as a background for the fatwas.[21] Furthermore, it emerged that he in part used methods and concepts from the same canon as the other muftis in my material.[22] This shows that the divides between trends are not necessarily watertight.

I have chosen to focus on one trend among several, then, so this book does not aim to give a comprehensive overview of all fatwas being given in Western Europe.

---

19 See e.g. Gräf and Skovgaard-Petersen 2009, 1–12.

20 "Revival and Renewal," in *The Oxford Encyclopedia of the Islamic World*, hereafter: OEIW (Abukhalil 2009).

21 Conversation with Barkatullah Abdulkadir, London, 24 Feb 2009.

22 See further discussion of this "canon" in chapter 6.

Three Dimensions of Fatwa

A fatwa has three dimensions: the question, or indication of the issue at hand; the answer, or interpretation; and the justification. All three dimensions are visibly present in my material. The questions asked form a body of empirical evidence that may be used to study the social reality of Muslim women. Thus Jajat Burhanudin, in his article about the spread of Muhammad ʿAbduh's reform ideas in Southeast Asia through the *al-Manār* journal, studies the requests for fatwas rather than the fatwas themselves. He argues that the questions, more so than the fatwas, reflect the changing social and intellectual circumstances of Southeast Asian Muslims at the beginning of the 20th century.[23] Amalia Zomeño, too, indicates the importance of the questions: "The question is the most interesting part of the fatwas in terms of social data, but at the same time, it is the part of the fatwa that has more of a translation of social facts in legal terms."[24] I too will begin with the questions asked, and sort them into a typology as a point of departure for discussing the particular challenges faced by Muslim women in Western Europe.

The answers set out the muftis' views on these challenges. Apart from studying these views, I seek to answer the following questions: How are the texts formed with a view to the intended reader? How is the particular authority that Islamic literature accords to muftis communicated in the fatwas, and how does the mufti express his position vis-à-vis the questioner? How is gender constructed in the fatwas, and what content is given to the notion of the Muslim woman?

I do not focus only on the norms declared in the fatwas, but equally on the independent reasoning (*ijtihād*) that justifies the stated norm, and hereunder, on the concepts and methods used. Do these indicate that the muftis place importance on social and cultural reality in their independent reasoning? If so, what content is attributed to these concepts? The question is relevant in terms of the requirement, formulated in the *ādāb al-muftī* literature, that a mufti be familiar with the context in which a fatwa is given. Nonetheless, Islamic religious leaders' frequent lack of relevant language skills and limited knowledge of the context in which they work is a familiar theme in European public debate.

We have often seen that the statements and attitudes of Muslims have caused consternation, or even disgust. This is probably not because the majority dislikes Muslims in general. More likely, certain statements and attitudes

23 Burhanudin 2005, 10.

24 Zomeño 2008, 32.

give offence because they appear to conflict with the *common morality* of society, "the morality of ordinary people," a notion that the Norwegian philosopher Knut Erik Tranøy thinks deserves more attention among philosophers. Tranøy argues in *Det åpne sinn* (The Open Mind) that there are many different common moralities, and that in countries where Islam is the dominant religion, a common morality anchored in religion must be understood as Islamic morality.[25] The question, however, is whether common morality as interpreted by Tranøy has an Islamic theoretical equivalent that can serve as a model for explaining different views of "good" and "right". In this book I will argue that the theory of *maqāṣid al-sharīʿa*, which Ebrahim Moosa describes as "the ethical turn in Islamic jurisprudence",[26] represents such an equivalent.

The muftis we meet in this book all focus on the *maqāṣid al-sharīʿa* (objectives of Sharia) and the promotion of *maṣlaḥa* (utility) in their fatwa-giving. The notion of *maqāṣid al-sharīʿa* has been well known since Abu Hamid al-Ghazali (d. 1111), but is first and foremost tied to the Muslim scholar Abu Ishaq Ibrahim al-Shatibi (d. 1388), who is the subject of growing interest among contemporary Islamic scholars, also with regard to fatwa-giving.

According to Kamali, the *maqāṣid* concept was first used by Abu Abd Allah al-Tirmidhi al-Hakim (d. 932). The concept is referred to in the works of Imam al-Haramayn al-Juwayni (d. 1085), who was probably the first to classify the *maqāṣid al-sharīʿa* into the three categories of *ḍarūriyyāt* (vital necessities), *ḥājiyyāt* (needs) and *taḥsiniyyāt* (embellishments), which went on to become generally accepted. Al-Juwayni's student Abu Hamid al-Ghazali developed the idea of *maqāṣid* further. His contribution consisted not least in defining the contents of the *ḍarūriyyāt* category: the vital necessities are *dīn* (religion), *nafs* (life), *aql* (the intellect), *nasl* (offspring), and *māl* (property). This list, Kamali says, was clearly based on an interpretation of the prescribed punishments (*ḥudūd*) in the Quran and the Prophet's Sunna. The values that these punishments were meant to protect were defined as fundamental. Later Muslim scholars would expand this list of fundamental values, however. Kamali notes that Shihab al-Din al-Qarafi (d. 1285) added *ʿirḍ* (honour), and Taqi al-Din ibn Taymiyya (d. 1328) added the fulfilment of contracts, preservation of kinship ties, and respect for rights of one's neighbour's in this world, and love of God, honesty, trustworthiness and moral purity with regard to the next world. He thus revised a finite list of values into an open one, Kamali says. Ibn Taymiyya's approach has been endorsed by modern-day scholars, and is being

25 Tranøy 2001, 201.

26 Moosa 2014, 177.

built on inter alia by al-Qaradawi. In conclusion, Kamali claims the list seems ripe for further additions, which will depend on the priorities of each era.[27]

Central to the *maqāṣid* theory is the concept of *maṣlaḥa* (utility, interest).[28] Malik bin Anas (d. 795) is considered the first to have made decisions based on *maṣlaḥa*, even though he never referred to the term in his decisions.[29] Abu Hamid al-Ghazali defined *maṣlaḥa* as preservation of the purpose (*maqṣid*) of the law (*al-sharʿ*), which he defined as preservation of the five *ḍarūriyyāt*.[30] He further divided *maṣlaḥa* into three categories: *maṣlaḥa* that is endorsed by a textual proof, *maṣlaḥa* that is rejected by a textual proof, and *maṣlaḥa* for which there is no textual proof. This latter category (*maṣlaḥa mursala*) is acceptable as long as it is a matter of preserving *maṣlaḥa* with respect to the five objectives of Sharia. As for *maṣlaḥa* that falls under the categories of *ḥājiyyāt* (needs) and *taḥsiniyyāt* (embellishments), al-Ghazali held that supporting textual proof is required for the derivation of a norm. Ibn Qayyim al-Jawziyya (d. 1350) claims that the Sharia is based on *ḥikma* (wisdom) and *maṣāliḥ al-ʿibād* (the interests of God's servants), both in this world and the one to which they shall return, and defines the Sharia, in Muhammad Khalid Masud's translation, as "all justice, kindness, *maṣāliḥ* and *ḥikma*". These principles are of decisive importance for the derivation of norms: "… any rule which departs from justice to injustice … from maṣlaḥa to mafsada (harm) … is not part of Sharīʿa …"[31] According to Masud, *maṣlaḥa* as legal proof has been the most-debated concept in the history of Islamic law.[32] Certain theological and philosophical considerations, according to Masud, have placed limits on the legal validity of the concept. Muslim legal theorists have therefore tended to see *maṣlaḥa* as a means, and not as an independent proof regardless of textual proof.[33] Abu Ishaq al-Shatibi bases his theory of *maqāṣid al-sharīʿa* on *maṣlaḥa*. Masud writes of Shatibi: "In his doctrine of *maqāṣid al-sharīʿa*, Shāṭibī not only develops the concept of *maṣlaḥa* as the basis for rationality and extendibility of Islamic law to changing circumstances, but also presents it as a fundamental principle for the universality and certainty of Islamic law."[34]

---

27 Kamali 2008, 8–12.

28 A survey of research on the concept of *maṣlaḥa* is given in Masud 1995, 129–135.

29 "Maṣlaḥa" in *EI2* (M. Khadduri 2010).

30 Quoted in Masud 1995, 139.

31 Masud 1995, 149.

32 Masud 1995, 161.

33 Masud 1995, viii.

34 Masud 1995, viii.

According to Hallaq, the epistemic foundations of Shatibi's theory are "anchored in comprehensive inductive surveys of all relevant evidence, be it textual or otherwise".[35] He puts these method to radical use: "Al-Shāṭibī's inductive method is not confined to the identification of objects and values but also extends to commands and prohibitions, which may either be obtained from the clear text, or from a collective reading of a number of textual proclamations that may occur in a variety of contexts."[36] This method might allow for some flexibility in jurisprudence. According to Hallaq and Masud, Shatibi's development of *maqāṣid al-sharīʿa* theory is informed by the society of his day. Hallaq insists that Shatibi's theory aimed to restore the "true law of Islam" as a golden mean between two extreme ways of practicing Islam among his contemporaries, the lax attitudes of the muftis and the excessively rigorous demands of a majority of Sufis.[37]

Shatibi's book *al-Muwāfaqāt*, where he discusses his theory of *maqāṣid al-sharīʿa*, has been influential up to the present.[38] According to Masud, for example, Muhammad Abduh encouraged his students to read the book to gain insight into the "true" spirit of Islamic jurisprudence.

The theory of *maqāṣid al-sharīʿa* is highly topical, almost a fad in the early 2000s: Conferences have been held,[39] books published (some translated into English),[40] and the Al-Maqasid Centre in the Philosophy of Islamic Law (*Markaz dirāsāt maqāṣid al-sharīʿa al-islāmiyya*) was established in 2005 as a project of al-Furqan Islamic Heritage Foundation, with Ahmed Zaki Yamani (b. 1930) in a key role.[41] The founding director of the Al-Maqasid Centre, Jasser Auda, has published the book *Maqasid al-Sharia as Philosphy of Islamic Law: A Systems Approach*,[42] which has been translated into several languages. Auda is now also executive director of the London-based Maqasid Institute initiative.[43]

---

35 Hallaq 2003, 165.

36 Kamali 2008, 15.

37 Hallaq 2003, 163.

38 For an overview, see Masud 1995, 108–120.

39 For instance, two conferences at the International Islamic University of Malaysia, the "First International Conference on Maqasid al-Shari'ah" in 2006, and the "International Conference on Jurisprudence of Minorities in the Light of the Objectives of Islamic Law (Maqasid ash-shariah), Identity and Integration" in October 2009, as well as a conference on *maqāṣid al-sharīʿa* at the al-Furqan Foundation.

40 Ibn Ashur 2006; Attia 2007; al-Raysuni 2005.

41 See http://al-maqasid.net/ar/home.php.

42 Auda 2008.

43 Jasser Auda, personal communication, 26 Jun 2015.

The research literature offers descriptions and analyses of *maqāṣid al-sharīʿa*,[44] as well as concepts that fall under this theory, such as *maṣlaḥa* (utility) and *ʿadl* (justice).[45]

I will attempt a brief comparison of Tranøy's interpretation of common morality with *maqāṣid al-sharīʿa*. I seek to uncover a possible correspondence between the concepts of the two models, and to see whether they represent two different languages for the same moral concerns. Furthermore, I will explore whether Tranøy's theory of change in common morality can explain how the general expression "Islamic standards" can include different understandings of women-related questions.

Knut Erik Tranøy's theory of common morality may be read as part of his project of supplying the premises for a global normative ethics.[46] There are different common moralities, depending on their grounding. Tranøy points out that in countries where Islam is the predominant religion, a religiously grounded common morality must be understood as Islamic morality.[47]

A View of the Islamic Legal Tradition

My point of departure is a view of Islamic legal tradition as flexible. The fatwa institute has been attributed with a central role in the development of Islamic legal thought. Schacht describes it as follows:

> The doctrinal development of Islamic law owes much to the activity of the *muftīs*. Their *Fatwās* were often collected in separate works, which are of considerable historical interest because they show us the most urgent problems which arose from the practice in a certain place in a certain time. As soon as a decision reached by a *muftī* on a new kind of problem had been recognised by the common opinion of the scholars as correct, it was incorporated in the handbooks of the school.[48]

---

44 For a description of Shatibi's theory, see Hallaq 1997, 162–206. Masud 1995 analyses al-Shatibi's theory with particular regard to the relationship between legal theory and social change. On the role of *maqāṣid* in the relationship between legal thought and ethics, see Kamali 2009, 23–46. Ibrahim 2006 has written about Rashid Rida and *maqāṣid al-sharīʿa*.

45 An overview of studies on *maṣlaḥa* may be found in Masud 1995, 129–135. Krämer 2007, 20–37 gives a good introduction to the concept of justice in modern Islamic thought.

46 Tranøy 2001, 11.

47 Tranøy 2001, 201.

48 Schacht 1991, 74 f.

Schacht would restrict the importance of the muftis, however, to what he terms the formative period of Islamic law, in line with the thesis of the "closing of the gate of *ijtihād*."[49]

> ... Islamic law, which until the early ʿAbbāsid period had been adaptable and growing, from then onwards became increasingly rigid and set in its final mold. [...] It was not altogether immutable, but the changes which did take place were concerned more with legal theory and the systematic superstructure than with positive law.[50]

Hallaq, in his article "From *Fatwās* to *Furū*," interprets Schacht as follows:

> If we are to make sense of his statements, we must conclude that the *fatwās*, however important they may have been in his view, did not have an effect on the development of Islamic law sufficient to rid it of its rigidity and to set it on a path of continuous development—development commensurate with the changing needs of Muslim societies.[51]

Hallaq disagrees with Schacht, pointing out that some researchers support the view that fatwas on new issues were included in subsequent *fiqh* manuals (that is to say, in substantive law). Not only were fatwas included in the manuals, Hallaq claims, they were also instrumental to changing and updating the substantive law. He seeks to support this claim by showing a connection between the primary fatwa[52] as a legal discourse and as a social instrument. Muftis did not sit in isolation, away from the people, deriving norms through pure speculation.

49 Schacht 1991, 69.

50 Schacht 1991, 75.

51 Hallaq 1994, 30.

52 Hallaq 1994, 32 f. defines primary fatwas as fatwas that have been preserved more or less in their original form, whereas secondary fatwas have undergone editing, and often contain less detail on the circumstances of the question that prompted the fatwa. D. Powers 2002 develops the definition as follows: "A primary fatwa is one that mentions the names of the litigants, the location of the dispute, and the date of specific events; it may also include a transcription of one or more legal documents relating to the case. These details were eliminated when the primary fatwa was transformed into a secondary fatwa. [...] As a result [...] a narrative dealing with a specific and historically contextualised situation was transformed into an abstract case that refers to one or more nameless individuals living in an unspecified place at an undetermined time" (D. Powers 2002, 7).

Hallaq points to a number of legal texts from the four schools of law, showing how fatwas were in fact incorporated into substantive law, and thus came to play a key role in Islamic legal thought (*fiqh*).[53] He concludes: "Any enquiry into the historical evolution and later development of substantive legal doctrine must take account of the *muftī* and his *fatwā*."[54]

Jacob Skovgaard-Petersen, too, appears critical of Schacht, tying his criticism to the choice of texts studied by past specialists in Islam.[55] He lists the various categories of texts studied in the madrasas (places of learning in the religious sciences): *uṣūl* ("roots," the study of the sources of law); *mutūn* (shorter texts that gave concrete expression to the central doctrine of the school of law in question); *shurūḥ* (explanations and commentaries on the *mutūn*); and *fatāwā* (fatwa collections ascribed to famous muftis).[56] He comments: "The immutability of *mutūn* was used by earlier European scholars as proof of the rigid and unchangeable nature of Islamic law ..."[57] On the other hand, he sees the fatwas as the most dynamic part of the Islamic *corpus juris*, hence their value for research purposes.[58]

The Law: Sharia and Fiqh

The idea of a divine law is expressed through the terms Sharia and *fiqh*. The word Sharia, according to EI2, is

> ... common to the Arabic-speaking peoples of the Middle East and designates a prophetic religion in its totality, generating such phrases as sharīʿat Mūsā, sharīʿat al-Masīḥ (the law/religion of Moses or the Messiah), sharīʿat Madjūs (the Zoroastrian religion) or sharīʿatunā (meaning our religion and referring to any of the monotheist faiths). [...] Within Muslim discourse, sharīʿa designates the rules and regulations governing the lives of Muslims.[59]

53 Hallaq 1994, 31–62.
54 Hallaq 1994, 64.
55 Skovgaard-Petersen 1997 is a study of the history of an Egyptian religious institution, the fatwa body *Dār al-iftāʾ*, and those in charge of it.
56 Skovgaard-Petersen 1997, 4–5, drawing on Johansen 1994.
57 Skovgaard-Petersen 1997, 5.
58 Skovgaard-Petersen 1997, 5.
59 "SHarīa" in *Encyclopaedia of Islam, Second Edition*, hereafter EI2 (Calder 2009a).

The *Oxford Dictionary of Islam* defines Sharia as "God's eternal and immutable will for humanity, as expressed in the Qur'an and Muhammad's example (Sunnah), considered binding for all believers; ideal Islamic law."[60] The Quran speaks of Sharia as a divinely appointed way: "Then We gave thee the (right) Way of Religion: so follow thou that (Way) …"[61]

Fiqh, on the other hand, originally means "understanding" and "knowledge," and refers to the tradition of scholars describing and exploring the Sharia.

> In early terminology (to the end of the 700s), fiqh includes both theology and law. In time, however, a usage was established that restricted the concept to legal questions, particularly concrete opinions. The term may therefore be translated by the concept of jurisprudence. [… J]urisprudence is a formulation of Sharia in the form of concrete rules based in the source texts.[62]

To the believer, then, Sharia would refer to the divine quality of the law, whereas *fiqh* is the result of the interpretations of scholars through history. In practice, Western academic studies of religious law are studies of *fiqh*, since this is the only form of the law that is empirically available.[63]

The 19th century is a watershed in the history of religious law. New ideas and innovations from the West, the view of traditional Islam as backward, and the emergence of secular education systems that excluded traditional legal studies led to new approaches to the law.[64] Muslims in the administration, as well as reformists, held that the Sharia should be practical, and resemble Western codified law. The Western description of the Islamic legal tradition as "Islamic law," Norman Calder writes, was in turn adopted into the vocabulary in the Muslim world (in Arabic: *al-qānūn al-islāmī*, "the Islamic law").[65]

The idea of codifying the law won out in independent Muslim states. According to Schacht, this was an expression of Islamic modernism and modern Islamic thought.[66] Norman Anderson describes it as follows:

---

60 "Shariah" in *Oxford Dictionary of Islam* (Esposito 2003, 287 f.).

61 Quran 45:18. I have chosen to translate *ja'alnāk 'alā* as "We gave," rather than "We put thee on," as used in Yusuf Ali's translation.

62 Eggen 2001, 7.

63 Schacht 1991; Masud 1995; Kamali 2003; Hallaq 2005; Hallaq 1997; See e.g. Eggen 2001.

64 "Law: Legal Thought and Jurisprudence" in *OEIW* (Calder 2009b, 386).

65 "Law: Legal Thought and Jurisprudence" in *OEIW* (Calder 2009b, 381).

66 Schacht 1960, 99.

> It was not that ordinary Muslims, generally speaking, were dissatisfied with the law to which they were subject and began to demand its reform, but that these reforms were imposed on them by the government [...] So for the first time in the history of Islam, principles derived from the Sharīʿa were enacted as law by the authority of the State.[67]

The law in question was the Mecelle, the first attempt to codify parts of the Sharia. Introduced in the Ottoman Empire from 1870–1876, it was practised at so-called *nizamī* (secular) courts. Family and inheritance law was kept out, and was first codified in 1917.[68] Codification subsequently took place in many Muslim countries, and has become the norm in the Muslim world, with the exception of Saudi Arabia.

Joseph Schacht, however, takes a critical view of this "codification project" for the Sharia. Traditional Islamic law, he asserts, is more of a doctrine and a method than a law, and its nature is thus incompatible with codification.[69] He argues:

> The legal modernists in the Arab countries of the Near East cannot and will not get away from the spiritual ascendancy and the deeply ingrained influence of traditional Islamic law. [...] Their method of picking isolated fragments of opinions from the early centuries of Islamic law, arranging them into a kind of arbitrary mosaic, and concealing behind this screen an essentially different structure of ideas borrowed from the West, is unreal and artificial. This is [...] why modernist Islamic legislation often appears haphazard and arbitrary. Modernist Islamic jurisprudence and legislation, in order to be sound and permanent, is in need of a more solid and consistent theoretical basis.[70]

In the 20th century, concepts and methods for the derivation of norms have been a central topic in the debate on Sharia and *fiqh*, not least among those Muslim actors who call themselves reformists. In the tradition, correct use of concepts and method is considered important for the orthodoxy of the norms. Ann Elisabeth Mayer puts it this way: "In traditional Islamic law it was the use of recognized juristic methods of interpretation that guaranteed the ortho-

---

67 N. Anderson 1976, 15, 17.

68 "Mecelle" in *OEIW* (Findley 2009).

69 Schacht 1960, 108.

70 Schacht 1960, 119f.

doxy of results, so that diversity in the results could be tolerated …"[71] Different reformist actors have different approaches and make different contributions.[72] What they have in common is their view of Sharia's potential flexibility.

The Muslim arrival and presence in Western Europe involves a new challenge, and a new twist on the problems. What does the Sharia mean in a non-Muslim-majority context? And what is the relationship between the Sharia and national legislation? Confusion is rife among Muslims, not least where the contracting and dissolving of marriage is concerned. It is often forgotten that the Sharia does not exist *per se* in Muslim countries, but rather is codified in national family laws, while at the same time, many Muslims consider it highly important to adhere to the Sharia. This has led to a number of different practices, from orally contracting and dissolving marriage, to formalized Sharia councils with the ambition that Sharia gain public status for Muslims.[73] No matter how it is implemented, though, Sharia is about right practice in all life's matters large and small, from prayer, marriage, work and finances to brushing one's teeth. How to practice Islam in a European context is considered an important matter for the believing Muslim. Norms are derived through fatwa-giving as proposed solutions for the challenges faced by Muslims. Islamic law, however, is not backed by the power of sanctions. It is therefore mainly up to the individual conscience whether to adhere to the norms that are developed. There is more than one norm. A person may choose among several patterns of conduct in a given case.[74]

Against this background, I will define the Sharia as "a set of source texts assumed to be authoritative, and various methods and concepts for deriving normative statements, directly or indirectly, from these sources."[75] As I see it,

---

71 Mayer 1990, 194. The case of Abdullahi an-Naʿim exemplifies how methodological orthodoxy is required for the result to be acceptable. His theory of reform, changing the order of the abrogating and abrogated verses of the Quran, met with considerable resistance among Islamic scholars.

72 These actors span a wide range of attitudes to reform, from those who limit themselves to proposing new norms, to those who would also reform the use of concepts and methods.

73 Based on the author's own observations in Muslim communities. Among central actors in the French UOIF, informal marriage is considered a major problem. (Interviews and fieldwork observations in Paris, May 2008.) The Sharia Council in London is an example of ambitions to gain a formal status for Sharia, expressed not least by the Council's general secretary, Suhayb Hasan. ("Divorce Sharia Style," broadcast on Channel4, 3 Feb 2008).

74 One illustrative example is the question of shaking hands with a person of the opposite sex. Several positions exist side by side. Some accept it, some do not; both find support in the sources.

75 I have taken Knut Vikør's definition of Sharia as my starting point: "… Islamic law is no

this definition encompasses the diversity in my materials, and makes room for references to the Sharia as an ideal and to various interpretations and readings of this ideal.

Islam, Women, Fatwas—and Gender

I call fatwas about questions tied to the challenges faced by Muslim women "women-related fatwas". This includes fatwas about women, even if women have not themselves asked the questions. This choice does not involve what historian of religion Jeanette Sky calls a "peculiar state of affairs" in scholarship, in which religion is described in general terms first, followed by an isolated chapter on women at the end.[76] Rather, it's a question of making visible women's issues that are often made invisible in the description of religion, and not least, of Islam. Sky describes this approach as follows:

> If we are to believe most textbooks in the history of religions, religion is about people and their relationship with the divine, the sacred, the unique and exalted. It's about *religious* people; people without either gender or class. Therefore, for example, we hear that Muslims attend Friday prayers at the mosque. But they don't: Muslim *men* attend Friday prayers at the mosque. Women, to the extent they are allowed to be present, are to keep in the back. Islam has a religious obligation to attend Friday prayers in the mosque that applies to all men. Separate rules and separate exceptions apply to women.[77]

Where fatwas are concerned, we find both tendencies, both focusing strongly on women, and rendering women's affairs invisible. Whereas women are invisible as a topic in fatwa collections from the formative and classical period, the strong focus on women is a modern phenomenon that was introduced at the end of the 1800s.

---

more than a body of sources of revelation and a methodology for making rules from these sources" (Vikør 2005, 1). I have used "source texts" rather than "sources of revelation" because, as a historian of religion, I do not wish to place normative constraints on my definition. I also use "methods and concepts" rather than "methodology," to reflect the existence of different methodologies.

76 Sky 2007, 10.

77 Sky 2007, 9–10.

The fatwas in my material sometimes indicate relations between men and women, and I have faced objections to describing these fatwas as women-related, rather than *gender-related*. I would respond that my project does have a gender perspective, although men are not its topic. My project consists in establishing new knowledge in the field of women and fatwas, without laying claim to covering everything. It ought likewise to be possible to take the angle of studying male-related fatwas as such.

The use of the term "women-related fatwas" can in my view also be defended from a gender perspective in the study of religion. Sky asserts that we are indebted to the feminist movement of the 1970s, which rendered gender visible, inter alia by raising the topic of women in the history of religion. This, she claims, shattered the overall picture that had earlier been created by mainly male researchers in the field.[78] Feminist researchers and theologians embarked on the writing of a women's history of religion. But what began as a critical tradition turned idealizing and romantic: In some circles, the feminist analyses soon acquired a sacralizing character, and a separate feminist theology developed, according to Sky.[79]

The 1980s and 1990s have seen a turn from women's studies to gender studies, and men too have been drawn into this field of research. Sky claims that, a few exceptions aside, this turn is absent from the scientific study of religion. She comments:

> Though gender is often stated as the subject of inquiry, the subject is nonetheless first and foremost *women*. Thus, men are left out, and this is a problem for analysis. A failure to focus on men leaves the gender-critical analyses one-sided, at the same time as they may paradoxically contribute to strengthening the perception of woman as something other in the culture. The man remains a norm, to which the woman, as *other*, is opposed.[80]

A gender perspective on religion, which Sky sees as the ideal, involves having regard to both genders and to the social interaction between them prescribed by culture and religion.[81] I join Sky in her view of an inclusive gender perspective. However, I think that calling women-related fatwas "gender related" could imply rendering women's experience and specific challenges invisible.

78 Sky 2007, 15.
79 Sky 2007, 16.
80 Sky 2007, 19.
81 Sky 2007, 24.

I consider my own approach—dealing with the fatwas in my material as "women-related"—a fruitful one, not least as a compensation for and a middle ground between making women invisible and presenting them as something entirely *sui generis* in the Islamic tradition.[82]

The Iranian-British anthropologist Ziba Mir-Hosseini has made a central contribution to reflections over "Islam and gender" in her book by that title.[83] Through interviews with scholars in Iran and analysis of texts, she identifies three positions on women and gender relations. The premise, she says, is that gender roles and relations and women's rights are neither fixed, given nor absolute.[84]

(i) The *inequality position* starts from the biological differences between women and men, which imply unequal rights, and regulate gender relations. It is promoted by the traditionalists, who consider this to be the natural order, rooted in sacred tradition.[85] From this position, women are described as emotional, and men as rational and capable of acquiring objective knowledge.[86] These qualities are utilized in the organization of the family and distribution of family roles. It is best for a woman to stay at home, since her primary responsibility is to raise children. The man, on the other hand, is the provider and head of family. This also implies that the man has the superior capacity for reason, and that the woman owes him obedience. Societies, whether Muslim or Western, that consider it natural for women to take part in the workplace, are considered to be exploiting women. The emotional nature of women and the rational nature of men are also used as an argument for unequal access to divorce.[87]

82 The view that the concept of woman is in danger of becoming invisible is shared by others, too. From the vantage point of Swedish cultural life and academic knowledge production, Witt-Brattström 2009 argues that notions such as "woman" and "femininity" are on their way out, and with them the historical experience that, for better or worse, separates women from men. She ascribes this development to post-feminist and queer theory, in which "woman" has been replaced as an analytical category by a sexualized identity politics that seeks to dissolve all rigidly defined genders. Witt-Brattström is a professor of literature. However, I think that her argument may also have validity for religious studies, not least the study of Islam and women.

83 Mir-Hosseini 2000a. In describing the content of these positions as delineated by Mir-Hosseini, I have partly followed Therese Bogstad's discussion in her MA thesis (Bogstad 2009).

84 Mir-Hosseini 2000a, 6.

85 Mir-Hosseini 2000a, 23.

86 Mir-Hosseini 2000a, 57.

87 Mir-Hosseini 2000a, 60–64.

(ii) The neo-traditionalists, as Mir-Hosseini calls them, promote a position based on *balance and complementarity*. They defend the Sharia gender models as immutable, but accept the importance of time and place—and admit the need for change. They aim to find an Islamic solution to acute gender-related challenges, but even though they search for new interpretations of the Sharia, Mir-Hosseini says, "they dismiss equality in rights and duties as a Western concept with no place in Islam".[88] Women and men do not have equal rights, but equal worth. This equality is expressed in balance within the family and society, in which the rights and duties of men and women even out.[89] Because the man has more duties, he also has more responsibilities. Male and female complement each other in the family as a fundamental social institution.[90] Women's participation in society is desirable, but only on the condition that they use the hijab. Gender relations and sexuality must be controlled and regulated, or chaos will ensue.[91]

(iii) Many modernists, in their turn, wish to bypass *fiqh* to seek new answers to new questions, in the light of *gender equality* in the sense of equal worth, equal rights, and equal duties. But we also find examples of legal scholars who argue the same position with *fiqh* arguments.[92] Equality implies that biological sex is not a criterion for determining rights and duties. Gender is a social and human concept, and not part of the divine realm or a matter for the Lawgiver.[93] Human beings are subject to God's laws, which are not divided into laws for women and men. Each norm is the outcome of an agreement, not based in nature. Reason takes precedence over blind obedience, since human beings are capable of understanding the reason for God's commands.[94] Promoting equality within a *fiqh* paradigm involves distinguishing between Islam and the acts of Muslims.[95] Concretely, it is argued that equality implies the equal right to divorce.[96]

---

88 Mir-Hosseini 2000a, 83.

89 Mir-Hosseini 2000a, 117.

90 Mir-Hosseini 2000a, 133.

91 Mir-Hosseini 2000a, 89.

92 For instance Saʿidzadeh, an Iranian scholar who in Mir-Hosseini's book argues for equality from a *fiqh* perspective.

93 Mir-Hosseini 2000a, 249–250.

94 Mir-Hosseini 2000a, 256.

95 Mir-Hosseini describes the distinction in this way: "It was much later [...] that I realised why he [Saʿidzadeh] insisted so much on separating 'ideas from actions'. For Saʿidzadeh, such a separation was necessary for establishing the system of women's rights within feqh frameworks, for broadening its focus from specific answers to new avenues for dealing with contemporary issues" (Mir-Hosseini 2000a, 268).

96 Mir-Hosseini 2000a, 270.

I consider these three positions relevant as analytical categories for my material, not least for shedding light on the contradictory expectations that lie in the traditional Islamic principle of gender inequality that stresses women's duties and subordination, and the Western notion of the equal rights of both genders, stressing women's rights and equality before the law.

Research on Fatwas

Skovgaard-Petersen has commented that the first generation of Western students of Islamic law did not care about fatwas.[97] The *Encyclopaedia of Islam* offers one explanation, which may have some validity for the 20th century:

> The public function of futyā is without prejudice to the private exercise of the profession. However, with the introduction of codes and their provisions borrowed from European systems in almost all branches of law, the profession has fallen into disuse; even in those matters which, like personal status and waḳfs, are still generally governed by the principles of Islamic law, the practice of fatwās seems to be becoming obsolescent.[98]

However, the fatwa institution has shown itself to be viable, and has been a growing phenomenon. It has also become so well known that "fatwa" has been incorporated into European languages. This is not least clear from an Internet search for the word.

Despite scattered studies in the first half of the 20th century, interest in fatwa studies first gained momentum in the early 1970s. According to David Powers,[99] the *Kitāb al-Miʿyār* of al-Wanshirisi (d. 1508) has received special attention from historians because it brings us closer to the social practices of the time than do other texts. As a group, he says, these historians deal with *al-Miʿyār* as a source from which they can extract information, usually from the request for a fatwa, *istiftāʾ*: Hady Roger Idris has written on marriage in the Western Muslim world based on fatwas from al-Wansharisi, but has also studied maritime commerce and the status of non-Muslims with *al-Miʿyār* as the primary source; Vincent

97 Skovgaard-Petersen 1997, 10, citing Johannes Benzing, who in a 1977 dissertation listed the first European commentaries on the fatwa institution from the beginning of the 19th century.
98 Tyan and Walsh 2009.
99 D. Powers 2002.

Lagardère has studied judicial administration and water law; and others "have written about women and property, child marriage, endowments [...], and even Christian festivals".[100]

Fatwas from al-Andalus have remained a source for researchers. In Norway, Ragnhild Johnsrud Zorgati used fatwas from *al-Miʿyār* along with Christian sources to examine legal discourses on mixed marriage and conversion on the medieval Iberian Peninsula.[101] In his analysis of al-Shatibi's theory of the objectives of Sharia (*maqāṣid al-sharīʿa*), Muhammad Khalid Masud has included 40 fatwas by Shatibi, some of them from *al-Miʿyār*.[102]

Masud has played a central role in fatwa studies. In January 1990, he organized the conference "The Making of Fatwa". The aim was to study how fatwa-giving has manifested itself throughout history in Muslim societies. It resulted in the volume *Islamic Legal Interpretation: Muftis and their Fatwas*,[103] which remains a key reference for fatwa students.

Skovgaard-Petersen ascribes the interest in fatwa research to increasing awareness of the fatwa as a historical source—as he himself used it to chart the history of the Egyptian religious institution *Dār al-iftāʾ* and its leaders—and to its ever-stronger position as a result of a renewed interest in Islam in most countries since the end of the 1960s.[104]

Fatwas have also been the subject of theoretical studies, in a research trend described by Eggen as focusing on "... questions of method [...] and attempts to find methods to to understand the internal structure and premises of the [Islamic legal] science".[105] As Eggen mentions, Wael Hallaq is a representative of this trend. Hallaq's paper "From *Fatwās* to *Furūʿ*,"[106] in which he explores the role of the fatwa in changing religious law (*furūʿ al-fiqh*), has become another key reference.

Little research has been done on fatwas in the recent European context. Three exceptions are the respective works of Alexandre Caeiro, Karen-Lise Johansen Karman and Uriya Shavit on the ECFR. Caeiro takes a sociological approach to the ECFR, and deals with Islamic normativity in the encounter with the West, Sharia as a social construction, and fatwas and authority.[107] Karman

100 D. Powers 2002, 9–10.
101 Zorgati 2007.
102 Masud 1995, 87.
103 Masud, Messick, and Powers 1996.
104 Skovgaard-Petersen 1997, 12.
105 Eggen 2001, 2.
106 Hallaq 1994.
107 Caeiro 2002 and 2011 (see also 2010; 2006; 2004).

studies the ECFR as one of three fatwa-giving bodies, to see if a change in legal arguments directed at Muslims as a minority can establish a so-called minority jurisprudence (*fiqh al-aqalliyyāt*).[108] Uriya Shavit analyses fatwas from the ECFR as well as Salafi fatwas, contrasting supposedly flexible (*wasaṭī*) and rigid (*salafī*) approaches to a minority jurisprudence.

Less studied yet are women-related fatwas. One exception is the work of Judith Tucker,[109] who has used fatwas along with court records to study the view of female roles (wives, mothers, sisters and daughters) in Ottoman Syria and Palestine in the 17th and 18th centuries.

I have found two works on contemporary women-related fatwas. Barbara Freyer Stowasser and Zeinab Abul-Magd explore how legal understandings of the family in modern legislation and in the fatwa literature, differ from the view of marriage and its purpose in the provisions of the marriage contract in pre-modern Sunni fiqh, taking *taḥlīl* marriage as their case.[110] Therese Bogstad, in her MA thesis, has studied fatwas on divorce from the IslamOnline.net website in a women's perspective.[111]

The present book on women-related fatwas is a contribution to the research on contemporary fatwas in the European context. I will examine fatwas as proposed solutions to the challenges faced by Muslim women in Western Europe, as these are expressed in the requests for fatwas. The analysis of the fatwas will stress the concepts and methods used in the fatwa-giving as much as the questions and answers themselves. I thus follow the example of Kate Zebiri's analysis of a fatwa collection by Mahmud Shaltut, which Skovgaard-Petersen describes as follows: "Zebiri analyses his use of the Quran, the Sunna and the texts of classical *fiqh* and then proceeds to investigate his application of *ra'y* (independent opinion) and *ijmāʿ* (consensus), as well as his references to empirical evidence".[112] I think it is a fruitful approach to evaluate a fatwa both in terms of its content and its justification. I further attempt to shed light on the legitimacy and authority of the fatwas. I make use of anthropologist Hussein Ali Agrama's perspective on what he calls the built-in ethical dimension and

108 Karman 2008.

109 Tucker 1999.

110 Stowasser and Abul-Magd 2008. *Taḥlīl* may be defined as "making licit what is by default forbidden". *Taḥlīl* marriage may occur when a couple cannot marry again after the triple divorce. If the wife marries another man and divorces him, she may marry her former husband again if she so wishes.

111 Bogstad 2009.

112 Skovgaard-Petersen 1997, 18.

authority of the fatwa,[113] with the caveat that as Agrama's argument is based on oral fatwas given by the so-called Fatwa Council at al-Azhar in Egypt, one needs to consider whether this theoretical perspective is also valid for written materials. This book is not about the reception of fatwas. That would have been extremely interesting to explore, but would have been a whole research project on its own.

History of the Project

This book, and the research questions and problems it deals with, have grown out of a decade of watching and listening to women asking questions at Muslim gatherings, as well as being present at telephone counselling for women seeking help. It was clear to me that answering women's questions, and helping women who ask for it, makes up a considerable share of the tasks of Muslim leaders, whether they are salaried or volunteers. Some leaders are contacted more often than others. This does not necessarily depend only on their level of Islamic education, but also on their reputation among women. I found that it was at least as important what leader was known for having "good views" on women and was considered able to contribute to solving the problems that arise. However, this activity—answering Muslim women's questions and helping them solve their problems in contemporary Western Europe—is invisible to the surroundings, and little research has been done.[114] This book's focus on muftis and their fatwas is an attempt to render this activity visible.

After formulating the idea for this book in 2001, I took part in a meeting in Malmö with Muslim participants from all over Europe. Among them were Mohamed al-Mansoori and Tahar Mahdi, both members of the ECFR, the work of which I had decided to include in my project.[115] Both would in the course of my project provide insights into a mufti's way of thought and his everyday situation, respectively. With al-Mansoori, I discussed the relations between religious experts and "engineers,"[116] that is, the highly educated people without

113 Agrama 2010, 2–18.

114 One exception is research on the Sharia Council (UK) (see e.g. Bano 2007).

115 Mohamed al-Mansoori is from the United Arab Emirates. In 2001, he was living in Scotland, and working on a PhD thesis on women's rights. He has been legal advisor to the shaykh of the Ras al-Khayma emirate, and has held a high profile as a human rights activist. Tahar Mahdi lives in a suburb of Paris. He is member of the Dar al-Fatwa, teaches *fiqh*, and is active on the grassroots level among Muslims in the Paris region.

116 Kari Vogt uses the expression "engineer Islam" for the phenomenon, criticized by Muham-

traditional religious schooling who have played an important role in the institutionalization of Islam in Western Europe and who have partly acted as experts due to the lack of religious scholars. I also talked with al-Mansoori about how a mufti thinks when giving a fatwa, and about the considerations that are weighed, not least what al-Mansoori called "the politics of fatwa," which I interpret as informal considerations that are taken into account in fatwa-giving. Al-Mansoori was available for questions and discussions from 2001 to 2006. During several visits to Tahar Mahdi in Paris up to 2006, I gained insights into the grassroots commitments of a mufti: his typical day, the questions that may come, the solutions he envisages, his view of women and of women's options, and how his specific fatwas are expressions of a solution-oriented attitude.

My reflections on fatwa-giving have benefited from the contributions of these two as well as other muftis in my materials. I have not only had access to written sources, but also to conversations and discussions with the muftis. In this way I have been able to discuss with them how they react to fatwas, I have looked into the personal relations among muftis, and I have learned about the considerations that are taken into account not only when fatwas are given, but also in the preceding debates. In other words, I have gained insight into the process around *Sharia as a social construction*.[117]

To learn more about the background for the materials that I analyse, I also attended sessions of the ECFR, five sessions in all (2002–2006). This provided insight into the "politics of fatwa" in practice: differences between public and private fatwas; how muftis primarily act as "guardians of tradition," but sometimes also as "custodians of change";[118] various hierarchical structures among muftis; and views of women's issues in practice and in relation to other topics, e.g. finances. When appropriate, I will draw on these background insights in my analysis of the fatwas.

Furthermore, I carried out fieldwork in London in 2006, gathering materials and talking to the actors, and again in 2009 to gather information about the Model Muslim Marriage Contract. I attended the large annual gathering of the UOIF at Le Bourget in Paris in 2008. I also met several of the same actors in France (2004, 2005, 2006), Cairo (2006, 2007, 2008, 2009), and Istanbul (2006). I gained access to the field through contacts I had made while work-

---

mad al-Ghazali and Yusuf al-Qaradawi, of engineers and others without the appropriate education acting as religious experts (Vogt 2005, 109–110). The issue is not restricted to Europe.

117 The expression "Sharia as social construction" is used by Caeiro 2004.

118 The expressions "guardians of tradition" and "custodians of change" are used by Zaman 2002.

ing on my second-cycle thesis on Islam and conversion in the Norwegian context.[119] Through my work on the projects "New Directions in Islamic Thought and Practice" and "Gender Equality in Muslim Family Law,"[120] and my activities in Islamic volunteer work, I have retained and developed contacts with actors who have also been relevant in this project. These contacts have also opened the doors to other sources.

In short, through interviews and participant observation I have learned about the fatwa field and gained tools for understanding the complexity that may characterize fatwa-giving in a minority context.

In my interaction with the actors, I follow the lead of anthropologist John Bowen: "I prefer to look for naturally occurring arguments, presentations, and debates, and to draw out of those events certain ways of acting and reasoning that can help account for other actions".[121] Bowen's events include "social chats and dinnertime conversations but also arranged conversations" (p. 5). Similarly, I have preferred conversations and events that take place through an already established social connection, rather than interviews. I have seen this as a fruitful means of entry, since I have met the actors in several different arenas, and have therefore been able to form more nuanced pictures of them than formal interviews alone could have afforded. This choice of method is tied to the increasing width and depth of my access to the field since 1993.

The Data

Iftā' or fatwa-giving is fundamentally an oral phenomenon. It may take place face to face between the *mustaftī* and the mufti, or in a live TV programme with a well-known scholar answering callers.

Most fatwas are given orally, outside public space, and unknown to the public. This implies severe constraints on the gathering of empirical data. "Since this form of delivery leaves no documentary trace, the historical incidence of oral questions and answers is unknown," say Masud and co-authors, though they mention one exception: "The single reported instance concerns the extremely bureaucratized Ottoman system, where in the late period ques-

119 Larsen 1995.

120 These two international workshop series with Muslim scholars have resulted in the publications Vogt, Larsen, and Moe 2009 and Mir-Hosseini et al. 2013. They were organized by the Oslo Coalition on Freedom of Religion or Belief, where I am programme director.

121 Bowen 2007, 5.

tioners could request an oral fatwa from a specially designated functionary".[122] Fatwa sessions under the auspices of established fatwa institutions offer one possible contemporary point of access to such materials, but have been little documented in the literature.[123] Radio and TV programmes are another source of contemporary oral fatwas. There is enormous interest in fatwas in the media, not least since the Rushdie fatwa, which turned fatwas into a global media phenomenon.[124] Every channel has its own shaykh giving fatwas, often on his own show, and often with callers asking questions on the phone. The most widely known TV programme has been *Sharīʿa wal-ḥaya* (Sharia and Life) on the al-Jazeera channel, which is the frame for Yusuf al-Qaradawi's treatment of various questions, including fatwa-giving.[125]

Written fatwas are far easier for the researcher to relate to. They are available in fatwa collections, court documents, home pages on the Internet, newspapers and journals. There are print editions of both fatwas from premodern muftis in manuscript form, intended for a limited readership, and the collected fatwas of modern muftis, with potentially unlimited distributions. Fatwa collections are important for the documentation of mufti activities, and a stream of these has been produced from the mid-900s up to the present.

Still, most fatwas are given orally, and this applies also to the fatwas of Syed Darsh, the ECFR, Barkatullah Abdulkadir, or the UOIF's Dar al-Fatwa. These are all examples of religious experts who are accessible to grassroots Muslims. At the same time, their profiles differ.

The activities of the French Dar al-Fatwa consist of giving oral fatwas through a helpline service and fatwa sessions at the *Institut européen de sciences humaines* (IESH) in Paris. Little of their work is documented in writing, but one written exception from this oral fatwa culture is a study in which Larabi Becheri presents the independent reasoning behind a fatwa he gave at the UOIF mass gathering at Le Bourget in 2008.

Barkatullah Abdulkadir, who is based in London, also represents the oral fatwa culture as an individual actor.[126] He was among the founders of The

122 Masud, Messick, and Powers 1996, 23f., citing Heyd 1969, 47.

123 One exception is Hussein Ali Agrama's fieldwork and attendance at the open sessions of the *Lajnat al-fatwā* (Fatwa Council) at al-Azhar University in Cairo, where people could come and get fatwas directly.

124 Masud, Messick, and Powers 1996, 29.

125 See e.g. Roald 2001b, 29–55.

126 Abdulkadir has also participated in a number of decisions of The Sharia Council (TSC, later renamed the Islamic Sharia Council) that have been recorded in writing. The TSC, however, is not part of my material.

Sharia Council in 1982, and is responsible for the Islamic Helpline phone counseling service. A written exception is the Model Muslim Marriage Contract, launched in London in 2008, of which Abdulkadir may be said to be the architect. This marriage-contract form contains fatwas and forms part of my materials, along with the independent reasoning behind the fatwas, which Abdulkadir presented to me in the course of two interviews.

Like the Dar al-Fatwa and Barkatullah Abdulkadir, Syed Darsh was available for questions, whether from Muslims lining up after Friday prayers, or in telephone conversations. However, Darsh has also given written fatwas, and I have included those that relate to women.

The same holds for written women-related fatwas from the European Council for Fatwa and Research. Although the ECFR also has extensive oral fatwa activities through a helpline, both at the Dublin secretariat and the local branches in England and France, I have dealt with their written fatwas.

In the course of the project, I discovered that fatwa-giving forms part of a broader practice that also includes counselling. Representatives of the Dar al-Fatwa were clear that in addition to fatwas, they also give *naṣīḥa* (advice).

The relationship between *naṣīḥa* and fatwa has not, to my knowledge, previously been explored in the academic literature. In the next section I therefore examine and compare what the theological literature has to say about these notions.

Naṣīḥa

Naṣīḥa is defined as "a statement implying the wish to [promote] righteousness and prevent immorality."[127] Lane offers two definitions among others that expand this semantic content: "Direction to that which is for the good of the person who is the object, by words, or deeds …" and "benevolence: desire for what is good for the person who is the object …"[128] The scholars refer to the tradition *al-dīn al-naṣīḥa* ("religion is sincerity"), defining sincerity toward all people as seeking their best interest in all their concerns, as an norm of obligation for all Muslims (*ḥukm taklīfī*).[129] Eggen defines a *ḥukm taklīfī* as "the [norm] that imposes on the subject of the norm the requirement of performing an action or refraining from it or choosing between performing it and refraining from it."[130] The above-mentioned tradition specifies the requirement of

127 *Mawsūʿat al-fiqhiyya*, 40:324.

128 "Nasīḥa" in *Lane's Lexicon*, 2:2801.

129 *Mawsūʿat al-fiqhiyya*, 40:325.

130 Eggen 2001, 19.

sincerity to mean that one should be sincere towards "Allah, His Book, His Messengers, the leaders of Muslims and the public."[131] The encyclopedia *Mawsūʿat al-fiqhiyya* cites scholars who claim that *al-dīn al-naṣīḥa* may be considered a fundamental pillar of Islam, and that it embraces the three aspects of Islam: *al-islām* (the five pillars), *al-imān* (belief) and *al-iḥsān* (beautiful deeds).[132] *Naṣīḥa*, then, can be a piece of sincere advice that covers religio-legal, moral and/or spiritual matters.[133]

The scholars differ over whether giving advice is a personal or only a collective obligation. According to the Maliki school, giving sincere advice is *farḍ ʿayn* (a personal obligation), whether or not one is asked for advice, if one believes it to be useful, because this is part of commanding the good (*amr bil-maʿrūf*). Al-Nawawi, on the other hand, relates from Ibn Batal that giving sincere advice is *farḍ kifāya* (a collective duty): The obligation of the community is considered fulfilled as long as someone takes on the responsibility.[134]

Giving sincere advice to the public implies giving guidance with regard to this life and the next, to prevent them from harm, to teach them what they do not know about their *dīn*, to help them by word and action, to conceal their weaknesses (that is, professional secrecy), to protect them against hunger, to give them advantages, and to command the good and forbid evil (*amr bil-maʿrūf wa-nahī ʿan al-munkar*).[135] There are requirements as to *how* to give advice. Sincerity and kindness are required. One is also obliged to wish for the recipient of advice the same good one wishes for oneself, and not tolerate what one does not oneself tolerate.[136] Another important principle, according to the scholars, is that advice is to be given secretly, without letting others know, because a piece of advice is a matter between the giver and the recipient. The rationale is simple: If advice is publicly given, it takes on a character of reproach rather than loving concern and advice.[137]

---

131 Hadith no. 7 in the *Kitab al-arbaʿin* (Forty Hadith) by Nawawi, who cites the *Ṣaḥīḥ Muslim* as the reference.

132 The contents of the three aspects are defined in hadith no. 2 in the Forty Hadith of Nawawi.

133 Examples of the relationship between the Islamic message as a whole and the giving of good advice may be found in the Quran, where Nuh has "fulfil[led] … the duties of [the] Lord's mission" and given sincere advice (7:62), Hud is a "sincere and trustworthy advisor" (7:68), and Salih and Shuaib have given good counsel (7:79, 7:93).

134 *Mawsūʿat al-fiqhiyya*, 40:325–326.

135 *Mawsūʿat al-fiqhiyya*, 40:328.

136 *Mawsūʿat al-fiqhiyya*, 40:326.

137 *Mawsūʿat al-fiqhiyya*, 40:329.

The giver of advice must possess solid knowledge of the Sharia, as well as general knowledge of the circumstances in which people live, of time and place, and of how to balance between multiple alternatives. In other words, knowledge, good sense and a balanced vision of the good are required. Someone lacking in these qualities is likely to commit mistakes, say the sources, and should therefore refrain from giving advice.[138]

We can identify several differences between *naṣīḥa* and *fatwā*: While a fatwa is the derivation of a religio-legal norm, *naṣīḥa* also includes ethical and moral aspects, and its subject matter could be just about anything. Where a fatwa focuses on the norm, the focus of the *naṣīḥa* is the human being receiving advice. We have seen above that when giving a fatwa, a mufti is considered to speak on God's behalf; in the giving of sincere advice, the stress is on fellow humanity. People are seen as each others' mirrors, and urged to wish the same good things for each other as for themselves. A *naṣīḥa* sometimes involves a holistic assessment of the individual's situation, and a weighing of different commands. This *may* result in an apparent conflict between the advice and the religio-legal norm that a fatwa would have stated in the same matter.[139] An important difference between advice and fatwa is that advice should be given in private, while a fatwa may also be public.

History of the Data and My Experiences as a Researcher

As a Muslim, I have done research into my own culture. This means that my sources and I possess "mutual knowledge," which, according to Wadel, may enable one to understand what one observes, while at the same time posing the challenge that things may be taken for granted, and hence not as easily discovered and put into words.[140]

One may reasonably assume that my experiences in gathering data for this project were also shaped by the fact that I am a woman and a Muslim. I will therefore present some bits of the history behind the data. Let me begin with the meetings of the ECFR.

After contacting the ECFR secretariat, I was accepted as a *murāqib* (observer) during the 2002 ECFR session at the UOIF headquarters in Paris. The setting was as follows: Council members sat around a long table in the middle of the room.

138 *Mawsūʿat al-fiqhiyya*, 40:331.

139 An example of such an apparent conflict of norms between fatwa and *naṣīḥa* will be shown in the presentation of Tareq Oubrou in chapter 2.

140 Wadel 1991, 18–19, citing what sociologist Anthony Giddens calls "mutual knowledge".

The observers were placed along one of the walls, with women and men seated apart. During the lunch break, the male observers sat with the Council members. Communications between Council members and the male observers were informal, and issues connected with the previous session were discussed and commented.[141] As one of two ladies, I was placed at a table some distance away, without the same opportunity to participate and benefit from the conversation around the table. We were subject to Islamic etiquette for behaviour between men and women, which excluded informal communications with the muftis in public.

To gather my data, then, I had instead to ask for personal appointments with members of the Council. Face to face with the muftis, my experience was nearly the opposite to the one I had had during the breaks. In these meetings, I experienced the muftis as friendly, helpful people, who very patiently shared with me their knowledge and experience. I relate this to the Muslim ideal of masculinity.[142] Virtues such as helpfulness, friendliness, accessibility and patience, which I found among all the muftis I interviewed, function, I would hold, as an operative Muslim ideal of masculinity. This kind of experience has been described as follows:

> In recent years, for instance, much has been written on women's methodological experiences as researchers in the field. The picture is not quite unambiguous. Many female observers in milieus that include male actors, report that they have been viewed as creatures in need of protection. This may have the positive outcome that they receive extra help and information. Due to their female role, they may be seen as harmless, and actors may not be very guarded about them. On the other hand, parts of male culture may be screened from them.[143]

When I attended the 2003 sessions in Stockholm as an observer, there were more women present—one researcher, the wives of some of the members, and local "sisters"[144] from Stockholm. The "women's corner" had its own dynamics. This became clear during the breaks. Conversations around the table were about the lives of the women, not least as mothers, and the local Islamic activ-

---

141 Author's conversation with a male observer who was also doing research on fatwas at the time.

142 Skarsaune 2006, 73 f.

143 Repstad 1993, 50, cited in Skarsaune 2006, 22 (translated from Norwegian).

144 "Sister" is a common form of address among women in some Muslim groups, including the field that I have studied.

ities in which they were involved at home. The dynamics and communication within the women's groups gave me insight into the culture in which the wives of the shaykhs live, its ideals and expectations. Fatwas and discussion of the previous session, however, were entirely absent from the conversations around the table. As a woman, I was considered to "naturally" belong in this category. The fact that I had years ago converted to Islam also aroused interest, and I was asked to tell about the conversion process. During the following meetings in London (2004), Dublin (2005) and Istanbul (2006), the women's group developed, and conversations began to revolve around more personal and private matters.

As the sessions proceeded, I (like other observers) was given the opportunity to speak and comment on the ongoing discussions. During the London session in 2004, I commented on a discussion of women's issues, whereupon I was invited to present a contribution on the challenges of Muslim women in Western Europe at the next meeting (in Dublin, 2005). In this paper, I presented the topic in light of *modern common morality*, that is to say, on the terms set by the majority community.[145] In the ensuing discussion among the members, I found myself participating on an almost equal footing. Both strong disagreement and support for my views were expressed, with various reasons given. One reason cited by ECFR member Rachid al-Ghannouchi may be worth mentioning: One should be tolerant of my critical comments, as I was a practising and active Muslim. Al-Ghannouchi let it be known that he had known me for years, and knew that I was a good "sister".

In the "women's corner," during the sessions, and in conversations with the shaykhs, I found myself confronted with my different identities. While I basically saw myself as a researcher who happened to have an advantage with regard to getting access because I was Muslim, the actors in the field primarily saw me as a Muslim and a woman. In time, it would also become clear that we placed different meanings on being an "active Muslim". I probably appeared a "feminist," and this would be remarked on later.

In 2014, I was invited to present a paper on *Musawa al-mar'a wa-maqāṣidiha* (the equality of women and its objectives), after it became known that besides completing my Ph.D., I had also been a leader of the project *Justice Through Equality in Muslim Family Law* of the Oslo Coalition on Freedom of Religion or Belief, which resulted in a book and a report.[146] This time, I had the very differ-

145 Larsen 1995, unpublished.

146 Mir-Hosseini et al. 2013. The accompanying report (Mir-Hosseini et al. 2013b) may be downloaded from http://www.jus.uio.no/smr/english/about/programmes/oslocoalition/docs/justice-through-equality.pdf.

ent experience of participating on a completely equal footing. For one thing, I was not confined to the "women's corner", but was seated at the same table as the members of the Council during my presentation and the ensuing discussion.

My experience with fieldwork and qualitative interviews correspond to the thoughts of British-Iranian anthropologist Ziba Mir-Hosseini on being a "native anthropologist": "'Doing anthropology' is more than an academic discipline, it is a way of life; it is a means of making sense of, belonging to and yet being able to transcend both the society into which I was born and the society which I now inhabit".[147] In my case, it is not a question of two different societies, but of my twofold work: in the traditional Muslim religious community, and in the promotion of the rights of Muslim women. Mir-Hosseini cites anthropologist Barbara Tedlock's description of the "native ethnographer":

> Native ethnographers [...] have worked to bridge the gulf between Self and Other by revealing both parties as vulnerable experiencing subjects, working to coproduce knowledge. They have argued that the observer and the observed are not entirely separate categories. To them theory is not a transparent, culture-free zone, not a duty-free intellectual market hovering between cultures, lacking all connection embodied in lived experience. They believe that both knowledge and experience from outside fieldwork should be brought into our narratives and that we should demonstrate how ideas matter to us, bridging the gap between our narrow academic world and our outer wider cultural experiences. These strategies should help us simultaneously deepen and invigorate our writing and our selves.[148]

My project was carried out within the tradition of the scientific study of religion, and I have focused on research on fatwas. But other disciplinary traditions have also played a role in my evaluation of the data, not least Islamic Studies, Arabic language, and theories about religion in a gender perspective. In other words, the approach has been inter-disciplinary. I have employed what religious studies expert Wendy Doniger calls the *toolbox approach*,[149] letting the material itself suggest appropriate tools of analysis. It has been commented that: "In the toolbox approach, it seems [...] as if the relation between the-

147 Mir-Hosseini 2010, 189.

148 Tedlock 1991, 80–81, cited in Mir-Hosseini 2010, 189–190.

149 Doniger O'Flaherty 1982, 5–6.

ory and method constantly varies, in an almost arbitrary way, as the researcher takes up a new tool or puts another one down".[150] I have not seen the relation between theory and method as an arbitrary one, and I have not thought that letting the material itself suggest appropriate tools of analysis implies that theoretical and methodological questions can be set aside, as has been objected to the toolbox approach.[151] I see the approaches I have used as fruitful for my project, even if experts within each particular field spanned by this project would have done things differently. It is by drawing in perspectives from across disciplinary boundaries that this book may contribute new knowledge, a new view of and analysis of the material, and make an original contribution to studies of Islam, in general, and fatwas in a gender perspective, in particular.

The Structure of This Book

This book is divided into eight chapters. *Chapter One* offers an introduction to fatwas on women's issues in historical perspective. We follow one trajectory of ideas from the emergence of the fatwa institution in the classical Islamic tradition and its development into a separate category of the legal literature, to the muftis who have contributed to shaping the discourse on women-related questions among Muslims in Western Europe today. Women became a central topic of the late 19th-century Egyptian public debate, which was reflected in Islamic discourse throughout the 20th century. The "new era" had profound effects on Islamic discourse, restructuring fiqh books and fatwa collections with "women" and "the family" becoming central organizing categories.

The target audience for fatwas has also changed. Once directed at other scholars and students, fatwas now often target the broad Muslim public. This is connected with the democratization of access to knowledge, which has gone hand in hand with the increasing importance of mass media in the dissemination of knowledge and preaching. This development has placed the mufti and his authority under increased pressure. Against this background, the muftis have dealt with issues, concepts and methods that define one trend among muftis in Western Europe: Those who consider "time and place" important considerations in fatwa-giving. In *Chapter Two*, I present the muftis and fatwa institutions I have selected. How do they view their own work as muftis, on what concepts and methods do they base their fatwa-giving, and how do they

150 Cavallin 2006, 17.

151 Cavallin 2006, 17.

designate their fatwas? I go on to examine the context in which they act. By drawing the profiles of these actors, we gain knowledge of *iftāʾ* (fatwa-giving) on European soil, knowledge that will help frame and inform the presentation and analysis of fatwas later in the book. The reason for including the UOIF in the presentation was that it was behind the establishment of the ECFR, and that the Dar al-Fatwa is considered a branch of the ECFR.

In *Chapters Three* and *Four*, I present the fatwas of Syed Darsh and the ECFR. The questions I seek to answer in these chapters are: What questions are posed? What women-related answers are given? How are they justified? What view of women is drawn in the fatwas? How and to what extent do the muftis argue that the fatwa has adapted for Muslim women in Western Europe? In *Chapter Five*, selected fatwas are analysed with regard to legitimacy and authority. The analysis takes its cues from John Bowen's use of the concept "field of reference and debate" as part of "a transnational public space," and from Hussein Agrama's exploration of how the authority of the fatwa is created. The discussion shows that the fatwa has two axes of authority: a horizontal axis among scholars, where the use of certain concepts, methods, and references, as well as the personal qualities of the mufti, are important determinants of whether a fatwa will gain recognition; and a vertical axis between the learned and lay Muslim, where the authority of the fatwa consists in being a guidance to become a better Muslim and feel that one belongs to the tradition. *Chapter Six* analyses fatwas on topics connected with contracting marriage. The marriage issue affects many Muslims in Europe—and raises many other questions besides the requirement of validity. It is a complex topic, where Islamic jurisprudence, European national legislations, and the legislations of Muslim countries all play a role.[152] The questions the chapter seeks to answer are: What concepts and methods are used in the arguments on which the fatwas are based? To what extent and in what ways are the muftis' arguments affected by local circum-

152 This book is not a study of law. The point here is only to show the range of challenges with regard to Muslims and marriage-related topics. The questions surveyed may illustrate challenges to Islamic jurisprudence, and in some cases challenges in the relationship between Islamic norms and national legislation. Among legal scholars, Marie Clair Foblets has worked on questions regarding the Moroccan Mudawwana and Moroccans abroad. Katja Fredriksen, a research fellow at the University of Bergen, has done research on Sharia before Norwegian courts (see http://www.forskning.no/Artikler/2006/desember/1165999803.1). In the UK, Samia Bano has studied the relationship between informal religious systems of family law and Muslim women in the UK and Europe (see http://reading.academia.edu/SamiaBano). In Germany, Mathias Rohe has worked on the development of Islamic law in the European context (Rohe 2007).

stances? *Chapter Seven* discusses European and Islamic fundamental values in terms of theories of the objectives of Sharia and modern common morality. I argue that the muftis' arguments for their fatwas are translatable into a more widely accessible language that allows clarifying fundamental values and their interpretations. I will argue that the *maqāṣid* theory forms one Islamic counterpart to the theory of a *modern common morality*, "the morality of ordinary people," as spelled out by the Norwegian philosopher Knut Erik Tranøy.[153] I seek to uncover a possible correspondence between the concepts of the two models. According to these theories, the categories of *ḍarūriyyāt* and "bio-moral values," respectively, are fundamental values that serve as a basis for any society. Conflicts may emerge when these fundamental values are to be interpreted. I present Tranøy's theory of competing common moralities, which could help understand the "clash of moralities" and hence the unease of multi-religious societies. In light of the current situation in Europe, however, where some of the most burning political controversies rage over "Islam" and "Muslims", I end this chapter with a pessimistic view on whether texts and authors can be approached, translated, and evaluated according to common values at present.

Chapter Eight offers concluding reflections.

153 Tranøy 2000.

PART 1

Women, Fatwas, Actors

CHAPTER 1

Continuity and Change: Fatwas and Fatwa-Giving on Women's Issues in Historical Perspective

The Fatwa in Early Islamic History

In Islamic tradition, the fatwa institution is considered to be as old as Islam itself. Its point of departure is found in the Quran. According to Wael Hallaq, the expressions *yas'alūnaka* ("they ask you") and *yastaftūnaka* ("they ask your opinion") serve as a Quranic model for *iftā'*.[1]

The fatwa institution is based on the view of the Quran as divine revelation to humanity through the Prophet Muhammad. Masud et al. describe the work of Muhammad as follows:

> Guided by the revelations, Muhammad instituted a series of rules and practices in the areas of ritual behavior, purity, social relations, and the economy. Inevitably, perhaps, these innovations occasionally met with expressions of incomprehension or resistance from the nascent Muslim community […] These reactions may be reflected in a literary structure that occurs repeatedly in the Quran: "When they ask you (yas'alūnaka) concerning … Say …"[2]

The encyclopedia of jurisprudence *Mawsū'at al-fiqhiyya* indicates, citing the Quran, that God himself has given fatwas to his servants:[3] "They ask thy instruction concerning the women […]; say: Allah doth instruct you about them […]" (4:127); "They ask thee for a legal decision. Say: Allah directs (thus) about those who leave no descendants or ascendants as heirs […]" (4:176). On this account, those parts of the Quran that form answers to questions may be considered fatwas.[4] Based on the Quranic formula, later scholars have interpreted

1 Hallaq 1994, 64. Hallaq also states that *yas'alūnaka* (and its variants) appear in 126 places in the Quran, and *yastaftūnaka* in nine places.

2 Masud, Messick, and Powers 1996, 5.

3 *Mawsū'at al-fiqhiyya*, 32:23.

4 Masud, Messick, and Powers 1996, 331 cite the literary genre *asbāb al-nuzūl* (occasions of revelation) as a good source of examples that parts of the Quran may be considered fatwas. One example concerns the revelation of 4:7, which designates "a share for men and

 | DOI: 10.1163/9789004367852_003

Quranic fatwas as a three-way communication between God, Muhammad, and the Muslim community.[5]

In the hadith literature, on the other hand, norms are derived through two-way communication between Muhammad and the Muslim religious community. Masud et al. point out that the hadith connect the authority of fatwas with the Quran 4:64: "We sent not a messenger, but to be obeyed [...]." The Quran is also cited as proof that the mufti function was part of Muhammad's prophetic mission: "[...] and We have sent down unto thee (also) the Message; that thou mayest explain clearly to men what is sent for them [...]" (16:44).

According to Islamic literature, the Companions assumed responsibility for managing and transmitting orthopraxy, as they had known the Prophet personally. Islamic sources count 120 or 130 Companions that acted as muftis.[6] According to Masud, the *futyā* (fatwa-giving) that was practiced by the Companions is connected with the preservation of the Sunna of the Prophet. The fatwas of the Companions are called *fatāwā saḥābī*.

Legal activities in the first century appear to have revolved around fatwa-giving. Hallaq describes this as a logical development, given that the emerging religion depended on those experts best acquainted with the law.[7] He also refers to Schacht, who claims that the generation of experts that were contemporaries of Ibrahim al-Nakhaʿi (d. 713/714) were above all muftis. Schacht writes:

> The pious specialists owed their authority and the respect in which they were held both by the public and by the rulers, to their single-minded concern with the ideal life according to the tenets of Islam, and they

a share for women" in inheritance. It is said to have been revealed shortly after a widow had complained to the Prophet that her in-laws had refused her and her daughters a share in the inheritance, citing a pre-Islamic custom that limited inheritance rights to fighting men.

5 Masud, Messick, and Powers 1996, 5.

6 See e.g. Masud, Messick, and Powers 1996, 7 and *Mawsūʿat al-fiqhiyya*, 32:22, which refers to the *Majmūʿ* of al-Nawawi. Three of these should be mentioned: The Prophet's secretary, Zayd b. Thabit (d. 666), was head of *futyāʿ* from 632 until he died. Ibn Abbas (d. 687) was the most prominent mufti among the Companions. His fatwas were collected in a twenty-volume work by the great-grandchild of the Abbasid caliph al-Ma'mun (al-Qasimi 1986, 35). According to Guergah n.d., A'isha, one of Muhammad's wives, was among the seven most prominent of the 130, as well as among the *al-mukathirūn* (those who transmitted the most hadiths). Fatwas ascribed to her are found in the hadith literature.

7 Hallaq 1994, 62–63.

gave cautelary advice on the correct way of acting to those of their co-religionists who asked for it.[8]

Hallaq ascribes to the muftis a quite central role in the development and changing of legal doctrines within the schools of law: "… the juridical genre of the fatwā was chiefly responsible for the growth and change of legal doctrine in the schools, and […] our current perception of Islamic law as a jurists' law must now be further defined as a muftīs' law".[9] Ibn al-Qayyim (d. 1350) compares the mufti to a minister signing on the king's behalf: If the latter's status is a lofty one, how much loftier is the status of the mufti, who signs on behalf of "the Lord of the earth and the heavens".[10] Hallaq writes of the muftis: "Standing at the top of the legal hierachy, they saw themselves as the guardians of the law and of the community at large".[11] Indeed, the aim of the traditional *madrasa* was the education of muftis.

The Fatwa Literature

In the centuries after the death of the Prophet Muhammad, a separate literature on fatwas emerged. Masud et al. comment: "The emergence of the fatwa collection as a discrete literary genre points to the increasingly important role played by the mufti in the judicial process."[12] According to Skovgaard-Petersen, fatwa collections were a category of literature studied at the madrasas by future scholars. The study of fatwas focused on their underlying rationale, as its main concern was with method.[13] A separate literature discussing methods and concepts for the derivation of norms arose, and became known as *uṣūl al-fiqh* ("the roots of jurisprudence"), whereas the literature on norms applied in various cases was called *furūʿ al-fiqh* ("the branches of jurisprudence").[14]

---

8 Schacht 1991, 27.

9 Hallaq 1994, 65.

10 Ibn al-Qayyim, cited in *Mawsūʿat al-fiqhiyya*, 32:23.

11 Hallaq 1994, 59.

12 Masud, Messick, and Powers 1996, 10.

13 Skovgaard-Petersen 1997, 3.

14 In the Hanafi school, for example, fatwa collections fall under the category of *wāqiʿāt*, legal rulings that were not dealt with by Abu Hanifa or the early masters of the school, but were solved by later jurists. *Wāqiʿāt* is one of the three categories by which *furūʿ* works are classified. The others are *ẓāhir al-riwāya* and *masaʾil al-nawādir*. *Ẓāhir al-riwāya*, at the top of the hierarchy, includes works by Abu Hanifa (d. about 767) and his two disciples, Abu

Fatwas may be given orally, in writing, or by signs.[15] Whether oral or written, the giving of fatwas is subject to a number of conditions. These conditions are found in the *uṣūl al-fiqh* literature,[16] and in a separate literary genre called *ādāb al-muftī*.[17] One of the texts consulted, according to Muhammad Khalid Masud, is the *Ādāb al-fatwā wal-muftī wal-mustaftī* by Yahya b. Sharaf al-Nawawi (d. 1277).[18]

This text has also been translated to English in a somewhat abridged edition. It discusses the meaning of *iftāʾ*, the proper etiquette, requirements of the mufti, various types of muftis ranked by their qualifications,[19] and directions for fatwa-giving. Some noteworthy requirements: The answer must be absolute, categorical and detailed. If the answer is given orally, the mufti must speak slowly, so that the questioner may understand the answer. If in writing, it should be short and precise, and with no spaces in the document that others might fill in. Question and answer are to be written on the same sheet.[20] Writing "permitted," "not permitted," "true" or "not true" will suffice. There are also purely formal requirements. The fatwa is to begin with the *basmala* formula, and end with *bi-llāhi tawfīq, wa-Allāhu aʿlam* or *wa-Allāhu al-muwafaq*.[21] Rules of etiquette also apply to the *mustaftī* (the questioner), who is enjoined to seek out the best-qualified mufti, show good manners, and know how to pose questions. One may gather from the translator's foreword to the English edition of Nawawi's text how the *ādāb al-muftī* genre is also considered relevant in our age:

Yusuf (d. 807) and Shaybani (d. 804), plus a few cases ascribed to Zufar and al-Hasan b. Ziad. *Masaʾil al-nawādir* are legal works and cases ascribed to the same persons, but lacking the same authority, as they have not been passed on through a name chain of highly qualified legal scholars, or through many parallel name chains (Hallaq 1994).

15 A fatwa may be given by signs if they suffice to convey the aim of the fatwa. The following hadith is cited as an example: "The Prophet said: 'Allah will not punish or reward either the tears of the eye or the sorrow of the heart, but on account of this'," and he pointed to his tongue. Narrated by al-Bukhari in *Fath al-bārī*, quoted in *Masūʿatu l-fiqhiyya*, 32:41f.

16 See e.g. Skovgaard-Petersen 1997, 3.

17 See e.g. *EI3*, "Adab al-Muftī" (Masud 2010).

18 It is found in the introduction to Nawawi's work *Kitāb al-majmūʿ: sharḥ al-muhadhdhab lil-shīrāzī*.

19 The text distinguishes between independent and "non-independent" muftis, and paints a picture of the knowledge required in the two categories. Norman Calder 1996, 137–164 has dealt with Nawawi's typology of muftis and its significance for a general theory of Islamic law.

20 Al-Nawawi, 107–110.

21 Al-Nawawi, 108.

> This [rules for *iftā'*] is a subject which is of the highest importance in Islam (and its branches of knowledge) but which can become dangerous if in the hands of the wrong people (due to it being abused). The translator has personal experience of seeing its open abuse by those who are less qualified, claiming that they have the status of a 'MUFTI', hence causing chaos in the lives of many innocent people. Therefore we hope that this text will be an Authority, Guidance and protection for those who strive to be counted amongst the people of 'the saved group' (Ahl as-Sunnah wal Jamaʿa).[22]

Regarding such texts, Caeiro comments: "The composition of an adab al-fatwa treatise is usually presented by its author as a mere reiteration of a well established [...] Islamic discipline. [But] the end product of such efforts inevitably involves a selection, re-valorization, and re-interpretation of the old discipline."[23] He concludes that *ādāb al-fatwā* manuals supply information on more than just religious and legal matters, since they were articulated as responses to "specific social conditions". Accordingly, they tell of "... the shifting normative criteria that have defined the correct performance of a religious act and, in so doing, tell a story of changes in the moral economy of Muslim societies."[24] Among other examples, he mentions writings in the field by Yusuf al-Qaradawi and Tareq Oubrou.[25]

> Qaradawi's fatwa methodology is inseparable from his *taysir*, which is less a hermeneutical tool than an assessment of the contemporary requirements for the formation of pious Muslim selves. Oubrou's "negative fatwas" are theoretical constructs that epitomize his own misgivings towards the production of fatwas: circulated in the mass media, fatwas have seemingly become "badges of piety" rather than tools for its *cultivation*.[26]

Fatwas and Women-Related Questions

Fatwa collections could be organized in various ways. Often, fatwas were ordered according to the order in which questions were asked or fatwas given,

22 Al-Nawawi, 12.

23 Caeiro 2006, 663.

24 Caeiro 2006, 677.

25 With reference to al-Qaradawi 1995 and Oubrou 2004.

26 Caeiro 2006, 678.

Hallaq says,[27] commenting on this practice: "Clearly, this arrangement proved unsatisfactory in a tradition with strong inclination toward systematic ordering of legal subject matter. We know, for instance, that Muḥammad b. Hārūn al-Kinānī and ʿAbd al-Raḥmān al-Qaysī rearranged Ibn Rushd's *fatwās* according to *fiqh* subject matter."[28]

In what does this organization of subject matter consist? And where do we find women-related questions? One possible answer may be found in one of the earliest written fatwa sources, the *Muwaṭṭaʾ* (The Beaten Path) of Imam Malik (d. 795).[29] Dutton considers it an early example of a book of hadith, a prototype *ḥadīth ṣaḥīḥ* collection, and at the same time Malik's chief legal work.[30] It contains statements by the Companions and the following generation (*al-tābiʿūn*) and hadith about the Prophet, as well as hadiths about the practice of the Medinans. Malik's statements (what Calder terms "the *qāla Mālik* items") fall at the end of most of the chapters. Abdel Majid Turki describes the book as a *muṣannaf* hadith collection organized by subject, and not a *musnad*, which is organized by transmitters of the hadiths. "Le plan du *Muwaṭṭaʾ* est celui d'un ouvrage de fiqh," Turki writes.[31] The book may be divided into two main parts. First come subjects tied to the *ʿibādāt* (ritual actions) category: *ṣalāh* (ritual

27 Hallaq 1994, 36. Hallaq refers inter alia to al-Nawawi; Ibn Nujaym, a scholar associated with the Hanafi school (d. 1563); and Ibn Rushd (d. 1126).

28 Hallaq 1994, 37. According to Hallaq, *fiqh* manuals tend to vary as to the organization of the different subjects. Many jurists divided *fiqh* into four major fields: ritual, economic transactions, marriage, and injuries. Each major *fiqh* subject was dealt with in a *kitāb*, what we would call a "chapter". A *bāb* (subchapter) might be further divided into *fusūl* (sections), *masāʾil* (questions or issues) and *furūʿ* (specific cases). Hallaq also remarks: "It must be said that the synchronic and diachronic variations in the organization of these works within and across the school both remain a fertile subject of enquiry." Hallaq 2009, 551.

29 Dutton 2002, 22 ff. discusses the authenticity and age of the *Muwaṭṭaʾ*, concluding that it must have been available before the death of Imam Malik in 795. Norman Calder claims that legal theory is more developed in the *Muwaṭṭaʾ* than in the *Mudawwana*, and therefore considers the *Mudawwana* the oldest (Calder 1993, 24). He dates the *Muwaṭṭaʾ* to about 270/883 (1993, 37). Brockopp 2005, in turn, claims, based on the study of a text fragment, that the text he identifies as the *Mukhtaṣar* (Minor Compendium) of Ibn Abd al-Hakam (d. 829) may be the oldest, and that this is the first known text authored by a single person—in contrast to the *Muwaṭṭaʾ*, which he holds should be seen as an edited work with several persons involved (he uses the German term *Kolleghefte*).

30 Vikør 2005, 44; Dutton 2002. Dutton describes *al-Muwaṭṭaʾ* as "… a composite picture of what Mālik considered to be the essential aspect of the *dīn* in action" (Dutton 2002, 3).

31 Turki 1997, 10.

prayer), funerals, fasting, *i'tiqaf* (solitary retreat in the mosque in the month of Ramadan), *zakāh* (the welfare tax) and *ḥajj* (the pilgrimage). Then follow subjects that fall under the category of *mu'āmalāt* (social transactions), roughly: family and household, economic activities, issues concerning the legal system, individual practice, and moral ideals.[32] Except for marriage, divorce and *raḍā'* (see below), which may easily be categorized as women-related issues, it is clear that "women" as a category is not an ordering principle in the *Muwaṭṭa'*.

I submit that the fatwas given in the hadiths of the *Muwaṭṭa'* offer insight into the emergence of Islamic law based on lived experience, rather than on theoretical construction as found among later scholars. The chapter on *raḍā'*, which the *Encyclopedia of Islam* defines as "the suckling which produces the legal impediment to marriage of foster-kinship,"[33] may serve as a good example: The question was raised by A'isha after the hijab verse had been sent down (*ba'd 'an unzila al-ḥijāb*).[34] A new situation had arisen for the wives of the Prophet. Only a *maḥram* (male relative forbidden in marriage) was exempt from the new restriction. Since *raḍā'* would create a kinship tie that made marriage forbidden, it would form an exception from the restriction. Two main questions are posed: How many times must an individual be suckled before a foster relation is established? Can foster relations be established through suckling both for adults and children, or is this only possible during the child's first two years? In the chapter on *raḍā'* of adults, we find A'isha asking her sister and her nieces to suckle the men she wanted to visit her. The background was that the Prophet

---

32 According to Aisha Abdurrahman Bewley's translation of the *Muwaṭṭa'* (Mālik ibn Anas 2001), the subjects that fall under *mu'āmalāt* are: the book of jihad, of vows and oaths, of sacrificial animals, of slaughtering animals, of game, of the *'aqīqa* (a ceremony the week after the birth of a child), of fixed shares of inheritance, of marriage, of divorce, of suckling, of business transactions, of *qirād* (division of crops), of sharecropping, of renting land, of pre-emption in property, of judgements, of wills and testaments, of setting free and *walā'* (loyalty), of the *mukatab* (slave who wishes to be free), of the *mudabbar* (leadership), of *ḥudūd*, of drinks, of blood money, of the oath of *qasāma* (see "Ḳasam" in *EI2*; Schacht 1991, 24, 184), of Medina, of the (divine) decree, of good character, of dress, of the description of the Prophet, of the evil eye, of hair, of visions, of greetings, of various matters, of the oath of allegiance, of speech, of *jahannam* (hell), of *sadaqa* (alms), of knowledge, of the supplication of the unjustly wronged, and of the names of the Prophet.

33 "Raḍā' or Riḍā', also Raḍā'a" in *EI2* (Schacht and Chelhod 2010). On *raḍā'*, Schacht notes: "From the manner in which the Ḳur'ān presents its ruling, it may be supposed that the question was already familiar to those addressed." The hadiths quoted above, in my view, confirm this supposition. According to J. Chelhod, the ban against marriage between foster-siblings dates from the pre-Islamic period.

34 Referring to Quran 33:53.

had allowed Sahla bint Suhayl to establish a *maḥram* relation by suckling her adopted son Salim five times. They lived in a single room, and it was difficult to prevent him from entering at times when she was not properly covered for non-*maḥram* men. The Prophet's other wives did not accept the kind of practice A'isha suggested, and argued that the Prophet's permission to Sahla bint Suhayl applied to her alone, and was not generally valid. We may clearly see that the possibility of establishing *maḥram* relations between adults is narrowed in the hadith of a man who came to Umar ibn al-Khattab and told him that his wife tried to prevent him from having sexual congress with the slave girl by suckling her. Umar said he could go to the slave girl, as kinship by suckling was only possible for small children.[35]

It is interesting to see these women's creativity in their encounter with new norms. A'isha clearly did not want to be barred by a new, restrictive rule from communicating with men who were not *maḥram*, whereas the wife who sought to suckle the slave girl did so to avoid having to share her husband with her. These hadiths are also interesting as regards *ijtihād* (independent reasoning) and *iftāʾ*: A'isha and the other wives of the Prophet differed over whether the norms were general (*ʿamma*) or valid only in one case (*khaṣṣa*). The hadith about the man who came to Umar is an example of a *fatwā ṣaḥābī* (fatwa by one of the Companions).

The *Muwaṭṭaʾ* served as a prototype for the structure of later *fiqh* manuals, a structure that was also the model for editing fatwas.[36] The first fatwa collections were published in the second half of the 900s.[37] One of the earliest collections is the *Kitāb al-Nawāzil*, which contains fatwas given by a number of Hanafi jurists, collected and organized by Abu Layth al-Samarqandi (d. 983). Later, it became customary for a jurist's students to collect and edit his fatwas by fields of law.[38] For example, the most important fatwa collection in the Hanafi

35 *Al-Muwaṭṭaʾ*, ch. 30: Suckling, section 30.2 (Mālik ibn Anas 2001, 12–13).

36 Hallaq 1994, 36–37 refers to Ibn Nujaym's preface to *al-Fatāwa al-Zayniyya*, where Ibn Nujaym (who served as mufti from 1557) relates that he had first organized his fatwas in the order he had given them, but then edited them according to the structure of *fiqh* manuals. Nawawi (d. 1277) expressed the wish that others would reorganize his fatwas on the model of *fiqh* manuals, and this editorial work was later carried out by Ibn Ibrahim al-Attar. Hallaq also refers to modern-day editing work, such as that of Nizam Yaʿqubi from Bahrain on the *Fatāwa* of Ghazali.

37 Masud, Messick, and Powers 1996, 9.

38 Two examples are *Majmaʿ al-nawāzil wal-wāqiʿāt* of al-Natifi (d. 1054) and *Fatāwā Qādīkhān* of Qadikhan (d. 1195); Masud, Messick, and Powers 1996, 10. The authors refer to the article on "Nāzila" i *EI2*, and point out that the terms *fatāwā* og *nawāzil* (cases) were used interchangeably to signify "legal opinions issued by jurisprudents".

school, *al-Fatāwā al-ʿĀlīmjiriyya*, gives a systematic account of authoritative Hanafi doctrine, and ranks next to the *Hidaya*, the most prominent Hanafi *fiqh* manual.[39] *Al-fatāwā al-ʿĀlīmjiriyya* offers its own definition of a fatwa as an authoritative and accepted opinion within the Hanafi school, and not necessarily an answer to a question. Masud et al. tie this definition to the Indian subcontinent, where a work was characterized as a "fatwa collection" if it was about issues that arose in practice.[40]

A similar, expansive use of the term fatwa is also found in our time. According to Hallaq, publishers in the Muslim world seem to be giving loose connotations to the term by publishing works with titles including the word "fatwa".[41]

One may further mention the most important fatwa collection in the Maliki school, the *Kitāb al-miʿyār*, compiled by Ahmad al-Wansharisi (d. 1508). This is a collection of about 6,000 fatwas by 150 muftis living between the years 1000 and 1496 in the large towns of North Africa and al-Andalus. The fatwas are grouped according to the standard categories of Islamic jurisprudence (*fiqh*), "such as ritual practices ('ibādāt); marriage; divorce; exchange and sale; partnership; inheritance; testimony, etc."[42]

The main categories as formulated in the *Muwaṭṭa'* have been the prevailing paradigm in Islamic jurisprudence, be it in *fiqh* manuals or fatwa collections, up to the modern age. This means that "women" were not the subject of a chapter of their own, but were subordinated to the structure we find in the *Muwaṭṭa'*.

Today, the picture looks quite different. The position of women is intensely debated among Muslims in Western Europe, and the women's issue is central to the encounter between Islamic identity and Western societies. This also finds expression in the production of fatwas, with "women" and "family" becoming categories of Islamic legal discourse. However, this discourse did not arise on its own in contemporary Western Europe. Its roots lie in Egypt in the late 1800s. In the following, I will present the historical line of this discourse—the actors,

39 *Al-Fatāwā al-ʿĀlīmjiriyya* was collected by a group of forty scholars led by Shaykh Nizam of Burhanpur (d. 1679) on the order of the Mogul ruler Awrangzeb Alamgir (1618–1707).

40 Masud, Messick, and Powers 1996, 14–15.

41 As an example, Hallaq mentions the *Majmuʿ Fatāwā Shaykh al-Islām Aḥmad Ibn Taymiyya*. The work is a collection of many theological and legal works by Ibn Taymiyya, and it also contains a number of fatwas, but technically, it is not a fatwa collection, argues Hallaq 1994, 32 n. 17. *Fatāwā Ibn Taymiyya* appears to be viewed as a major work in what one might call an "Islamic reference library," often published as software on CDs. For example, the Kuwaiti ministry of religion has published *al-Maktaba al-islāmiyya al-jāmiʿa*, a set of seven CDs, of which one is the *Fatāwā Ibn Taymiyya*.

42 Zorgati 2007, 17.

the arguments, the method and the concepts—since it is directly relevant to the topic of *iftāʾ* in Western Europe, and is an example of the transnational character of Islamic jurisprudence.

Women in Focus—a Twentieth-Century Trend

Late 19th-century Egypt saw a shift in the position of women as a subject of Islamic discourse.[43] The idea of social reform had taken root, particularly with regard to women's issues. Its framework was the idea of the Egyptian nation, which Rifaʿa Badawi Rafiʿ al-Tahtawi (d. 1873) had been the first to try to explain and legitimate.[44] Hourani describes Tahtawi's demands for reform of women's conditions:

> Girls must be educated as much as boys, and on the same footing [...] The teaching of girls was necessary for three reasons: for harmonious marriages and the good upbringing of children; so that women could work, as men work, within the limits of their capacity; and to save them from the emptiness of a life of gossip in the harem. [...] Polygamy is not forbidden, he maintains, but Islam only allows it if the husband is capable of doing justice between his wives.[45]

Similar ideas were developed further by the jurist Qasim Amin[46] and published in 1899 in the far more famous book *Taḥrīr al-marʾa* (Women's Liberation), which grew out of a public polemic over family life and nation in Egypt.[47] The book takes a Darwinian perspective. The dangers to Egypt's development, Amin held, lay in the challenge posed by the civilization of the West:

---

43 The discussion here is limited to Egypt, since this is relevant for the line of muftis that leads to my materials.

44 Hourani 1987, 69.

45 Hourani 1987, 77–78.

46 Qasim Amin (1865–1908) was of Kurdish origin, born in Egypt, educated in France and worked as a judge.

47 According to Laading 1986, Francois Charles Marie, Duc d' Harcourt, in 1893 published the book *L'Egypt et les égyptiens*. He criticized the decadence and stagnation of Egyptian society, the roots of which he traced to Egyptian family life and to women's lack of knowledge, esteem and freedom. The book made waves and was discussed both privately in Eugenie Le Brun Rushdi's salon for women, which prepared the ground for the later women's movement, and publicly, in princess Nazli Fazil's salon for men, a political and intellectual centre of Cairo.

> Western civilization, speeded by steam and electricity, is advancing and has expanded from its origins to all parts of the earth. [...] Whenever Western civilization enters into a country, it seizes the wealth and resources of that country including agriculture, industry, and commerce. [...] whenever Westerners encounter a country like ours—a country with a former civilization, with historical traditions, religion, laws, and customs and with some form of elementary organization [...] they usually intermingle with the inhabitants, interact with them, and live with them amicably for a while, and then eventually acquire their most important resources of wealth.[48]

The reason for Egypt's weak position, Amin claims, is not biology, but the loss of moral fortitude and social virtues due to *ignorance*, as well as the corruption of Islam "from outside".[49] The "social core" of the problem could be found in the position of women, the improvement of which would strengthen the "moral standard of the nation."[50]

Amin's book may be considered part of a nationalist project: liberating Egypt from Ottoman domination and Western colonialism. He demanded mandatory education of girls, at least on the "elementary level," the abolition of face veils and sex segregation, the right of women to decide for themselves on contracting marriage, a ban on polygamy, and delegation of the unilateral male right of divorce (*ṭalāq*) to the judiciary.[51] These demands implied a new interpretation of the Sharia and a reform of the legal status of women in family law. Amin blamed the religious scholars for the situation of women, since they defended the *status quo* through *taqlīd* (imitation), as an argument for rejecting all demands for reform.

Amin was a student of, and belonged to the circle around, Muhammad Abduh, the architect of Islamic modernism.[52] Modernism was based on the

48 Amin 1992, 62f.

49 Hourani 1987, 164.

50 In English translation, the heading of the introduction to *Taḥrīr al-mar'a* runs: "The Status of Women in Society: A Reflection of the Nation's Moral Standard."

51 Qasim Amin uses the term "hijab" when discussing face veiling and segregation. The point of departure is the Quran 33:53, which applies to the wives of the Prophet, and where "hijab" is interpreted as a curtain. It is clear from Amin's text, however, that the demand for removing the "veil" refers to the face veil: "The disadvantages of veiling are without a doubt the reason the Sharīʿa allows the woman to uncover her face and her palms. I am not asking for more than what the Sharīʿa allows" (Amin 1992, 41).

52 Muhammad Abduh was a theologian, a jurist, and for the last six years of his life, the Mufti

view of the Muslim world as decadent and subordinate to the West. The modernist project consisted in bridging the gap between traditional Muslim culture and modern Western influences, without going against central Islamic dogma, such as the teaching about one God (*tawḥīd*), and that the Quran is the word of God as revealed to the Prophet Muhammad. The modernists accepted an evolutionary perspective on world history, with the West at the summit of the hierarchy of civilisations. They recognized modern sciences and supported democracy, a divide between religion and politics, and the promotion of women's rights. A "reform from within" was to contribute to resisting Western domination and the secularization of Egyptian society. This involved a certain interpretation of Islam, Islamic sources, and Islamic history. "It was their [the modernists'] contention that an Islam correctly interpreted and set free of traditional ballast was able to provide a viable system of beliefs and values even under the changed circumstances of modern times."[53]

With *Taḥrīr al-mar'a*, Qasim Amin gave the women's question a central place in the modernist agenda. The argument for women's liberation was based on Muhammad Abduh's project of reform or *tajdīd* (renewal).[54] Abduh had a central role in its publication. Muhammad Ammara, known for the compilation and editing of the collected works of Muhammad Abduh, claims that *Taḥrīr al-mar'a* was written to order for Abduh by Qasim Amin, his student, and that they each wrote part of the book, Amin the general argument, and Abduh the *fiqh* arguments. Ammara believes this can be seen in different styles of language in the text.[55]

Abduh's point of departure was the distinction between *'ibādāt* (worship) and *mu'āmalāt* (social transactions). Whereas specific rules are given for *'ibādāt* in the Quran and in the Sunna of the Prophet as expressed in the hadith literature, only general guidelines are given for subjects connected with *mu'āmalāt*. This fact legitimated and necessitated *ijtihād* (independent reasoning) to

---

of Egypt. He was trained in traditional disciplines at al-Azhar, and had belonged to the Shadhiliyya order in his youth. Abduh and Amin were close friends, and they both frequented Nazli Fazil's salon for young men in Cairo.

53 Philipp 1978, 278.

54 *Tajdīd* has been described as: "The attempt by Islamic modernizers and Salafiyah advocates to introduce more Islamic influences into the lives of Muslims who have been subject to Western currents of thought and practice particularly in the wake of the Napoleonic invasion of Egypt. [...] A distinction should be made here between the strict and orthodox Salafiyah trend and the reformist trend championed by people such as Muhammad 'Abduh." *OEMIW*, "Revival and Renewal" (3:431).

55 Conversation with Muhammad Ammara, Cairo, March 2008.

seek "new answers to new questions". In re-interpreting, Abduh stressed two methods of interpretation that legitimated change and adaptation: *maṣlaḥa ʿamma* (public interest) and *talfīq* (selection and composition). *Maṣlaḥa ʿamma* made it possible that "a jurist using his own reason might interpret the law in the light of public interest"[56]—with regard to *muʿāmalāt*, and in those cases not covered by texts. *Talfīq* offered the option of choosing between the four schools of law to find a suitable interpretation for a case. The legitimation of *ijtihād* and the use of *maṣlaḥa* and *talfīq* enabled the justification and implementation of legal reforms that met the changed needs of society.[57] In 1900, Abduh worked out an eleven-point proposal expanding women's right to demand divorce. The legal proposal was based on the practice of the Maliki school, and supported Amin's demands for reform.[58] Abduh also argued against polygamy in what would become published as *Tafsīr al-Manār*:[59] "… Polygyny is in contrast to the original nature of marriage. Verily the origin is for a man to have one woman, and he is towards her as she is towards him."[60]

Taḥrīr al-marʾa drew unprecedented attention.[61] It "shook Egypt" and prompted a number of reactions,[62] and Amin was both praised and contested. Huda Sharawi, the founder of the Egyptian Women's Union, called him "the father of Egyptian feminism".[63] Other reactions were far more skeptical. The Egyptian nationalist Taʿlat Harb "… rejected Amin's interpretations of the religious precepts and the claim that woman was man's equal in moral, physical and mental terms."[64] He felt that women's liberation would weaken the Egyptian nation, and accused Amin, who was of Kurdish origin, of meddling in internal Egyptian affairs.[65]

---

56 Esposito, cited in Laading 1986, 58.

57 Laading 1986, 59.

58 The eleven points are reproduced in Amin 1995, 89 ff. The report was approved by al-Azhar rector Salim al-Bishri on 2 Aug 1899 (6 Rabiʾ Thani 1318).

59 Muhammad Abduh's lectures at al-Azhar were later published as *Tafsīr al-Manār* (Sedgwick 2009, 85 ff.).

60 Translation in Roald 2001a, 202.

61 *Al-Manār* 3 (32) (6 Feb 1901): 850.

62 Adams 1968, 231 refers to a contributor to the *al-Siyāsa* newspaper, who claims that "… in studying the works of Ḳāsim and the replies which they evoked, he had discovered no less than thirty books and pamphlets written to refute his books or to attack him personally."

63 Laading 1986, VI.

64 Laading 1986, 140.

65 Philipp 1978, 279.

> From conservative religious quarters, especially those concentrated around al-Azhar, Amin was attacked for subjecting sacred revelation to personal, rational evaluation, and he was accused of heresy. His claim that legal reform was necessary for the progress of society was seen as a direct attack on religion, and his methods of reform were roundly rejected.[66]

Muhammad Rashid Rida's support for Qasim Amin, on the other hand, is apparent in the introduction to the review of *al-Mar'a al-jadīda* (The Modern Woman, 1900), which Amin had written as a reply to the critics of *Taḥrīr al-mar'a*. Rida panegyrically praises the two books of Amin: like "twin brothers" and "thoroughbred horses," they stem from the same "fresh spring". He also criticizes the opponents of Amin's books, calls them "foolish" and accuses them of having weak arguments.[67] For all this, Rida considered Amin mainly a theoretician, not a practical man.[68] However, Amin's position in the judicial system, as a judge and Chancellor of the Cairo National Court of Appeals, may have given him insight into the practical challenges faced by Egyptian women, not least with regard to divorce. Muhammad al-Ghazali (d. 1996), too, defends Qasim Amin in the book *Les problemes de la femme entre les traditions et la modernité*.[69] According to al-Ghazali, his fundamental contribution lay in defending Islam against the attacks in Duc de Harcourt's book *L'Égypte et les Égyptiens* (1893).[70] Al-Ghazali is clearly referring to Amin's *Les Égyptiens: Réponse à M. le Duc d'Harcourt* (1894). It is interesting that al-Ghazali, when defending Amin, refers to the book that defends traditional interpretations in order to stress the excellence of Islam, and not to *Taḥrīr*.

In more recent times, too, Amin is criticized. Ahmed accuses Amin of bending his knee to Western colonial attitudes:

> [... T]he fundamental and contentious premise for Amin's work was its endorsement of the Western view of Islamic civilization, peoples, and customs as inferior, whereas the author's position on women was profoundly patriarchal and even somewhat misogynist. The book merely called for the substitution of Islamic-style male dominance by Western-style male dominance.[71]

---

66 Laading 1986, 137.

67 *Al-Manār* 3 (32) (6 Feb 1901): 850.

68 Rida's obituary.

69 Al-Ghazali 1994, 25–27.

70 Al-Ghazali 1994, 26.

71 Ahmed 1992, 162. The author refers to the views on Islam and women of lord Cromer

Nergis Mazid, convinced of Amin's sincerity, takes a more amicable view: "... he found compabilities between his interpretations of Orientalism and Islam regarding women's morality and the nation's strength."[72] Laading comments that Amin's critique and views held challenges:

> In many ways, Amin stood at the intersection of the two orientations: secularisation of society through a reform programme modeled on the West, or Islamisation of society, defense of one's own norms and values and rejection of all Western influence. In *Taḥrīr*, Amin sought a middle road by following Abduh's programme of reform and using Islam as the uniting factor in further development.[73]

Amin is controversial, and some see him as a threat to Islam.[74] We may conclude that Amin through his book contributed to making women a central issue on the modernist agenda, viewed in the light of (i) the Muslim world's relations with the West and (ii) new methods of interpretation in the encounter with the new era. However, it was more about nation-building than about women's rights. Yvonne Haddad writes:

> For those who participated in the [nation-building] endeavor, change in the role of women was from the beginning among the most important concerns, especially in the areas of education, seclusion, polygyny

(British consul general to Egypt, 1883–1907): "... the reasons 'Islam as a social system has been a complete failure are manifold.' However, 'first and foremost,' he asserts, was its treatment of women. [...] Whereas Christianity teaches respect for women, and European men 'elevated' women because of the teachings of their religion, Islam degraded them, Cromer wrote [...] However, it was in his activities in relation to his own country that Cromer's paternalistic conviction and his belief in the proper subordination of women most clearly declared themselves. This champion of the unveiling of Egyptian women was, in England, founding member and sometime president of the Men's League for Opposing Women's Suffrage." Ahmed 1992, 152 f.

72 Mazid 2002, 42.

73 Laading 1986, 135.

74 I personally experienced being criticized by the moderator during a session of the XIX Conference of the Supreme Council of Islamic Affairs, Cairo, 27–30 Mar 2007, where I gave a paper on women as a subject of Islamic debate from 1899 to present-day Western Europe, titled "Islam facing Everyday Challenges: Islam and Women in a Historical Perspective". The moderator commented: "How could you think of mentioning Qasim Amin in the same distinguished company of scholars such as Muhammad Abduh and Muhammad Rashid Rida?"

> and divorce. The survival of the nation was seen as contingent on these changes, not so much out of the innate equality of male and female as for the utilitarian goal of achieving parity with Europe.[75]

This process of nation-building included legal reforms, which meant structural changes[76] and centralization. Whereas so-called Sharia courts had held jurisdiction over urban Muslims, Sharia law was now limited to governing family law and the *awqāf* (religious foundations). By bureaucratizing the Sharia courts according to Western principles, the Sharia was incorporated into a modernizing state, Asad writes. "Law began to disentangle itself from the dictates of religion, becoming thereby both more modern and more secular."[77] Asad describes this change as follows: "[… W]hat happens to the *sharīʿa* is best described not as curtailment but as transmutation. It is rendered into a subdivision of legal norms (*fiqh*) that are authorized and maintained by the centralizing state."[78] In this new landscape, the "family" emerges as a category that covers the subject areas of the Sharia courts as described by Muhammad Abduh in an 1899 report.[79] Focusing on the family as a category, then, is in line with the modernization of Egyptian society. "So if Muhammad Abduh regards the family as the basic unit of society, it is not because he invokes a nostalgic past but because something new is now emerging in the changing social structure."[80]

In this light, Asad interprets Amin's *Taḥrīr al-marʾa*, which he characterises as the most well-known example of the Egyptian upper-class discussion of "the ideal family": "Among the upper urban classes, Western-type schooling (in European languages) and the adoption of Western domestic styles and manners also produced a discourse of the ideal family—typically expressed in terms of 'the problem of the status of Muslim women' […]"[81]

The modernist heritage may be traced in what Margot Badran styles secular feminism:

> 'Secular feminism' has been used to signify the feminisms developed by Muslims as citizens within the context of nation-states rather than as Muslims solely within the framework of their religious community

75 Haddad 1998, 4.
76 For the various legal systems in Egypt before the legal reform, see Asad 2003, 210.
77 Asad 2003, 211f.
78 Asad 2003, 227.
79 Asad 2003, 228.
80 Asad 2003, 232.
81 Asad 2003, 232f.

> (*ummah*) [...] The Islamic scrutiny to which Muslim women as incipient feminists subjected practices said to be ordained, such as female domestic seclusion and face veiling, and their moves to reject practices they discovered not to be ordained by religion would be a hallmark of Muslims' secular feminisms.[82]

The modernist heritage was also preserved by secular jurists, which led to the codification of family law around the Muslim law. The Tunisian family law adopted in 1956 is particularly well known because it bans polygamy. "[... B]y legislation enacted i 1956, Tunisia has put herself in the forefront of the movement of legislative modernism," Schacht comments on this law.[83]

Muhammad Abduh as a Mufti

Muhammad Abduh was appointed Mufti of Egypt in 1899. During his time as mufti, he gave nearly a thousand fatwas.[84] Muhammad Ammara divides Abduh's fatwas into three categories by subject matter: economics (728 fatwas), family and marriage ("more than a hundred"), and killing and retribution (29 fatwas).[85] A number of his fatwas have been published in recent years. A selection of 184 fatwas was published by Muhammad Ammara as part of the publication of the collected works of Muhammad Abduh.[86] Abduh's role as a mufti was also central to the centennial of Abduh's death observed by *al-*

82 "Feminism" in *OEIW* (Badran 2009, 246–247).

83 Schacht 1991, 105–108.

84 Skovgaard-Petersen 1997, 121, citing *Fatāwā al-islāmiyya*, vol. 1: 34–35, gives the official number as 1,044. The number may vary depending on whether some of the attached documents are considered fatwas in their own right.

85 Skovgaard-Petersen cites Kemke, who "... concludes that Abduh's fatwas fall squarely within the limits of standard Hanafi works on waqf, so that while Abduh in his political and theoretical works argues against taqlīd, he is himself in practice following Hanafi fiqh, in his fatwas on *waqf*. This may, however, be explained by the lack of references to *waqf* in the Koran and hadith; it is not a field where the mufti can make a new *ijtihād* based on a new reading of the central Koranic passages." Skovgaard-Petersen 1997, 122.

86 Skovgaard-Petersen 1997, 121. Skovgaard-Petersen also mentions Rashid Rida, who devoted 72 pages to Abduh's work as a mufti in "Tarīkh al-ustādh al-imām al-shaykh Muḥammad 'Abduh," *al-Manār* (1931): 646–718.

Jamaʿiyyat al-khayriyyat al-islāmiyya, which saw the publication of 191 of Abduh's fatwas in a collection edited by the then Mufti of Egypt, Ali Jumʿa.[87]

Jumʿa's collection is divided into two main parts: *ʿibādāt* and *muʿāmalāt*, with the latter taking most of the space. Financial matters are central, and fall mainly under the subjects of *waqf* (57 fatwas) and inheritance/testaments (*al-mawārith*, 54 fatwas). The fatwas on inheritance follow a traditional Hanafi interpretation of the Quran. Thirteen fatwas concern the contracting of marriage, whereas divorce is dealt with in ten fatwas. The fatwas are interesting, not because they go beyond the existing *fiqh*, but because they clearly form answers to detailed questions tied to actual challenges of everyday life—not general treatises on hypothetical cases. Adams explains that Abduh, unlike his predecessors, allowed individual petitions for fatwas.[88] Adams describes Abduh's fatwas as follows: "The many 'fatwās' which he delivered [...] were characterized by a spirit of liberality and a freedom from bondage to tradition and a desire to render the religion of Islām entirely adaptable to the requirements of modern civilization."[89] One example is the fatwa on whether marriage solemnized by German authorities is valid in Egypt.[90] Abduh replies in the affirmative, on the grounds that any marriage contracted "in Germany or another European country" is valid as long as the requirement of two witnesses is satisfied and the bride is of the *ahl al-kitāb*. The fatwa is not the product of a reformist interpretation, however; it represents a classical Hanafi position on the matter of witnesses.[91] As we have seen above, Abduh presented an eleven-point programme of divorce reform. There are ten fatwas on divorce in Jumʿa's collection of Abduh's fatwas. Abduh's close contact with ordinary Muslims shows through in the questions. But does he follow his own principles of reform? Skovgaard-Petersen refers to Kemke, who claims that Abduh's fatwas on *awqāf* fall inside the framework of the Hanafi school, and comments: "Still, it seems that in the overwhelming majority of fatwas Muḥammad Abduh never resorted to the *ijtihād* which he so warmly advocated."[92]

87 Jumʿa 2005, 4. *Al-jamaʿiyyat al-khayriyyat al-islāmiyya* was founded in 1896 in response to the threat of British colonization, with the aim of offering education and financial support for Egyptian citizens.

88 Fatwas requested by public authorities were to follow the Hanafi school, whereas an "unofficial fatwa" would follow the *madhhab* of the questioner (Adams 1968, 80 f., n. 6).

89 Adams 1968, 80.

90 Jumʿa 2005, 196 (fatwa no. 102).

91 Al-Marghinani 1989, 1:75.

92 Skovgaard-Petersen 1997, 123.

According to Badawi, Abduh's contribution to Islamic thought consisted in "… a method, albeit imprecise, rather than a complete interpretation of Islam."[93] In his evaluation,

> Abduh's legal reform […] consisted primarily of resurrecting an old principle […], *talfīq*, […] the use of all schools of thought and the works of all *Ulema* as a source from which to select the most suitable legislation for any current problem. However, he never deviated from the established schools of law. In essence, therefore, what Abduh was calling for was the abandonment of specific taqlid in favour of a general one.[94]

Mark Sedgwick holds that Abduh did not write at any length on methodology, and in general spent little or no time examining the basis for a conclusion. It seems that he was more concerned with the conclusion than with the methodology used to reach it. This also went for his objection to polygamy, which according to Sedgwick was a conclusion reached based on his readings on the topic, his reflections, and his experience over the years.[95]

However, Abduh's women-related fatwas have not, to my knowledge, been examined with a view to the methods and concepts used to derive the norms, as would be necessary to confirm or disconfirm Skovgaard-Petersen's view.

The Salafiyya Movement

The modern Salafiyya movement[96] stressed *ijtihād* at the cost of *taqlīd* ("blind imitation").[97] The most prominent members of the movement belonged to the tiers of society that were the most exposed to European thought, and according to Skovgaard-Petersen, they had adopted the social, ethical and political values of the 19th century, which they felt accorded with the message of Islam

---

93 Badawi 1978, 95.

94 Badawi 1978, 80 f.

95 Sedgwick 2009, 100.

96 The modern *Salafiyya* reform movement, founded by Jamal al-Din al-Afghani and Muhammad Abduh, must be distinguished from *Salafī* thought, which may be traced back to pre-modern *Salafiyya* on the Arabic Peninsula, such as the *Wahhābī* movement founded by Muhammad ibn Abd al-Wahhab (d. 1792). See "Salafiyah" in OEIW (Shahin 2009); Roald 2001b, 50.

97 "Taqlīd" i *Dictionary of Modern Written Arabic*: "[uncritical] adoption of the legal decision of a madhhab" (Wehr 1976, 786).

and could be implemented in society right away. It was necessary, however, to interpret the juristic materials anew, or even better, disregard them in favour of new studies of the Quran itself, that is, *ijtihād*. "Thus *ijtihād* and *taqlīd* come to mean the rational, authentic (and modern) way of life, as opposed to a tradition that dares not to consult the Koran and the Sunna to see how much it has degenerated."[98]

The one who carries out independent reasoning (the *mujtahid*) is therefore expected to be "the modern man who knows enough about history to realize that humans are limited in their understanding, and often wrong, and that consequently every man should go through the proofs by himself and consult all the scientific knowledge available on the subject."[99] Dissemination of knowledge becomes a main concern of the leading Salafiyya, who make use of the printed word to reach the public through their own publications. As early as 1884, Muhammad Abduh and Jamal al-Din al-Afghani published *al-ʿUrwa al-Wuthqā* (The Firmest Bond) in Paris. The leading publisher, however, would be Rashid Rida, who founded *al-Manār* (The Lighthouse), the mouthpiece of the Salafiyya movement, and edited it from 1898 to 1935.[100] *Al-Manār* was first published weekly, then bi-weekly, and finally monthly. The page number increased from eight to 80 pages per issue, except for a decline during World War I. According to Rida, the press should serve the *umma* (the Muslim society or nation) and has three aims: *taʿlīm* (education), *khatāba* (preaching) and *iḥtisāb* ("promoting good and prohibiting evil"). As we will see, the fatwa institution was to play an important role in this regard. Traditionally, contacts between scholars and laymen had been limited to sermons and fatwas. Whereas sermons were directed to groups, *iftāʾ* was usually a private matter. This changed when *al-Manār* in its third year got a separate fatwa column. "A special section of each issue was given to answers to questions of morality and practice sent by the readers to the periodical—and perhaps sometimes contributed by the editor himself."[101] The fatwas were not addressed to a specific person, but to the reader, who might not even have considered the subject of the fatwa. Since following a fatwa is not mandatory, but is up to the believer, the *al-Manār* fatwas primarily functioned to enlighten the populace, not least with regard to new social phenomena. The Salafiyya fatwas often involved a new *ijtihād* at the

98 Skovgaard-Petersen 1997, 67.
99 Skovgaard-Petersen 1997, 68.
100 My description of the Salafiyya press and the fatwas in *al-Manār* is based on Skovgaard-Petersen 1997, 69ff.
101 Hourani 1987, 237.

expense of the established norms (*aḥkām*) of the schools of law. New norms in the *fiqh* literature are fatwas by definition.

Muhammad Rashid Rida

Muhammad Rashid Rida gave a total of 2,592 fatwas in *al-Manār*. He based the fatwas on the Quran, hadith and *ʿaql*, the use of the intellect.[102] Rida distinguishes between the unchangeable and the changeable.[103] The former category includes *ʿibādāt* and some general ethical rules of *muʿāmalāt*. The latter category includes most of *muʿāmalāt*, which is of a social and political character, and may therefore be changed. Moreover, Rida's use of *istiḥsān* (juristic preference) opened for extensive novel interpretations. In 1927, he gave a fatwa on whether an uneducated Muslim (*āmmī*) may depart from the *taqlīd* of the four schools of law.[104] Rida answered in the affirmative, basing his reasoning on a discussion of the method and conceptual apparatus of the Salafiyya movement, in which Islamic tradition itself was used as an argument to reject *taqlīd* and go beyond the four schools of law in order to uncover the right practice.[105] The point is not to practice Islam based on the *opinions* of the scholars, but to examine these opinions in light of the Quran and Sunna, which are seen as the superior authority. Unequivocal texts require uniform practice, whereas texts with several meanings, or the absence of text, cannot be made into a general law. How, then, is the right practice to be determined? In his fatwa, Rida places the onus on the questioner, *al-mustaftī*, who must be aware that a mufti is not a legislator and cannot force his opinion on the questioner. When one asks an *ʿālim*, it is in order that one may decide for oneself whether or not to follow the answer or not. Faith in a *ḥukm* (norm) should depend on the conscience of *al-mustaftī*, and should be based on his confidence that he is following the norm

102 Masud, Messick, and Powers 1996, 31.

103 The presentation of Rida's theories is taken from Skovgaard-Petersen 1997, 73, which refers to Rida's book *Kitāb muḥawarāt al-muṣliḥ wal-muqallid* as it is presented in Kerr 1966, 190.

104 *Al-Manār* 28 (6) (1927): 427–430.

105 Rida lists the *ẓahiriyya* of Ibn Hazm along with two Shiʿi schools of law as an argument that "the four" have not reigned supreme, and points out that earlier practice involved elements from various schools of law. He also mentions the use of method as an argument. For instance, there is no consensus on the use of *qiyās* (analogy). Some reject it, while others differ over how to use it.

of God, and not just the opinion of a scholar.[106] This is not a novel approach. According to Rida, the first Muslims, who are held up as models for the modern Muslim, focused on knowledge of "what God says," and in seeking to partake of this knowledge, they did not restrict themselves to one single person. Rida's argument holds the lay Muslim responsible for acquiring knowledge, and this has an impact on the view of the authority of the scholar.

Rida's References

When Rida draws on all four schools of law for *iftā'*, his model is Taqi al-Din Ahmad ibn Taymiyya, who rejected *taqlīd* and supported *ijtihād* based on a literal interpretation of the sacred sources, and who condemned the cult of saints, discursive theology (*'ilm al-kalām*), philosophy and metaphysical Sufism. Ibn Taymiyya's chief doctrine consisted in a view of the Quran, Sunna and early Muslims (*al-salaf*) as the foremost authority.[107] By virtue of living after the four Imams, he had a unified knowledge of them that the Imams had not themselves possessed. Moreover, he had knowledge of innovations and traditions (such as those mentioned above) of which the Imams had not been aware. Ibn Taymiyya applied this accumulated knowledge in his fatwas. He pointed to differences and arguments among the four Imams, and went on to examine the proofs and to give a reasoned presentation of the proofs he felt carried the most weight. According to Rida, the governing principle of most of Ibn Taymiyya's fatwas was "justice".[108]

In his fatwa on *iftā'*, Rida also refers to Ibn Qayyim al-Jawziyya's (d. 1350) book *I'lām al-muwaqqi'īn 'an rabb al-'ālamīn* (Instruction to Those Who Sign on Behalf of the Lord of All the Worlds), a work of *'uṣūl al-fiqh* intended as a theoretical and practical manual for muftis. It offers a theoretical background for the collected fatwas of Ibn Taymiyya, and also refers to a number of them. According to Skovgaard-Petersen, its interest lies in the instruction that the

---

106 Rida uses the expression *ḥāka fī ṣadrik*, which may be understood as "something gnawing in the breast," which he, with a contemporary reference, defines as "conscience".

107 "Ibn Taymīyah" in OEIW (Nettler 2009, 502) According to Nettler, Ibn Taymiyyah was persecuted and imprisoned in Syria og Egypt inter alia for his idiosyncratic legal judgments about divorce. Laoust 2010 states that "... he was criticized for denying the validity of uniting three repudiations into one single ..." ("Ibn Taymiyya, Taḳī al-Dīn Aḥmad Ibn Taymiyya" in EI2).

108 *Al-Manār* 28 (6) (1927): 423f.

mufti should work independently. In the 1920s, Rida edited works by Ibn al-Qayyim, prompting a renaissance for his thought that has lasted up to the present.

Ibn al-Qayyim attacks *taqlīd* and supports the method used by Ibn Taymiyya in his fatwas, namely, comparing and contrasting the four schools of law. Ibn al-Qayyim defines Sharia as follows:

> The Sharīʿa is founded upon the administration of justice (*al-ḥukm*) and the interests of the servants of God (*al-ʿubbād*) in their earthly existence and in the hereafter: It is all justice and mercy and benefit and wisdom. No ruling can go against justice, mercy, wisdom or the benefit of the believers and still be part of the Sharīʿa.[109]

This places demands on the mufti. He must not only have knowledge of the Quran, Sunna and jurisprudence, but also understand his own age and its needs. Skovgaard characterizes Ibn Qayyim al-Jawziyya as follows: "A wide definition of the Sharīʿa with a change of emphasis from the rules of the *fiqh* manuals to the interests of the community is what most of all makes Ibn Qayyim al-Jawziyya valuable to the reformers at the turn of the century."[110]

Rida was the leading student of Muhammad Abduh, the one that carried on his legacy and interpreted his doctrines.[111] Adams asserts about Rida that: "He has attempted no independent work in either theology or philosophy, but in editing the works of his master and in his notes and comments on the same he shows his grasp of the subjects involved."[112]

Rida and Women's Issues

Hourani, however, states that "[t]he limits of his sympathy with the modern world, and the strength of his roots in tradition, were shown most clearly perhaps in the discussion of women, a contribution to the discussion started by Qasim Amin."[113] Rida dealt with women's rights on the principle "… that every woman should have a legal guardian, to give her all she needs to be an hon-

109 Ibn Qayyim al-Jawziyya, *Iʿlām al-muwaqqiʿīn ʿan rabb al-ʿālamīn*, Cairo: Dār al-ḥadīth, 1987, vol. 2, book 3, p. 1, quoted from Skovgaard-Petersen 1997, 77.

110 Skovgaard-Petersen 1997, 77.

111 Adams 1968, 177.

112 Adams 1968, 180.

113 Hourani 1987, 238.

ourable virgin, a virtuous wife, a careful mother, and a respected grandmother. She who is prevented from being wife or mother is not thereby prevented from enjoying protection and honour."[114] This principle is clearly based on a biological argument, which also has conseqences for his view of women's rights. "There is an equality of rights, but there is an inequality of fact, for men are stronger, more intelligent, more apt for learning and most types of action. So they have a predominance over women …"[115] He also took a more positive view of polygamy than did Muhammad Abduh: "… indeed polygamy is always justified if it does not contradict the principle of justice and if there are advantages derived from it."[116] Here, we see a more conservative turn compared with Qasim Amin's and Muhammad Abduh's views on women-related questions.

Already in 1901, writes Muhammad Qasim Zaman, Rida had published selections from the contemporary English press purporting to show that some English women had themselves come to see polygamy as a solution to the ills afflicting their societites.[117] He did the same in the book *Nidāʾ lil-jins al-laṭīf* (A Call to the Fair Sex, 1932). This sums up Rida's view of women:

> Rida argues that Islam treats women and men equally in terms of their religious obligations and their ability to earn God's favor. Women have the right to choose a spouse (although entering into marriage requires a male guardian), and they have clearly stipulated rights and responsibilities in a marriage, just as men do. Men are the heads of the household, but this, he reasons, eminently suits the good of all parties concerned. The book has sections on veiling, on the etiquette of good Muslim women, and on divorce. The heart of the book is, however, a defense of polygamy, together with the discussion of the Prophet's polygamous household.[118]

According to Zaman, the book was ostensibly addressed to Muslim women, but was also equally intended for an imagined European audience whose lingering ignorance and reservations about Islam it seeks to dispel. Only their lack of acquaintance with the teachings of Islam prevented European women from following them.[119] Clearly, the modernist view of Europe as a model is no longer

114 Rida, *Nidāʾ ilā al-jins al-laṭīf*, 121, quoted in Hourani 1987, 239.

115 Hourani 1987, 238.

116 Hourani 1987, 239.

117 Zaman 2012, 196.

118 Zaman 2012, 200.

119 Zaman 2012, 200. Zaman also explains how Rida aimed his book at women in the West, a fascinating story that is also an example of the globalization of Islamic debates.

present. The book seems to be part of a shift in the focus of Rida's work, partly as a result of World War I and its consequences, together with the fall of the caliphate.

Changing Views of the West

Before World War I, Europe was in a superior position, and laid down the terms in which progress and development would be viewed. This engendered a feeling of subjugation in the Muslim world. Kramer writes:

> By the late nineteenth century, reformers could posit the existence of an almost universal Muslim predicament, one of subjugation to the West, and they held that discord within the community of believers was partly to blame for their tribulations. The affective affinity of Muslims on the plane of theory was not sufficient. What was required was effective solidarity.[120]

As new media and means of communication allowed Muslims to communicate far more easily across national borders, the idea of Muslim unity or "pan-Islam" emerged, and various initiatives arose to realize it.[121] Rashid Rida was an eager spokesman, and used *al-Manār* to spread the idea of holding a congress.[122] He saw the congress as his own idea, and worked for the five Muslim congresses arranged from 1924 to 1935: Mecca (1924), after the supporters of the Hashemite Hussein bin Ali (d. 1931) had declared him a caliph the same year;[123] Cairo (1926), on the initiative of leading al-Azhar scholars, who declared the

120 Kramer 1986, 3.

121 Ottoman intellectuals had since the 1860s been writing about Muslim unity as a potential political weapon against fragmentation of the Ottoman Empire, and Sultan Abdülhamid (governed 1876–1909) used this idea as a political strategy. Jamal al-Din al-Afghani (d. 1897), too, is known for promoting the idea of Muslim unity. "Pan-Islam" in *OEIW* (Landau 2009). In the Arabic-language newspaper *al-ʿUrwā al-wuthqā* (The Firmest Bond), published by al-Afghani and Muhammad Abduh, pan-Islam was one of the chief subjects. The newspaper is said to have been influential, despite appearing for only one year. "Al-Afghani, Jamal al-Din" in *OEIW*, 1:35–39.

122 Kramer 1986, 30 mentions the publication of Abd al-Rahman's Arabic dissertation *Umm al-qura* (a name for Mecca) in 1900. It argued for an end to the Ottoman caliphate, and the establishment of an Arab "Qurayshi" caliphate in cooperation with a large Muslim congress.

123 Kramer 1986, 80.

aim of the congress to be the appointment of a new caliph after the fall of the Ottoman caliphate in 1924;[124] Mecca (1926), held by Ibn Saʿud (d. 1953), who had seized power, and restricted the congress theme to improving logistics for pilgrims;[125] Jerusalem (1931), in support of a Muslim Palestine; and Geneva (1935), which dealt with an issue that is still of current interest today, reform of Islamic education in Europe, but ended in no result.[126] The congress themes are good indicators of political events and changes after the fall of the caliphate, and they form the backdrop to the growth of new movements in the later 20th century and their rhetoric. One of these was the Muslim Brotherhood (*al-Ikhwān al-muslimūn*), established in 1928 by Hassan al-Banna. The Muslim Brothers considered themselves part of the modern reform movement associated with the names of Jamal al-Din al-Afghani, Muhammad Abduh and Rashid Rida.

> The Society of the Brothers, according to this view, was the 'practical' (*ʿamali*) extension of the previous movements.[127]

> [The Muslim Brothers] did not attempt to build on the intellectual venture the modern Salafiyya had undertaken in legal, political and educational reform. [… Instead] these movements focused on reforming the morality and beliefs of the Muslim individual …[128]

But they kept the Salafiyya movement's focus on the press as a means of communication in order to disseminate the message and respond to the challenges from their opponents.[129] One of the publications was *al-Manār*, which Hassan al-Banna took over from the heirs of Rashid Rida, and which appeared until 1941. That year, Egyptian authorities withdrew its license to publish, and *al-Manār* passed into history. However, the Muslim Brothers have continued their publishing activities up to the present, with a number of different publications.

One of the contributors in the first part of the 20th century was Muhammad al-Ghazali, who published his first article in *al-Manār* in 1939, after it was rejected by *Risālat al-ikhwān*. Most of al-Ghazali's articles in the 1940s were published in the magazine *al-Ikhwān al-muslimūn*, and he gradually became

124 Kramer 1986, 86.

125 Kramer 1986, 106.

126 Rashid Rida died in 1935, just before the last congress was held.

127 Mitchell 1969, 321.

128 "Salafiyah" in OEIW (Shahin 2009, 34).

129 Mitchell 1969, 185. Publishing activities began in 1932 with *The Letter of the General Guide*.

one of the most controversial and popular preachers in Egypt.[130] By his death in 1996, many sympathizers of the Brotherhood considered him "*the* great scholar of our time" (*al-ʿallāma*).[131]

Muhammad al-Ghazali

Muhammad al-Ghazali was educated at al-Azhar and a member of the Muslim Brothers until he was excluded in 1953.[132] He held a number of prominent posts, inter alia serving as state secretary in the *Wizārat al-awqāf* (Ministry of Religion), director of the Mosque Department, and director general of the *Daʿwa al-islamiyya*, all in Egypt. He taught at al-Azhar University (Egypt), the King Abd al-Aziz and Umm al-Qura universities (Saudi Arabia), and in Qatar, and was academic director of the Amir Abd al-Qadir Islamic University in Algeria.[133] He was also known for his ability to mobilize the masses.[134] Skovgaard-Petersen describes him as an "eminent mufti," who focused on "great" fatwas, that is, fatwas that address Muslims in general, a target group that sometimes appears as an imagined *mustaftī*.[135]

Only one of al-Ghazali's more than forty books—"Ghazali's accessible and continuing legacy," according to Khalafallah—is a question-and-answer-book, *Miʾat suʾāl ʿan al-islām* (A Hundred Questions on Islam).[136] The book deals with various subjects in the form of answers to questions posed by Khalid Muhammad Khalid.[137] They begin with the question, What is Islam? There is a

130 Khalafallah 1999, 56.

131 Roald 2001a, 279.

132 Al-Alwani, quoted in Khalafallah 1999, 68. Al-Ghazali was considered rebellious after he criticized the new Guide of the Muslim Brothers, Hassan al-Hudaybi, for his perceived autocratic style.

133 "Ghazālī, Muḥammad al-" in *OEMIW* (Ayubi 1995).

134 Khalafallah 1999, 68. In the 1960s, al-Ghazali exhorted president Nasser to introduce a standard dress code for men and women, which was met with public ridicule and a satirical poem published in the government-controlled press. His aim was "... among other things, to protect Egypt from Western cultural invasion and moral decay" (Khalafallah 1999, 69). Al-Ghazali's intervention, which Khalafallah terms "eccentric," gained "overwhelming" support, and "Islamic dress" became a special term for a certain dress code also beyond Egypt's borders.

135 Skovgaard-Petersen 1997, 382 f.

136 Izzi Dien 2004, 144; Khalafallah 1999, 107. The book has seen several printings since it was first published in 1984.

137 Information from Essam Tallema, in conversation in Oslo, October 2007. Tallema is the

pedagogical discussion of topics connected with the *ʿaqīda* (articles of faith), the five pillars, jihad, Islam as a solution in this life and the next, cinema, arts and music, the Quran and its role, freedom of belief in Islam, renewal of Islamic Thought, *ijtihād*, arguments for methodology and concepts, financial questions, the 99 names of Allah, the angels, women-related questions, and Islam in historical perspective. As an overall impression, I would claim that the book is first and foremost a presentation of al-Ghazali's interpretation of Islam, and that it could be seen as a programmatic statement for this interpretation. It ties in with his view of *fiqh* as a political and social project rather than a legal one: "[T]he [work of the] four fuqaha and others are no more than programs for disciplinary, social, economic and political reforms. Others have the right to join [these programs] or keep away from them. These are not [divine] texts."[138] According to al-Qaradawi, al-Ghazali did not consider himself a *faqīh* (legal scholar). His interest in *fiqh* was above all related to *daʿwa* ("invitation to Islam," mission), and not to the detailed application of the legal sources (*ʿuṣūl al-fiqh*).[139]

Women were a chief topic for al-Ghazali even in his early works. In *Dustūr al-waḥda al-thaqafiyya bayna al-muslimīn* (Principles of Cultural Unity Among Muslims), he comments on Hassan al-Banna's programme *Twenty Points*, and adds ten more points he thinks are needed in an Islamic society. The first point concerns women and their role. "Women are men's sisters. Seeking knowledge is a duty unto both sexes, as is commanding good and forbidding evil. Within the limits of Islamic *ādāb* (rules of etiquette), women have the right to take part in building and protecting society."[140] But al-Ghazali's ten additional points have a different focus from al-Banna's original twenty. Whereas al-Banna's points have an organisational focus, and are intended as a platform for agreement among Islamic organizations and foundations, al-Ghazali's points have a broader aim: how to understand Islam in the 20th century.[141]

---

author of a biography of Muhammad al-Ghazali (Tallema n.d.). Khalid Muhammad Khalid (b. 1920) was also a scholar, and a close friend of al-Ghazali's. The focus of Khalid's work shifted from social justice and reform in the 1950s to Islamic authenticity in the 1980s. He also wrote the book *Min huna nabda* (Hence We Begin, 1950), which moved al-Ghazali to reply with Islamic arguments under the title *Min huna naʿlam* (Hence We Know).

138 Khalafallah 1999, 95.

139 Al-Qaradawi 2000a, 157.

140 Al-Ghazali, quoted in al-Qaradawi 2000a, 34.

141 Conversation with Essam Tallema, September 2007.

According to Khalafallah, methodology was a chief focus of al-Ghazali's work, and he also used women-related topics to exemplify his method.[142] *Min huna naʿlam* (the 1950s), *Fiqh al-sira* (1975) and *Sunna al-nabawiyya bayna ahl al-fiqh wa-ahl al-ḥadīth* (1989) are three milestones of al-Ghazali's oeuvre, in terms of the method for deriving norms. In *Min huna naʿlam* (Hence We Know), al-Ghazali attacked Western ideas that he thought menaced Islamic norms, including what Khalafallah names "modern concepts of gender".[143] He used hadith and selected *fiqh* positions, combined with a biologically argued view of women, as the point of departure for deriving the norm of women's ineligibility to public functions.[144] One of the references he cited in support of this stance was the hadith that no good would come to a people that handed leadership to a woman.[145] Al-Ghazali cited the Quran as "proof" of the hadiths that he quoted. With regard to the question of women judges, he referred to 2:228, which states that men are a degree above women, and concluded with a rhetorical question: A judge requires respect and authority. How can women hold authority over men in general, when "Islam" gives the man authority over the woman in the home?[146]

In 1975, while al-Ghazali was living in Saudi Arabia, he wrote *Fiqh al-sīra* (Understanding the Life of the Prophet Muhammad).[147] In the preface, he accounts for his hadith methodology. In contrast with *Min huna naʿlam*, the Quran and the Sunna of the Prophet have now become the bases for evaluating hadith.[148] As long as the *matn* (wording) of the hadith is in accordance with the Quran and Sunna, al-Ghazali finds it acceptable, whether it is considered

142 According to al-Qaradawi 2000a, 157, al-Ghazali deals with various aspects of Islamic culture in his books, such as faith, morality, the biography of the Prophet, and Quranic exegesis. However, he did not deal with *fiqh* and *ʿuṣūl al-fiqh*.

143 Khalafallah 1999, 110.

144 Khalafallah 1999, 138 f. Khalafallah offers two examples of al-Ghazali's biologically argued view of women: "… in contrast to a woman, a man was characterized by strength in mind and ability to persevere" and "… it has been noted that the bodies of men are more beautiful and closer to perfection than women."

145 Khalafallah 1999, 141.

146 Khalafallah 1999, 143.

147 Al-Ghazali 1997.

148 Sunna means "practice," whereas hadith means "reporting". Eggen quotes Zafar Ishaq Ansari, who describes the relationship between the two concepts as follows: "As for sunna, it referred to an established religious norm. Thus, hadith provided the documentation of the sunna, but was not the sunna itself […] As against a hadith, therefore, sunna constitutes an established norm of practical life …" (Eggen 2001, 45).

sound (*ṣaḥīḥ*) or weak (*ḍaʿīf*).[149] The hadith is no longer the point of departure, but has gained a confirming and explaining function.

This function of the hadith is the starting point of *al-Sunna al-nabawiyya bayna ahl al-fiqh wa-ahl al-ḥadīth* (The Sunna of the Prophet Between the People of Fiqh and the People of Hadith),[150] where al-Ghazali confronts the Salafi movement's literalist interpretation of hadith, which in al-Ghazali's robust turn of phrase promotes *fiqh badawī* ("beduin fiqh" or primitive fiqh).[151] He describes his methodological frame of reference as follows:

> The school that I consider myself a leader in and contributor to, is one based on the full use of all intellectual achievements as well as on all fiqh schools. It believes in using discoveries in the disciplines of psychology, sociology, politics, economics and history. This in conjunction with the correct comprehension (fiqh) of the Book [the Quran] and the Sunna [Prophetic precedent].[152]

Izzi Dien claims that "Ghazali states that Muslim jurists always remained close to the prophetic tradition, drawing attention to ʿĀ'isha's attitude regarding the understanding of the Sunna's text through legal analogy and the circumstances of its occurrence."[153] A'isha was not least known to be skeptical of the transmissions of some of the Companions, a fact that al-Ghazali would seem to wish to highlight. Khalafallah, referring to an interview with al-Ghazali, writes: "He encouraged his Azhari students to write their doctoral dissertations on the *fiqh* of ʿA'isha, the wife of the Prophet, noting that she was one of the highest Muslim scholars of all time and contending that when Muslims ignored ʿA'isha's scholarship, especially her critique of hadith, they may have incurred serious intellectual losses."[154]

The methodological change in the relative weighting of the Quran, the Sunna and the hadith[155] in interaction with social and political reality also

149 The main categories by which the hadith are classified as to their authenticity is "strong" (*ṣaḥīḥ*) and "weak" (*ḍaʿīf*). The criteria for this classification include both the chain of transmitters (*isnād*) and the wording (*matn*).

150 Al-Ghazali 1989; Aisha Bewley has published an English translation, al-Ghazali 2009.

151 In the book al-Ghazali uses this expression repeatedly.

152 Khalafallah 1999, 104.

153 Izzi Dien 2004, 131.

154 Khalafallah 2006, 47.

155 Khalafallah claims that al-Ghazali understands the Sunna of the Prophet as principles for

led to a change of norms, not least with regard to women-related questions. Al-Ghazali now advocates equality between women and men (with reference to the Quran 3:195 and 16:97), equal *diya* (compensation for killing and physical injury) for women and men, and the right of women to hold public office, including as judges and heads of state; and he opposes face veiling. Khalafallah apparently also interprets him as holding that male–female equality also applies to the *imāma*, ritual prayer leadership, which according to al-Ghazali depends most of all on knowledge and skill at the recitation of the Quran.[156] According to Khalafallah, al-Ghazali referred to the hadith of Umm Waraqa, who was instructed by the Prophet to lead the ritual prayer in her home, as she was the most knowledgeable in *fiqh* and the best at reciting the Quran. He made this hadith relevant to today's faithful, she writes:

> In his usual manner Ghazali threw a dead end question: "for me [is it possible for] a woman such as Dr. ʿAisha ʿAbd al-Rahman[157] … to pray behind a man who is a junior scholar?" Having blown up a considerable tradi-

guidance, as opposed to hadith in the form of texts living their own context-free life among Muslims (Khalafallah 1999, 168).

156 Khalafallah 1999, 168 and 2006, 48, referring to an interview with al-Ghazali by Safinaz Kasim on the premises of the International Institute of Islamic Thought, Zamalek, Cairo, in 1990. Female leadership of ritual prayer has proven a controversial issue, and I have elicited reactions to Khalafallah's claim. Both Mohamed al-Mansoori, a member of the European Council for Fatwa and Research (ECFR), and Kamal Helbawi, a personal friend of al-Ghazali's (London, August 2007) strongly doubted the claim that al-Ghazali defends the possibility of a woman being imam for women and men. Kamal Helbawi thought that he might have said "there is no impediment to …," without presenting any elaborate argument to advocate this as a cause. Al-Mansoori thought it was not clear whether this applied to prayer in a mosque, or in a less public setting. They both thought that the recordings would have to be examined in order to find out what al-Ghazali actually meant. In my conversation with Muhammad Ammara (Cairo, March 2008), he rejected the possibility that al-Ghazali might have opened up for women leading women and men in *salāh*. He said he had attended the meeting where the recording was made. It would seem, therefore, that Khalafallah may be somewhat optimistic about al-Ghazali's zeal for reform in this area, but the question cannot be settled without a closer examination of the recordings.

157 A'isha Abd al-Rahman (1913–1998) was an Egyptian writer and a professor of Arabic language, literature and Quranic studies. Writing as Bint al-Shāṭi' ("Daughter of the Coast"), Abd al-Rahman penned over sixty books on Arabic literature, Quranic exegesis and the lives of Muslim women (particularly the women in the Prophet's family). "ʿAbd al-Raḥmān, ʿĀ'isha" in *EI3* (Hoffmann 2010).

> tional prescription, Ghazali, as usual, hastened to qualify the rule, adding that of course not just any woman could be an imam of prayers.[158]

Khalafallah describes the method of Ghazali's books as follows: "He demonstrates the dynamic three-way relationship between an Islamic scholarly text, its socio-political context, and the given content of Islamic doctrine at a given place and time."[159] One example is the book *Qadāya al-mar'a bayna al-taqālid al-rākida wal-wāfida* (Women's Issues Between Rigid and Foreign Traditions).[160] The foreword says that al-Ghazali "presents, explains and analyses the position of woman in Islam," and that the book is "the fruit of a positive confrontation between his theological knowledge and his experience".[161] The book is divided into four parts: "Understanding Islam," "Folded Pages" (Ar. *ṣafḥat al-maṭwiyya*, a poetic expression used here to mean "neglected subjects"), "Let's Start With The Home" and "Views That Need Correcting". The main aim is *daʿwa*, inviting people to Islam, and the underlying idea is that right understanding is conducive to right practice. Mainly, however, the book would seem to be an argument for Islam as a counter-culture to Western influence, and for a mobilization in favour of Islamic collective and individual morality. The perspective is more optimistic than in the 1950s *Min huna naʿlam*, though. Khalafallah comments that "[i]n his later works, a Muslim woman appears to be less a usual target of endless prohibitions and more an untapped source of energy and *taqwa* (concern for God), on the same level as the modern Muslim man."[162]

Yusuf al-Qaradawi

Yusuf al-Qaradawi first became acquainted with Muhammad al-Ghazali through his texts in the Muslim Brothers' weekly *al-Ikhwān al-muslimūn* in the

158 Khalafallah 1999, 168.

159 Khalafallah 1999, 61.

160 According to Stowasser, the book was first published in 1990. It is a combination of articles published in a column titled "al-Ḥaqq al-murr" ("The Bitter Truth") in the magazines *Majallat al-muslimīn* and *Al-Shaʿab* in the 1980s, and articles written especially for the book. (Information from Essam Tallema in conversation 11 Dec 2007). The book has also been translated to French as *Les problèmes de la femme entre les traditions et la modernité* (Beirut: Dar al-Bouraq, 1994).

161 Al-Ghazali 1994, 6 f.

162 Khalafallah 2006, 48.

mid-1940s. They first met in 1948.[163] This was the beginning of a lifelong friendship, and al-Ghazali was al-Qaradawi's shaykh and source of inspiration until his death in 1996.

Al-Qaradawi gave fatwas as early as the 1950s. He had his own fatwa column, *Yastaftūnaka* (They Ask You) in the *Minbar al-islām* magazine, signed "Yusuf Abdullah" with the last name omitted.[164] His first book was *al-Halāl wal-ḥarām fil-islām*, first published in 1960.

The Egyptian ministry of religion (*wizarāt al-awqāf*) had been advised by "some Egyptian embassies in Europe and America" that Muslims in these countries needed easy-to-read, modern books communicating knowledge of Islam.[165] Al-Qaradawi was invited by al-Azhar's Institute of Islamic Culture to participate in what he called "... an academic project of writing easily understandable books or pamphlets which, when translated into European language, would introduce Islam and its teachings to Europe and America, educating the Muslims who reside there and attracting the non-Muslims toward Islam."[166]

His special task was to write a book on what is *ḥalāl* (permitted) and *ḥarām* (forbidden) to a Muslim, based on given topics. Already al-Qaradawi's chosen way of structuring the book heralds a new era:[167] First, he describes general principles of *ḥalāl* and *ḥarām*; next, how these principles can be applied in the private life of a Muslim (food and drink, intoxicants, dress, house and home, work and living); in marriage and family life (the contracting of marriage, the relations of husband and wife, contraception, divorce, parents and children); and in everyday life in society (faith and customs, financial transactions, spare time and games, social relations). According to Gräf and Skovgaard-Petersen, however, to al-Qaradawi the individual believer is important only as a part of the community, which is his main focus.[168]

163 Al-Qaradawi 2000a, 17. They were both prisoners, on their way to the Tur prison in Sinai. They were placed in the same part of the prison, where al-Ghazali led the five prayers, gave Friday sermons and led study groups (*halaqāt*) together with Sayyid Sabiq.

164 Al-Qaradawi 2004, 2:292.

165 Al-Qaradawi 2004, 2:292.

166 From al-Qaradawi's preface to the 1960 edition, translated into English and included in the 2003 edition of al-Birr Foundation (p. xiii). In the preface to *al-Ḥalāl wal-ḥarām fil-islām*, al-Qaradawi accounts for the background to the book, the significance of its topic, and the method he has followed. Al-Qaradawi has used the same structure in introductions to later works in his opus.

167 As noted by Gräf and Skovgaard-Petersen 2009, 5.

168 Gräf and Skovgaard-Petersen 2009, 5.

In the preface, al-Qaradawi accounts for his method: *ijtihād* based on all four schools of law (*talfīq*), *tafsīr* (interpretation of the Quran), hadith and general manuals of fiqh.[169] He also explains his trademark principle, *al-wasaṭiyya* (the middle path or golden mean), here the middle path between those who, in al-Qaradawi's view, have let themselves be dazzled and dominated by Western culture, and those whose views on the forbidden and permitted are set in stone.[170] The book might be characterized as a blend of fiqh manual and fatwa collection, in that the aim is to uncover the norms in the matters discussed, but its structure is a novel departure from these classical genres. Women's topics, in particular, have been prominently placed under headings of their own, rather than the classical *furūʿ* categories.

Methodologically speaking, *Al-Ḥalāl wal-ḥarām* belongs to the legacy of Muhammad Abduh and Muhammad Rashid Rida, but it marks a turn from intellectual discourse to questions of faith and morality for individual Muslims. Thus, the book naturally situates itself within the moral programme of the Muslim Brothers, not least with regard to the women's issues it covers. According to Izzi Dien, al-Qaradawi's choice of topics, such as the hijab, shows some continuity with that of Muhammad al-Ghazali.[171] Nearly one third of the book is devoted to marriage and family life, directly or indirectly thematizing women. New issues arise. Not least the chapter on plucking one's eyebrows (*al-nams*) has come to symbolize what it means to be a "righteous Muslim woman" in the West,[172] along with the use of head coverings (hijab) to facilitate female partic-

---

169 By choosing freely from among the four schools of law, al-Qaradawi naturally situates himself within what Roald calls "the idea of eclecticism," a modern phenomenon that she characterizes as follows: "The notion of 'the return to the pure sources' which was implicitly stated in the thought of the salafiya movement of the nineteenth century and was later repeated in Ḥasan al-Bannā's thought, was initially expressed in terms of eclecticism in that one could choose freely from the legal rules of the four Islamic law schools. This is apparent in a book by a member of the Muslim Brotherhood, as-Sayyid Sābiq, *Fiqh as-sunna* (The Jurisprudence of the Sunna), written in the 1940s." Roald 2001a, 106.

170 Al-Qaradawi 2003a, xiv–xv. The *wasaṭiyya* concept stems from the word *wasaṭ* (centre, middle path) and the Quranic expression *ummatan wasaṭan* (2:143). The term has been used before in Islamic history, e.g. by Tabari (d. 927), al-Ghazali (d. 1111), Ibn Taymiyya and Muhammad Rashid Rida; see Gräf 2009, 215.

171 Izzi Dien 2004, 133.

172 Al-Qaradawi 2003a, 76. I draw here on my own experience in Muslim women's circles in the early 1990s. It was an ongoing discussion whether plucking eyebrows was permitted, and whether it forms a part of right practice for women, along with the type of hijab. I particularly recall an episode with a young Muslim woman in Stockholm, who apparently

ipation in public life, sex segregation in the workplace and the public sphere, idealized female roles in keeping with the woman's life cycle, and a certain type of femininity.[173]

As a relatively small book, aimed not only at the experts but at "ordinary people," *Al-Halāl wal-ḥarām fil-islām* marked a watershed in fiqh literature.[174] The ground had been prepared as early as the 1940s, when Sayyid Sabiq wrote the three-volume *Fiqh al-sunna* (The Jurisprudence of the Sunna), which refers to the Quran, the normative example of the Prophet (*sunna*), theologians and the various schools of law. In the preface to *Fiqh al-sunna*, Hassan al-Banna commends Sayyid Sabiq for his exemplary presentation of fiqh, avoiding difficult and complicated concepts and hypothetical details, and connecting with the Quran and the Sunna of the Prophet. Sabiq also points to the utility of the norms, al-Banna writes, so that the readers feel themselves in touch with Allah and His prophet, and thus the book may encourage them to seek further knowledge.[175]

In al-Qaradawi's own view, *al-Halāl wal-ḥarām fil-islām* is modern in thought, culture and language, while also preserving its Islamic roots and culture.[176] Stowasser has a more sober take on the book: "He [al-Qaradawi] has written a traditionalist text that emphasizes women's obligation to safeguard social morality through circumspect demeanor in public and obedient behavior."[177]

The book was greeted with much interest and approval by Muslim scholars in Egypt, Syria and Pakistan, and it laid the foundations of al-Qaradawi's fame in the Muslim world. This is not least interesting because the book was written based on questions relayed from Europe and America, and on al-Azhar University's focus on Muslims in diaspora. A pertinent criticism was that of Muhammad Abdullah al-Saman, reviewing the book in *Majallat al-Azhar* in 1961:

---

felt obliged to explain at length why she had to pluck her eyebrows. The issue remains topical today on numerous Islamic web pages; in one closed online forum, I have seen a woman be verbally attacked with allegations that she plucked her "devilish eyebrows".

173 Zuhur 1992, 87.

174 The Syrian scholar Mustafa al-Zarqa told his students that every Muslim family ought to be required to own a copy, according to al-Qaradawi 2004, 2:299.

175 Sabiq 1987, 5–6.

176 Al-Qaradawi 2004, 2:300.

177 Stowasser 2009, 185.

> If the point was to write a book to be translated into English, so that people can learn about Islam in Europe and America, the author would have had to be familiar with many traditions (*taqālid*) and customs (*ʿādāt*) of those societies in order to be able to present the view of Islam in these [societies]. This is not clear from the book.[178]

Al-Saman's was not the only critical voice. For example, the Saudi writer Salih al-Fawzan in 1976 penned a book criticizing al-Qaradawi's views and presenting his own, stricter ones.[179] Salafi groups in the West have ironically renamed the book *al-Ḥalāl wal-ḥalāl fil-islām* (The Permitted and the Permitted in Islam), according to Caeiro and Saify, who refer to Salafi-oriented websites. The book has also aroused interest beyond the borders of Sunni Islam. The Iranian ministry of culture and religious guidance has published a critical edition.[180]

The book was first translated into Turkish, then into European languages, including English, French, German, Bosnian and Albanian.[181] In France, however, it was banned on 28 April 1995 as supposedly contrary to "public order". The ban was soon reversed, after Dalil Boubakeur, rector of the Mosquée de Paris, complained to the French ministry of the interior.[182] Al-Qaradawi himself drily comments in his autobiography that the ban was allegedly lifted due to "administrative error".[183]

In 1961, al-Qaradawi moved to Qatar. When Qatari television started broadcasting in the 1970s, he was invited to host the show *Hadī al-islām* (Guidance of Islam) and answer questions.[184] The show was broadcast throughout the Gulf, and gave rise to the first of four volumes of *Min hadī al-islām: fatāwā muʿāṣira* (Contemporary Fatwas), published from 1988 to 2009.[185] The fatwas were written down and edited with a view to publication in book form on the grounds that both their topics and their reasoning could be of general interest.[186] The main group of women-related fatwas is gathered under the heading

178 al-Saman 1961, 1152.
179 Gräf and Skovgaard-Petersen 2009, 20–21.
180 Caeiro and al-Saify 2009, 120.
181 It has also been translated into Urdu and a number of other languages on the Indian subcontinent, plus Malay, Indonesian, Swahili and Chinese, says al-Qaradawi 2004, 2:300ff.
182 Caeiro and al-Saify 2009, 120.
183 Al-Qaradawi 2004, 2:302.
184 http://www.tbsjournal.com/Archives/Fall04/interviewyusufqaradawi.htm.
185 The first volume is not dated, but Stowasser 2009 describes its fatwas as first issued in 1988.
186 Al-Qaradawi 2000b, 1:7.

"*al-Mar'a wal-usra* (Woman and family)", and mostly deals with issues of private moral and religious practice, in a way that may strike a modern Western reader as misogynist, alien, and fixated on trivial details. Headings such as "Is woman entirely evil?," "Using a wig and going to the hairdresser's," "Use of nail varnish," "Licit lies among spouses," "May a man see the woman before engagement?," "Water that has been in contact with a menstruating woman," "Love and marriage," and "When the family wishes a girl to marry someone else than the one she has promised to marry" may serve as examples.[187] In the preface, al-Qaradawi stresses that the fatwas are given in a modern language that people can understand, without difficult words and expressions. The target group, namely, is a diverse one in terms of age, education, profession, and culture.[188] The second volume contains studies of more overarching topics, and fatwas written on them.[189] Two of the fatwas deal with women's political participation: One with women standing for parliamentary elections, the other discussing an earlier fatwa from al-Azhar that denies women political rights. Both fatwas are presented as independent reasoning (*ijtihād*)—without being answers to questions posed. They should none the less be taken as fatwas.[190] Stowasser analyses these fatwas as follows:

> A comparison of these two fatwas, on the one hand, and, on the other, the more person-focused, often family law related "responsa" [… in *Fatāwā mu'āṣira*, vol. 1 …] yields some important insights into al-Qaraḍāwī's intellectual position on society and politics as a whole. It highlights the Shaykh's pragmatism in finding the most effective methods of strengthening the Islamic fibre of the public realm (government and politics) while preserving the authority of traditional law over the private spaces. […] I would argue that Qaraḍāwī's way of thinking […] differs from the methodological approaches of many modernist intellectuals who approach the issue of gender equality in Islam as a human rights question, meaning that its individual implications are primary and its collective implications secondary. […] Even the notion of women's "equality" with men in Qaraḍāwī's oeuvre bears this distinction, in that he prefers not to use the term *musāwat* ("equality," "equal rights") but *iqtirān* ("simultaneous

187 Al-Qaradawi 2000b, see the table of contents on pages 790–797.

188 Al-Qaradawi 2000b, 1:13 f.

189 Telephone conversation 11 Dec 2007 with Essam Tallema (who was al-Qaradawi's secretary in 2000).

190 See Masud, Messick, and Powers 1996, 14.

interaction," "connectedness"); this enforces the notion of "gender equivalence" in the private realm but can on occasion connote "gender equality" in public matters.[191]

The third volume deals with both detailed and general questions, from "a father's love for his daughters" to "the absence of Muslim women from knowledge, thinking, culture and innovation". In addition, we find a new focus: Questions relating to Muslims as a minority. Al-Qaradawi has developed a different structure from that of earlier fatwa books. First comes a preface outlining the background of the book, current problems al-Qaradawi is dealing with in his work, and the methods and principles behind the fatwas in the book. Then, the fatwas are presented under the following headings: "The Quran and the Quranic sciences" and "Hadith and the sciences of hadith"; "The science of *uṣūl*"; "The articles of faith"; "*ʿIbādāt* (Ritual acts)"; "Women and family issues"; "Society, social relations and transactions"; "Politics and government"; "Health and medical science"; and "*Fiqh al-aqalliyyāt* (Jurisprudence of minorities)".

The prefaces to the four books allow us to follow al-Qaradawi's work as a mufti both with regard to his topics and to the method he articulates. In the third volume, for example, he argues for the method and principles that he follows in fatwa-giving. Al-Qaradawi's trademark notion of *wasaṭiyya* is presented as the equilibrium between detailed texts and the higher objectives of Sharia. Al-Qaradawi refers to al-Shatibi, who claims that the best mufti is the one that pulls people towards *al-wasaṭ* ("the centre," "the golden mean"), as this is suitable for most people.[192] The intention of the law-giver (God), according to al-Qaradawi, is moderation: neither too much nor too little. He also looks at this from the perspective of the questioner: Rules that are too strict and limiting will lead to hatred of *al-dīn* (a way of life based on Islam), but if the rules are too permissive, one might be suspected of following one's lusts and desires.[193] The fatwas are arranged under a few main headings, which al-Qaradawi says are simpler than the classical *furūʿ* categories.[194] Like the first two volumes, the women's fatwas are mainly placed under the headings *Shuʾūn al-marʾa wal-usra* and *Fiqh al-aqalliyyāt*. Women-related topics take up considerable space in all four volumes. The reason may simply be that he gets most of the questions from women, of all ages. Al-Qaradawi comments that women in general

191 Stowasser 2009, 207.

192 Al-Qaradawi 2003b, 3:8.

193 Al-Qaradawi 2003b, 3:8 f.

194 Al-Qaradawi 2003b, 3:7.

seem to be more interested in their *dīn* and more concerned about a negative balance (on the Day of Judgement) than men are.[195]

Questions and answers about Muslims as minorities are found in the third volume, in the last main chapter, *"Fī fiqh al-aqalliyyāt"* (Jurisprudence of Minorities). Women's issues take up 21 out of 49 fatwas. The topics include rules related to polygamy, the husband's permission to get a haircut, women biking, the husband's presence at childbirth, who should arbitrate between spouses in the West, divorce claims when the bride turns out not to be a virgin, and women's participation in children's dancing games. Not all of the fatwas seem to have any immediate connection to Muslims as a minority. The reason may be that the chapter contains fatwas given in response to queries from Muslims living as minorities, but not selected for their exclusive relevance to the life of Muslim minorities.[196]

In volume four, the focus is broadened beyond Europe, and the reader learns that al-Qaradawi's fatwa-giving activity extends far beyond the fatwas that get printed. He says that he gets questions from all over the world, and only a few selected fatwas have been included in the book. The preface is short by al-Qaradawi's standards; in summary, the purpose of the fatwas is what al-Qaradawi terms "relief for Muslims in the modern age".[197] *Al-mar'a wal-usra* ("woman and family") is one of the topics, and female circumcision takes up the most space in this chapter. *Fatāwā muʿāṣira* may be described as a key work in al-Qaradawi's literary opus, not least because a number of the fatwas are reproduced at IslamOnline.net[198] and adopted by the European Council for Fatwa and Research. We see the outline of the future legacy of al-Qaradawi, whom Gräf and Skovgaard-Petersen aptly characterize as a "global mufti".

Al-Qaradawi claims not to have changed his position on women-related questions in the course of his career. "Qaraḍāwī denied that he had changed his position on women's issues in any remarkable way, but said that some of the issues 'had become clearer' (*aṣbaḥat akhtara wudūḥan*) to him during the more recent past," writes Barbara Stowasser, who interviewed him in 2006.[199]

---

195 Al-Qaradawi 2000b, 1:33 f.

196 Telephone conversation with Essam Tallema, 11 Dec 2007.

197 Al-Qaradawi 2009, 4:10. The word "relief" should be understood in terms of al-Qaradawi's figurative description of his fatwas as taken from *al-saydaliyya al-islāmiyya* (the Islamic pharmacy), an expression I have noticed him using every so often.

198 See discussion of IslamOnline.net and OnIslam.net in chapter 2, n. 57 and chapter 4, p. 159 f.

199 Stowasser 2009, 183.

The same may apply to al-Qaradawi's *wasaṭiyya* principle, which has gained a number of new meanings over time. He has described it as a method between two extremes, in the book *al-Ḥalāl wal-ḥarām fil-islām*; as a political alternative between capitalism and socialism, in the 1970s; as a principle of *fiqh*; as an intermediary position between old and new fatwa-giving methods; and as the ideal position of the Islamic movement between stagnation and extremism.[200] The middle position is also expressed in the titles of al-Qaradawi's books, where the topic of the book is nearly always cast as a mean between two extremes.

Iftāʾ in Europe: The Concerns of the Mufti

In 1988, al-Qaradawi published a small book titled *al-Fatwā bayna l-inḍibāṭ wal-tasayyub* (The Fatwa Between Discipline and Chaos). The text was originally intended as a preface to *Fatāwā muʿāṣira*, but it was published as two articles in the magazine *al-Muslim al-muʿāṣir* (The Modern Muslim), and later as a book, in order to reach a broader public than the readers of what al-Qaradawi calls an intellectual magazine (*majalla fikriyya*). *Al-fatwā* presents methods and rules for *iftāʾ*, the place and signficance of the fatwa in Islam and in people's lives, requirements regarding the knowledge and morals of a mufti, and dangers and obstacles to the fatwa in our time.[201] Al-Qaradawi is concerned that people declare even "the gravest matters" *ḥalāl* or *ḥarām* without adequate qualifications for *iftāʾ*. Some of these young people, Qaradawi says, are thought to belong to the Islamic awakening (*al-ṣaḥwat al-islāmiyya*), which gives rise to criticism of the movement itself.[202] *Al-fatwā* thus appears to be a manual of fatwa-giving with a view to defending the Islamic movement against the fragmentation of scholarly authority.[203] The blurb on the back cover lists the required qualifications of a mufti, and serves as a kind of warning sign for the lay Muslim reader. Caeiro describes the publication of *al-Fatwā* as paradoxical, as it also functions as "… a ready-to-use manual for an extended readership of would-be muftis not formally trained in the classical Islamic disciplines, further contributing to the fragmentation of religious authority that the author sought to counter in the first place."[204]

200 Gräf 2009, 218–227.

201 Al-Qaradawi 1995, 3.

202 Al-Qaradawi 1995, 4.

203 Al-Qaradawi 1995, 4.

204 Caeiro 2006, 670.

Al-Fatwā follows the pattern of the *ādāb al-fatwā* genre, as Caeiro describes it: "The adab al-fatwa usually starts with a discussion of the social and religious relevance of fatwas, and often includes a section on the role of the muftis at the time of its composition. The genre can thus be said to be animated by a sense of *contemporaneity*."[205] I think the view of the questioner (*al-mustaftī*) in *al-Fatwā* is a case in point. He or she is exhorted to seek knowledge.[206] Caeiro characterizes this as an expression of the Salafiyya movement's stress on individual responsibility for oneself and one's conscience.[207] On the other hand, there are dangers connected with the quest for knowledge. Al-Qaradawi writes:

> They [the young] cannot venture into this extensive and sophisticated discipline without the guidance of such reliable scholars who can interpret and explain obscurities, define terms, and point out similarities and the relationships between the parts and the whole. Those who venture into it alone will meet with the same catastrophic results which would certainly befall the unskilled swimmer who ventures into deep waters.[208]

Qaradawi's argument in *al-Fatwā* may also be interpreted as a response to the democratization of access to knowledge about Islam, which began in earnest when the Salafiyya movement in the early 20th century began making use of the printed word as a means of preaching and teaching.

This trend was reinforced by the development of technology and mass media in the 20th century. The Muslim Brothers have played a central role by publishing books, treatises, magazines, and cassettes, and adopting TV and Internet media. The Islamic movement has also established new institutions of learning, including study groups in the mosques and *daʿwa* centres. Al-Qaradawi's reputation as the foremost scholar in contemporary Sunni Islam is not least tied to his use of the media, TV as well as the Internet. The result is a democratization of religious authority.

Hirschkind describes this trend in relation to taped sermons, claiming they have enabled a culture of public debate in which the divide between laymen and scholars has been abolished. This implies a structured, informal debate across divides of age and gender, a debate on the correct interpretation of the

205 Caeiro 2006, 664.
206 Al-Qaradawi 1995, 52–56.
207 Caeiro 2006, 671.
208 Al-Qaradawi 1991, 71.

sources, and a familiarity with the bases and style of Islamic reasoning. For the participants, the aim of such debates is to advocate right practice as they see it. The lay Muslim is no longer just a seeker of knowledge, but an actor, in other words, a *dāʿī*.[209]

The spreading of the Islamic message through mass media may be said to promote dialogue, discussion and debate. At the same time, it has a disciplining effect. It presents Islam as both a *model of* and a *model for* reality—an ideal implying expectations to be met.[210] However, it is not a question of one model, but several competing ones—the choice is up to the believer.

The scholars find their authority at stake. Kari Vogt invokes the notion of "engineer Islam," citing a fatwa by shaykh Kutty at IslamOnline.net on scholarship. Kutty refers to Muhammad al-Ghazali and Yusuf al-Qaradawi as having stressed that "… it is a tragedy that people with inadequate training, such as engineers, suddenly act as ulama and experts. The result is that we lose good engineers and are left with lousy scholars. The solution is to insist on specialized Islamic knowledge, as in the past."[211]

The "engineer Islam" trend has materialized in its own way in Western Europe. It is usually highly educated people with informal knowledge of Islam that have established and are running Islamic institutions, and appear as authorities and spokesmen in certain segments of Islam in Western Europe. This provokes reactions. According to Mohamed al-Mansoori, member of the ECFR, it is time for the scholars to "take back Islam" and take on the role of guiding the believers to Islamic legal thought.[212] The ECFR, in al-Mansoori's view, was precisely such an initiative.

The first known seminar on the *fiqh* challenges to Muslims in the West was held in France as early as 1992. On the grounds of "care for the needs of Muslims in their new environments," the Union des Organisations Islamiques de France (UOIF) invited scholars to the event *Muslims in the West: A Fiqh Seminar* (13–15 July 1992). The aim was "to tackle the pressing shariʿa questions facing those who are trying to preserve identity of the Muslim Communities in Western Society."[213] The seminar was the first of its kind in that Muslim scholars addressed the concrete challenges facing Muslims in the West with regard to *fiqh*. Women-related questions such as hijab, marriage and relation-

209 Hirschkind 2005.

210 Geertz 1993, 95.

211 Vogt 1995, 109 f., citing Kutty. Re-translated from Norwegian.

212 Personal conversation in the summer of 2001.

213 Darsh, 4.

ships were on the agenda, but only as "subordinate detailed questions of fiqh" along with questions of ritual burials, dietary rules, work and business transactions, interest-based loans to finance purchase of a home, and finally, the relations between Muslims and non-Muslims. The overarching issues concerned the legality of taking up residence outside Muslim countries, and obtaining citizenship in a non-Muslim country.

The choice of topics reflected the agenda of Muslims and the needs that were reported in the beginning of the 1990s. The question of residence and nationality was often debated in Muslim circles at the time. There was a great deal of uncertainty as to whether one could take up permanent residence in a non-Muslim country, let alone adopt a European citizenship.[214] "There are a large number of fatwas from colonial times banning Muslims from adopting European citizenship. To become French is to be a *murtadd*, an apostate from Islam, a traitor."[215] It is characteristic that hijab was raised as a separate topic; it had been a burning issue since the late 1980s.[216]

The discussions at the seminar were interesting because they involved *ijtihād* with particular regard to Muslims as a relatively new minority. Two *fiqh* concepts are named as relevant to Muslims in Europe: *ḍarūra* (necessity) and *wāqiʿat ḥāl* (the actual situation). According to the report, these concepts were used in the discussion on the overarching issues, whereas the discussion on the hijab focused on its obligatory nature. Clearly, the same flexibility did not apply to all the topics, as seen in the point on hijab:

> So far we have been trying to compare between advantages and disadvantages of issues under discussion. But the question of hijab has to be taken out of this comparison. If it means that the young girls may lose their education, let it be.[217]

The participants were well pleased with the seminar. Darsh reports:

---

214 This stems from the notion of the division of the world into *dār al-islām* (the House of Islam) and *dār al-ḥarb* (the House of War). See "Dār al-Ḥarb" in *EI2* (Abel 2010).

215 Vogt 1995, 50, quoting from Vogt's conversations with Abdallah Ben Mansour, the then secretary general of UOIF, in Paris, 27 Jun and 9 Dec 1994.

216 Vogt 1995, 206.

217 Darsh, 18. This view has subsequently changed. Not least, al-Qaradawi has asserted that education is so important that the hijab may be taken off if this is required for going to school. This fatwa was given based on the "hijab struggle" in France. See discussion in chapter 4.

> It was a good start in building up a Fiqh tradition dealing with situations which are new in the life of the Muslim communities in Western societies. [...] It was felt too, that such seminars should continue to find Islamic legal answers to many new developments faced by Muslims in the West.[218]

The first step had been taken. The UOIF was also behind the next seminar, held in 1994, which formed another step on the way to the first permanent fatwa institution on European soil, *al-Majlis al-ūrūbī lil-iftāʾ wal-buḥūth* (the European Council for Fatwa and Research, ECFR). The ECFR was established on al-Qaradawi's initiative, in cooperation with the UOIF. Caeiro and Sayfi claim that by this time, al-Qaradawi "had arguably become the most charismatic living Muslim scholar of his generation".[219] He was unanimously elected head of the Council when it was founded.

> By then Qaradawi viewed himself as a scholar who may never have resided in Europe, but nevertheless "carries the worries and anxieties of their [*sic*] fellow Muslims in Europe, visits them on a frequent basis and appreciates their conditions and living situations".[220]

We will examine al-Qaradawi's contributions to the ECFR in the next chapter, not least the concept of *fiqh al-aqalliyyāt*, which serves both to legitimate the existence of the ECFR, and as a method for deriving norms for Muslim minorities.

Conclusion

In this chapter, we have seen how the fatwa institution emerged in the classical Islamic tradition and developed into a separate category of the legal literature. Fatwas may be seen as responses to the encounter between text and social reality. The *Muwaṭṭaʾ* offers us a glimpse of how pre-Islamic custom was modified and redefined into rules of correct Islamic practice. Fatwas (and interpretations) in early 20th-century Egypt exhibit different responses to British colonial administration, the fall of the caliphate, and the contemporary struggle over Islamic identity.

---

218 Darsh, 21.

219 Caeiro and al-Saify 2009, 113–114.

220 Caeiro and al-Saify 2009, 114.

The muftis, fatwas, and fatwa collections presented in this chapter exemplify both continuity and change in the concept of fatwa. The questions may be real or constructed. A fatwa may be considered a fatwa even if a question has not been posed; the discussion of a given topic may start from a fictional *mustaftī*. The addressee of fatwas as teaching aids has also changed: once directed at other scholars and their students, fatwas now often target the broad Muslim public. This is connected with the democratization of knowledge, which has gone hand in hand with the increasing importance of the mass media for the dissemination of knowledge and preaching. Another modern phenomenon is the emergence of collective fatwa councils, such as the European Council for Fatwa and Research (ECFR).

Women did not form a topic under their own heading in classical fatwa collections or fiqh manuals, which followed a traditional *furūʿ* division on the model of Malik bin Anas' *Muwaṭṭaʾ*. This changed at the end of the 1800s. Qasim Amin followed Rifaʿa Badawi Rafiʿ al-Tahtawi in his choice of topics for *Taḥrīr al-marʾa*. Women became a central topic of the Egyptian public debate of the time, which was reflected in Islamic discourse. Interest has continued until the present, and women-related questions are central topics of transnational Islamic discourse.

Qasim Amin's demands for reform received support from Muhammad Abduh, "the architect of Islamic reform," who advocated easing the requirements for women seeking to obtain divorce, and restricting polygamy. Abduh, Muhammad Rashid Rida, Muhammad al-Ghazali and Yusuf al-Qaradawi represent a trajectory in the history of ideas that has contributed to shaping the discourse on women-related questions among Muslims in Western Europe today. Together, they have contributed issues, concepts and methods that define one trend among muftis for Muslims in Western Europe: those who consider "the time and place" important considerations in fatwa-giving. In the next chapter, I will present people and institutions that belong to this trend.

CHAPTER 2

The Muftis and the Fatwa Institutions

This chapter introduces the muftis and fatwa institutions I have selected. How do they view their own work as muftis, on what concepts and methods do they base their fatwa-giving, and how do they designate their fatwas? I go on to examine the context in which they act. By drawing the profiles of these actors, we gain knowledge of *iftāʾ* (fatwa-giving) on European soil, knowledge that will help frame and inform the presentation and analysis of fatwas later in the book.

Syed Mutawalli Darsh

Syed Mutawalli Darsh (1930–1997), "the first real mufti of Western Europe,"[1] came to London in December 1971. He had been posted there by Egypt's al-Azhar University,[2] and worked as an imam in the London Central Mosque until 1980. When his al-Azhar contract expired, he was hired by the then *wizārat al-iftāʾ wal-buḥūth al-islamiyya wal-daʿwa wal-irshīd* (Ministry of Fatwa, Research, Invitation to Islam and Guidance) of Saudi Arabia.[3] He was also a member of the Saudi fatwa authority *Dār al-iftāʾ*.[4] Darsh's main interest lay in *daʿwa* (invitation to Islam), and the new position seems to have suited him very well:

> I set my own timetable, I was much more free. I was mainly with the Islamic societies at the universities, talking here and there. It gave me a much wider chance to go out … In fact, the period I spent in the Central Mosque, I consider to be more PR, than dedicated hard Islamic work.

---

1 Conversation with Fuad Nahdi, editor of *Q-News* magazine, Istanbul, July 2006.

2 Darsh was trained at the al-Azhar faculty of *ʿuṣūl al-dīn*, and had studied moral philosophy at the University of Aberdeen. Information from conversation with Syed Darsh in Oslo, 25 Nov 1993, in connection with my second-cycle thesis (Larsen 1995).

3 Similar arrangements were made for the Azhar-educated Sadiq Sharif and Mahmud Mujahid in France, when their contracts with al-Azhar expired. After Darsh's time, the ministry was restructured and split in two. *Iftāʾ* now comes under the *wizārat al-awqāf*, whereas *daʿwa* is an independent unit. (Information from Usama Hasan, 15 Jun 2010.)

4 Information from Suhayb Hasan, secretary of the Islamic Sharia Council and a close friend of Darsh's.

 | DOI: 10.1163/9789004367852_004

> There are so many people coming who want to sit and talk, ask so many questions. That didn't give the chance to know the wider Islamic society.[5]

Darsh described the ministry as part of a Saudi strategy to establish educational institutions and run missionary work as a competitor to al-Azhar.[6] He said that the Saudi initiative stressed Hanbali fiqh and Salafi theology, unlike al-Azhar, which was based on the thought of the Ashʿari school,[7] with the option of studying all the existing schools of law. Until the early 1980s, the ministry recruited employees educated outside of Saudi Arabia, and being trained at al-Azhar was, as Darsh put it, "fair enough." As Saudi universities have trained their own candidates, it is increasingly their graduates that are hired and sent as missionaries.

In the early 1990s, Darsh had a weekly show on the London Arabic-language television channel MBC,[8] and worked as *khaṭīb* (preacher of the Friday sermon) at the Muslim Welfare House in East London.[9] Acccording to Fuad Nahdi, editor of *Q-News* magazine, people would line up after the Friday prayer to get advice and answers to the questions that concerned them. One Friday Nahdi joined the line himself, not to have a personal question answered, but to invite Darsh to have a fiqh column in *Q-News*. The column was started based on two premises: No question was too trivial or too big to answer, and the language of the answers was to be youth-oriented. According to Nahdi, the column was read by 10–15,000 people a week.[10] Until then, Darsh had hardly been known among young people; he was just an ancient *ʿālim* who meant nothing to them.[11] This would change with the column. As Nahdi remarked in a conversation with Kari Vogt:

---

5 Conversation with Syed Darsh, Oslo, 25 Nov 1993.

6 The competition between Egypt and Saudi Arabia is described e.g. in Skovgaard-Petersen 1997.

7 The Ashʿari school of theology was founded by Abu al-Hasan al-Ashari in the 10th century, and established itself as an intermediate position bridging the rationalism of the Muʿtazila and the literal interpretations of the Hanbalis. The Ashʿari school considered revelation the only source of certainty, but supported by reason. It further considered the Quran the uncreated word of God, held that anthropomorphisms such as "the hand of God" should be accepted without knowing how, that eschatological themes should be literally interpreted, and that human acts are created by God and acquired by humans (Watt 1979, 85–86).

8 Vogt 1995, 54.

9 Information from author's fieldwork in England in July 1993.

10 Conversation with Fuad Nahdi, Istanbul, July 2006.

11 Vogt 1995, 124.

> To Shaykh Darsh, it means that he gets in touch with a large group of people and has gained a far more significant role than if he had remained in his Sharia Council giving fatwas on the Gulf War and suchlike [...] In my view, the interest in Darsh reflects a tendency: Muslims in this country may be faithful to tradition, but they want a new interpretation of the tradition. They want the classical law made topical and relevant for our time. This is precisely what Darsh is doing.[12]

The column uses the expressions "questions" and "answers" for the derivation of norms for actions, which is, technically, fatwa-giving. The avoidance of the word "fatwa" may be due to the requirement that the language of the column address young people. However, it may just as well be connected with Darsh's view of himself and his own role as a mufti: Darsh carefully stressed that he was not capable of *ijtihād* (independent reasoning). He held that the encounter with the Western environment did not require a new interpretation or new categories, such as *fiqh al-aqalliyyāt* (minority jurisprudence),[13] arguing as follows: "... in the traditional books of Islam[ic] law we find every possible point of view. This shows the greatness of the law."[14] However, he did stress the importance of understanding the conditions in which Muslims live. The changing conditions of Muslims' lives must be taken into account when norms are defined.[15] The most prominent methodological element in Darsh's answers was how he compared the arguments and positions of the schools of law, and advocated that school which, in his view, was the most relevant to Muslim circumstances. "What we do in the present situation is to find that which is the more appropriate to the Muslim community, and then we accept the particular point of view."[16] This is *takhayyur*, a method defined by Wael Hallaq as "an amalgamated selection from several traditional doctrines held by a variety of schools."[17] Darsh further followed the principle of *taysīr* ("easing").[18]

---

12 Vogt 1995, 124 (re-translated from Norwegian).

13 Vogt 1995, 54 none the less points out one case in which Darsh argues for a new interpretation: concerning the custody of a child after divorce. He claims that the best interests of the child determine which parent should have custody. He further asserts that according to Sharia, the woman is considered best suited, *even* if she remarries. This is a break with the legal literature. Vogt remarks: "But a learned shaykh may also advance his own interpretations!"

14 Roald 2001a, 116.

15 Roald 2001a, 116.

16 Roald 2001a, 116.

17 Hallaq 2003, 210.

18 Conversation with Suhayb Hasan, Istanbul, July 2006. Hassan was a close colleague and

Darsh was characterized as a "grassroots mufti," accessible to "the common man." This probably colors his answer to a question about the validity of an oral fatwa:[19]

> A fatwa is usually a personal matter. Someone is coming to inquire about a particular religious point of view. It's something of interest to the person. But if it becomes [...] of interest to the community, there's no difficulty in writing it down. Otherwise fatwas, all through the time of the Prophet (SAAW), were oral fatwas [...] Nowadays people are taking to reading and writing, and written material is available everywhere. [... T]he fatwa is of interest to so many people, and that's why people are writing fatwas and publishing them [...] to make them available to the ordinary person, who may not have the religious authority available [...] It depends upon the situation. If it is an intimate matter, she will pick up the phone and speak about very intimate matters. I don't know who she is. She wants be be anonymous, to have a fatwa. [...] Once you have faith in a person knowledgeable about this particular thing, you ask him. That's enough.

Darsh's commitment extended not least to women- and family-related issues. According to Fuad Nahdi, Darsh was not afraid of raising taboo questions, and he made it legitimate to discuss topics such as violence in relationships, sexual abuse of children, and AIDS.[20] Darsh was also the protector of the British Muslim women's group An-Nisa Society.[21] Humera Khan, the head of the society, describes his commitment to the organization as follows:

---

friend of Darsh's. Together, they revised Yusuf Ali's rendering of the Quran (1987–1988), and established the Sharia Council in 1982. Sano 2000, 152 explains the concept of *taysīr* in its relation to *iftāʾ*: The mufti's task is to make it easier for people to understand things and practise them.

19 This was a question I posed to Darsh in our 1993 conversation. The background was the Rushdie affair, when a fatwa promising a reward for the killing of Salman Rushdie, the author of *The Satanic Verses*, was issued in Iran. Fatwas thus became a hot topic in the early 1990s, and it was interesting to have a scholar shed light on them.

20 According to Nahdi, he did so behind closed doors, by arranging conferences on these topics. For example, Darsh gave the keynote at the conference "Towards Understanding the Dynamics of Child Abuse and its Healing Within the Muslim Community," organized by the Amana Projct and supported by *Q-News* (18 Feb 1993).

21 An-Nisa's homepage informs us that the society was founded in May 1985 by a group of young British Muslim women, to respond to the needs of Muslim women and their families (http://www.an-nisa.org/).

> The most unique feature of ad-Darsh was the way he treated women and encouraged their spiritual and intellectual development. Women found him always eager to exchange ideas and comprehend their situation before issuing appropriate fatwas ('edicts'). His work with the An-Nisa Women's Society, for instance, exemplified the wisdom, commitment and trail-blazing nature of his work.[22]

In an obituary, Fuad Nahdi describes Darsh's *Q-News* column as an "agony uncle column" in which Darsh answered questions ranging from contraception and marriage to interest (*ribā*) and lotteries.[23] Questions about divorce, however, were notably absent. Divorce matters were nonetheless an important part of Darsh's work—in The Islamic Sharia Council, which he founded in 1982.[24] The aim was to assist women who were not granted Islamic divorce by their husbands. Darsh described this work as follows: "What I do […] is only to relieve women who are strained in difficult relationships and in difficult situations in life."[25] Ataullah Siddiqui states that the Sharia Council gave women direct access to an authority where they could discuss matters of marriage and inheritance, instead of having to go to their home country to resolve such matters. The Sharia Council brought together scholars of various traditions and ethnic backgrounds. Barkatullah Abdulkadir, who was involved in its founding, describes Darsh this way: "He was like the glue bringing everybody together. He was an Arab, of Azhari background and with a certain personality, hence he had the moral authority."[26]

The European Council for Fatwa and Research (ECFR)

History

The European Council for Fatwa and Research (ECFR, *al-Majlis al-ūrūbī lil-iftā' wal-buḥūth*) was established in 1997 by the Federation of Islamic Organiza-

22 Quoted from the obituary Humera Khan wrote for Darsh, see http://www.independent.co.uk/news/obituaries/obituary-sayed-ad-darsh-1235728.html.

23 http://www.iol.ie/~afifi/Ad-Darsh/obituary.htm.

24 According to the promotional brochure *The Islamic Shari'a Council of Great Britain and Northern Ireland: An Introduction*, the Council was founded in 1982, at a meeting joined by scholars from many British mosques. See the Council's homepage (http://www.islamic-sharia.org/).

25 Roald 2001a, 116.

26 Conversation with Barkatullah Abdulkadir, London, 24 Feb 2009.

tions in Europe (FIOE, *al-Ittiḥād al-munaẓẓamāt al-islamiyya fi-ūrūba*).[27] It was intended as an interim solution for the "chaotic" contemporary situation in Islamic jurisprudence[28]—pending the graduation of the first Muslim scholars from another FIOE initiative, L'institut européen des sciences humaines (IESH).[29] At the founding meeting in London in 1997, Yusuf al-Qaradawi and Faysal Mawlawi—two eminences of modern Islam with a long-standing special interest in the Muslims of Europe[30]—were elected president and vice-president of the ECFR, respectively. The Mauritanian scholar Abdullah bin Bayyah figures as a third, Maliki, "pillar" of the ECFR.[31]

Fifteen scholars attended the meeting on the invitation of the FIOE. They adopted a "draft constitution of the ECFR".[32] Ambitiously, they expressed the hope that the Council would become an "indispensable reference" for European Muslims and would represent their aspirations to religious and public institutions throughout Europe.[33] They sought to achieve this aim by bringing together the scholars living in Europe, and unifying their views on jurisprudence with regard to the main fiqh issues; issuing collective fatwas to meet the needs of Muslims in Europe; and publishing legal studies and research to

27 Caeiro 2002 gives a description of the FIOE, referring to Frégosi, who calls it the shadow of the Muslim Brotherhood in Europe. The FIOE was founded in 1989, and functions as an umbrella for a number of organizations and activities. Particularly relevant in our connection is L'institut européen des sciences humaines (IESH), established in Chateau Chinon in 1990, with two departments in France and one in Wales, and the European Council for Fatwa and Research, which I describe in the following.

28 Caeiro 2002, 15.

29 Education at the IESH is described below.

30 Faysal Mawlawi (1941–2011) was born in Lebanon. He initiated the founding of the Union des Organisations Islamiques en France, and became its first *murshid* (religious leader) when it was established in 1983. Mawlawi was the secretary general of *al-Jamā'a al-islāmiyya* in Lebanon. http://www.onislam.net/english/news/global/452177-prominent-muslim-scholar-mawlawi-dies.htmlhttp://www.islamonline.net/servlet/Satellite?cid=1119503615017&pagename=IslamOnline-English-Ask_Scholar%2FFatwaCounselorE%2FFatwaCounselorE.

31 Caeiro 2002, 40. Bin Bayyah (b. 1935) was a minister of education, minister of justice, and vice president of Mauritania, before political upheaval took him to Saudi Arabia, where he teaches at King Abdulaziz University. He is also a member of the Islamic Fiqh Council in Saudi Arabia. Bin Bayyah's sphere of influence, too, reaches beyond the Muslim world, especially through one of his students, the American Hamza Yusuf.

32 ECFR 2002a, 1.

33 Caeiro 2002, 16.

resolve the issues arising in Europe in a manner which would realize the objectives of Shari'ah and people's interests.[34]

Fatwas and *qarārāt* (resolutions) made in the name of the ECFR are passed during its regular sessions, "… by virtue of a consensus where possible, or by absolute majority. A member who has objections or reservations to the Fatwa has the right to record his reservation according to what is customary practice in Fiqh Councils."[35]

Following Muhammad Qasim Zaman, the ECFR may be seen as an example of an attempt to institutionalize religious authority—the "aspiration, effort, and ability to shape people's belief and practice on recognizably 'religious' grounds"—through a collective *ijtihād* envisioned as representing a new consensus (*ijmāʿ*).[36] The Council's claim to represent the consensus with regard to European Muslims is at the same time a claim to have the power to define the substance of such consensus vis-à-vis other collective fatwa bodies.

Who could be a member of the new council? The conditions for membership are given by the statutes:[37] Members are required to have university-level qualifications in Sharia or *ijaza* from recognized scholars, as well as knowledge of Arabic; to be of good conduct and commited to the Sharia; to be residents of the European continent; and to be approved by the absolute majority of the members.

At the same time, the statutes allow the ECFR members to elect as members scholars who live outside Europe and hence do not fulfill the third requirement. This requires an absolute majority. The share of such members, however, was not to exceed 25 percent. This quota has subsequently been raised, so that more than a third of the members now hail from outside Europe.

Considerations behind the Composition of the ECFR

What other considerations were taken into account and weighed against each other when the council was composed?[38]

34 Lightly rephrased from ECFR 2002a, 1ff.

35 From the statutes, which may be found at the ECFR homepage (http://www.e-cfr.org).

36 Zaman 2012, 29, 95. As examples of other sites of collective *ijtihād*, Zaman mentions Egypt's *Dār al-iftāʾ* (est. 1895) and Academy of Islamic Research (est. 1961), the transnational *fiqh* academies of the Muslim World League (est. 1961) and the Organization of the Islamic Conference (OIC) (est. 1983), and the *fiqh* academy in India (est. 1989).

37 ECFR 2002a, 5.

38 On the various concerns that were taken into account in the composition of the ECFR, see also Caeiro 2002, 20–65.

Those who see the ECFR as an organ for the Muslim Brothers often seem to imagine the organization as homogeneous and place little weight on individual variations: the fact that there are different interpretations of the methods and principles of fatwa-giving, and that individual members may represent different orientations.[39] The council member Suhayb Hasan may serve as one example. Hasan was trained at the University of Medina, and came to Great Britain in 1976, posted there by the Grand Mufti of Saudi Arabia, Bin Baz,[40] to carry out Salafi *daʿwa*. Bin Baz is also said to have supported the election of Hasan to the leadership of *Jamiʿat Ahl-e Hadith*. Hasan stresses Bin Baz as a role model, and they stayed in touch until Bin Baz died in 1999.[41]

There are fundamental differences between the Muslim Brothers and the Salafi movement, which has roots in *wahhābiyya*.[42]

This conflict is also present in Europe. Hasan has been criticized for being a member of the ECFR, because it is not a pure Salafi council. A response to this criticism stresses the importance of having Salafi views in a body like the ECFR:

> The European Council for Fatwa and Research (ECFR) is a representative body where scholars from different backgrounds and schools of thought meet and discuss the problems confronting the Muslims in Europe. The participation of Shaikh Suhayb is based upon making sure that the Salafi view point is represented in important matters of Fatawa and Fiqh and in trying to influence the council, so that its decisions are made in accordance with the Sunnah and the Salafi Manhaj.[43]

Abdullah Judai, of Iraqi origins, also represents a different position from that of the Muslim Brothers. He was a co-founder of the ECFR, and served as its

39 Author's observations during ECFR sessions and in conversations with the members.

40 Abd al Aziz bin Abd Allah bin Baz (d. 1999), Grand Mufti of Saudi Arabia until the end of his life, was a prominent authority in Salafi Islam.

41 Hasan et al., 5.

42 Roald 2001a, 50f. "The *wahhābī* movement developed in a close, non-colonised atmosphere, and it evolved trends particular to such a society. The two other movements [Salafiyya and the Muslim Brothers] developed in an atmosphere of western colonisation of Muslim countries, so that their understanding of Islam was a result of the encounter between the traditional and the modern. […] Some scholars, such as Muḥammad al-Ghazzālī (d. 1996), have compared the conflict between these two movements to the differences between the historical stand of the people who adhered to the hadiths and the people who believed in the scholars' opinions."

43 Hasan et al., 16.

secretary general from 1998 to 2000. He received a broad Islamic education from Iraqi scholars, and according to Mohamed al-Mansoori, he has been a student of Muhammad Nasir al-Din al-Albani (d. 1999), of whom Stéphane Lacroix claims that he was known as the foremost scholar of hadith in his generation.[44] He has authored a number of books.[45] He has specialized in assessing the authenticity of hadith.[46] Judai is considered a progressive on women's issues, not least where the hijab is concerned, but there is also disappointment that he does not participate in debates and promote his views, since he could have given legitimacy to new interpretations of women-related topics.[47] In my conversation with Judai, it emerged that he thinks civil marriage fulfills Islamic requirements of a validly contracted marriage, and the same applies to divorce, which in his view should not become a symbolic issue that leads to the establishment of a Sharia court.[48]

Even though the ECFR was established by and for Muslims in Europe, the FIOE leadership decided to invite persons from outside Europe as well. This composition of scholars may serve several functions: ensuring the *authority* of the mufti, and avoiding rejection by stricter, more Salafi-oriented groups.[49] People such as Yusuf al-Qaradawi (based in Qatar), Faysal Mawlawi (based in Lebanon) and Abdullah bin Bayyah (based in Saudi Arabia) give the council needed *legitimacy*. Al-Qaradawi and Bin Bayyah are considered to be *mujtahidūn* (qualified to perform *ijtihād*, independent reasoning),[50] and this matters for new issues that have arisen in the wake of Muslim immigration to Europe. However, it may also have to do with the scholars' attempt to *control* the development of Islamic thought in Europe. Since the establishment of the ECFR, representation from the Muslim world seems to have become as important as representation from Europe. The Council lists 32 members on its website. A number of European countries are represented, mostly by one or two members each.[51]

---

44 Lacroix 2008, 6.

45 A list of his books is at http://web.archive.org/web/20061025084522/http://www.islamicforumeurope.com/live/ife.php?doc=newsitem&itemId=1833 (captured 25 Oct 2006).

46 Conversation with Abdullah Judai, London, 9 Jul 2004.

47 Conversation with Batool al-Toma, responsible for the "New Muslims project" at the Islamic Foundation in Leicester.

48 Conversation in London, 9 Jul 2004.

49 Caeiro 2002, 24.

50 Mohamed al-Mansoori described them in these terms at the seminar "Ideal and Practice: A Seminar about Sharia in our Everyday Lives," Oslo, 26 May 2007.

51 The list of members is at http://e-cfr.org/new/?post_type=members, accessed 12 Feb 2014.

The exceptions are France and Great Britain, with respectively five and six members each, forming the main axes of the council. The second session of the ECFR agreed to set up two subcommittees for *iftāʾ* (fatwa-giving), one in France and one in Great Britain. The aim was to relieve the workload of the ECFR by answering questions between its sessions.[52]

The Sessions

Until 2000, the ECFR held one session a year, from 2000 to 2005 it held two sessions a year, and since 2006 it has again held one session a year. Since 2005, the sessions have mainly taken place in Istanbul.[53] I have attended five of the sessions, in Paris, Stockholm, London, Dublin and Istanbul (2002–2006), and also participated in the 2014 session.

The *lajnat al-amāna* (secretariat) prepares the content and organization. It decides what matters shall be tabled for the meeting, and specifically requests members to prepare studies on the subject. The *lajnat al-amāna* also distributes the questions it receives to the members for fatwa-giving.

A huge logistical apparatus is also set in motion before and during each session, including cooperation with a local organization in the city where the session is held. The local organization is responsible for airport transport, hotels, meals and a public meeting for local Muslims. Members of the Council often also depend on visas to enter the country. The organizational challenges and the level of effort is reflected in the concluding declaration of the Council, with thanks to all those who have made the session possible.[54] As an illustration, the concluding declaration of the 19th session held in Istanbul on 30 June–4 July 2009 cordially thanks the Turkish government for facilitating the event on Turkish soil, not least for allowing the members to enter Turkey. Local organizations are thanked for helping arrange the session. Last but not least, the board of the Council is mentioned, together with various "brothers" and "sisters" who have helped make the session a success.[55]

52 ECFR 2002a, 7. The French Dar al-Fatwa, associated with the UOIF umbrella, considers itself the ECFR's fatwa committee in France. The British committee is based in Manchester. The committee in Paris consists of the ECFR members from France. See Karman 2008, 73–74.

53 With the exception of Sarajevo (2007) and Paris (2008). The choice of Istanbul as the venue may be connected with visa restrictions for members living outside Europe.

54 The concluding declarations used to be found at the Council's website (http://www.e-cfr.org/en/index.php?cat_id=339, accessed 24 Jun 2010). The Arabic version may be consulted at http://e-cfr.org/new/?cat=2, accessed 12 Feb 2014.

55 The concluding declaration of the 19th session was accessible at the Council's website, but has since been removed.

The sessions usually last for four days. Administrative matters are dealt with in a closed meeting, followed by meetings in which prepared studies on given topics are presented. The studies are then discussed, for the purpose of agreeing on *qarārāt* (resolutions). Such a resolution most often is not an answer to a specific question, but springs from the members' initiatives on topics they consider important for Muslims in Europe. Then comes the fatwa session. The fatwas given by the Council are often worked out in advance by one of the members, or a small group of members, in response to a questioner (*mustaftī*). The Council seeks to give unanimous fatwas, and the text of the fatwa is often edited to include various points of view among the members. If they are accepted, they are considered to be the Council's fatwas.[56] At the end of the session, the concluding declaration, which includes both fatwas and *qarārāt*, is read out loud, and the members give their assent.

The Council is centrally concerned with publishing the fatwas, through several channels. In addition to the concluding declaration, posted on the Council's website, they are also included in the annual publication *al-Majalla al-ʿilmiyya*. Some of the fatwas have also been published on the IslamOnline.net website, where they are often edited into texts together with other fatwas on the same topic.[57] A number of fatwas were also published in a joint edition of the first and second fatwa collection, which contained fatwas and resolutions given up until the seventh session (January 2001). A long-awaited third collection was published in 2013. It consists of fatwas and resolutions from the establishment of the Council in 1997 to 2010.

According to Council member Mohamed al-Mansoori, the fatwas are distributed to Islamic centres all over Europe, where they only seem to end up in a drawer. In al-Mansoori's view, they should be translated and be made available to everyone, not least because they should be read and discussed.[58]

---

56 Conversation with Ounis Guergah, member of the Council and the then head of the Dar al-Fatwa (Paris), in Le Bourget, Paris, 11 May 2008. The literature on fatwas gives examples to show that the term "fatwa" is not only used for answers to questions, especially in Central Asia and India: "… a work was characterized as a 'fatwa' collection if it concentrated on issues that arose in practice" (Masud, Messick, and Powers 1996, 15).

57 Conversation with staff from the IslamOnline.net fatwa desk, Cairo, March 2007. IslamOnline had a "fatwa bank" until 2010. After a crisis between the Qatar-based management and the Cairo-based staff, which was responsible for all content on the site, the Cairo staff set up a new website, OnIslam.net. This site features some of the ECFR's fatwas under the categories "Ask the scholar" and "Ask about Islam". On the crisis in IslamOnline.net, see Abdel-Fadil 2011.

58 Lecture at the seminar "Ideal and Practice," Oslo, 26 May 2007. For example, al-Mansoori

The Questions

The work of the ECFR, however, extends far beyond the annual session and the publications. According to Hussein Halawa, secretary general of the ECFR, the Council receives questions from all over Europe.[59] Most of the questions are posed in writing, by letter, e-mail or fax.[60] Halawa himself answers what he describes as "simple" questions that do not require the full Council. As examples, he mentions questions about marriage, divorce, and inheritance. He passes on some of the questions to the fatwa committees in the UK and France. The answers are sent directly to the questioner (*al-mustaftī*). Questions that might be of general interest are sent to the Council.

More women than men contact the ECFR with questions. Halawa says the ratio of women to men is seven to three. Topics common to women and men are divorce, *ṭalāq* (unilateral repudiation), or *khulʿ* (where the woman is granted divorce against compensation), which make up about 60% of the questions. Women often ask if the husband's *ṭalāq* is valid. According to Halawa, *ṭalāq* does not have to be registered to be valid, but the husband is asked to register it, that the woman may enjoy her rights. In conversation, Halawa also stressed that a public divorce signed by the husband is considered a divorce in Islam. Beside divorce, Halawa says, women's questions fall under the following main headings: menstruation and other women's health issues; whether to go to university; conflicts with children, not least in the father–child relationship; and domestic violence, including violence against children (the latter topic accounts for 25% of all the questions posed). Halawa was plain that differences of opinion on these questions between Eastern and Western cultures can be challenging in themselves. Men mainly ask about financial issues, specifically contracts, loans, and business affairs.

The Sources

The sources the ECFR may use to give fatwas are stated as the Quran, the Sunna of the Prophet, consensus (*ijmāʿ*) and analogy (*qiyās*), on which the majority of Muslim scholars agree. However, writes the Council, it will also make use of

---

notes that people are still asking whether the sunset and night prayers (*salāt al-maghrib* and *salāt al-ʿisha*) may be joined in the short North European summer night. Al-Mansoori says that this fatwa was given early on in the history of the Council, and it ought to be public knowledge.

59 Conversation with Hussein Halawa, Cairo, 18 Mar 2008.

60 Halawa stated that, as a daily average, there were ten oral queries by telephone, ten questions by e-mail and three to four questions by fax; weekly, they also got five questions by letter.

other sources if it is in the interest of the Muslim religious community to consider them.[61] These are: *istiḥsān* (consideration of reasonableness), *maṣlaḥa mursala* (utility with no textual evidence for or against), *sadd al-dharāʾiʿ* (preventing the use of lawful means to reach an unlawful goal), *istiṣḥāb* (presumption that a circumstance continues to apply), *madhhab al-ṣaḥābī* and *sharʿ min qablinā* (laws from pre-Islamic time)—provided that these are known to the *ahl al-ʿilm* (Islamic scholars).

The Council stresses that it does not intend to compete with fiqh councils in the Muslim world, such as the *Majmaʿ buḥūth al-Azhar* (the al-Azhar research center), *Majmaʿ al-fiqhī li-rābiṭa al-ʿālam al-islāmī* (the *fiqh* academy of the Muslim World League), or the *Majmaʿ al-fiqhī al-islāmī* (the *fiqh* academy that sprang from the Organization of the Islamic Conference, OIC, in 1981). The ECFR is intended as a supplement to these councils, specializing in issues of *fiqh al-aqalliyyāt* (jurisprudence of minorities).[62] Thus, the ECFR also lays claim to authority over European Muslims, by virtue of their minority status. The Council's use of the term *fiqh al-aqalliyyāt* may therefore be interpreted as a strategy to position it as independent and equal in rank to other fiqh bodies, at least on the Council's European preserve. The concept has become the "trademark" of the ECFR, and forms the framework for the principles, concepts and methods used to derive norms. It is also a hot topic of discourses on Muslims in the West, not least with regard to Muslim families and Muslim women.[63]

Fiqh al-aqalliyyāt

According to Muhammad Khalid Masud, *fiqh al-aqalliyyāt* is a new concept that will grow in importance and affect the future of Muslims living in the West.[64] Central questions are at stake.[65] Muslim minorities are considered part

61 ECFR 2002a, 3.

62 ECFR 2002a, x.

63 In addition to the following section, see Caeiro 2011; Hassan 2013.

64 Muhammad Khalid Masud, "Fiqh al-aqalliyyat: Toward another civil rights movement?" (http://www.maruf.org/?p=101, accessed 11 Jun 2010, now defunct). Masud refers to Khalid Abd al-Qadir, *Fiqh al-aqalliyyāt al-muslima* (Lebanon, 1998) as probably the first book devoted to this topic. Karman 2008, 44, however, holds that the idea of a particular fiqh for Muslim minorities belongs to Taha Jabir al-Alwani, former head of the Fiqh Council of North America (FCNA).

65 Uriya Shavit describes *fiqh al-aqalliyyāt al-muslima* as the field of jurisprudence that examines the legitimacy of voluntary, modern migration to and residence in non-Muslim societies and addresses specific, everyday challenges that Muslim minorities confront. Shavit 2015, 2.

of the Islamic religious community (*umma*), and other Muslims expect them to abide by Islamic norms. Many Muslims think that Muslims can only temporarily take up residence outside what is considered *dār al-islām* (the House of Islam), and that they should protect their religious and cultural identity for the duration.[66] Masud describes scholars with such views as follows: "These jurists are obviously restrained by the methodology as well as the worldview of the old laws; to the extent that they still use the term 'enemy countries' for the abode of the Muslim minorities."[67] Other Muslim scholars find it acceptable for Muslims who have come to the West to stay.[68] This implies categorizing the world differently than into *dār al-islām* and *dār al-ḥarb*. Taha Jabir al-Alwani, who promotes the idea of *fiqh al-aqalliyyāt* in his small book *Towards a Fiqh for Minorities* (2003), divides the world into *dār al-islām* and *dār al-kufr* (the House of Unbelief): "… *dār al-islām* is anywhere a Muslim can live in peace and security, even if he lives among a non-Muslim majority. Likewise, *dār al-kufr* is wherever Muslims live under threat, even if the majority there adhere to Islam and Islamic culture."[69] Al-Alwani also describes the *fiqh al-aqalliyyāt* as a "fiqh of coexistence" suited to the world we live in, in contrast to what he calls the "fiqh of conflict" of earlier times.[70] It is a view shared by Andrew March, who based on studies of modern works on the subject claims that *fiqh al-aqalliyyāt* "… is an attempt to provide an Islamic foundation for a relatively thick and rich relationship of moral obligation and solidarity with non-Muslims."[71] Al-Alwani describes *fiqh al-aqalliyyāt* as follows:

> Fiqh for minorities is a specific discipline, which takes into account the relationship between the religious rulings and the conditions of the community and the location where it exists. It is a fiqh that applies to a specific group of people living under particular conditions with special needs that may not be appropriate for other communities.[72]

---

66 Masud refers to *Muslim Minorities: Fatwa regarding Muslims as Minorities*, by the late Grand Mufti of Saudi-Arabia, Bin Baz (d. 1999), and to the Islamic scholar Muhammad ibn al-Uthaymeen.

67 http://www.maruf.org/frames/Articles/article-10.htm (accessed 1 Dec 2008; now defunct).

68 See e.g. Darsh, 13 (unpublished).

69 Al-Alwani 2003, 28.

70 Al-Alwani 2003, 11.

71 March 2009, 34–35. March has read texts by Khalid Abd al-Qadir, Yusuf al-Qaradawi, Abdullah bin Bayyah and Taha Jabir al-Alwani among others.

72 Al-Alwani 2003, 3.

According to al-Alwani, the *fiqh al-aqalliyyāt* is to solve the problems of Muslims through a new vision, based on *maqāṣid al-sharīʿa* (the objectives of Sharia), and through the exercise of *ijtihād*.[73] It is a collective concern, and should not be practiced individually; experts in different fields should participate on equal terms with religious scholars.[74] Al-Alwani also describes *fiqh al-aqalliyyāt* as a project to establish a separate area of law. This requires knowledge, and he suggests that institutes of *fiqh* and Sharia be established within the framework of "existing institutions and associations of Muslim social scientists," as a step in the development of such institutions.[75] Al-Alwani's document on *fiqh al-aqalliyyāt* takes a theoretical perspective, and argues for the use of methods and concepts in a style reminiscent of a project proposal.

The foundations of the ECFR's use of the *fiqh al-aqalliyyāt* concept have been formulated by Yusuf al-Qaradawi, president of the Council, in the book *Fī fiqh al-aqalliyyāt al-muslima: ḥayāt al-muslimīn wasṭ al-mujtamaʿāt al-ukhrā* (Islamic Jurisprudence of Minorities: The Lives of Muslims in Non-Muslim Societies), published in 2001.[76] The book is in two parts, the first presenting the theory, and the second applying it to practical questions.[77]

Al-Qaradawi's point of departure is that Muslims in the West find themselves in a new situation and face challenges because they live in societies under non-Muslim laws, and they lack the framework and support for a natural socialization into Islamic practice. Many of these challenges are *fiqh*-related.[78] Regarding women-related issues, al-Qaradawi poses the following questions: What is the status of a civil marriage contract in Islam? What about divorce granted by a non-Muslim judge? May one marry a second wife when the laws of the country do not allow more than one wife? What rights does a second wife

73 Al-Alwani 2003, 13.

74 Al-Alwani 2003, 34.

75 Al-Alwani 2003, 36.

76 According to al-Qaradawi 2001, 5, the book results from a request by the leadership of the Muslim World League (*Rabiṭat al-ʿālam al-islāmī*) for a study of fiqh challenges confronting Muslims in the West.

77 It is interesting that the English translation only includes Part II, the practical questions.

78 To give an impression where al-Qaradawi believes the shoe pinches, some of the questions he raises are: Can a Muslim take up permanent residence in a non-Muslim country if he fears for his religious practice and that of his children? What about citizenship? What is the norm concerning jelly, cheese and meat? May one work in a restaurant that serves pork and alcohol? May a Muslim attend a wedding where pork and alcohol are served? May one buy a house with a normal bank loan? (al-Qaradawi 2001, 25–28)

have in the case of conflict? Is an imam in an Islamic centre allowed to marry the husband to a second wife in such cases? May a woman marry without a guardian? Is a woman who converts to Islam obliged to divorce her husband if he does not follow suit?[79]

According to al-Qaradawi, the *fiqh al-aqalliyyāt* keeps one eye on the Islamic heritage and the other on *al-wāqiʿ* ("reality").[80] It relates the global character of Islam to various social realities; it strikes a balance between detailed texts and *maqāṣid al-sharīʿa* (the overall objectives of Sharia); it weighs the norms by priority in relation to one another, in the light of the sources; it changes according to *ʿurf* (custom); and it aims to preserve a "good Islamic personality" in the encounter with the surrounding society, to which one should relate and into which one should integrate.[81]

The foundations of *fiqh al-aqalliyyāt* are what al-Qaradawi calls "correct" *ijtihād*, defined as a set of selected Islamic norms that are either inherited from traditional fiqh (*ijtihād intiqāʾī*, "selective independent reasoning" in which a choice is made between existing possibilities), or discovered throuh *ijtihād inshāʾī* ("creative independent reasoning"). Al-Qaradawi considers the latter type of *ijtihād* the most important. He presents and argues the case for concepts and methods that should be used in *ijtihād*. Most scholars, al-Qaradawi says, agree on the Quran, the Sunna of the Prophet, *ijmāʿ* and *qiyās*; he goes on to present what he terms the more controversial sources: *maṣlaḥa mursala, istiḥsān, sadd al-dharāʾī*, *ʿurf*, *sharʿ min qablinā*, *istiṣḥāb* and *qawl ṣaḥābī* (the sayings of the Companions).[82] These sources are identical with the ones mentioned in the ECFR statutes.[83]

Al-Qaradawi claims that this kind of *ijtihād* is part of the renewal (*tajdīd*) that the Prophet has said will take place in every century. He thus stakes a claim for the recognition of *fiqh al-aqalliyyāt* as an integral part of the Islamic fiqh tradition.[84] Al-Qaradawi's book seems to have twofold agenda: to promote a

79 Al-Qaradawi 2001, 27.

80 Tariq Ramadan renders this term as "the social and human context" (Ramadan 2009a, 102).

81 Al-Qaradawi 2001, 35–36.

82 Al-Qaradawi 2001, 39.

83 ECFR 2002a, 3.

84 The concept of *tajdīd* ("renewal") is often used in connection with modern Islamic movements, but it has pre-modern roots. Pre-modern *tajdīd* was usually tied to a named *mujaddid* (renewer). According to a hadith, such a figure will appear at the beginning of every century to renew the Islamic faith and practice. ("Tajdid" in the *Oxford Dictionary of Islam*, Esposito 2003, 265).

conceptual and methodological canon, and thus assert authority, among other scholars; and to promote his view among lay Muslims by applying this canon to particular examples that may be relevant to them.[85]

Abdullah bin Bayyah also defends the use of the concept *fiqh al-aqalliyyāt*, with reference to the ECFR's resolution on the matter at its twelfth session in Dublin in 2004.[86] In Bin Bayyah's view, the *fiqh al-aqalliyyāt* seeks to find guidelines for Muslim minorities that will (i) preserve their collective and individual faith and way of life; (ii) remind the minority of their duties to the other groups with which they live, that religion might be a bridge tying people together, not a fence; and (iii) ease and simplify the religious life, because religion is not intended to cause man pain and suffering.[87] This should follow the principle of integration, which represents what Bin Bayyah calls *wasaṭiyya*, a middle position between isolation and assimilation. According to Bin Bayyah, the general situation of Muslims outside the Muslim world may be described one of *ḍarūra* (vital necessity). He thus upgrades the *ḥāja* (a less pressing need than *ḍarūra*),[88] and joins *ḍarūra* and *ḥāja* into one category.[89] Thus, Bin Bayyah makes the *ḥāja* subject to the legal maxim "necessity makes the forbidden lawful," a rule of license (*rukhṣa*) in all cases of of necessity.[90] The above principle is one of six maxims on which Bin Bayyah bases *fiqh al-aqalliyyāt*: i) relieving

85 The book is also found in English translation, titled *Fiqh of Muslim Minorities: Contentious Issues & Recommended Solutions* (al-Qaradawi 2003c). The theoretical part has been heavily abridged compared with the Arabic edition, but the second part, focusing on concrete issues, is translated in full. It seems that the target audience of the translation is not an academic one, but Muslims as a minority, and that the book is intended as *daʿwa* (invitation to practice Islam) addressed to this group, whereas the Arabic version is aimed at other Muslim scholars.

86 See below.

87 Bin Bayyah 2007, 167.

88 The point of departure is the three categories of *ḍarūr(iyy)āt*, *ḥājiyyāt* and *taḥsiniyyāt* in the theory of *maqāṣid al-sharīʿa* (objectives of Sharia). The Moroccan jurist Ahmad Raysuni defines *ḍarūrāt* as "… things which are essential for the achievement of human beings' spiritual and material well-being. If these essentials are missing, the result will be imbalance and major corruption in both this world and the next." He defines *ḥājiyyāt* as "… the interests which, when fulfilled, contribute to relieving hardship and difficulty and creating ease in the lives of those accountable before the Law" (al-Raysuni 2005, 108–109). I briefly elaborate on this three-way division in chapter 7.

89 Bin Bayyah 2007, 167.

90 Eggen 2001.

pain and suffering, ii) a fatwa changes with time and place, iii) *ḥāja* (need) is upgraded to *ḍarūra* (vital necessity), iv) regard should be had to *ʿurf* (custom), v) regard should be had to *maʾālāt* (consequences), vi) the Muslim community may act in place of the *qāḍī* (judge). This is not the place to delve into the contents of the argument, of which only keywords have been given here in order to show how the scholars discuss the concept of *fiqh al-aqalliyyāt*.[91]

Within the Council, however, there are different views of the development of a *fiqh al-aqalliyyāt*.[92]

The subject of *fiqh al-aqalliyyāt* was discussed at the Council's twelfth session in Dublin (2004). A number of members presented studies on various aspects of the concept. The Council passed a resolution (*qarār*) on the topic, defining *fiqh al-aqalliyyāt* as fiqh norms concerning Muslims living outside Muslim countries. The Council also agreed to use the concept in its work. There is no point in disagreeing over this concept, as it is already in use in our time, the Council wrote in its *qarār*.[93]

The use of *fiqh al-aqalliyyāt* may be read as an argument that the fatwas are adapted to the situation of Muslim minorities, and as a strategy to bolster the ECFR's legitimacy vis-à-vis Islamic scholars and fatwa councils outside Europe. In this way, according to Caeiro, "a fictional account of the legal primacy of shari'a in Muslim majority countries" is constructed.[94] As a result, authority lies with the recognized scholars of the Muslim community, who are entrusted with the responsibility of guiding Muslim believers.

Union des Organisations Islamiques de France (UOIF) and Dar al-Fatwa

The Union des Organisations Islamiques de France was established as a challenge to the monopoly of the Mosque of Paris (*La grande mosquée de Paris*) with its focus on an "official" Algerian Islam.[95] The members were students from Muslim countries, who had come to complete their studies in France. The core

91 Bin Bayyah 2007.

92 Some of these views are presented in Karman 2008, 86–89.

93 *Al-Majalla al-ʿilmiyya* 4–5:471–472.

94 Caeiro 2011, 109.

95 Laurence and Vaisse 2006, 104. The Paris Mosque, established in 1926, has had close ties to Algerian authorities, who inter alia appointed the head of the mosque, the rector, until 1992 (Vogt 1995).

of the UOIF consisted of Tunisians with ideological ties to the Mouvement de la tendence islamique (MTV), which became the al-Nahda party in 1989. The spiritual guide was the Lebanese jurist Faysal Mawlawi.[96] At that stage, the activities of the UOIF consisted in producing a calendar with prayer times for the major cities of France, organizing pilgrimages to Mecca, and focusing on the family with activities for women and a summer camp—a huge annual gathering that has since developed into the UOIF's mass meeting at Le Bourget, Paris.[97] The aim of the activities was the care and guidance of Muslims *during their stay* in France. However, the UOIF's view of Muslims as foreigners in the French context would change. The 1987 internal charter of the UOIF referred to *la communauté musulmane de France*. In Ladmiral's view, this implied a definition of Muslims as French citizens.[98] A natural further development took place in 1990: the organization changed its name from "Union des Organisations Islamiques *en* France" to "Union des Organisations Islamiques *de* France". According to Ladmiral, this change implies the development of a separate "school" with the aim of promoting Islamic practice adapted to the local context—based on the principles of the golden mean (*wasaṭiyya*) and making the rules easy (*taysīr*).[99]

According to Caeiro, the UOIF is "the most dynamic organisation at the grassroots level, [...] gathering together over 200 associations," and it is "one of the few organisations in France systematically engaging with religious texts and thus able to posit itself as a religious authority, rather than as a mere (political) representative of Muslims."[100] The UOIF is a member of the Conseil Français du Culte Musulman (CFCM), the Muslim representative body and interlocutor with French authorities.

The UOIF, the CFCM, and the French Authorities

The Conseil Français du Culte Musulman (CFCM) was founded in 2003. This was the culmination of a lengthy consultation with Muslims in France, initiated in 1999 by the then minister of the interior Jean-Pierre Chevènement. The CFCM has been extensively described in the scholarly literature.[101] According to Caeiro, many European countries have engaged in the promotion of national

96 Ternisien 2002, 149. Faysal Mawlawi was a member of the ECFR until his death. Ternisien cites Gilles Kepel's *Les Banlieues de l'islam* as a main reference work about the founding of the UOIF.

97 Ladmiral 2006, 33.

98 Ladmiral 2006, 34.

99 Ladmiral 2006, 35.

100 Caeiro 2005, 73.

101 See e.g. Vogt 1995; Laurence and Vaisse 2006; Frégosi 2008.

forms of "Islam," not least a "French national Islam," which he describes as "a cultural, linguistic, financial, political and theological enterprise"—a liberal Islam with a Sharia "*bien tempérée à la française.*" The French government's strategy for the adaptation of Islam in France consists in organizing the Muslim religion in a "church."[102] Laurence and Vaisse describe this "church" as "… the equivalent of the Catholic Conférence des Évêques, the Jewish Consistoire Central (1807), and the Protestant Fédération (1905), all of which serve as national and regional interlocutors for the state."[103]

The French Ministry of the Interior, headed by Nicolas Sarkozy (minister of the interior 2002–2004), was deeply engaged in the founding of the CFCM, not least with regard to the composition of the council.[104] According to Laurence and Vaisee,

> [t]he government-led creation of the [… CFCM …] was an attempt to reduce foreign influence on France's Muslim population. Rather than simply tolerate the existence of Islam *in* France, the government has made it a policy goal to create an Islam *of* France […][105]

Frégosi describes the involvement of Sarkozy as total and personal, with the minister himself drawing up the outlines of the future CFCM in December 2002; internally, the CFCM would largely be made up of the Mosque of Paris, the UOIF and the Fédération Nationale des Musulmans de France.[106]

This involvement extended to holding the founding meeting of the CFCM at the residence of the interior minister, and using "stick and carrot" to get the delegates to agree and sign on to Sarkozy's proposal. Frégosi comments as follows on this meddling in what should have been an internal Islamic matter:

> This insistence on expecting everything from the State is surprising in a regime of *laïcité* where the state is supposed not to interfere in the organisation and functioning of the religions. At the same time, it is a confession of the responsible Muslims' relative inability to bring out a real consensus among themselves on common objectives.[107]

---

102 Caeiro 2005, 71.

103 Laurence and Vaisse 2006, 154.

104 Frégosi 2008, 298.

105 Laurence and Vaisse 2006, 138.

106 Frégosi 2008, 298. When the CFCM was established in 2003, the Mosquée de Paris got the presidency, while the two other organizations each got a vice-president.

107 Frégosi 2008, 300.

According to Frégosi, the UOIF is the French Muslim actor with the most to show for its participation in the consultation process and other negotiations with the public authorities. It has become an indispensable partner for the government.[108]

Vincent Geisser considers the UOIF a political actor in French society: "It produces political meaning *pour soi* (existing, being recognized as a representative organization) and *en soi* (socializing, supervising and mobilizing the 'Muslim base')."[109] He cites the speech of Thami Breze, president of the UOIF, who at its 2005 general assembly summed up *la réalité de l'UOIF* as a media contact point for questions on Islam, an organization recognized by public opinion and Muslim opinion both. The UOIF, then, may be described as an interest or pressure group.[110] At the same time, the UOIF is in a clear client relationship to the public authorities,[111] as an intermediary between the authorities and the Muslim grassroots. This has affected the UOIF in certain "sensitive matters," according to Geisser, who points to a number of issues over which the UOIF has struck compromises based on theological arguments: the headscarf affair of 2003–2004, the battle against Salafism, the Palestinian question, the dialogue with the Jewish council CRIF in 2004, the Tariq Ramadan affair of 2003–2004, and security in the 2005 crisis in the *banlieus*.[112] Geisser's comment on the UOIF's line is harsh: "It is in a way about 'pleasing' a 'political patron' who was the first to recognize the full legitimacy of the UOIF in the French public space."[113]

Geisser's view may help explain what I will call the "fatwa-collection affair" of 2005, which was probably a "sensitive matter" for an organization with ambitions to be an actor in French society at large. In 2005 the publisher Éditions Tawhid, with Yamin Makri as editor-in-chief, was in the process of publishing a French translation of the second ECFR fatwa collection. The translation of 37 fatwas was done, and the well-known intellectual Tariq Ramadan had been invited to write an introduction and commentary, as he had done for the French edition of the ECFR's first collection.[114] However, the publication was stopped by the UOIF,[115] even though Éditions Tawhid had permission from

108 Frégosi 2008, 311–312.
109 Geisser 2006, 85, italics added.
110 Geisser 2006, 87.
111 Geisser 2006, 93.
112 Geisser 2006, 96.
113 Geisser 2006, 97.
114 Conversation with Tariq Ramadan, Oslo, June 2008.
115 Conversation with Yamin Makri, in Paris, 10 May 2008.

al-Qaradawi himself. It was only an oral permission, though, and to no avail against the UOIF's veto. Xavier Ternisien claimed in *Le Monde* that the UOIF feared the publication would harm the organization's reputation with authorities and non-Muslim public opinion.[116] He tied this to two fatwas in particular: One on polygamy, with a wording likely to conflict with the view of European common morality ("Rather than calling for the abolition of this right, it would be fairer, as far as possible, to put a stop to all the abuses that certain Muslims engage in ..."). The other, on Palestine, urged every effort to resist the occupation and liberate Al-Quds (Jerusalem).

The publisher's editor, Yamin Makri, also tied the veto to the fatwa on Palestine, which might be seen as controversial and at odds with the UOIF's project of representing Islam in France. Makri stressed that Éditions Tawhid had no problem with controversial contents, as it was a publisher, and not a "political actor" like the UOIF.[117]

The next day, *Le Monde* published a disclaimer from the UOIF, pointing out that the UOIF had not received any request to approve publication of the fatwa collection, and claiming a certain ownership of the ECFR: "It's the UOIF that set up this European Council for Fatwa," said Thami Breze.[118] The concluding claims that the UOIF had not even been aware of the collection seem far-fetched, considering the relationship beween the UOIF and the ECFR, and the fact that the collection was already published in Arabic. The protest shows the challenges faced by the UOIF in juggling relationships and expectations at the intersection between the French authorities and the French public, the scholars of the ECFR, and the UOIF itself, as both the independent representative of Muslims vis-à-vis French authorities, and closely tied to the ECFR. The result may seem like the *double langage* the UOIF is often accused of using. The protest may also have been a strategy to retain control over a publication in which the UOIF was involved.

The UOIF and the Muslim Brotherhood

A recurrent topic of the scholarly literature on the UOIF is the question whom the organization "really" represents, and in particular, its relation to the Muslim Brotherhood.[119] Recurring issues in this discussion include the organizational affiliation of its founders in their country of origin, the selection of lecturers at the annual mass gathering in Le Bourget, the conduct of the UOIF in the hijab

116 *Le Monde*, 23 May 2005.

117 Conversation with Yamin Makri, in Paris, 10 May 2008.

118 *Le Monde*, 24 May 2005.

119 See e.g. Kepel 1997; Ternisien 2002; Deltombe 2005; Geisser 2006; Peter 2006; Frégosi 2008.

affairs of 1989 and 2003, which actors are talking to each other, and whether the UOIF is a threat to French society. Vincent Geisser describes how such analyses attempt to "unveil" the UOIF as a French branch of the Muslim Brothers allegedly seeking, under cover of religious worship, to win political power and take "quasi-totalitarian" control over the Muslim community in France.[120]

Gilles Kepel, the French expert on modern Islam, early on characterized the UOIF as an Islamist organization with ties to the Muslim Brotherhood in his book *Les banlieues de l'islam* (1984), which set out to describe the causes and effects of "the birth of a religion in France".[121] Kepel mapped the landscape of Islamic traditions and organizations, including the UOIF, which he described at the time as a union of 31 local Maghrebi and Turkish organizations aligned with the moderate Muslim Brothers or the Turkish National Salvation Party.[122] He devoted space not least to a description of *Le Groupement Islamique en France* (GIF), which joined the UOIF in 1984. The GIF, Kepel wrote, enjoyed the intellectual backing of the Muslim Brothers in the Middle East through its "guide," the Lebanese shaykh Faysal Mawlawi. Mawlawi would later become the vice-president of the ECFR and held the office until he died in 2011. Kepel commented on a lesson by Mawlawi on how to "command the good and prevent evil" while living as a Muslim in France, and concluded with the claim that: "To unite the Muslim populations into one community tending towards the building of the Islamic State, such is the ambition of our preacher …"[123]

Kepel would later explain the UOIF's change of profile in the early 1990s in terms of changing aims, from seeking an Islamic state in the Muslim homeland, to participating in a democratic experiment as a political factor of influence representing Muslims in France. According to Kepel, this was based on a new interpretation of France as part of *dār al-islām* (the House of Islam), a concept defined by Abdullah Ben Mansour, the then head of the UOIF, as any territory where Muslims were safe and might freely practice their religion. "In the long term, the Union hopes to become the representative of the Muslim 'minority' and defender of its specific interests, which it stamps with its own conception of Islam," Kepel claims.[124]

Xavier Ternisien describes the Muslim Brotherhood as a network, and seeks to clarify the position of the UOIF within this network relative to the Muslim

120 Geisser 2006, 84.

121 Kepel 1987, 9.

122 Kepel 1987, 267. The Turkish organizations eventually left the UOIF and formed their own organization.

123 Kepel 1987, 258 ff.

124 Kepel 1997, 197–198.

Brotherhood in Egypt. The Egyptian group and the foreign "branches" refer to the same ideology. Ternisien distinguishes the Brotherhood's organization (*tanẓīm*) from its "school" or movement of thought (*madrasa*),[125] and claims it is a fact that there are no formal relations between the UOIF and the Muslim Brothers.[126] By urging respect for religious scholars such as Yusuf al-Qaradawi and Faysal Mawlawi, the UOIF nevertheless places itself within the frame of *fikr al-ikhwānī* (the thought of the Muslim Brothers).[127]

According to Tareq Oubrou, a key person in the UOIF, it is precisely a matter of the "school"—or as it is more frequently called, the "thought" (*fikr*):[128]

> For young Muslims who wanted to reflect and act, the literature of the Muslim Brothers was the only one available. It introduced us for a movement that was reformist, modern, alluring. We went on to make our way and contextualize our action. It was indeed a thought born in the Muslim world, a reality that did not correspond to a secularized society, the one we lived in. So we fashioned our own reading of the relation of Islam to society.[129]

Expanding on this, Caeiro claims that the UOIF has distanced itself from transnational religious authorities such as al-Qaradawi and Mawlawi. Instead, "lo-

---

125 Ternisien 2002, 155.

126 Ternisien 2002, 158 points out that the Union des Organisations Islamiques d'Europe (UIOE), of which the UOIF is a member, in 1991 resolved not to depend in any way on the Muslim Brotherhood of Egypt. On the relationship between the central Brotherhood and the various national organizations, and the growing independence of the latter, see Brooke 2012; Baylocq 2012.

127 Ternisien 2002, 158.

128 The concept of *fikr* (thought) and *haraka* (movement) are more often used than *madrasa* (school), because it is considered more open than a "school", which suggests a closed relationship between teacher and student. Information from Basim Ghozlan, March 2009.

129 Maillard 2006, 19. There is reason to believe that Oubrou is here referring to books published by the Kuwait-based International Islamic Federation of Student Organizations (IIFSO). In the 1970s and 1980s, the IIFSO translated and published books in 70 languages, including French. Among the titles, we find books by well-known Islamists within what Roald calls "the *ikhwān* trend of thought", such as Hassan al-Banna, Sayyid and Muhammad Qutb, Yusuf al-Qaradawi and Muhammad al-Ghazali. Roald also refers to a study by Pernilla Ouis on "… how a certain understanding of islam became pervasive in Europe due to the influence of these IIFSO books. She claims that oil wealth enabled the spread of this interpretation of Islam so that it came to be regarded as the only true version." (Roald 2001a, 55)

cal" scholars like Tareq Oubrou and Ahmed Jaballah are promoted as "spiritual reference points."[130] This is a result of French authorities conducting, since the mid-1990s, a policy toward Muslims Caeiro calls "containment through engagement."[131] As discussed above, this policy resulted in the founding of the CFCM in 2003, and the UOIF has been included in this process.

Thomas Deltombe ties the French public's perceptions of the UOIF to the French media's construction of Islam as a potential threat to French identity. In *L'islam imaginaire*, he critically surveys the dominant media discourse on "Islam in France" from 1975 to 2005. He identifies three stages of this "history of construction": (i) The first, from the mid-1970s to the end of the 1980s, was marked by the revolution in Iran and the settlement of immigrants in France. Through an odd kind of optical illusion, Deltombe writes, images of Iran were transfered onto immigrants in France. As a result, Islam was seen as a problem, something the media liked to think "incompatible" with French society.[132] (ii) The second stage, in the 1990s, mainly revolved around the establishment of an *islam de France* and the attempts of television to change its language. "At the same time as it portrays a widening 'gap' between the 'Muslim world' and the 'Western world', it chops the 'Muslim community' of France into two poles: the 'moderates', who should be defended, and the 'Islamists', who should be fought."[133] (iii) The third stage began with the events of 11 September 2001, and has been characterized by a combination of media efforts to find the "invisible enemy" and the transformation of the political elite's concern with security into a question of identity. One seeks to protect oneself against a perceived threat. *La République* becomes a magic notion seen as the solution to all social problems, in contrast to Muslims as a group, who symbolize the "Islamic menace".

> Terrorism, communalism, anti-Semitism, sexism: it all seems to go together to impeach a 'Muslim community' said to be eaten from the inside by an Islamism the contours of which are nevertheless hard to make out.[134]

These three stages form the backdrop to Deltombe's discussion of the media's interest in and treatment of the UOIF, which he claims is part of the debate

130 Caeiro 2005, 74.
131 Caeiro 2005, 74.
132 Deltombe 2005, 10.
133 Deltombe 2005, 11.
134 Deltombe 2005, 12.

on French identity and the adaptation of Islam in France.[135] He ascribes the interest of the media to three events in 1991: the establishment of an institute of theological education in Nièvre, the annual conference in Le Bourget, and more indirectly, the FIS victory in the first round of the 1991 parliamentary elections in Algeria.[136] The view of the UOIF as a threat was reinforced when the media discovered the connection between the UOIF, the conference, and the institute. "On the public network newscast, Abdallah Ben Mansour, the president of the UOIF, would suddenly become 'one of the key persons of the Islamic movement in France' and a 'very influential man in the Islamic world.'"[137] Accusations of close ties between the UOIF and the FIS evaporated, but accusations that the UOIF was using a *double langage* proved far more tenacious. Differing texts in the French and Arabic versions of the introductory brochure of the Nièvre institute were used as proof.

The German expert on Islam Frank Peter claims in an article on Muslim discourses in France that the public French discourse and the Islamist vision are mirror images of one another:

> The debate on immigrants in the Republic indirectly impacted in important ways the articulation of certain segments of Muslim populations. [... T]he problematic issue of immigrants and that of the banlieues had increasingly come to be perceived as a problem of Muslim immigrants. The latter issue, in turn, was debated primarily via the ongoing conflicts around the Muslim headscarf in public school. The debate on immigrants had thus set the stage, since the early 1990s, for continuing scrutiny of France's 'Muslim' population with regard to the possibility of their integration and their loyalty to the Republic [...]. It is crucial to point out that in most cases underlying this scrutiny was a specific vision of Islam. Not only was Islam considered to be an essentially public religion which was supposed to have a significant, although rarely specified, impact on the believers' attitudes and behaviour in society, but was also mostly seen as a religion whose normative dimensions, Islamic law, was deemed an inseparable part of it. [... T]hese debates define Islam mainly via (often uninformed) interpretations of Islamic scriptures [...] Islam, as it was constructed in the course of the French public debates, overlaps in important ways with an all-encompassing understanding of Islam, as defended

135 Deltombe 2005, 166.
136 Deltombe 2005, 166f.
137 Deltombe 2005, 167.

> notably by Islamists: not only because of its essentialized vision of Islam, but even more so because of the emphasis on its normative dimension.[138]

Peter states that the UOIF has from the very beginning had strong ties to Islamist groups in North Africa and the Middle East, and to prominent persons in the Islamic movement. This, however, is not a satisfactory criterion for defining the thinking of the organization, and the emphasis placed on proximity to the Muslim Brotherhood in analyses of the UOIF is misleading, Peter writes.[139] When the UOIF claims a place in French society, it addresses a twofold audience, both Muslims and non-Muslims. Accordingly, they have to meet both expectations of loyalty to the French Republic, and demands for Islamic legitimacy. The UOIF leadership has therefore, according to Peter, developed a rhetoric stressing what he calls "the harmonious union of Islam and French citizenship."[140] This does not correspond well to the Islamist ideal of Islam as a comprehensive system structuring both the private and the public sphere. Peter points to the UOIF's notion of the good Muslim citizen, who respects the laws of the state and casts his vote in political elections, as an example why "Islamic reformism" is a more fitting description of the UOIF's attempts to find its place in French society.[141] Based on Peter's analysis, the UOIF does not quite seem to fit on either side of the mirror image referred to above.

Dar al-Fatwa

Answering questions has been an integral part of the UOIF's activities since its founding in 1983.[142] This field gained more and more attention, and in 1992 and 1993, the UOIF was behind *fiqh* seminars in which Muslim settlement was a

138 Peter 2006, 445–446.

139 Peter 2006, 456.

140 Peter 2006, 449–450.

141 Peter defineres reformism as the "… elaboration and defense of a legal and more generally, hermeneutical methodology which was supposed to re-establish the essential flexibility and evolutionary capacity of islam and to enable the 'Islamic civilization' to catch up with the West." Islamism, too, stresses flexibility and reform of Islamic jurisprudence and education, but it "… pursued this endeavor only insofar as it would achieve the more precise aim of constructing a coherent and comprehensive Islamic system." The main difference between reformism and Islamism is the aim of the reform: The former seeks to appropriate desirable features of Western modernity, the latter seeks an Islamic state as the means to establishing an Islamic system (Peter 2006, 448).

142 A committee was formed from the very beginning in 1983, with members who took a particular interest in this field. Faysal al-Mawlawi, the founder and spiritual guide of the UOIF, was a member of this committee.

main issue.[143] These fiqh seminars were the starting point for the initiative of the UOIF, in cooperation with Yusuf al-Qaradawi, to establish the ECFR in 1997. Five of the ECFR's members are from France. Four of them are described by Hussein Halawa as "the French fatwa committee (*lajnat al-fatwā*) in the ECFR," which is so to speak identical[144] to parts of the "inner circle" of the Dar al-Fatwa in the UIOF.[145] The Dar al-Fatwa was established in 2001, on the occasion of the UOIF's annual gathering in Le Bourget. The founding may be seen as the formalization and institutionalization of the "questions-and-answers session" that had been a regular item on the programme at previous Le Bourget gatherings. Dar al-Fatwa is part of the UOIF organizational structure on the national level, and belongs to the department for *affaires religieuses et Dar al-Fatwa*.[146] The department is responsible for

> … dans le sens le plus large, des besoins culturels des musulmans de France. Il s'appuie pour cela sur Dar al-Fatwa, une institution de réflexion et de recherche qui élabore, à partir des données théologiques et canoniques musulmanes et en tenant compte des conditions de vie en France, les éléments conceptuels théoriques et les modalités permettant aux musulmans de vivre leur religion de façon authentique, loin de tout gêne et en bonne conformité avec leur contexte.[147]

In addition to the inner circle, the Dar al-Fatwa consists of imams and shaykhs in the cities where the UOIF is represented, as well as teachers and graduates of the *Institut européen des sciences humaines* (IESH). Three of the latter are women.[148]

---

143 The 1992 *fiqh* seminar is referenced in chapter 1.

144 The difference seems to consist in who their questioner is. As a local committee under the ECFR, the *lajnat al-fatwā* gets questions forwarded by the secretary general in Dublin, whereas the Dar al-Fatwa gets questions directly from *mustaftīs* in France.

145 According to Ahmed Jaballah, *le cercle constraint* consists of the four members of the ECFR along with Tareq Oubrou, the head of the association Les Imams de France, and Zin Al-Abidin, the secretary of Dar al-Fatwa. Conversation with Ahmed Jaballah, Cairo, 30 Mar 2007.

146 Daho 2006, 55. The other departments are: Secrétariat national, Département des activités nationales, Département de relation avec les associations, Département de l'information et de la communication, Département de l'enseignement, Département des affaires culturelles, Département de l'éducation et de la formation des cadres, Département du dialogue interreligieux, Département des finances et du développement des ressources, and Département des relations publiques.

147 Daho 2006, 56.

148 Conversation with Ahmed Jaballah, Cairo, 30 Mar 2007.

In 2004, they offered a total of eight hours' phone service a week, with the four members Ounis Guergah, Bishri Larabi, Ahmed Jaballah and Tahar Mahdi manning the phone.[149] The offer has since expanded a great deal, and in 2008, the phone service was offered five days a week (not Fridays and Sundays) for a total of 33 hours. The staff of muftis has been expanded with Tareq Oubrou in Bourdeaux and Zin al-Abidin, the UOIF secretary.[150] Beside phone calls, the Dar al-Fatwa receives questions by e-mail and fax. According to Ahmed Jaballah, the phone is constantly ringing during the service hours, and ten questions an hour are answered on average. Between 60 and 70% of the callers are women. Apart from questions on the five pillars, which are equally distributed between men and women, the young women's questions are mainly about marriage, *wilāya* (guardianship), parental permission to marry, and civil versus "*ḥalāl*" marriage contracts, whereas the older women's questions are often about duties and rights in marriage and about *khulʿ* (when the woman requests divorce against compensation). The men's questions are often about loans and investments for business purposes, a frequently recurring theme being interest-based loans.

According to Ahmed Jaballah, some of the questions require a therapist, someone to listen to the callers' complaints. In such cases the fatwa is often given as a piece of advice, *naṣīḥa*, which Jaballah describes as "a moral and spiritual response." Comparing the concepts of *fatwā* and *naṣīḥa*, he stresses that all fatwas may be seen as *naṣāʾiḥ*, but not every *naṣīḥa* is a *fatwā*.

The Annual Gathering of the UOIF

Once a year, during the annual gathering of the UOIF, *Rencontre annuelle des musulmans de France*, the muftis of Dar al-Fatwa are available in the so-called fatwa tent, where one may get answers to questions *sur place*. At the 2008 gathering, there were seven tables, each serviced by one person. (The number of tables in service might vary from five to seven.) The tables were staffed by young volunteers, both men and women.[151] They were all graduates of three-year Sharia studies at the IESH in Paris, or its sister institution at Chateau Chi-

149 Conversation with Ahmed Jaballah, Cairo, 30 Mar 2007.

150 According to the leaflet *Permanence de la Dar Al-Fatwa de l'UOIF* that I found in the reception when I visited the IESH in Paris in May 2008. This overview contains the hourly schedule of the telephone service, indicating who can be reached when, and the phone number of each mufti. (IESH in Paris, 12 May 2007).

151 This was the first and only time in the course of my research for this book that I found female muftis giving fatwas in Europe.

non. Ounis Guergah or Larabi Becheri were present most of the time, so the other muftis could turn to them in case of doubt.[152]

I spent 9–11 May 2008, the last three days of the conference, close to the tent, watching the fatwa activities. The tent was open between 10am and 1pm, and from 3pm to 7pm. People were lining up for fatwas. The line was shortest in the morning, and grew in the afternoon. People came on their own, or in the company of spouses or friends. Each session followed a certain pattern. First, the mufti and *mustaftī* would greet each other. The mufti then asked what was the matter, and the *mustaftī* stated his problem. Often, a discussion followed, before the mufti finally gave his fatwas. Judging by body language, the questioners seemed pleased with the fatwas they got.

Although the fatwa activities of the Dar al-Fatwa take place in clearly organized forms, whether the phone service, the fatwa tent or the *rencontre mensuel* (monthly meeting) at the IESH in Paris,[153] they place little weight on recording and publishing fatwas in writing.[154] The oral and private character of the fatwa thus limits the researcher's access to the primary sources, the fatwas themselves. My interviews with Ounis Guergah and Larabi Becheri, as well as a female mufti, Kamilia, nonetheless disclose two important aspects of the Dar al-Fatwa's activities: premises and guidelines that the muftis of Dar al-Fatwa are required to follow in fatwa-giving, and the contents of their education with regard to *iftāʾ*.

Premises and Guidelines for iftāʾ

Kamilia[155] holds a bachelor's degree in *al-sharīʿa wa uṣūl al-dīn* from the IESH (Chateau Chinon), and volunteered as a mufti in the Dar al-Fatwa tent during the 2008 conference. Not officially a member of the Dar al-Fatwa, she describes herself as a supporting member. Her ambitions, however, are clear: Her dream is to obtain a doctorate in the Sharia, and to become a member of the ECFR in time. Speaking of her view of *iftāʾ*, she said: "In the beginning I was afraid of fatwas." Kamilia says that women, couples, and young boys come to her with their questions because she is a woman. Half the questioners seek advice for marri-

152 In the course of my two interviews with Ounis Guergah, I saw the other muftis ask him for advice on what answer to give.

153 See e.g. the website of the IESH in Paris (http://www.ieshdeparis.com).

154 One exception is a so-called "fatwa sheet", a four-page document titled *Avis théologique: L'assise théologique de la participation des musulmans á la vie politique dans les sociétés á majorité non musulmane* (Theological Justification for the Participation of Muslims in the Political Life of Non-Muslim Majority Societies).

155 Conversation with Kamilia, Le Bourget, Paris, 10 May 2008.

tal problems, 25 % of the questions concern interest-based loans and financial transactions, and the remaining 25 % concern various other matters. Education and how to live in Europe are frequent topics. Asked whether the questioners seem content with the answers, Kamilia says they do—several come back, year after year.

The fatwas are given with regard to certain references and a certain method. The point of departure is the Quran and the Sunna of the Prophet. All four schools of law may be used, but since most of the questioners belong to the Maliki school, the Maliki and Hanafi schools are most often referred to. The concept of *wasaṭiyya* as defined by al-Qaradawi is also used as a guideline for fatwas. The ECFR's fatwas serve as references and directions for the fatwas given, with one exception: registration of marriage, where the fatwa of the Dar al-Fatwa is much clearer than that of the ECFR.[156] However, there is also space for the mufti's personal assessments of the questioner. Kamilia says that she gives simple answers to those she calls "closed" people, while more "open" people are presented with various options, whereupon she as the mufti gives grounds for recommending one of the alternatives she has outlined.

Ounis Guergah makes consideration of the questioner (*mustaftī*) the very criterion for whether the answer should be seen as merely an "answer," the reproduction of a previously given fatwa that represents the prevailing view in the school of law; or whether it is an actual fatwa, representing an interpretive effort and taking new circumstances into account. The Paris mosque, according to its rector Dalil Boubakeur, does not issue fatwas, but only answers questions within the frame of the Maliki school.[157] Guergah gives the example of couples who have cohabited outside of marriage:

> As an example we may take a man who lives with a woman without being married. An answer from e.g. the *Mosquée de Paris* will place weight on the Maliki school and say that the couple must be separated for three months, and that any children are from *zina* [fornication]. We are aware that this may make the situation difficult for the parties, not least with regard to finding a temporary place to stay. Just think of the rental prices here in Paris! In the Dar al-Fatwa we base ourselves on a fatwa from the ECFR that not only offers an answer, but also suggest a course of action

156 On the relationship between civil and religious marriage, and the requirement of public registration of marriage, see Larabi Becheri's study *al-Muslimūn fī-ūrūbā bayna al-zawāj al-ʿurfī wal-zawāj fil-qānūn al-madanī*, which I summarize in chapter 6.

157 Conversation with Dalil Boubakeur in the Mosque of Paris, October 2006.

> that takes the situation of the person into account. This consists in: (i) *tawba* (repentance), (ii) cessation of sexual relations, (iii) that the parties separate for a month and (iv) that they contract civil marriage as soon as possible, which may be followed by a religious ceremony. In case there are children in the relationship, the father must go to city hall and acknowledge his paternity. As muftis, we are in the physician's role: Giving the right medicine to the patient. This is where *ijtihād* and *takhayyur* based on the principle of *maṣlaḥa* enter the picture.[158]

The *fiqh al-aqalliyyāt*, which the ECFR considers a pillar of its methodology, was not mentioned in my interviews with the Dar al-Fatwa muftis. When asked directly, Jaballah considered that there would be less and less need to use this concept as Muslims become "finally established". Guergah considered the concept a premise for *iftāʾ* in the Dar al-Fatwa, citing two fatwas in which it had been directly useful: on holding Friday prayers early, and on letting a woman stay married to her non-Muslim husband after conversion. In his view, this would not have been possible in a Muslim-majority country. Both these fatwas were given by the ECFR.

The Education of Muftis

The necessary qualifications for issuing fatwas are obtained through the study of *al-sharīʿa wa uṣūl al-dīn* at the IESH. The institute's description of the course gives an overview of the curriculum and of the competences required of a future mufti.[159] Candidates should be acquainted with the status of *futyā*, the requirements of a mufti, the qualities one must have to be able to issue fatwas, the rules to be followed, how to practice them with regard to social realities, the methods of classical scholars as well as scholars in the modern age, and collective fatwas issued in our time.

The curriculum is divided into a theoretical and a practical part. The theoretical part is covered at the IESH in Chateau Chinon (correspondence courses are also offered), with a text from the book *Uṣul al-daʿwa* by Abdulkarim Zaydan, an introduction to the four notions of *mustaftī*, *muftī*, *iftāʾ*, and *fatwā*. At the IESH in Paris, Ounis Guergah, the head of Dar al-Fatwa, has produced a text titled *Muḥaḍarāt fil-futyā wa-manāhijihā: mudhakkira li-ṭullāb al-sanat al-thāniya sharīʿa wa-ʿuṣūl al-dīn* (Lectures on Fatwa-Giving and its Methods:

158 Conversation with Ounis Guergah, 10 May 2008 at Rencontre Annuelle.

159 Information from the preface to the compendium *Fatāwa* (*al-sanat al-thālatha līsāns*), department for distance education, IESH (Chateau Chinon).

Memorandum for Second-Year Students of Sharia and the Roots of the Law). Both texts explain the institutional conditions that regulate *iftāʾ*, and so belong to the *ādāb al-muftī* literature.[160]

Both IESH texts argue for the use of certain concepts and a certain method in *iftāʾ*. They state that a fatwa is not forever, but changes with time and place (*al-zamān wal-makān*). Zaydan presents four conditions for change: A fatwa may be changed if the norm (i) is based on a country's *ʿurf* (custom), and this custom has changed; (ii) is based on an idea, and this idea has changed; (iii) is given with regard to a specific place or a specific time; or (iv) has a certain objective, and following the norm would no longer attain the objective, but would on the contrary lead to unwanted consequences. Guergah ties the mutability of the fatwa to the purpose of deriving new norms: promoting justice, commanding good actions and preventing the bad ones, and having regard to *al-awdāʿ* (the conditions) and *al-wasāʾil* (the means), within the framework of common morality (*al-akhlāq al-ʿāmma*).[161] According to Guergah, the mutability of the norms is also clearly limited by the principle of *lā ijtihād maʿa al-naṣṣ* ("no independent reasoning if there is a [clear] text"), that is, the Quranic texts that express clear norms (*āyāt al-qaṭʿiyya*) may not be re-interpreted.[162]

Both Zaydan and Guergah argue that a single school of law (*madhhab*) is not binding either on the questioner or on the mufti. Zaydan argues from the perspective of the questioner. Any scholar may be asked, regardless of school. Locating oneself within one school of law means only that the school acts as a guide to the law of God. This implies that one may follow a different school than one belongs to if it seems right. Certain principles must apply, however. If one is in danger of following one's own desires, one should follow one school of law. If one belongs to a certain school of law, one has to accept receiving answers accordingly.

Guergah, for his part, argues from the mufti's perspective. The use of *takhayyur* (selection) as a method has several advantages, he writes. One advantage is that people do not incur needless burdens because they belong to a *madhhab*, if outside the *madhhab* there are norms that make things easier for them.[163]

---

160 Cf. Caeiro 2006, 663. On the *ādāb al-muftī*, see also chapter 1.

161 Guergah n.d., 47.

162 Guergah n.d., 55.

163 Guergah mentions several examples, such as precepts for purity concerning dogs; the definition of women's *ʿawra* (parts of the body that should not be shown) where non-Muslim women are concerned; inheriting non-Muslim relatives; and the question whether three pronunciations of *ṭalāq* at the same time are counted as one.

This brings up yet another principle for *iftāʾ*, namely *taysīr* ("easing"). Zaydan again argues from the viewpoint of a *mustaftī*, citing the Quran.[164] A questioner who gets several fatwas on the same matter, should choose the easiest of the solutions. Guergah, too, stresses *taysīr*—understood "in accordance with the texts and the principles and the general spirit and purpose of Islam"—as a principle to take into account in fatwa-giving. With reference to the Quran and to the theory of the objectives of Sharia (*maqāṣid al-sharīʿa*), he claims that *taysīr* is a *maqṣid ʿazīm*, a "significant objective" of the Sharia.[165] The mufti is urged to take into account the difficulties Muslims face in our time, and to give fatwas that do not add to their burdens, but encourage them to practice Islam. This was the method of the Prophet, the Companions and the "true scholars," Guergah writes.[166] Among the requirements of a mufti, Guergah mentions *ijtihād*, which requires knowledge of the Quran and the Prophet's Sunna, *uṣūl al-fiqh*, Arabic language, and the pronouncements of the scholars on various matters. The most mature mufti, Guergah claims with reference to al-Shatibi, is the one who convinces people of the golden mean between excessive strictness and laxity.[167] Guergah also refers to al-Qaradawi's two-part definition of the concept, *al-ijtihād al-intiqāʾī* ("selective independent reasoning") and *al-ijtihād al-inshāʾī* ("creative independent reasoning"). The former type is individual *ijtihād*, and involves making a selection of scholarly views that are seen as relevant to the reality and circumstances in which people live. The latter type of *ijtihād* is applied by a scholar, or jointly by the scholars, to new issues.[168]

The practical part of the curriculum consists of a number of contemporary fatwas. Fatwas from the first and second collection of the ECFR are studied.[169] So is a selection of fatwas including medicinal topics (human-milk banks, norms for breastfeeding, abortion, organ donations, embryos and organ transpants, scientific experiments); the polar regions as a challenge to jurisprudence (e.g. prayer times); financial and legal questions (bank loans for buying a house, divorce granted by a non-Muslim judge); and, in a category all of its own, whether a woman's conversion to Islam requires divorce from her non-Muslim

164 Quran 2:185.
165 Quran 2:185; 5:6; 22:78.
166 Guergah n.d., 38–39.
167 Guergah n.d., 28–29.
168 Guergah n.d., 29.
169 ECFR 2002a.

husband.[170] We may conclude that IESH candidates are trained in a conceptual apparatus and method closely connected with the ECFR's approach to *iftāʾ*.

Tareq Oubrou

One of the Dar al-Fatwa members, Tareq Oubrou, is based in Bourdeaux, where he is the *recteur* of the al-Huda Mosque. Alexandre Caeiro describes his work as follows: "Oubrou leads the prayer, delivers the Friday *khutba*, interrogates would-be converts, gives religious advice, organizes imam-training seminars, receives journalists and answers social scientists ..."[171] In other words, Caeiro says, he fits the classical description of an Islamic scholar who "studied, taught, and gave advice."[172] In the French landscape, however, Tareq Oubrou has made his mark with the concept *sharia de minorité* (minority Sharia) or *sharia relative*,[173] through which he formulates a theory of Islam's relationship to French secular society. The perspective is clear: It is possible to practice an Islam that is in line with both the Sharia and with French law.[174]

Oubrou's theory implies a "relativization of Sharia". The Sharia is not universal and unchangeable, but subject to influence in time and space, based on a set of given premises. Oubrou formulates this relativization on five different levels. On the first level, Sharia is subordinated to theology, and itself includes a hierarchy of norms. Oubrou places *ʿibādāt* (ritual acts), which he characterizes as the "vertical" expression of belief, at the summit of this hierarchy. It is followed by *akhlāq* (morality), which is a matter for each individual conscience. At the bottom of the hierarchy is *le droit*, or *muʿāmalāt* (social transactions), also described as the "horizontal" part of Sharia. Oubrou chooses to disregard this latter aspect of Sharia, since in his view it requires a formal legal system and is reserved for state authorities.[175] Oubrou's understanding of Sharia includes French law, rather than Islamic jurisprudence. The French legal system has become the legal system of Muslims. This is the second level

---

170 The selected fatwas are found in an unpublished compendium that is distributed to IESH students.

171 Caeiro 2005, 48.

172 Caeiro 2005, 48.

173 Oubrou defines *sharia de minorité* as a legal (*canonique*) notion, not a demographic one. It refers to a social, political, and cultural exception in time and space (Oubrou 2004, 207). Oubrou spells Sharia in various ways; I have chosen *sharia* here. Caeiro has described Oubrou's theory (2006; Caeiro 2005).

174 Oubrou 2004, 206.

175 Oubrou 2004, 160.

of relativization of the Sharia.[176] Oubrou legitimates this turn away from the legal content of the Sharia by recalling that "individuals are tied to the Republic [...] by the contract of citizenship, which, in the eyes of the Sharia, is a moral contract to be respected."[177] Islamic normativity, Oubrou claims, is like the solution to an equation with three quantities: *le donné revelé* (the given revelation), *le facteur humain* (the human factor, i.e. interpretation), and *le contexte* (the context). The answer may be *al-ḥukm* (the norm) or *la fatwa*.[178] *Al-ḥukm* is constant, and is characterized by *adialecticité* with regard to culture and context, whereas a fatwa, by its nature, takes human, social and psychological circumstances into account, and is a necessary and central element of Sharia in a minority situation.[179] Oubrou goes as far as to claim that in a minority situation, an approach to Islam in the form of *ʿibādāt* and *akhlāq* can only take place through the fatwa. He promotes the idea of a "minimalist fatwa," with the fewest possible ritual and moral provisions (this, he claims, is a Quranic principle). A fatwa is not just statements marked by the circumstances; it is also a *méthodologie fondamentale principiologique*, a fundamental methodology of the sources of law. This is a third level of relativization of *sharia de minorité*.[180] A fatwa, then, is a movable norm, or as Caeiro puts it: "In principle, for Oubrou, the fatwa is *auto-biodégradable*, in that it contains in its very formulation the ingredients and time-space criteria of its validity and life-length."[181]

Oubrou distinguishes between different forms and levels of fatwas given in a *laïque* minority situation. A fatwa may be positive (explicit) or negative (implicit). It can also be common/public or situational and individual. *La fatwa positive, par articulation* may thus be divided into *la fatwa positive commune* and *la fatwa situationelle ou individuelle*. He describes the difference as follows: "... the *fatwa commune* is of a theoretical nature, related to French law, and the *fatwa situationelle* is of a practical nature, closely related to the culture of the majority."[182] In contrast to *la fatwa commune*, which represents a normative spectrum of possibilities for Muslims who wish to practice, a *fatwa situationelle* involves a set of norms that shed light on individual practice. In this sense, *la*

176 Oubrou 2004, 161.
177 Oubrou 2004, 208.
178 Oubrou 2004, 206.
179 Oubrou 2004, 161.
180 Oubrou 2004, 222.
181 Caeiro 2006, 675.
182 Oubrou 2004, 165.

fatwa situationelle may be considered a minority fatwa, compared to *la fatwa commune*. This is the fourth level of relativization of *sharia de minorité*.[183]

La fatwa situationelle ou individuelle can also be *négative par omission volontaire*, or *mutisme canonique principiel*. The aim of this kind of fatwa is to "... always strive for the best within the human and contextual limits." This is the fifth and final level of Oubrou's relativization of Sharia.[184] In conversation, Oubrou offered an example of this kind of fatwa, which might perhaps also be viewed as an "anti-fatwa".[185] A girl asks: "Should I take the hijab off at school?" Oubrou poses a counter-question: "Do you want an education?" The girl answers yes, and the fatwa goes: "Take off the hijab."[186] He legitimates the answer inter alia by reference to Ibn Taymiyya, who did not hesitate to make exceptions even if they allowed the reprehensible (*makrūh*) and skirted the borders of the formally prohibited.[187]

Why doesn't Oubrou use the notion of *fiqh al-aqalliyyāt*? In part, he explains it by reversing the common view of the changeability of fiqh and Sharia respectively. Whereas *fiqh*, in the sense of the sum of norms (*aḥkām*) is constant, the Sharia is dynamic, and changes through the fatwa. He also explains the use of "Sharia" as a communication strategy:[188] "The word *fiqh* is not strong enough to express the legality of our minority situation and what it implies as practices conditioned by the non-Muslim majority context ..."[189] By taking Sharia to include French law, Oubrou says he aims to include Islam in European history, and let Muslims take root in France as Europeans, without experiencing a deep division between the legal orders of society and religion.[190] The fatwa, then, plays a role in what Caeiro calls "constructing the borders of a distinctive French Islam," on which he comments: "Fatwas must tie the individual to his (French) culture, however that is defined, rather than act as a 'homogenizing factor' under global conditions."[191]

A fatwa may also be called a contribution to the cultivation of piety. Here, Sufism or Islamic mysticism enters the picture. Oubrou describes Sufism as *la*

---

183 Oubrou 2004, 225–226.
184 Oubrou 2004, 230.
185 This is an example of Oubrou's distinction between public and private fatwas.
186 Conversation with Tareq Oubrou, Bourdeaux, 31 Oct 2006.
187 Oubrou 2004, 227.
188 Conversation with Tareq Oubrou, Bourdeaux, 31 Oct 2006.
189 Oubrou 2004, 216–217.
190 Conversation with Tareq Oubrou, Bourdeaux, 31 Oct 2006.
191 Caeiro 2006, 675, 678.

porte royale de l'islam en occident, and gives it a central position in his *iftāʾ*.[192] A fatwa is "mediation with the divine," in light of Islam as "preparation for eternity". It is an "inner and moral education," where the fatwa is to secure a minimum of spiritual stability for the believer. The circle is thus closed: Sharia is not relativized ad infinitum, but leads back to the point of departure, theology, which is above Sharia on the uppermost level of Oubrou's minority Sharia.

Tareq Oubrou bases his fatwa-giving on two main principles, *ʿadl* (justice) and equality. He defines the former as an "experience of what is considered to be justice in a given context," whereas equality implies a principled approach to topics whether they relate to women or men.[193] Oubrou criticizes differentiation between men and women where requirements of practice are concerned. A great deal of understanding is shown for working men who cannot make it to the Friday prayer (which is *farḍ*, obligatory, for men, according to Islamic jurisprudence), whereas women are not shown the same flexibility with regard to wearing head coverings. Influences carried by the internet and satellite dishes contribute to preventing new thought that would take into account the local context and the actual challenges faced by Muslims. Reform, in Oubrou's view, presupposes a dynamics between academics and Islamic scholars. Reform will never be carried out by *des universitaires*, but by *des barbus*; however, the questions posed by the "university people" must be taken seriously by the "bearded ones".

Tareq Oubrou is a member of Dar al-Fatwa, which is considered identical with the French fatwa committee of the ECFR. He was invited to be a founder of the ECFR, but says he did not accept the invitation, because it conflicted with his principle of direct contact between the sources and the social context. He also thought that the ECFR was interpreting the texts in the light of Arab culture, and thus spreading a cultural understanding that prevented integration.[194]

192 Conversation with Tareq Oubrou, Bourdeaux, 31 Oct 2006.

193 Oubrou holds that Muslim women may marry non-Muslim men, and he is willing to defend this view in public. He raises two points in justification: the conditions for contracting marriage, and the conditions for the validity of a marriage contract. The conditions for contracting marriage must be defined broadly to include more than religious belonging, they should e.g. include level of education, Oubrou claims. Taking marriage as a contract, he further argues that the contract is no less valid even if not all the conditions for the contract are fulfilled. It is of the utmost importance, however, that any children be raised as Muslims, and that the Muslim spouse be able to practice Islam, e.g. by fasting in Ramadan.

194 Conversation with Tareq Oubrou, Bourdeaux, 31 Oct 2006. Bowen 2010 and Baylocq 2012

Barkatullah Abdulkadir

In 1993, on my first trip to London and the UK to do fieldwork for a thesis on converts to Islam, I was received by a certain Barkatullah Abdulkadir, who had been assigned to find me shelter in London. I next heard of him in 2008. He was named as the "architect" behind the so-called Model Muslim Marriage Contract that was launched in London in August 2008. Since I discuss his relevant fatwas in chapter 6, he must be briefly introduced here. There does not seem to be any previous account of Abdulkadir in the scholarly literature.

I met him for a conversation about the Model Muslim Marriage Contract at the fashionable Landmark Hotel in London, during the "9th Annual Islamic Finance Summit" held by Euromoney Seminars, a division of the investment company Euromoney Institutional Investor PLC.[195] Abdulkadir was one of the speakers at the conference. He is known as an advisor on Islamic banking for several banks and financial institutions.[196]

Barkatullah Abdulkadir came to England in the late 1970s. He was trained as a mufti at the Darul Uloom in Deoband,[197] but continued his education to get an MPhil in computer science from the University of Wales in 1992. Abdulkadir also headed a hadith database project in the 1980s, and founded the Islamic Computing Centre. He has been a member of the Islamic Sharia Council, and has what he describes as "long experience of dealing with socio-cultural issues of Muslims living in the UK"[198] He is also responsible for the operation of Islamic Helpline, a telephone service that gets questions on a number of topics (including inheritance, loans, student loans, pilgrimages, ritual prayer, alcohol and drug abuse), with marriage-related questions dominating. 40 % of the questions come from women, and 60 % from men.[199] Abdulkadir has also answered questions as a host of call-in shows on radio and television.[200] He is currently also teaching at Ebrahim College, which apart from a secondary-

---

do not seem to have noticed the difference between Oubrou's *sharia de minorité* and the concept of *fiqh al-aqalliyyat*.

195 See http://www.euromoneyseminars.com/Default.aspx.

196 Including Lloyds TSB, al-Buraq Arab Banking Corporation, and the UNB, according to documentation Abdulkadir gave me.

197 Darul Uloom of Deoband, India, was founded in 1866.

198 Conversation with Barkatullah Abdulkadir, London, 24 Feb 2009.

199 According to information from Barkatullah Abdulkadir.

200 Radio Ramadan, Q&A Programme, East London (2002); Vectone TV Islamic call-in Show (2003, 2004); Islam Channel TV Islamic Q&A Call-in Show (2004); Unity TV Islamic Finance Live Show (2007).

school curriculum offers an Islamic education as well as a study programme for the training of Muslim scholars.[201] Abdulkadir has appeared as a "moderate" since, as a board member of the Finsbury Park mosque, he got Abu Hamza al-Misri thrown out for preaching militant Islamism and jihadism.

In connection with the launch of the Model Muslim Marriage Contract, the well-known writer, TV presenter and expert on Islam Ziauddin Sardar wrote:

> My friend Mufti Barkatullah is an unusual chap. He is a fully qualified "mufti," a traditionally educated and recognised expert in Islamic law. You cannot guess by simply looking at him, and his attire would definitely fool you, but in western terms he is also highly educated. He is just the kind of person who can combine tradition and modernity to produce something new that retains the best features of the old …[202]

Conclusion

In this chapter, we have introduced actors in the fatwa field who also represent part of the on-going institutionalization of *iftāʾ* on European soil. The London-based Syed Darsh is described as the first mufti of Western Europe. He himself claimed that he did not carry out *ijtihād*, but only answered questions, and that "everything" was already there in the tradition.

A red line may be seen from Darsh's work to the establishment of the European Council for Fatwa and Research (ECFR) in 1997. The purpose of the Council, according to its statutes, is to guide Muslims in the West and solve their problems through unified fatwas. Through the use of the *fiqh al-aqalliyyāt* concept, the Council seeks legitimacy vis-à-vis fatwa institutions in the Muslim world, and it claims authority vis-à-vis Muslims in Europe. Nonetheless, the Council may be said to be part of transnational Islam, or what the anthropologist John Bowen characterizes as "the global field of reference and debate."[203] This is not least evident in the arguments for concepts and methods for fatwa-

201 See the school website (http://www.ebrahimcollege.org.uk/).

202 Ziauddin Sardar, "Modern marriage", *New Statesman*, 4 Sep 2008 (http://www.newstatesman.com/religion/2008/09/muslim-marriage-islamic-mufti).

203 Bowen claims that transnational Islam creates and implies a global public space and debate. This transnational Islamic space is found in the idea of a worldwide community of belief (the *umma*) that transcends borders, based on a set of supernational social norms—the many interpretations of Sharia and God's plans and commands (Bowen 2004, 882–883). This transnational space is discussed further in chapter 5.

giving. But the other fatwa actors, too, through their own arguments for methods and concepts, are part of the same global field, whether they work in a London setting like Syed Darsh, or on the national level, like the Dar al-Fatwa.

Behind the Council's expression "the fatwa committee (*lajnat al-fatwā*) in France," we have uncovered a whole segment of French Islam, including the Dar al-Fatwa and the education of future muftis. The initiative to form the ECFR came from "brothers" in the Union des Organisations Islamiques de France (UOIF). As a visible actor in France, the UOIF faces accusations that it belongs to the Muslim Brotherhood. Among the French public, much weight is placed on a claimed *organizational* belonging, which may be analysed as a construction created by the media. This contrasts with the actors' own focus on the development of a method and conceptual apparatus that I will call *fikr al-ikhwānī* (the thought of the Muslim Brothers), and that thus rather represents a connection in terms of *ideas*.

But the Dar al-Fatwa also features another line of thought, represented by Tareq Oubrou and the concept of *sharia de minorité*. I have devoted some space to his theory, as an example of how the use of concepts and methods forms part of a mufti's identity, is tied to authority, and plays as large a role as the fatwas themselves. This is also confirmed in the training of future muftis, who are equipped with a methodological and conceptual "toolkit" that they are expected to use in their work. The content of the concepts is not given once and for all, however, as we have seen with regard to the concept of *fiqh al-aqalliyyāt*.

Barkatullah Abdulkadir has a different background than the other fatwa actors, but he worked with Syed Darsh in the Islamic Sharia Council until Darsh's death in 1997. He entered the Muslim limelight through his contribution to the Model Muslim Marriage Contract that was launched in 2008, an attempt to help British Muslims based on his experience from the Islamic Sharia Council.

Most fatwas are given orally, and are difficult to document, as is the case of the Dar al-Fatwa. The next two chapters, however, will present written fatwas, respectively by Syed Darsh (chapter 3) and the European Council for Fatwa and Research (chapter 4).

PART 2

The Fatwas

CHAPTER 3

Agony Uncle: The Fatwas of Syed Darsh

Introduction

Syed Darsh had his own column in *Q-News* magazine from 1992 to 1997. The column was titled "What you ought to know," under the header "Helpline". Under Darsh's picture, the caption said that Dr. Syed Mutawalli Darsh answered questions every fortnight, and the reader was encouraged to submit questions.[1]

The fatwas in the column consisted of "questions" and "answers". The questions were signed with name and place of residence, sometimes replaced with "name and address withheld".[2] The questions resemble letters to the editor; the *Q-News* editor, Fuad Nahdi, described this as "a normal procedure in the press".[3] Darsh, however, thought the questions should be anonymous, and fought the practice. It also turned out that people whose name and address had appeared in print had experienced problems later. In time, *Q-News* ceased to give this information.

A large number of questions reached *Q-News*—far more than the column could answer. The editors made a list of the questions, and indicated which ones they thought important. The list was sent to Darsh, who went over it and made a final prioritized list. According to Fuad Nahdi, Darsh gave fatwas in two different ways. Most of the fatwas were written down by the editors, who would call Darsh on the phone, by appointment, and record the conversation on cassette tape, as he answered those questions that required no further investigations. The questions were taken from the editors' list. The answers were transcribed and edited for style, as oral language and written presentations will differ. The text was then sent back to Darsh, to check that the message of the fatwa was the same as he had given orally. He would also check the English rendering of Arabic terms. In the end, Darsh would sign the fatwas, and they would be published in the *Q-News* column.

1 This was before the age of e-mail, so the mailing address of *Q-News* was given.

2 This recalls the *Fatāwa al-Manār*, where questions were signed with name and country.

3 The following information about the editorial process and fatwa-giving was given in a telephone conversation with Fuad Nahdi, who was editor of *Q-News*, on 28 Sep 2009.

 | DOI: 10.1163/9789004367852_005

Some of the questions were considered to need elaboration before they could be answered. As one example, Fuad Nahdi mentioned sexual abuse. The background to the question about sexual abuse was that a woman had contacted the An-Nisa Society and told them she had been abused. The question was passed to Darsh, who asked for a meeting to be arranged with sexually abused women. This meeting resulted in the conference *Towards understanding the dynamics of child abuse and its healing within the Muslim community*, with Darsh as one of the main speakers.[4]

Some questions recurred so many times that Darsh would deal with them in the form of an article, such as "The Question of Marriage".[5] This article dealt with arranged marriage, choice of partner, conflict with the family, procedure for contracting marriage, early marriage, equality in marriage, and the role of the guardian.

One way to answer as many questions as possible was to join several questions into one. This, however, was only done with questions on the Ramadan fast and the hajj (pilgrimage), which are answered in general books of *fiqh*. Questions such as whether one may go on the hajj with a credit card would be dealt with separately, though, since this was a new problem tied to the present social reality. All other questions were presented as asked.

The questions bear the mark of a certain social and cultural reality, are posed by people in specific situations, and often address topics outside the legal field. These points are exemplified by the following question: "I wish to marry my cousin but my mother is objecting to the marriage simply because the girl is a year and a half older than me. Is there any Islamic basis for her objection?"[6] In other words, the questions concern real people and the challenges they face; they are not the product of a mufti's own creative formulation of questions. Hallaq uses the term "primary fatwas" for such fatwas, in which question and answer have been preserved with more or less their original form and content.[7]

The column is sometimes structured by topic (e.g. marriage, pilgrimage); sometimes, it is a collection of various topics. The fatwas are often of current interest at the time they are given. Fatwas on fasting in the month of Ramadan and the pilgrimage (hajj) exemplify the relevance of the fatwas to the ritual cal-

4 The meeting took place on 18 Feb 1993.

5 *Q-News*, 9 Oct 1992.

6 *Q-News*, 9–16 Jul 1993.

7 Hallaq 1994, 32.

endar.[8] Among women-related topics, in January 1993 we find two questions on current events in the 1990s Balkans conflict: (i) "Would abortion be allowed for our sisters who suffered in notorious rape camps in Bosnia (the idea in this case being to make them bear children which will then be taken and raised as Serbs)?" (ii) "The British government has told local authorities to relax bureaucratic controls easing the way for concerned families to adopt Bosnian babies born from raped Muslim mothers. In such circumstances is it better for the natural mother to raise the child, or should Muslim families be prepared to adopt these children and bring them up as Muslims?"[9]

According to Fuad Nahdi, there was no-one able to take Darsh's place when the column was discontinued a few months before his death in 1997. However, his fatwas have been given a new lease on life in other media. A selection is published in book form as *Questions and Answers about Islam*.[10] The purpose is stated in the book's brief introduction: "… making them [the questions and answers] more readily accessible to a more general readership, for they deal in a practical manner with issues and situations which in fact affect almost everyone today, in a society in which it is not always particularly easy to follow Islam in its totality …"[11]

The book is structured by topic, and includes non-fiqh topics such as "Allah," "The Prophet Muhammad," "Qur'an and Hadith," and "In the Beginning". Women-related topics are naturally found under "Marriage," "Parents and Children," "Adoption and Fostering," "Hijab," "Clothes and Jewellery," and "Hair". But they are also found under other headings, such as "Mosques and Islamic Centres," "Prayer," "Hajj and 'Umra," and "Death and Funerals". The sense of current interest found in the *Q-News* column is gone, for several reasons: the thematic structure, the omission of the sender's name and address (included in the first years of the column's existence), and the omission of fatwas tied to specific events, such as those on rape and abortion in the Bosnian war of the 1990s. Editorial choices and a new "packaging" make the fatwas appear more of a timeless document than in the *Q-News* column.

8 For example, the fatwa columns in *Q-News* 5–12 Mar 1993 and 14–21 May 1993 coincided with Ramadan and the hajj, respectively, in the Hijri calendar.

9 *Q-News*, 22 Jan 1993.

10 Darsh 1997.

11 Darsh 1997, "Introduction".

Darsh's fatwas also live a new life on the Internet.[12] Marriage-related questions seem to have the greatest recycling value.[13]

Muslim Women's Challenges as Revealed by the Questions

A survey of the media discussed above shows that Darsh has answered 117 women-related questions.[14] As we have seen, "women-relatedness" is not an organizing principle for these materials, so I have made an overview of the questions to see if there naturally emerge categories by which they can be structured. Focusing on the questions offers insight into what Muslim women themselves consider the challenges.

I have sorted the questions into the following categories, with the number of questions in each category in brackets: different types of marriage (9); before

---

12 The homepage http://www.iol.ie/~afifi/Ad-Darsh/darsh.htm has material titled "Shaykh Dr. Ad-Darsh column". Heading the page is the Quranic verse encouraging the asking of questions: "… If ye realise this not, ask of those who possess the Message" (21:7). There follows a picture of Darsh, who is presented as a *shaykh*, a *faqīh* (expert in Islamic jurisprudence) from al-Azhar university in Cairo, and head of the UK Sharia Council. He is said to answer questions "ranging from contemporary to family issues". Beneath the picture, Darsh's death is noted by a brief obituary. An archive of questions and answers follows.

The questions are reproduced nearly literally from earlier versions, but they have been classified and tagged with key words. Clearly, the editor of the web page has created his own categories. For example, marriage-related questions are named "marriage and divorce (*munakahat*)", "family relations", "clothing", or "social relations." In the 1996 archive we find 34 questions, of which 15 women-related ones. The ratio falls in 1997, when three out of 28 questions relate to women.

Darsh was also a reference for IslamOnline.net, which in its heyday in the 2000s was one of the largest Islamic websites. Five of Darsh's fatwas were included in IslamOnline's fatwa section, three of them women-related. In one case, he was cited in a so-called Live Dialogue, a forum that for a set period would accept and answer questions on a given topic. After a conflict over the running of IslamOnline, OnIslam.net was established by the IslamOnline staff in Cairo, who held property rights to the site contents, and transferred some of them, including some of Darsh's women-related fatwas. That site, too, is now defunct.

13 The website http://mehbooba.co.uk, which has marriage as its main topic (*mehbooba*: "beloved"), features "Questions and Answers on Marriage". It says the questions are taken from *Trends*, a magazine targeting young Muslims, which in turn, according to Fuad Nahdi, took them from *Q-News*.

14 "Women-related question" means that the topic relates to women, not that the *mustaftī* has to be a woman.

marriage (23); contracting marriage (14); marriage (12); body and care/sexuality/reproduction (15); social relations (17); child-raising/education/work (5); and *ʿibādāt* (acts of worship) (22).[15] I thus follow the usual divisions of Islamic jurisprudence, where all acts are divided into the categories of *ʿibādāt* (ritual practice) or *muʿāmalāt* (social transactions).[16] This is an important distinction for several reasons, including the question of changeability. The *Oxford Dictionary of Islam* specifies the divide between *ʿibādāt* and *muʿāmalāt* as follows: "The distinction is important because the principle in all matters involving ibadat is that they are not susceptible to innovations or change (ittiba). In muamalat, however, there is considerably more room to develop and change the law to facilitate human action and promote justice."[17] The first criterion by which I structure my material is what is changeable or not. Most of the questions (96) fall under the *muʿāmalāt* category, and far fewer under *ʿibādāt* (22), so I have chosen to gather all the latter into one catch-all category, rather than setting up a separate category for each of the pillars plus the rules of ritual purity. The questions do not all unambiguously fall into one single category. For example, the question about women in the mosques pertains to ritual life, but also to social relations. I have chosen to place it under *ʿibādāt* to show how women's experiences also make them ask questions about ritual practice.

"Hijab" forms a separate category in the book *Questions and Answers about Islam*. The questions on hijab mostly turn out not to be about the hijab per se, but about the use of hijab in a specific context. The questioners do not appear to focus on the norm as such, but on how they should deal with various situations, e.g. when meeting a potential suitor (the category "Before contracting marriage"), in the workplace or in sports ("Child-raising/education/work"), and I have chosen to include these questions in the various appropriate categories.

The issue of divorce is conspicuous by its absence from Darsh's answers. Even when answering a frustrated husband who claims that both he and his wife are unhappy, and asks whether this is sufficient reason to divorce, Darsh shifts the topic from divorce to realistic expectations of marriage.[18] According to Fuad Nahdi, the topic of divorce was omitted according to Syed Darsh's wishes, as the column targeted second- and third-generation British Muslims:

15 Compare how Judith Tucker (1999), working on 17th- and 18th-century fatwas from Ottoman Palestine and Syria, structured the discussion of marriage-related topics mainly by the different phases of marriage: "The purposes of marriage"; "Arranging a marriage"; "Entering a marriage"; "Living a marriage"; and "Marriage in the courts".

16 See the *EI2* entries on "ʿIbādāt" (Bousquet 2010) and "Muʿāmalāt" (Bernand 2010).

17 "Muamalat" in the *Oxford Dictionary of Islam* (Esposito 2003, 208 f.).

18 *Q-News* 14–20 Jul 1995.

"To them, the problem isn't divorce, but how to get married," Nahdi claimed.[19] The age of the target group may also explain the absence of questions on inheritance.

The *complexity* of the challenges women face in the various categories is evident from the questions as I have structured them (Table 1).

TABLE 1 *Categorization of women-related subjects*

Different types of marriage	**Before marriage**
arranged marriage	choice of partner
polygamy	possible or suitable partners
"eternal marriage"	conflicts with parents
marriage between a Muslim woman and a non-Muslim man	how to propose
	engagement
temporary marriage	the bounds of communication during engagement
forced marriage	hijab
secret marriage	dowry/bride-gift
civil marriage	
Contracting marriage	**In marriage**
early marriage	changing gender roles
equality in marriage	hygiene
wilāya (guardianship)	obedience to the husband
persons authorized to solemnize marriage	domestic violence
conditions in the marriage contract	relations with parents-in-law
weddings and identity	divorce
filming weddings	

19 Telephone conversation with Fuad Nahdi, 28 Sep 2009. This partly alludes to the age of the target group, which indicates that they are not yet married, and partly to the challenge of finding a marriage partner in a minority context, which may be greater than in a Muslim country.

Body and care/sexuality/reproduction	***'Ibādāt***
the postpartum period	what breaks the fast
the act of sexual intercourse	women on hajj
artificial insemination	women's access to the mosque
contraception	nail polish/hair colouring/makeup and ritual purity
prostitution	voiding of ritual purity
child adoption after rape	the full ritual ablution after sexual relations (ghusl)
physical-fitness role models	women and funerals
moisturizers	using drugs to delay menstruation
haircuts	
Child-raising/education/work	**Social relations**
choice of profession	rules for relations between men and women
parents of different confessions	hijab and work activities
sports/work and hijab	types of hijab
housemaids	jewelry
	women and cemeteries
	the religio-juridical definition of maturity

The Women in the Questions

The women are present in the questions in various ways, with varying distance to the reader. At times they are not there at all. Their presence finds expression both in content and form. Regarding content, the questions may be divided into three main types:

1. Questions asking about a norm directly, without explaining the background to the question.
2. Questions that account for the background to the question or problem.
3. Questions that contain arguments as well as background.

The type of content often corresponds to the form of the question. Distance and presence may be measured through the use of pronouns, with "I" and "you" giving the impression of proximity, whereas the third person or indefinite pronoun conveys distance. We find both forms in the questions. In the first category, asking about a norm directly, women are often absent or appear in the third person as objects of the request for clarification of the norm, e.g.: "At what age do men and women become legally responsible?"[20] "Can a husband's sperm be used by his wife for artificial insemination after his death?"[21] In the second kind of question, the situation report is often made in the first person, as in a woman's question whether a wife is reunited with her husband in the beyond: "I have heard that a wife is united with her husband in Paradise. I live with my husband for the sake of my children and put up with his violence and intolerable, miserable behaviour. It seems unfair that in trying to gain Allah's pleasure and Paradise that I would have to put up with him for eternity?"[22]

Women can however also appear in the third person in questions where the background and problem are presented, as illustrated by a father's request for a fatwa to help him advise his daughter:

> Does Islam dictate the exact style of hijab which a Muslim woman has to wear? Recently my daughter has taken to experimenting with wearing a variety of hijabs from different Muslim cultures, some of which I believe are not Islamic. Can you tell me which hijab styles are allowed so I can advise my daughter accordingly?[23]

In the third category, questions containing arguments, the questioner may express the view that something is injust or discriminatory. The question often seems to be made in the hope that the questioner's view will be confirmed. For example: "Am I correct in understanding that Islam allows a man to marry women of different faiths but that a woman who marries a non-Muslim man becomes an immediate apostate? Isn't that discriminatory?"[24] In some cases, the answer requested is clearly meant to serve as an argument in an ongoing discussion:

> Both my sisters are of marriageable age, and are attracting many *rishtey* (marriage proposals). However my father cannot agree to any of the proposals because he says he spent all his money on my wedding, dowry and all the elaborate arrangements and functions and is waiting until he has saved up some more. While my father saves up, I feel that the girls will get

20 *Q-News*, 29 Sep–5 Oct 1995.
21 *Q-News*, 23–30 Jul 1993.
22 *Q-News*, 7–14 Apr 1995.
23 *Q-News*, 23 Oct 1992.
24 *Q-News*, 26 May 1995; http://www.iol.ie/~afifi/Ad-Darsh/darsh.htm, 25 Oct 1996.

too old and the proposals will dry up. If I argue with my father he says that Islam encourages big weddings because it is important to announce it to as many people as possible. Is this correct?[25]

The Fatwas

A fatwa may be short, and may consist of just the single word "permitted" (*ḥalāl*) or "forbidden" (*ḥarām*). Darsh's fatwas[26] are longer, more complex, and not so easily reduced to one of the two categories. Often, the fatwas are just part of a piece of advice (*naṣīḥa*) based on a reflection on the textual sources, Darsh's own experience, and his personal taste. In this sense, they reflect the questions, which do not always ask for clear-cut yes/no answers. One example is the husband who considers marrying a second wife. He has obtained the first wife's permission. Still, he wonders if it is a good idea, considering that polygamy is forbidden under British law. The answer opens with a piece of advice: "If you are asking my advice, I would say that one wife is more than enough. One is quite a handful for any husband, let alone two."[27]

More than half the fatwas relate to the topic of marriage. In his answers, Darsh presents a number of ideas about the ideal marriage and its function, which serves as one of several nodal points in his message about "what is right".[28] Marriage is a life-long experience.[29] Getting married for a limited time is not permitted.[30] One does not get married as an experiment, or for "fun and play".[31] Marriage is a very important relationship, and should be a source of "peace, happiness and tranquility" for those concerned. A "solemn, important bond" is tied between the spouses.[32] The aim of marriage is to build a life together, "to enjoy each other's company and to bring up children". If the marriage is successful, it is "a great social and moral bond, creating a prosperous

25 *Q-News*, 6 Nov 1992; Darsh 1997, 102.

26 In presenting the fatwas, I wish to reveal Darsh's message about the categories by which I have structured the materials. Accordingly, I join several fatwas together under each category. Darsh's views have been gathered from the fatwas published in *Q-News*, in Darsh 1997, and at IslamOnline. Exact page references are not available for all the quotations.

27 *Q-News*, 18–25 Mar 1994.

28 I use the term "nodal point" following Jørgensen and Phillips 2002, 26.

29 *Q-News*, 9 Oct 1992.

30 *Q-News*, 13–19 Oct 1995.

31 *Q-News*, 9 Oct 1992.

32 Darsh 1997, 97.

relationship between the parties concerned". Darsh also holds that a successful marriage contributes to fulfilling the parents' wish for "a decent, happy, successful future" for the young.[33]

Darsh exhorts the young to get married as soon as they are physically mature and able to take care of themselves, not least in financial terms. The aim is clear: Avoiding sexual immorality. Sex belongs within marriage.[34] Darsh does not shy away from criticizing extravagant weddings, which he finds immoral, and sees as a potential obstacle to young people getting married, because they or their parents lack the means for a wedding.[35]

Marital happiness depends on finding "the right person". In Darsh's view, this is not as easy for Muslims in the West as in their parent's home country. He claims that the best marriage method is arranged marriage, despite its flaws, on which he does not elaborate. Arranged marriages have been practiced for centuries, and are based on "sound reasoning" and a common position on religion and the raising of children. However, Darsh is aware that the questioners find themselves in a new social context, and that traditional ways of finding a spouse will not necessarily work. In this connection, he wags a warning finger at parents: They are responsible for avoiding conflict and social discord, not least by refraining from forcing their children. A marriage contract entered into under duress is invalid. If parents think they have the power of veto, the consequences will be conflict in the family. It is important that they accept their daughter's own choice, as long as the husband is a decent, respectable and God-fearing person able to support her. Young Muslims in the West, in their turn, should not fight their parents, who have life experience, especially as the young live "besieged by a powerful aggressive culture that is both un-Islamic and anti-Islamic". They are at risk of being influenced by Western immorality. As a remedy, as well as a possible arena for meeting a suitable future spouse, Darsh points to Muslim student societies. "There, they can talk, study, mix in an appropriate environment and surroundings."[36]

The exhortation to think innovatively about how to find a spouse may be read as a balancing act between a number of considerations: a new social reality, the role of the parents, the possible social influence on the morals of Muslim youth, and the requirement that the spouse be a Muslim, which Darsh thinks is a minimal requirement.

---

33 *Q-News*, 9 Oct 1992.

34 *Q-News*, 9 Oct 1992.

35 *Q-News*, 6 Nov 1992.

36 *Q-News*, 9 Oct 1992.

The criteria for an acceptable partner are the topic of eleven of the questions posed. Darsh refers to the hadith literature for four things that should be considered when proposing to a woman—beauty, wealth, nobility of descent, good upbringing and religiosity—and goes on to recommend stressing the latter (though not necessarily disregarding the other three).[37] Then, the marriage will be a success. The same goes for women regarding men. Muslim men may marry women from the Peoples of the Book, defined as Jews or Christians. Women have the full liberty to practice their religion without being forced to switch faiths. Women are not allowed to marry non-Muslim men: The man is the head of the family, and has the final say. The religious status of the Muslim woman, therefore, is not safeguarded in such a marriage, according to Darsh, who rhetorically defends what he calls the "faith rights" of the woman (i.e. guarding her Islamic allegiance and faith), and rejects what he calls "human rights".[38]

However, Darsh asserts that marriage between a Muslim man and a non-Muslim woman is "undesirable" (*makrūh*). He justifies this by reference to his own experience with many cases before the Islamic Sharia Council, which he headed, as well as to the second caliph, Umar ibn al-Khattab (d. 636), who cited *social* reasons against the practice.[39] With regard to securing their future marital happiness, the parties are also advised to look to culture, family background, age and level of education.[40] That does not mean being limited to marrying someone from the same country, caste, or family.[41] It is, however, important for future marital happiness that the man be the woman's social equal.[42] Since the man is the head of the family-to-be, the woman's status would be weakened if the man came from a lower social stratum. This may be a valid reason for the woman's guardian to declare the marriage invalid, Darsh claims, referring to the Hanafi school.[43]

---

37 *Q-News*, 9 Oct 1992.

38 *Q-News*, 19–26 May 1995.

39 *Q-News*, 10–17 Mar 1995.

40 Darsh 1997, 95.

41 Darsh 1997, 92–93; *Q-News*, 14–20 Jul 1995.

42 This refers to the concept of *kafā'a*, equivalence of social status, fortune, and profession as a requirement for marriage. Darsh simply uses the word "equality", somewhat obscuring the sense, since "equality" is easily associated with the division of roles in marriage. In ordinary usage, the word *kafā'a* has several meanings at once: "equality, parity and aptitude", according to *EI2*. In Islamic jurisprudence, *kafā'a* is seen as the woman's right. See "Kafā'a" in *EI2* (Linant de Bellefonds 2010).

43 According to the *EI2*, this position of the Hanafi school, allowing the guardian to attempt to have a marriage declared invalid if the man is not the woman's social equal, should

Central to the question of partner choice is the fact that parents and youths have different wishes. Darsh advocates intergenerational dialogue.[44] Even though both a boy and a girl can choose their own partner, and Islamic rules do not preclude the alliance, the question is: Is their love strong enough to survive a possible conflict with the family?[45] Often, Darsh does not answer the questions about what the individual should do, but rather gives arguments pro and contra, and asks the questioner to think carefully through all the contingencies.

The engagement period is the topic of two questions. Darsh presents the norm: The parties are only allowed to meet in the family setting and with a chaperone present. Private meetings alone are forbidden. An engagement is only a promise, Darsh says, and it can be retracted. Meeting in public out on the town could compromise the girl's and her family's honour. He recommends not dragging out the engagement period. At the same time as he refers to the norms, though, he also expresses his understanding for Muslims in the West. They face resistance from a society with norms and traditions opposed to Islamic teachings, and they may find it hard to practice the Islamic rules.[46] In these fatwas, Darsh expresses awareness that Islamic teachings and the West represent competing sets of norms, and an underlying criticism of the non-Muslim majority society.

The marriage should be contracted in Arabic, but this is not required, since it is not a matter of a ritual like the ritual prayer.[47] The couple need not be married by an imam or scholar for the contract to be valid according to Islam. In the UK, which is the setting for the answer, the authorities are responsible for the registers of births, deaths, and marriages, Darsh says. An imam or religious leader with the authority to solemnize and register marriages therefore has a legal function. Therefore, one can do without an imam, Darsh claims with a twinkle in his eye, especially if the imam seems prone to turn a joyous event

---

be seen in light of the school's granting every woman of age the right to marry without a guardian. In countries that followed the Maliki school, it was not possible to marry without a guardian, which was seen as a guarantee for the wife's family. The aim of allowing claims for the dissolution of a marriage where the parties are not social equals seems to be to provide a safety valve to secure *kafāʾa* as the woman's right, in case she has not secured it herself, as well as her family's right. For a Hanafi view of *kafāʾa*, see al-Marghinani 1989, 1:110.

44 *Q-News*, 9 Oct 1992; Darsh 1997, 93–94.

45 *Q-News*, 14–20 Jul 1995.

46 Darsh 1997, 90–92.

47 *Q-News*, 19–26 Mar 1993.

into a drab and boring one.[48] It is a good Islamic tradition, he says with reference to a hadith, to hold the ceremony in the mosque, followed by entertaining.

The groom gives the *mahr* or bride-gift to the bride. One is not required to pay a dowry to the family of the groom.[49] Darsh refers to the Islamic legal literature, which defines the *mahr* as "the wealth to which the wife has a right from her husband as a result of the contract of marriage after consummation".[50] The amount depends on the tradition of a society. Darsh points to the practice of a previous age, when the *mahr* might reflect the status of the parties. In the present age, however, families consider the *mahr* a symbolic gesture. The *mahr*, according to Darsh, is an expression of the man's love and care, and the woman's dignity.[51]

Darsh offers ethical and moral advice on the wedding party (*al-walīma*), with reference to the Prophet, who held simple weddings. A tradition has the Prophet saying that the best wedding party is the one that costs little. This, however, does not preclude entertaining the guests with food and singing (*qawwali*). Darsh describes large, expensive weddings as a social phenomenon, a reflection of a certain culture, and as wrong, because it is wasteful. Darsh cites a tradition that the worst wedding dinner is one that is given for the rich and denied to the poor.[52] There is nothing to prevent the bride from wearing a wedding gown, provided it's not too extravagant, even if some would consider it as imitating a British wedding. The wedding party is an occasion for the couple to dress up.[53] Darsh thinks there is no harm in going on a honeymoon trip, quite the contrary. Unlike the questioner, who insinuates that honeymooning is imitation of Western customs, Darsh claims that the West has copied the Muslims, as it is *sunna* for the newlyweds to spend seven days together alone.[54]

Within Marriage

In Darsh's view, the marital relationship is based on the equal worth of the man and the woman, but the man is above the woman as the head of family with the overall responsibility. Darsh argues this view with reference to a Quranic

---

48 *Q-News*, 10–23 May 1996.
49 *Q-News*, 10–23 May 1996.
50 Darsh 1997, 98.
51 Darsh 1997, 99.
52 http://www.iol.ie/~afifi/Ad-Darsh/18.10.96.htm.
53 *Q-News*, 16–22 Jun 1995.
54 http://www.iol.ie/~afifi/Ad-Darsh/16.8.96.htm.

commentary by Ibn Abbas (d. 687/88), who describes the husband-wife relationship as follows: "I look after myself, I dress myself nicely, I use perfume. Why? Because when I ask my wife to look her best for me, then I too have to look my best for her."[55]

There are three questions on the division of roles, given that women are out in the workplace contributing to the household. In one of the cases, the wife has the greater earnings and controls the finances. What does this do to the division of roles between the spouses? Darsh's answer deals with finances and housework. With regard to the finances, Darsh advocates a traditional position: from an Islamic point of view, it is not acceptable that women become breadwinners. The man has a duty to get work to support the family. The woman may, however, take over the man's role if he has nothing against it. When the woman is the provider, however, Darsh does not consider it to be *nafaqa* (maintenance). He merely notes, with reference to a hadith, that a woman who spends her money on the household gets a double reward, for using her money for her family and for giving alms (since she is not obliged to do this). According to Darsh, there is no reason why women's work outside the home should lead to changes in the fundamental roles of men and women.[56] He is careful, however, to underline that these are minimum requirements. He argues for the importance of good manners, and reminds readers that the marriage contract is not an agreement on slavery. "It is the husband's duty to care for his family and home, not just sit in the front of the television for hours on end while his wife does the cooking and looks after the children. This is unfair."[57] He recalls that the man has a duty both to cook, do the washing, go shopping, and otherwise be of assistance in every way. Women are not vacuum cleaners or dishwashers, but partners.

Nevertheless, Darsh does point out that the marriage contract gives the woman the right to *nafaqa* "on account of her staying at home". One implication, Darsh says, is that she may become responsible for her own expenses, especially if marital conflict arises.[58] This is an interesting twist on the traditional tie between *nafaqa* and *ṭāʿa* (obedience), but the Islamic legal literature does not explicitly make this contingent on whether or not the woman is out at work earning money.[59]

---

55 *Q-News*, 19–26 Mar 1993.

56 Darsh 1997, 108–109.

57 *Q-News*, 1–7 Mar 1996.

58 *Q-News*, 19–26 Mar 1993.

59 In *The Distinguished Jurist's Primer*, Ibn Rushd cites agreement among jurists that a wife is entitled to *nafaqa*, being maintained; but he also notes differences among jurists over

Darsh does not shy away from the topic of domestic violence, the open discussion of which is often taboo in Muslim circles.[60] The question is whether the husband has a right to beat his wife. One of the questions is from the son or daughter of a man who has beaten his wife ever since they got married, claiming a right to do so. The answers do not feature the evasive apologetics that are often used to address the topic (such as restricting the definition by saying "Muslims do not beat their wives; if they do, they're not Muslims"). Darsh expresses his sympathy and assures the readers that, from an Islamic point of view, beating one's wife is completely unacceptable. He bases this claim on a traditional interpretation of the Quranic *wa-aḍribūhunna* ("beat them," 4:34),[61] which holds that the act is only to be symbolic and comparable to beating her on the the shoulder with a toothpick, as well as on a tradition that the Prophet Muhammad never beat his wives. Beating implies a lack of respect for the "honour and feelings" of women and children. A person who fails to control his anger and beats others has a psychological problem, Darsh states. It may be because the husband feels stigmatized by unemployment and inability to provide for his family, or he may feel that he is living in a hostile environment. Regardless, a solution has to be found, and both the one who beats and the one who is beaten must be helped. This is not least a responsibility for the "community elders," Darsh claims.[62]

No question is too small to answer if it plays a role in marriage. One woman complains that her husband has greasy hair, uncut fingernails and smells of tobacco, and doesn't accept her talking to him. However, the wife adds, he has high morals, is intelligent, and is Islamically aware. Darsh is surprised that

---

the time, the amount, who bears the duty and who holds the right. One contested topic is whether the *nafaqa* is a compensation for the wife's availability for sexual congress, or for her being "confined" on account of her husband. Another is whether unruly (*nushūz*) women are entitled to *nafaqa*. The *nafaqa* may therefore appear to be linked to *ṭāʿa* (obedience). Ibn Rushd 2000, 2:63–65.

60 Based on the author's personal experiences in Muslim communities over 20 years, and fieldwork for this book.

61 Traditionally, this word has been understood as "beating". At present, however, there are examples of arguments that the word may have other meanings. For instance, Abdulhamid A. Abu Sulayman, in his little book *Marital Discord: Recapturing the Full Islamic Spirit of Human Dignity*, discusses the word *ḍaraba* and concludes that it should be taken to mean "to go away" (Abu Sulayman 2003). Laleh Bakthiar would seem to follow this interpretation, as she has used the same wording in her Quran translation, *The Sublime Quran* (2009).

62 *Q-News*, 19–26 Mar 1993.

the wife describes her husband as having high morals and Islamic awareness. Hygiene, including cutting one's fingernails, is a religious duty, and it is her duty to remind her husband. Darsh declares smoking to be *makrūh* (reprehensible), saying he follows the Hanafi school, which rejects frivolous use of the concept of *ḥarām* (forbidden).[63] One man worries that his wife cooks meals without taking a bath after sex. Darsh replies without hesitation that his wife can cook without taking a bath. But if she is a Muslim, he ought to worry that she does not seem to take the five daily prayers seriously, since *ghusl* (full washing of the body) is obligatory after sex in order to perform the ritual prayer.[64]

Sexuality and Reproduction

Darsh describes the marriage contract as *ʿaqd istimtāʿ*, defining it as "… an agreement allowing all parties to enjoy themselves in that intimate relationship."[65] The column also answers questions on sexual intercourse. Darsh gives general answers to specific questions, reminding the questioner that public discussion of such topics is "disreputable" and "dishonourable". Sexual acts belong to the private sphere.[66]

There is no concept of rape within marriage, as the marriage contract implies consent. Darsh points to a tradition that the wife should not deny her husband if he wants to be with her, but he reminds readers of the ethics of relationships: "… there are etiquettes and decent norms of behaviour to be observed by the husband."[67]

Use of contraceptives is permitted, on the condition that the spouses agree. It is not a decision for one spouse to make alone.[68] Sterilization is forbidden under all circumstances. Artificial insemination is possible, as long as ovum and sperm come from the marriage partners. But the husband's stored sperm may not be used after his death. Death terminates the relationship, and the wife is in *ʿidda* (the waiting period of four months and ten days to see if she is pregnant with her late husband).[69]

---

63 *Q-News*, 19 Feb 1993.

64 *Q-News*, 28 May–4 Jun 1993.

65 *Q-News*, 1–7 Mar 1996.

66 Darsh 1997, 113–114.

67 *Q-News*, 24–31 Mar 1995.

68 Darsh 1997, 110.

69 *Q-News*, 23–30 Jul 1993.

Darsh does however discuss voluntary or involuntary sexual relations outside of marriage—in the cases of prostitution and wartime rape. With regard to prostitution, Darsh argues against decriminalization, based on two points. First, there is a clear prohibition in the Quran, and laws are made to regulate its violation.[70] Darsh relates it to the mission of the Prophet, which was to enjoin what is good and forbid what is evil (*amr bil-maʿrūf wa-nahy ʿan al-munkar*).[71] Moreover, it is a threat to the family, the protection of which is one of the objectives of Sharia (*maqāṣid al-sharīʿa*).[72] According to Darsh, the solution lies in the Islamic regulation of sexuality, which is to say, its expression within the framework of marriage.[73]

The war in Bosnia in the early 1990s gave rise to three questions: on whether abortion is permitted after rape, on adoption, and on family names. Darsh stresses that the raped women have suffered a criminal act and carry no guilt or shame whatsoever. But abortion is not permitted, and does not improve matters: Two wrongs do not make a right. The children should be given their mothers' family names, since the fathers are not known, nor do they have any right to the children. The mother is obliged to raise the child herself. Regarding orphans, Darsh stresses the responsibility of the Muslim society as a whole for raising such children, lest they lose their Islamic identity.[74]

Returning to the consequences of sexual intercourse within marriage, there are two questions related to birth and the post-partum period. The questioner refers to Maryam, who was advised to sit down in the shade under a palm tree (19:23), and asks if this does not entail Quranic support for so-called natural childbirth. Darsh rejects this interpretation, asserting that there is nothing wrong with easing a childbirth through modern methods.[75] He also rejects the tradition that a woman should not leave the house the first 30 to 40 days after giving birth. This only pertains to her being ritually unclean and unable to pray as long as she is bleeding. Otherwise, she is free to go wherever she likes.[76]

70 Darsh refers to the Quran, chapter 24.

71 See Quran 7:157.

72 Here, Darsh describes the family as one of the *ḍarūriyyāt*, the five vital necessities to be protected (see chapter 7). In the *uṣūl al-fiqh* literature, the word *nasl* (offspring or descendants) is used. The word "family" is not mentioned. In the contemporary period, however, *nasl* is used nearly synonymously with "family," not least as shown in Darsh's rhetoric.

73 http://www.zawaj.com/articles/prostitution_smd.html.

74 *Q-News*, 22 Jan 1993.

75 Darsh 1997, 116.

76 *Q-News* 18–25 Dec 1992.

Darsh's replies here are down to earth. The message seems to be that the texts should not be over-interpreted, and that norms do not exist for every least detail of various cultural practices.

Social Relationships

An overarching theme in social relations is the organization of gender relations. The historian Judith Tucker describes public space as "gendered space".[77] It is a dominant view that there has to be a divide between the genders. What does this norm of gender segregation entail? One female questioner is clearly skeptical about men and women not being allowed to look at or talk to each other if they are not married. "Apart from total segregation, leading to a breakdown of understanding between men and women in society, this rule is also difficult to enforce as it breaks down as soon as you get out on the street, board the bus, take a lift, talk to teachers, etc."[78] In our time, goes the answer, men and women may mingle if the woman uses hijab. This applies in situations where other people are present. *Khalwa*, a man and a woman who are not married being together on their own, is not allowed. The implication is, for example, that "brothers" may not drive "sisters" home after an Islamic event. Darsh, however, cautiously formulates the answer in terms of his personal preference for public transportation, since private transportation could lead to "familiarity" and situations that are undesirable according to Islamic norms.

This reply sets the tone for the rest of the answers on gender relations. The free mingling of the genders, without women using the hijab, is limited to family members, and specifically, to persons one cannot marry (*maḥram*). Adopted children do not fall among the latter. The explanation is taken from the Quran. The aim of these rules, Darsh says, is for family life to be "happy, relaxed and comfortable".[79] Outside the home, the tone should be different, even among spouses. It is not recommendable for a husband and wife to walk hand in hand, even though it is not forbidden.

When are young men and women considered legally accountable in the Islamic context, that is, responsible for fulfilling their duties according to the Sharia? In his answer, Darsh presents different sources. The Quran gives "marriageable age" as an indicator of maturity. Opinions differ as to how this is

77 Tucker 2008, 175.

78 *Q-News*, 20 Nov 1992.

79 *Q-News*, 28 May–4 Jun 1993.

determined, ranging from signs such as the onset of a girl's menstruation, to age in calendar years, such as the 18 years mentioned in the Hanafi school.[80]

Hijab plays a central role in regulating the shared space. Usually, the woman's hijab is in focus. A number of questions deal with hijab. What is considered hijab? What should be covered? Is the female voice *ʿawra*, i.e. part of what must be covered up in front of non-*maḥram* men? What if one cannot find clothes that are large enough? In that case, could one buy men's clothes, as they are often found in larger sizes and reasonably priced? May one show men pictures of oneself from before one started using the hijab? As we see, the queries do not question whether the hijab is required; rather, they seek practical solutions for concrete situations.

Darsh states that women's hijab consists in covering all the body except the face and hands. The clothes should be loose-fitting, and not diaphanous. That apart, one may choose whatever style one likes.[81] Citing a tradition, Darsh recalls that women and men should not imitate one another, and it might be a good idea to have the clothes made by a tailor—a widespread tradition in the Muslim world. We cannot expect the western clothing industry to take Islamic rules into account in fashion development, and we should find our own solutions based on the Quran and traditions, Darsh asserts.[82] The female voice, however, is not a part of the woman's *ʿawra* in need of covering. Citing the Quran (33:32), he shows that the wives of the Prophet were not prohibited from talking to men. Since they represent the supreme example for Muslim women, this clearly also applies to Muslim women in general, Darsh states.[83] The duty of hijab entails that one may not be seen by men when one is not covered. This extends to pictures taken without the hijab.[84]

When one wishes to start using the hijab, frictions may arise. What should a daughter do when her parents oppose her choice? Darsh voices support for girls who wish to use the hijab, as this in his view is an Islamic duty. He explains the parents' attitude as a lack of knowledge of Islam mixed with uncertainty over Islamic identity. It is also a matter of wanting to be accepted in non-Muslim social settings. Darsh advises the woman to listen to her parents at home, but to use the hijab when she goes out, citing the tradition: "There should be no obedience to that which constitutes disobedience to Allah."[85]

80 *Q-News*, 29 Sep–5 Oct 1995.
81 *Q-News*, 29 Oct–5 Nov 1993.
82 *Q-News*, 30 Apr–7 May 1993.
83 *Q-News*, 23 Dec–6 Jan 1995.
84 *Q-News*, 16–22 Jun 1995.
85 http://www.iol.ie/~afifi/Ad-Darsh/27.9.96.htm.

The organization of gender relations, including the hijab, is also a challenge women face in their choice of profession and their participation in sports activities. What about the nursing profession? May one wear a nurse's uniform, and may one treat patients of the opposite sex? May one take the hijab off for a job interview? Is playing tennis in front of a mixed audience acceptable?

Regarding the nursing profession, Darsh points out that there is a large need for Muslims working in healthcare. The nurse's uniform can be adapted to Islamic requirements for covering, he says, pointing out that the healthcare authorities are flexible in this area, which is a matter of non-discrimination. There is an old debate over caring for people of the opposite sex. Darsh finds support in the opinion of the Hanbali jurist Ibn Qudama (d. 1223) that there is nothing wrong with nurses treating patients of the opposite sex, as the reasons are medical.[86] Here, Darsh appears very focused on finding solutions.

One lady seeking a job worries that she might experience discrimination because she wears the hijab. Could she take it off for interviews? Darsh does not recommend that she take it off, as she might face challenges anyway if she gets the job and wears the hijab while working. He comes across as a realist with regard to hijab in the workplace, and mentions a number of obstacles that Muslim women with hijab face when looking for work. He ascribes it to "a narrow-minded, prejudiced attitude against the Muslim population of Europe," and reminds the Muslim community that it has a duty to support Muslim women and their right to wear the hijab in society at large.[87]

The question whether it is acceptable to play tennis before a mixed audience, comes from the mother of a promising ten-year-old player. Darsh declares that it is not just a question of hijab, but also one of morality versus degeneration. The life of a tennis professional entails a great deal more than playing before mixed audiences: the deprivation of childhood, loneliness, being treated as a commercial product, relationships, parties, the pressure to make achievements at any cost—Darsh has a long list. He recommends that the mother should not deny her daughter tennis, but should try to keep her from being swallowed up by what he calls a professional circus. The moral is clear: Muslims should develop athletic arenas where they can compete in a wholesome atmosphere that stresses athletic achievement, team spirit, and genuine fun.[88]

86 *Q-News*, 19 Feb 1993.

87 *Q-News*, 2–9 Jun 1995.

88 *Q-News*, 2–9 Apr 1993.

Clearly, uncertainty over the relationship between women and men extends even into death. May a man see the face of a deceased woman? May a man perform the ritual washing of his deceased wife before the funeral, and the other way around? The norm concerning the face of a dead person goes back to the death of the Prophet, Darsh relates. Abu Bakr, the first caliph, uncovered the Prophet's face, and said that he was beautiful. Based on this report, Darsh days that men and women may look at a man, but it is better that only those men who have blood ties to a woman see her face.[89] As to the husband washing his dead wife or vice versa, Darsh points out that this is accepted by three of the schools of law (the Malikis, Shafiʿis, and Hanbalis; the Hanafis rejected it on the grounds that the marriage comes to an end when one of the spouses dies). If there is no husband to wash the deceased wife, another *maḥram* may wash her, on the condition that she be covered by a shroud. If there is no *maḥram*, and no other women, there should be only a symbolic ritual of purification without water (*tayammum*).[90]

Not everything is about segregation, though. There is also the question of visiting the graves of deceased family members. Is it permitted? Darsh points to a tradition that Muslims are allowed to visit graves, because it reminds them of the next life. Darsh's advice is that women may visit graves, but should keep in mind that making social events out of such visits is unacceptable, as is loud wailing.[91]

Bodily Care

The encounter of Islamic identity with non-Muslim culture is the underlying theme of a question about setting up an exercise group for Muslim women. What about Jane Fonda as a role model? And what about the music, with its sometimes powerful rhythms? Advice is sought. In his response, Darsh analyses the question in order to identify relevant subjects of Islamic norms. The only real matter, Darsh says, is that such classes should be free of men. Music is acceptable, as long as the lyrics are not indecent. However, he points out, surely it is the exercise and not the music that matters most to those who want to get in shape.[92]

---

89 Darsh 1997, 191–192.
90 *Q-News*, 21–28 Oct 1994.
91 *Q-News*, 12–18 Jul 1996.
92 *Q-News*, 18–25 Dec 1992.

Darsh also takes a down-to-earth approach when responding to whether animal-tested lotions are permitted. Affirming that they are, he nevertheless advises against using such products, since the needless exploitation of animals is unethical.[93]

Three other questions deal respectively with the use of hair dye, nail varnish, and makeup cream as it concerns ritual purity (*ṭahāra*). This leads us over into the field of *ʿibādāt*, acts related to ritual practice, which are incumbent on all Muslims of age, including the five pillars and the regulations on ritual purity. *ʿIbādāt* is discussed at the beginning of hadith collections and manuals of jurisprudence.[94]

ʿIbādāt

The questions about hair dye, nail varnish, and makeup cream are all about whether they prevent water from reaching the hair, scalp, nails, and face, which all have to be washed as part of ritual purification. The answers are short and precise: Nail varnish does not let water reach the nails, and should therefore be avoided,[95] but use of makeup cream is acceptable if it does not form a film on top of the skin. Dyeing one's hair is a different matter, since hair dye does not prevent the water from reaching the hair and scalp. Moreover, dyeing one's hair is recommended when it turns grey, Darsh says. Women are entirely free to choose their hair colour and hairdo to smarten themselves for their husbands. Men, on the other hand, face a restriction: They should not colour their hair to make themselves look younger than they are.[96]

Some of the questions are more elementary. Do caresses among the spouses invalidate the *wuḍūʾ* ablution?[97] In what does *ghusl* (the major purification ritual) consist?[98] Does one have to wash one's hair every time? The responses form an elementary education in right practice, and thus function as a pedagogical aid.

93 *Q-News*, 11–18 Jun 1993.

94 "ʿIbādāt" in *EI2* (Bousquet 2010).

95 *Q-News*, 18–25 Mar 1994.

96 *Q-News*, 30 Jun–6 Jul 1995.

97 Ablution (*wuḍūʾ*) consists in washing the hands, face, and arms, rubbing water over the hair and washing the feet before each prayer.

98 *Ghusl*: A bath taken in a particular way, required to become ritually pure after e.g. sexual intercourse, menstruation and childbirth.

One question concerns the limits on caring for the deceased beyond the ritual washing. Is it possible to put makeup on the deceased and ornament him or her with rose petals, as is the custom in the homeland? Yes, says Darsh, as long as the deceased has left behind financial means to cover the extra costs. The ethical ideal, however, is for material goods to benefit the living more than the dead.[99]

Concerning *ṣalāh*, the ritual prayers, their performance is of the utmost importance, even if it may seem mechanical and one experiences a loss of concentration.[100] *Dhikr*, the remembrance of God, and *duʿā*ʾ, free prayers, may also be made during the menses, unlike the *ṣalāh*.[101]

Darsh stresses that women's non-performance of the ritual prayers during the menses or after childbirth implies an exemption from a duty and a burden on days when one may feel worn out and tired.[102] It is interesting that Darsh frames this in a rights perspective. An argument based on equality is made in response to a question where a wife complains that her husband passed in front of her while she was praying. Darsh states that one should not pass in front of someone performing the ritual prayer, whether a woman or a man.[103]

The rights perspective emerges even more strongly when Darsh answers a question whether the *tarāwīḥ* prayer may be performed at home, because a certain mosque has such poor facilities for women.[104] Clearly, Darsh here measures social reality against women's right to come to the mosque, and finds it lacking. He replies by rephrasing the question, stating that it is not a matter of praying at home or not, but of women's access to the mosque. He criticizes Muslim men who build and furnish mosques with facilities for ten times more men than women. He ascribes this problem to the Hanafi school and its attitudes to women: "Sadly, they discourage women from going to the mosque."[105]

Fasting, too, gives rise to women-related questions. One question is about how intimate spouses can be with one another without breaking the fast, specifically about holding hands and caressing each other's cheeks. It depends, Darsh says, stating that any act that leads inevitably to ejaculation is forbid-

99 *Q-News*, 10–17 Mar 1995.

100 Darsh 1997, 32.

101 http://www.iol.ie/~afifi/Ad-Darsh/4.10.96.htm.

102 *Q-News*, 18–25 Dec 1992.

103 Darsh 1997, 38.

104 The *tarāwīḥ* prayer (the "resting prayer", as one makes a little pause after each prayer unit) is the prayer prayed each night in the month of Ramadan, and at which a certain portion of the Quran is recited.

105 Darsh 1997, 79.

den. He refers to the Companions of the Prophet, who apparently concluded that it depends on the age of the man. A young man is more easily aroused, and should therefore abstain completely from daytime physical contact during the fast. An older man, who is often less sexually active, is not subject to the same restrictions.[106]

Another recurring question is whether hormone pills may be taken to delay the monthly period. The question is topical both with regard to the fasting month, the hajj and the *ʿumra*. The answer is affirmative, on the grounds that this is not considered a permanent intervention against human nature. The norm is stated: "It is considered an act of regulation so that Ramadan and Hajj can pass free from anxiety."[107] One of Darsh's references for this fatwa is Abdulaziz bin Baz, mufti of Saudi Arabia from 1993 until his death in 1999.

The final topic is whether a woman may go on the hajj or *ʿumra* unaccompanied by a *maḥram* (the husband or a relative she is forbidden to marry). Opinions are divided, Darsh says. Whereas the Hanafi school holds that the woman should stay at home if she has no *maḥram*, except if the voyage takes less than three days, al-Shafiʿi finds it acceptable if women travel as a group. Darsh further refers to sources that allow women to go on pilgrimage without a *maḥram*. He cites inter alia a tradition that two of the Companions accompanied the wives of the Prophet in his absence. He also cites another tradition, according to which the Prophet said there would come a day when women could go on the hajj from al-Khira (a place in Iraq) without a *maḥram*; and the comment on this tradition by Ibn Hajar al-Asqalani (d. 1449), who interpreted it as saying there would come a time when Islam would be well established, and the conditions for traveling would change.[108] Since travel in our time is considerably less of a risk than at the time the sources refer to, Darsh probably takes this source, too, as support for his view that women may go on pilgrimage without a *maḥram* as long as they travel together with other women.

Characterizing the Fatwas

Darsh's replies are usually not pure fatwas in the sense of statements of norms; rather, they are combination of fatwas and advice (*naṣīḥa*). In the responses, the norms are linked with ethical reflection, often based on Darsh's own experi-

106 *Q-News*, 5–12 Mar 1993.

107 Darsh 1997, 68.

108 *Q-News*, 1–8 Oct 1993.

ence with Muslims where he worked, whether the questions concern marriage, personal care, or social relations. The advice is not given in a vacuum, but often with regard to a social setting. A piece of advice on searching for a marriage partner in the British context may serve as an example. Darsh gives advice both with regard to Muslims as a minority in a non-Muslim majority society, and to a potential generation gap, with a parent generation that have grown up in a Muslim country and have other expectations of the young than do the young themselves.

Darsh very rarely uses the category "forbidden" when stating norms, and he explicitly explains why. He relies on the Hanafi school, which, he says, seeks to avoid the careless use of this category. When considering smoking, for instance, he refers to other scholars declaring smoking *ḥarām*, forbidden, while he himself is content to use the category *makrūh* (reprehensible)—but *strongly* reprehensible (*makruh taḥrīmī*). He usually uses words like "advisable" and "recommendable" (*mandūb*).

By using the whole range of categories of obligation, not just compulsory or prohibited, Darsh is able to combine ethical ideals and legal norms.[109] This combination is particularly clear in his description of marriage, where he combines ethical ideals for marriage with concrete statements of norms. He gives explicit expression to this in his description of the nature of rules and norms: "They follow a rationale given in the Qur'an itself and reflect the spirit of care, compassion and reasoning. This is clearly stated in the Qur'an, giving the general framework of the Islamic legal system [...] Any particular issue has to be judged in the light of this general moral framework."[110] Discussing whether prostitution should be decriminalized, Darsh cites the principle of commanding the good and forbidding evil (*amr bil-maʿrūf wa-nahy ʿan al-munkar*) in the light of certain objectives one should seek to attain. In this case, the objective is to protect the family, which is the cornerstone of society. Darsh's argument places him within the theory of *maqāṣid al-sharīʿa* (the objectives of Sharia), where the family is considered an absolute necessity (*ḍarūra*). Without the family, a society or legal system cannot exist in a meaningful way, and its protection hence entails a utility (*maṣlaḥa*).[111]

---

109 The English terms for the categories of the norms that the subject of the norms (*al-mukallaf*) is bound by and held accountable for, are taken from Kamali 2003: obligatory (*wājib*), recommendable (*mandūb*), permissible (*mubāḥ*), reprehensible (*makrūh*) og forbidden (*ḥarām*).

110 http://www.zawaj.com/articles/prostitution_smd.html, accessed 12 Aug 2009.

111 On the *maqāṣid al-sharīʿa*, see the Introduction and chapter 7.

Darsh also shows himself familiar with the social reality in which the questions are posed, whether they concern the new challenges of finding a marriage partner when living as a minority in a new country, or hijab in the work place. Interestingly, he does not criticize Western society; he merely states that Western norms and rules for youth culture and gender relations do not accord with those of Muslims. He does not come across as a spokesman for identity politics. Instead, he calls for understanding young people, without compromising on what he describes as Islamic requirements for conduct. He expresses his sympathy and support for those facing challenges, and besides clarifying the norms, he often offers advice on solutions. The impression given is that of an intense presence in the fatwas and closeness to the reader. There are occasional glimmers of humour, as when he is asked whether a marriage must be solemnized by an imam: He replies by urging the questioner not to allow some imam to turn a joyous event into a drab and boring one. Sometimes, he appears as a supporter of the questioner, most clearly in his references to the exchanges of opinion he has had with people in charge of mosques about women's access. He not only supports the women questioners, he is himself an actor in the struggle for women's access to mosques.

Darsh claimed he was not capable of *ijtihād*, independent reasoning. By this he may have meant that he did not engage in re-interpreting the sources, which he thought contained all possible views.[112] His method consisted in choosing what he considered a correct Islamic answer conditioned by the social context in which the questioner stood, on the grounds that: "It is a matter of understanding the environment in which we live and a reflection of the changing positions and changing situations. We Muslims have to take these changes into consideration when we look into the life of the Muslim woman."[113] Understanding social reality is also part of the method: "What we can do is to look into what is recorded and the former points of view. What we do in the present situation is to find that which is more appropriate to the Muslim community, and then we accept this particular point of view."[114] In addition to the Quran and hadith, he refers to the Companions of the Prophet, the four schools of law, Muslim theologians through Islamic history, and the *maqāṣid al-sharīʿa*. The references are often paraphrased and presented in popular language, probably because the target group of the fatwas are young Muslims.

112 Roald 2001a, 116.
113 Roald 2001a, 116.
114 Roald 2001a, 116.

The Construction of Muslim Women

Above, I have characterized the questions as social data; that is, they tell something about the questioner's perception of reality, whether with regard to gender relations, partner choice, getting married, marital life, education and work, sexuality and reproduction, or *ʿibādāt*. This becomes clearer when they are grouped from the bottom up by categories suggested by the materials themselves, rather than in a top-down approach based on broad predetermined categories from *fiqh* manuals and fatwa collections, such as "women" or "the family". Some of the answers given may be described as liberating in the context of challenges faced by young Muslims, not least forced marriages or costly wedding arrangements. The woman does not need a guardian (*wālī*) for her marriage contract to be valid; the contract is invalid without the consent of the spouses-to-be; the *mahr* is a gift for the bride; no dowry is paid by the family of the bride to the family of the groom; one may marry regardless of race or caste. In these questions, the legal norms appear emancipatory compared to social practice.

Darsh also recalls the ideal relationship between a man and a woman in marriage as described in the Quran:

> And among His Signs is this, that He created for you mates from among yourselves, that ye may dwell in tranquillity with them, and He has put love and mercy between your (hearts): verily in that are Signs for those who reflect.
>
> 30:31

> … They are your garments and ye are their garments …
>
> 2:187

Darsh appears to interpret these verses as evidence for equality in principle in the relationship between man and woman. As such, they may be experienced as liberating.

Practical matters, however, are a different story. The marriage partners have equal worth, according to Darsh, but the man is the head of the family. This represents a traditional understanding of *qiwāma*, guardianship, as expressed in the Quran: "Men are the protectors and maintainers of women, because Allah has given the one more (strength) than the other, and because they support them from their means …" (4:34). The man is responsible for supporting the family, while the woman's primary responsibility lies in the home. This is not to say that they should not help each other out: the man in the home, the woman financially. However, the gender roles are fixed, even if women make a financial contribution. Interestingly, Darsh reminds women of the reward for such contributions in the life to come, but without using the expression *nafaqa* (maintenance). By not calling the woman's contribution maintenance, he avoids discussing the question of equal inheritance rights, which will inevitably be raised in a new social reality in which both spouses support the family.[115] And yet, a working woman has to accept paying her own expenses, because her right to maintenance is tied to her staying at home.

This view of marriage is used to argue for the traditional norms that a Muslim woman may not marry a non-Muslim man, whereas a Muslim man may marry a non-Muslim woman, even if Darsh for social reasons does not recommend it. It is justified in terms of protecting the woman's freedom to be a Muslim, and ensuring that the children are raised as Muslims. It is a matter of protecting religion (*ḥifẓ al-dīn*), the first of the vital necessities within the paradigm of the objectives of Sharia.[116] We see Darsh defending the traditional gender roles, while accepting that they are affected by time and place. He seeks to find Islamic solutions for what the questioners experience as acute challenges, but in his answers, he does not advocate equal rights and duties. Because the man has more duties, he also has more rights. Men and women complement each other in the family as a basic social institution. He takes a positive view of women's participation in society, but stipulates that they use the hijab. Gender relations and sexuality must be regulated in the interest of preserving society. Against this background, Darsh may be termed a neo-traditionalist, advocating the view of balance and complementarity.

However, this does not apply to *ʿibādāt*. Here, the ideal of equality applies. Women and men have equal duties with regard to purity prescriptions, prayer, fasting and pilgrimage. That women should not pray or fast during their menses or after giving birth is described as a freedom from a duty and a burden at a time when they are worn out and tired. Three issues are particularly interesting in a rights perspective: the use of hormone pills to delay menstruation, women going on pilgrimage without a *maḥram*, and women's access to the mosque. All these questions receive positive answers, and in particular, it is stressed that access to the mosque is a women's right, and that the current practice in many mosques is shameful. We see a fundamental ideal of equality, with a stress on women's rights. In this regard, the legal norms appear emancipatory with

---

115 In the modern Islamic legal literature, *nafaqa* is used as an argument why men should inherit twice as much as their sisters. See e.g. al-Qaradawi 2006, 23.

116 See chapter 7.

regard to social reality. We should be aware, however, that equal access to the mosques for both sexes is only part of the issues of gender equality in *ʿibādāt*. In the reality of ritual practice, men and women are not equal. In my materials, there are no questions on this issue, probably because the fatwas were given in the first half of the 1990s, when this was not yet a topic of public debate.

Against this background, I would argue that we do not find one unambiguous view of women in Darsh's fatwas. While asserting equality and rights in *ʿibādāt*, Darsh defends the equal worth of the sexes and stresses balance and complementarity with regard to social transactions (*muʿāmalāt*). It is interesting that Darsh throughout ties the norms to ethical perspectives. That way, the norms do not come across as mechanical, but as reasonable within the frame of the argument, which appears to be focused on finding solutions for the questioner.

CHAPTER 4

Women's Issues and Collective Fatwas: The Case of the ECFR

Introduction

Questions reach the European Council for Fatwa and Research (ECFR) from all over Europe, by telephone, fax, e-mail and letter. The general secretary of the ECFR, Hussein Halawa, estimates an average of 25 questions per day.[1] Most often, fatwas are requested in writing. However, only a small part of the fatwas that the ECFR issues in response to questions are published. In part, this is due to the different ways incoming questions are answered. Karman describes three different ways: immediate response, if the matter is urgent or there already is a recognized answer in Islamic jurisprudence; referral to the fatwa committee, which meets every other month, if the question requires further consideration; or to the annual ECFR session, if the question is considered of interest to the Muslim community.[2] The "simple" questions, as Halawa calls them, he answers himself. The fatwa committees give their answers directly to the questioner (*al-mustaftī*).[3] The questions that are raised at the annual meeting are distributed in advance among the members, who then present their proposed answers in the so-called fatwa session that lasts between half a day and a whole day during the meeting. The proposed answer is discussed, and comments and changes may be proposed, or the fatwa may be accepted without comment.[4] The Council's resolutions are reproduced in the concluding declaration (*al-bayān al-khitāmī*), which is published on its website (http://www.e-cfr.org) and in its publication *al-Majalla al-ʿilmiyya* ("Scientific Journal"). But the ECFR also has a fourth way of giving fatwas: carrying out studies on topics the Council members consider important, in order to make a joint decision, or produce a

1 Conversation with Hussein Halawa, Cairo, 18 Mar 2008. Halawa gives the following breakdown of questions by media: Ten questions by phone, ten by e-mail, three to four by fax, and one in writing.

2 Karman 2008, 74. In her dissertation, Karman only mentions the fatwa committee in England. There are two such committees, one in England, and one in France.

3 Conversation with Hussein Halawa, Cairo, 18 Mar 2008.

4 Author's observations during fatwa sessions in the Council. Karman 2008, 74 describes the same procedure in her dissertation on modern fatwa councils.

 | DOI: 10.1163/9789004367852_006

resolution (*qarār*) on the norm in the individual case. Whereas the fatwas are the result of a bottom-up approach, the resolutions (*qarārāt*) are the result of a top-down approach.[5]

The ECFR has published two fatwa collections in Arabic and English, and a recent third collection (2013) only in Arabic so far.[6] The first two contain fatwas and resolutions given up to and including the seventh session (January 2001).[7] The collections begin with an introduction by the Council's head Yusuf al-Qaradawi, followed by the ECFR statutes, fatwas and resolutions. Women-related fatwas make up a considerable percentage of the total number of fatwas and resolutions (*qarārāt*) published by the Council. There are two reasons: Women make up a far larger share of those contacting the Council than men,[8] and women-related topics are considered by Council members as the most important topics, tied to Islamic identity.[9] According to Alexandre Caeiro, the female body functions as a barometer of people's "Islamicness" (*islamicité*), as he calls it.[10]

The other ECFR publication, *al-Majalla al-ʿilmiyya*, is published at regular intervals as a single issue every six months, or a double issue once a year. The number of pages has increased since the journal's early days, and it has come to include summaries in English and French. The bulk of the material consists of studies presented in the preceding session. Then follows the concluding declaration, which among other things contains resolutions, fatwas, and the Council's recommendations to Muslims in Europe. By the 19th session, which took place in Istanbul in 2009, the ECFR had issued 73 *qarārāt*, of which 24

5 There is one exception. The resolution on whether a married woman who converts to Islam is obliged to divorce her husband if he does not become a Muslim, resulted from a question by a woman who faced this problem.

6 The first two fatwa collections, both in Arabic and English, have been published in two different editions, in paperback and in hardback with a gold-lettered imitation leather cover. The first of the two fatwa collections has also been translated and published in French with a foreword by Tariq Ramadan. The second collection was translated, but was stopped before publication (see chapter 2).

7 This makes it plain that *qarārāt* are considered fatwas. All decisions, fatwas and *qarārāt* are numbered as fatwas. This is also in accordance with statements made during my interviews with the Council's general secretary Husein Halawa.

8 See chapter 2. The same tendency is mentioned in Masud, Messick, and Powers 1996, 32, with reference to al-Qaradawi.

9 Conversations with Tahar Mahdi, Ali al-Qaradaghi, and Mohamed al-Mansoori, members of the Council.

10 Caeiro 2002, 118.

were women-related, and 94 fatwas, of which 46 were women-related.[11] These are the ones I consider in the present book. I have not covered the additions in the recent third collection, which brings the total up to 91 *qarārāt*, of which 31 are women-related, and 121 fatwas, of which 52 are women-related. Adding the two categories together, we find that about 40 percent of all the statements of norms were women-related. We see a clear shift in the relationship between fatwas and resolutions (*qarārāt*). In the course of the first two sessions, 42 fatwas were given. Later, the focus shifted to resolutions based on studies on topics the Council had agreed to raise (with the exception of the 13th session in London, 2004, where 13 fatwas were given). Karmen comments:

> To begin with, the council placed emphasis on issuing short answers (fatwas) to questions. Since then, however, it has gradually tended to become more concerned about the conduct of intensive research, and also begun to give further attention to urgent juridical issues related to the Muslim minority community; currently research constitutes the major part of the council's work.[12]

The Arabic and English editions of the fatwa collections are distributed for free, while the French translation, published by GEDIS (the publishing house of the UOIF) and Tawhid, is commercially distributed, and likely more easily available in the market than the English and Arabic editions. Caeiro discusses the target groups of the latter editions:

> The hardback edition, reminiscent of the heritage classics, seems to appeal to a religious elite (imams, Muslim intellectuals, advanced students), while the paperback version appears geared toward a much larger readership. If this is correct, the targeted audience of the ECFR's texts comprises both a (male) intellectual elite from the first generation of immigrants and a more general readership of Muslim youth (of both genders) socialized in Europe.[13]

As for the French editions:

---

11 Three of the matters were postponed, all of them women-related.

12 Karman 2008, 75. The turn toward more research is clear in the last issue of the Council's journal (nos. 14–15), which contains only studies in article form.

13 Caeiro 2010, 440–441.

> [... T]he translations of its fatwas have been commercially distributed only in that country [France]. The competition between GEDIS (the publishing house of the Union des organisations islamiques de France based in Paris) and the Lyon-based Editions Tawhid (close to the Young Muslim network inspired by Tariq Ramadan) yielded two translations of the ECFR's First Collection of Fatwas in 2002. By contrast to the situation in other European countries, these French collections responded to a previously untapped market demand.[14]

The Council's journal *al-Majalla al-ʿilmiyya* has a different target audience. According to to Karman, the journal is sent to ulama in the Middle East and Islamic institutions in Europe in order to inform them about the activities of the ECFR.[15] This target audience is clearly signalled by the design of the journal, every issue of which has the same neutral cover with the title and number, without pictures and with only the background colour changing, traits typical of a scientific journal.

Some of the fatwas were also reproduced in the so-called fatwa bank on the website IslamOnline.net. IslamOnline.net was established in 1997 on the initiative of Maryam Hasan al-Hajari, an IT expert from Qatar, and developed into one of the most visited Islamic websites giving fatwas in Arabic and English.[16] The page functioned as a portal to a number of sections, the most popular of which, according to Gräf, was the Sharia section, with its options for searching and receiving fatwas.[17] The fatwa bank was an electronic archive of previously issued fatwas, searchable by topic or mufti. Fatwas could be found both on the English and the Arabic webpage.[18] The ECFR was listed in the fatwa bank as a mufti, with eight Arabic-language fatwas, of which three women-related ones, and 54 in English, of which 21 women-related ones. There may be several reasons for the large difference in the number of fatwas. For one, an effort was made to reach out to non-Arabic-speaking Muslims, not least in Europe, which the ECFR claims as its "jurisdiction". For another, the majority of Arabic-speaking Muslims live outside Europe. To them, well-known Muftis and fatwa councils from the Muslim world may be a more relevant choice than

14 Caeiro 2010, 441.

15 Karman 2008, 75.

16 Gräf 2008.

17 Gräf 2008.

18 http://www.islamonline.net, accessed 29 Oct 2009.

the ECFR. At the similar OnIslam.net site, the ECFR was listed with 10 women-related fatwas on the English page, and 39 on the Arabic page.[19]

One possible way of issuing a fatwa is joining a fatwa that has been given before, if it meets the mufti's standards.[20] Where women-related fatwas are concerned, the Council has made use of this approach with fatwas previously issued by its head Yusuf al-Qaradawi. Nineteen of the Council's fatwas may be found in the third volume of his *Fatāwā muʿāṣira*, in the chapter titled "Fiqh al-aqalliyyāt."

The Council's adoption of Qaradawi's fatwas in particular is due to his position as its leader and the authority he enjoys in the Council. Caeiro and al-Saify puts it this way:

> It is [...] a measure of the chairman's scholarly authority that many of the fatwas of the ECFR borrow literally from Qaraḍāwī's texts, while very few [members] have explicitly gone against Qaraḍāwī's personal views. This seems to justify the association, common among Muslims in Europe, of the ECFR's fatwas with those of Qaraḍāwī himself.[21]

The Questions

By the time it published the proceedings of its seventeenth session, the ECFR had published a total of 70 women-related fatwas and *qarārāt* (resolutions). Eight of these questions fall under the category "Different types of marriage," five under "Before contracting marriage," nine under "Contracting marriage," 15 under "In marriage," eight under "Body and care/sexuality/reproduction," ten under "Social relations," one under "Child-raising/education/work," and two under "*ʿIbādāt*". Beside the themes of Syed Darsh's fatwas, there are two additional categories: "Divorce" (twelve questions) and "Inheritance" (two questions). We recognize many of the problems raised, but new ones have been added.

19 As of mid-2013. On IslamOnline.net and OnIslam.net, see ch. 2, n. 57.

20 Conversation with Mohamed al-Mansoori, Oslo, 20 Sep 2006.

21 Caeiro and al-Saify 2009, 114–115.

The Women in the Questions

The questions reproduced in ECFR publications are in part very different from those on which Darsh's fatwas were based. They are often short, focusing on the norm to be clarified. The following two questions may serve as examples: "If a woman fell in love with a man, is she considered to have sinned?" and "Can a husband prevent his wife from attending Islamic women gatherings?" Just as often, however, there is no question, just a topic that is clarified through a resolution (*qarār*) based on studies presented by the members. The fatwas on *ʿaqd al-zawāj fil-kanīsa* (getting married in a church)[22] and *taʾjīr al-raḥm* (surrogate mothers)[23] are examples.

Few questions are as personal and intimate as those posed to Darsh. Here is one exception:

> I got married to a man who is twenty years older than I. Nevertheless, I would not have seen the difference in age as a barrier that separates me from him or turn[s] me away from him, had he shown a cheerful face and a good tongue and love. Alas, he has deprived me of the cheerful face, sweet word and the active emotion that makes woman feel her femininity and her place in the heart of her husband.
>
> He is not mean when it comes to my clothing and expenditure, nor does he hurt me. But this is not everything a woman needs from her husband. I do not think I mean anything to him other than as a chef or a unit of pleasure whenever he wills. This makes me feel bored and hate my life especially when I see my friends and peeresses whose husbands are filling their lives with love and euphoria.
>
> Once I complained to him against this treatment and he said: Do you think I do not fulfill my duties towards you? Am I mean regarding your expenditure and clothing?
>
> For husbands and wives to know I raise the following question: Are the financial needs in term of food, clothing and accommodation the only Islamic duties that the husband owes his wife? Is the psychological aspect valueless in the Islamic view? According to my limited knowledge and by nature I do not think so. Please elaborate on this issue since it dramatically affects the continuity and happiness of the Muslim family.[24]

22 *Al-Majalla al-ʿilmiyya* 3: 361.

23 *Al-Majalla al-ʿilmiyya* 3: 360.

24 *Al-Majalla al-ʿilmiyya* 8–9: 352–353.

The questions in this material are posed by both men, women, and boards of Islamic centres: women asking on their own behalf, men wishing to assist in matters involving their wives or daughters, and boards facing challenges, whether with regard to solemnizing marriage or women's access to the mosque. Often, the question is posed in the third person, and it is not clear whether the questioner is a man or a woman.

The Fatwas

Marriage

Most of the fatwas and resolutions are related to marriage. They are based on the concept of the "objectives of marriage" (*maqāṣid al-zawāj*). With reference to the Quran, marriage is described as a solemn or sacred covenant (*mithāqun ghalīẓa*).[25] As willed by God, marriage should be the framework for the realization of tranquility, mercy and love: "And among His Signs is this, that He created for you mates from among yourselves, that ye may dwell in tranquility with them, and He has put love and mercy between your (hearts) …"[26] This is not limited to physical relations, but finds concrete expression in norms and moral bounds regulating the relationship.[27]

According to Essam Tallema, marriage is the framework of acceptable sexual relations; it safeguards the offspring (*nasl*, known paternity); it promotes knowledge and religious practice; and it has financial aspects that advance the objectives of Sharia with regard to the family.[28] Yusuf al-Qaradawi, too, stresses the family in his theory of the objectives of Sharia. He considers the building of a healthy, well-functioning family (*usra ṣāliḥa*) a concretization of the fundamental intentions of Islam, along with building a healthy and functioning human being, society, and Muslim religious community (*umma*), and inviting to what is best for humanity (that is, performing *daʿwa*). Qaradawi defines these as *kulliyyāt*, the overall principles to be realized in human lives that the detailed norms are all about.[29]

These perspectives form the point of departure and the framework for the ECFR's fatwas and declarations on marriage-related topics. The *intention* be-

---

25 Quran 4:21. Telephone conversation with Essam Tallema, 18 Feb 2010.

26 Quran 30:21. Telephone conversation with Essam Tallema, 18 Feb 2010.

27 Lecture by Essam Tallema on *maqāṣid al-sharīʿa* at Det Islamske Forbundet, Oslo, Jan 2010.

28 On *maqāṣid al-sharīʿa*, see the Introduction and chapter 7.

29 Al-Qaradawi 2006, 27.

hind the marriage is crucial. If a woman contracts marriage intending to divorce, in order to return to a husband from whom she has been thrice divorced (a *taḥlīl* marriage), it is not considered valid. Marrying in order to acquire a residence permit, perhaps to divorce once it is available, is forbidden (*ḥarām*). There are two reasons: The intent is something else than marriage itself, and it implies a marriage for a limited term. An argument against marriage for a limited term is that it resembles *zawāj al-mutʿa* (temporary marriage in Shia Islam). A tradition is cited to the effect that the Prophet Muhammad banned such marriages "until the Day of Judgment".[30] The ideal is stressed: "Marriage in Islam implies continuity in the relationship, stability and settlement."[31] Various scenarios and variations over marriage and residence permits are discussed in detail. Even if the man and the woman agree on the arrangement, and the legal requirements are met in the form of a registered civil marriage, it breaks the law of the country concerned; in this case, it is claimed, the non-Islamic law accords with the objectives of Sharia. If the woman is not aware that the man's intent in proposing is to get a residence permit and, possibly, a divorce, the woman is deceived, and two of the most basic elements of marriage are violated: the man's proposal and the woman's acceptance. One may be careless when marrying for a residence permit, and Muslim women are warned against marrying non-Muslim men. Since this is prohibited in itself, pro forma marriages of this kind are all the more prohibied.

If a woman is married, in a non-registered, Islamically contracted marriage (*ʿurfī* marriage), she may not conclude a civil marriage contract with another man, even if her *ʿurfī* husband wishes it in order to help his friend get a residence permit.[32] The fatwa refers to the Quranic ban on marrying married women.[33] Such a marriage is invalid in Islam, and the witnesses have sinned, since they would know that the woman was already married. This kind of eagerness to help might stem from the misunderstanding that a marriage contract is only valid if made in a mosque or an Islamic centre. The marriage contract, however, is explained to be valid "... provided the pillars [*arkān*] and conditions [*shurūṭ*] are fulfilled".[34] Here, we see *ʿurfī* marriage placed on a par with a registered civil marriage, on certain conditions.

30 Muslim, hadith no. 1406.

31 ECFR 2002a, 57.

32 *Al-Majalla al-ʿilmiyya* 8–9: 355.

33 Quran 4:24. The text of the fatwa explains that *al-muḥṣanāt min al-nisā* here means "married women".

34 *Al-Majalla al-ʿilmiyya* 8–9: 355.

The equation of civil and Islamic marriages implies that civil marriage is enough, if it fulfills all the conditions. However, there is nothing to prevent such a marriage from being confirmed in an Islamic ceremony on the date stated in the civil marriage certificate.[35]

This equivalence is also central to a fatwa on marriage for pay.[36] A woman has contracted a marriage with a man for payment, and has not seen him since. Later, she has met a Muslim, and has married him in the Islamic way at an Islamic centre. She asks if this is permitted in Islam, but she will find the answer disappointing: No, it is not permitted; she and her first husband have sinned, even if the marriage is valid in its external aspects. The Islamic marriage is invalid, since she was a married woman, and the relationship should be broken off until the first marriage is dissolved by divorce. The fatwa ends with a reprimand for the leaders of Islamic centres: They should do their duty to God, and not marry anyone before they are sure that the woman is not already in a civil or Islamic marriage.

Nor does it help if the parties have agreed to divorce, unless the divorce is already a fact. A father asks on behalf of his daughter: She has been married by a shaykh to a second husband, and is living with him, without having received divorce papers from her first husband, with whom she had also contracted an Islamic marriage. The first husband has gone back to his home country with the intention of issuing her a divorce certificate, but according to the questioner, he has not sent anything. He asks what to do about their dilemma, and asks the ECFR to make it easy on them. The Council, however, does not open up for any easy solutions.[37] It states that the first marriage contract remains valid. The daughter and her new husband are therefore unlawful to one another, and if they continue to share a bed after this statement, they are performing *zinā* (extramarital intercourse). The woman must get a divorce, either from her husband or a judge. Thereafter, she may marry the other man—after the *ʿidda* (waiting period for re-marrying) is over.

The husband is obviously not similarly required not to be married when entering into a marriage. Polygamy is dealt with in a resolution (*qarār*) under the heading: "the allowance [*rukhṣa*] of marriage to four women and the abuse of this allowance".[38] The norm is stated with reference to the Quran: A man may

35 ECFR 2002a, 58.

36 *Al-Majalla al-ʿilmiyya* 8–9: 354.

37 *Al-Majalla al-ʿilmiyya* 8–9: 338.

38 ECFR 2002a, 132–135. The resolution is an abridged version of a fatwa from Yusuf al-Qaradawi published in *Fatāwa muʿāṣira*, 3:582.

marry up to four women if he is capable of being just and realizing full equality among them. The man must also be able to support the women and meet their sexual needs. The resolution goes on to reflect on this permission. Islam is a realistic religion, and is not based on idealistic notions that may prevent solutions to the problems of daily life. Perhaps a second marriage represents a solution if the first wife is infertile, or if she has long menstrual cycles that leave the husband's sexual needs unmet. If the first wife is ill, too, a second wife can be a support for her. Becoming a second wife can also be a solution for a widow, or a divorcée with children. The resolution says this can solve the problem of a surplus of good women over capable men, especially in the aftermath of war and similar situations. It also rebuts the criticism that this permission may be abused. This is not a reason to withdraw the permission, but to establish bounds and rules against its abuse.

I have devoted space to this resolution since the issue it raises is a sensitive one in Europe, and has come to symbolize Muslim women's lack of rights in European eyes. The ECFR's statutes charge it with issuing fatwas to meet the needs of Muslims in Europe and help them regulate communications with European authorities.[39] The so-called fatwa-collection affair in France in 2005, over the aborted publication of the translation of the ECFR's second fatwa collection, which also included the fatwa on polygamy, indicates that this fatwa was not perceived to further such an aim.[40]

The validity of a marriage also depends on whether it was voluntarily entered into.[41] The girl's parents or other representatives are obliged to consult her about her marriage. If she accepts, the contract is valid, if not, it is invalid. The ECFR states that it is impossible to achieve the noble aims of marriage as described in the Quran (30:21) if it is contracted by force. The fatwa refers to hadith that she may not be married without her permission, that her silence is her consent, and that the Prophet allowed a woman who had been married against her will to choose whether to remain married.

The question of whether a *wālī* (guardian) is required for the marriage contract to be valid is also the topic of a fatwa.[42] The ECFR stresses that the marriage contract is one of the most important contracts, and that the consent of the *wālī* is intended to safeguard the girl's rights and protect her against "ill-hearted and evil opportunists". The scholars differ, however, over whether the validity of the marriage contract depends on the guardian's consent. The

39 ECFR 2002a, 2.

40 On the fatwa-collection affair, see chapter 2.

41 *Al-Majalla al-ʿilmiyya* 7: 415.

42 ECFR 2002a, 128–132.

majority of the scholars think not, citing a hadith in their support, whereas the Hanafi school holds that this is not a condition as long as the woman is *bāligha ʿāqila* (has attained majority)[43] and all other conditions are met.[44] However, the guardian may ask a judge to annul the marriage if the husband is not her social equal.[45] This also implies that the *wālī* has no right whatsoever to refuse the woman permission to marry the man she wants, as long as he is suitable. The most "suitable," according to the ECFR, is a practising Muslim with good manners.[46] Daughters, however, are urged not to go against their guardians, who only wish what is best for them. Fathers, too, get a piece of advice: They should make it easy for their daughters to marry, and consult with them about their suitors, without abusing the right that Islam has given them. Islamic centres, too, have a responsibility: They should appoint a *wālī* if the woman lacks one.[47]

One question that is carefully discussed is marriage to a *kitābiya* (Jewish or Christian woman).[48] The norms are stated: A majority of the scholars accept it, with reference to the Quranic text that Muslim men may marry chaste women among the believers (5:5). The minority rejects it with reference to the same verse. The ECFR sides with the former view. The text goes on, however, to list a large number of reservations. One should be aware that not everyone born of Christian parents in Europe has faith. They might be communists, or belong to a religion that Islam does not recognize, such as the Bahaʾi faith. Moreover, it is important for the woman to be decent, have a good reputation, and have no history of extramarital affairs. It is also important not to marry a woman from a hostile people before one knows that she does not share their attitude. Nor should the marriage entail any negative consequences. If the consequences are of a general nature, so is the prohibition; if they are specific, the prohibition is restricted to these specific matters. The examples of possible harms are frightening: Marriage to non-Muslim women could induce good young Muslim women to make lesser demands on themselves to be chaste before marriage; it could lead to morally corrupted offspring; the woman might influence the

43 ECFR 2002b, 123.

44 The term *bulūgh* implies sexual maturity, and the concomitant obligation to perform religious duties. This is a minimal definition where marriage is concerned. In a European context, it might be defined as "majority", since it implies that one has the legal capacity to conclude contracts and agreements on one's own behalf.

45 On *kafāʾa*, see n. 56 in this chapter.

46 *Al-Majalla al-ʿilmiyya* 8–9: 364.

47 ECFR 2002a, 128–132.

48 *Al-Majalla al-ʿilmiyya* 7: 416.

husband, with dire consequences; and not least, there is the question how she "disposes over his body and what he leaves behind when he dies" (*wal-taṣarruf bi-badanihi wa-tarakathu baʿd al-mawtihi*).[49] In other words, the Council voices the concern that the woman might not have the husband buried according to Islamic ritual and his belongings correctly distributed in accordance with Islamic rules of inheritance.

A Muslim woman may not marry a non-Muslim man. This is confirmed by the Council in the resolution (*qarār*) on a woman converting to Islam when her husband does not. The text is long, and presents an *ijtihād* behind the discovery of the norm. With a long list of reservations, the wife is allowed to remain married.[50]

Before Marriage

If a woman falls in love, has she sinned? No, goes the answer, not if it does not lead to forbidden acts. The Quran says that God does not require more of a human being than one can bear, and a tradition says that God has forgiven the Muslim religious community for what they have hidden in their hearts, as long as it has not been acted on. But there is a stern piece of advice: "… a man and woman must not indulge in any acts which would cause such emotions to overcome their hearts, as this may lead to sinful acts being committed."[51]

What about a man and a woman who have had extramarital sex? This question is the subject of a resolution.[52] If the man and the woman wish to lead a pure life, and get married, there is consensus among the scholars that the marriage contract is valid. Concerning a woman who has had sex outside marriage, the question of *ʿidda* (the waiting period before she can marry) is discussed in detail. The ECFR joins the Hanafi school, the Shafiʿi school, and Sufyan al-Thawri (d. 778) in holding that no *ʿidda* is incumbent on her, even if she is pregnant, because the child will belong to the one she marries, not to the biological father. In any case, the spouses may not have any sexual relations until the child is born if the child is not his.

Pre-marital medical examinations form the subject of another resolution.[53] It is a matter of venereal and other communicable diseases as well as hereditary diseases. The Sharia *does not ban* medical examinations, including genetic

49 *Al-Majalla al-ʿilmiyya* 7: 417.

50 This resolution is analysed in chapter 5.

51 ECFR 2002a, 175.

52 ECFR 2002a, 135–137.

53 *Al-Majalla al-ʿilmiyya* 7: 413.

tests for treatments, as long as they are confidential. Nor does the Sharia prohibit one of the parties from requiring the other to get genetically tested before marriage, or both parties from agreeing to get medical examinations (other than genetic testing), on the condition of confidentiality. One must not conceal potentially fatal diseases, and if one does, one is liable to divine punishment. One has the right to dissolve the marriage contract if the other party has such diseases, which are detrimental to the objectives of marriage.

Getting Married; Weddings

The presence of witnesses is a minimal requirement for the validity of a marriage. A man says that he married a convert to Islam, without others present. He explains that he left his home country to meet her in a different country, but for legal reasons, they were not able to get married there. He had been told that they could marry themselves, with God as their witness—and so they did, without *wālī* or witnesses. No, states the Council:[54] This contract is not valid. The minimal requirement is two witnesses; opinions differ as to whether a *wālī* must be present. The Hanafi school is cited as not requiring a woman to have a *wālī* if she is of age (*bāligha*). The questioner is required to freeze the relationship until a correct marriage contract has been made, and both parties are required to pray for forgiveness for extramarital sex.

Social equality as a requirement for marriage (*kafāʾa*) is also the subject of a resolution (*qarār*).[55] The equal standing of the spouses will contribute to securing a harmonious and lasting marriage, without problems caused by cultural and social differences. The Council notes that the scholars worked out the criteria of *kafāʾa* based on the circumstances of their own time—i.e., new times and circumstances might make for different criteria. The Council further refers to an independent reasoning (*ijtihād*) to the effect that equality of conduct may substitute for social and racial equality—there is a consensus that piety is the supreme criterion where equality of standing is concerned.[56] Where Muslims in Europe are concerned, the Council stresses that both bride and groom

---

54 *Al-Majalla al-ʿilmiyya* 4–5: 475.

55 *Al-Majalla al-ʿilmiyya* 7: 413 and 8–9: 364.

56 In the entry on "*kafāʾa*" in *EI2* (Linant de Bellefonds 2010), two scholarly views are cited: "On the one hand that of the scholars of Medina, who reduced *kafāʾa* to almost nothing, simply forbidding a pious woman to marry a libertine, and on the other hand the tendency of the jurists of Kūfa, from which the exacting theory of the Ḥanafī school has arisen, according to which a husband is well-matched with his wife only if he is of the same lineage, the same social status, of the same seniority in Islam, and of the same morality." As we see, the Council here cleaves to a minimal definition of the concept.

should consider equality of standing before they marry. This will help build a solid family, one of the most important objectives in Islam.

Getting married in a church is not approved by the Sharia, and it is prohibited (*ḥarām*) if it includes rituals tied to the Christian faith, or requirements that the children be raised in any religion other than Islam. The marriage may however be valid if it fulfills the *arkān* and *shurūṭ*, fundamental elements and conditions. In any case, it should be renewed in a non-church setting to ensure that the marriage is made known among Muslims. Young Muslims are also advised not to accept church weddings for the sake of courtesy to the women they marry. It could expose them to demands as to how the children should be raised.

Within Marriage

To what extent are the spouses equal, and how are they to function as partners? This topic prompts a lengthy resolution (*qarār*).[57] The ECFR considers the wife to be equal to the man in the marital relationship, referring to the Quran, which uses the term *zawj* (partner) for a spouse. Together, they form a whole. Each of them is required to look after the interests and needs of the other, which is the sign of a true partner. The Council cites several Quranic verses,[58] stressing that they all point toward gender equality.

Then come the reservations: "However, this equality in principle, does not contradict the fact that there are duties and responsibilities unique and specific to each part of this relationship …"[59] The roles are distributed according to what the muftis consider the gender-based strengths of each party.

Qiwāma (guardianship), defined as the man's responsibility to protect and support his family after having paid the *mahr* and set up the household, is mentioned first. Women's strength lies in the emotional field, and she is responsible for looking after the home. The spouses are also required to promote good and forbid evil vis-à-vis one another. The husband should exercise his protection according to " what is appreciated and acknowledged by people of sound minds, good tastes and people of wisdom."[60] Consultation is recommended, but if the spouses disagree, the husband has the final say. The wife is required to obey the husband as long as he keeps within the bounds of *maʿrūf* ("what is known to be good," generally recognised).

---

57 ECFR 2002a, 137–143.

58 Quran 30:21, 16:72, 2:187.

59 ECFR 2002a, 138.

60 ECFR 2002a, 141.

The question of permission to leave the home and travel without a *maḥram* is directly related to the *qiwāma* of the husband and the wife's duty of obedience.[61] Based on *ʿurf* (custom), it is said that work, study or shopping require only a general permission. The husband, in turn, should inform his wife of his travels or overnight stays. The woman's right to travel without a *maḥram* is limited. The husband may not allow his wife to visit certain persons if he feels that it would have a bad influence on her, on the children, or on the marriage in general. However, the husband is advised not to abuse his authority to keep his wife from going out because he is suspicious. It would be wrong for the wife to feel her home turning into a prison, the Council states. The same applies if the woman the wife wants to visit is not a Muslim. Wives should be treated with *birr* (kindness) and *qisṭ* (fairness).

With reference to a tradition that a woman should not travel without a *maḥram*, different opinions are presented, with both positions focusing on the woman's safety. Some scholars think it is forbidden, while others think it is accepted if she travels accompanied by a group of reliable people. The ECFR states that a woman may travel alone if her safety is guaranteed, whether by plane, train or bus. If there is an overnight stay, however, she must have her *maḥram* with her, or stay with a Muslim family, lest she be exposed to temptations. The ECFR offers some advice in the resolution: Parents are urged to teach their daughters, and husbands to teach their wives, to follow the norm of God, in the certainty that they will follow it if only they are properly taught.

What does the husband's duty of maintenance entail?[62] He is to support his wife and meet her needs according to his ability. The rule is that she should have the same level of support as other women with the same status and in the same circumstances. This includes food, clothes, medicines, and everything to do with the home, including furniture and home appliances. If the husband is stingy, the wife is allowed to help herself to money in order to meet her own needs and those of the children in accordance with *maʿrūf*. If she is working outside the home, she should cover her own work-related expenses. If the husband is poor, the wife may take it upon herself to support the household, if she is able to do so. This is an act of generosity on her part, for which she will be thanked and praised—and will have her reward with God.

Material support is not enough, though.[63] Many husbands mistakenly believe they have fulfilled their duties by providing food, clothes, and shel-

61 ECFR 2002a, 186–188.

62 *Al-Majalla al-ʿilmiyya* 7: 417–418.

63 *Al-Majalla al-ʿilmiyya* 8–9: 339–342.

ter. She is also in need—indeed, in greater need—of a kind word, a winning smile, a gentle touch, a small kiss, tender care and flirtation, to ease the burdens of life and create happiness. The Council holds up the Prophet Muhammad as a role model in this regard, with reference to a text by Ibn Taymiyya.

One of the questions is whether Islam allows the husband to send all his money home to his relatives abroad, and let the wife support him and the family by paying the rent, food and drink, clothes and so on. The answer is: No, he is not allowed to do so.[64] A husband may not live off his wife. How could he then be her guardian and the master of the household? The ECFR takes a clear stance: "We [...] dislike for a Muslim man to live in dependency upon his wife, even if she consented to that, particularly if he was able to bring an income."[65] The wife is not in any way obliged to spend her money on household expenses. If she does so, it is only out of goodwill, and it must not be due to emotional blackmailing. The woman is free to do with her money as she likes, with no restrictions of any kind, and may open a bank account in her own name.[66] The husband has no right to demand that the wife deposit her money in his account, or in a joint account for the upkeep of the household. The responsibility to provide is the husband's alone. The ECFR supports the view that a man and a woman should each have a separate account. Women are not least urged to save up for bad times and for the "behaviour swings" of husbands. Everyone is entitled to his or her property.

But marriage and family life has its challenges. Is a wife obliged to wait on her husband's guests if she is ill? The answer offers a broad introduction to the ECFR's view on the division of roles in the family.[67] When the woman is not obliged to wait on her own husband, goes the answer, how could she be obliged to wait on his guests? The woman is obliged to look after her husband and children, and thus fulfill the conditions for a good partnership, and attain equality in responsibilities and rights, as God has prescribed. The husband, in his turn, should work outside the home. If the wife works outside the home, it is only fair for her husband to help her, especially if they have children to look after. Back to illness and guests: Islam considers illness to excuse one from a number of duties, such as fasting in Ramadan. The Council also points out that e.g. an Arab Muslim married to a Western woman must take into account that she might not be used to receiving guests in the manner to which her husband's

---

64 *Al-Majalla al-ʿilmiyya* 1: 292; ECFR 2002a, 71–73.

65 ECFR 2002a, 72.

66 ECFR 2002a, 73–75.

67 ECFR 2002a, 66–68.

culture is accustomed. She in her turn should take the husband's upbringing and culture into account, and appreciate that taking good care of guests is customary in Islam. This is directly tied to faith.[68]

How should a wife behave with regard to problems that stem from cultural differences between her and her husband? The question is a specific one, but the answer is general.[69] Marriage, it is recalled, is a sacred tie, and the parties have to cooperate to bring about happiness and harmony. Each must show indulgence, patience, and tolerance for the disagreements that will always arise. They should not be governed by their feelings: "It is important that they both understand that emotions must never rule their marriage and that their life together must be governed by good behaviour and beautiful mannerisms."[70] They should seek to meet each other halfway. The Council recalls that there are no magic solutions to marital problems, which can only be solved through mutual understanding, kindness and patience, and through seeking support from God.

If domestic troubles become too serious for the parties to solve on their own, the Muslim community must intervene and arbitrate. In the case of Muslims living in a non-Muslim Western country, it is up to the Muslim community in each area to set up an arbitration council.[71] Such a council may consist of three trusted Muslims, one of whom should be knowledgeable in Islamic jurisprudence. The council may play an important role by solving problems and reconciling spouses in conflict.

Sometimes, the problems are of an emotional nature. One man wonders what to do: He has heard that his wife was in love with another man at her workplace before they got married.[72] The wife swears that it isn't true, but the man in question claims that she was running after him. The answer is that he is obliged to give her the benefit of the doubt if there is no evidence. The husband must stop listening to the man making such accusations. The Quran requires witnesses. The wife, however, is advised to find a new place to work, to avoid running into the man who is the cause of the conflict, and restore trust between herself and her husband.

What about domestic violence?[73] In one resolution, the Council defines violence as doing physical or mental harm to the other. The man may do violence

68 ECFR 2002a, 68.

69 ECFR 2002a, 75–77.

70 ECFR 2002a, 76.

71 ECFR 2002a, 79.

72 *Al-Majalla al-ʿilmiyya* 6: 268–269.

73 *Al-Majalla al-ʿilmiyya* 7: 418–420.

to his wife, parents to children, or the other way around; this includes physical violence, sexual violence, verbal violence, including threats, and worst of all, so-called honour killings. Violence may stem from a wrong understanding of religion, from a faulty upbringing and from growing up with violence, from the lack of a culture of dialogue and consultation within the family, and from poor living conditions, such as poverty and unemployment. Violence in the family may leave dangerous traces on spouses, children, and the rest of society. The Council declares violence in all its forms to be prohibited by the Sharia, pointing to a number of texts that ban injustice and harm of any kind. It is all the more so within the family, which should be based on goodness, tranquility and love. On these grounds, the Council recommends strengthening religious awareness and education that promotes a culture of dialogue and consultation in the family; being careful with one's choice of marriage partner; giving advice and guidance to show the dangers of injustice, beatings, swearwords and demeaning talk; and seeking help from two mediators to stop the violence and find a solution. If one of the spouses crosses the line, and the measures listed do not help, divorce is the last resort. The Muslim minority is advised to follow the example of the Prophet and refrain from violent methods in the family. Family violence may also have serious legal consequences.

Sexuality and Reproduction

May a man be present when his wife gives birth?[74] The answer is that it is permitted if he so wishes and believes it may help her. It may cause him to better appreciate both her and his own mother, who bore him in pain. Some may feel ill at ease because they see the private parts of the wife as she gives birth, and may claim that this is deprecated or in the worst case forbidden. The Council rejects this view, citing a hadith where the Prophet and A'isha, one of his wives, took a bath together after having sexual intercourse.

Giving birth can be exhausting, and one question answered in fatwa is whether the woman is entitled to rest in the postpartum period, or whether she is obliged to take care of guests coming to greet and congratulate her.[75] In this period, the Council declares, she is bleeding and is exempt from prayer and fasting. It is natural to let her rest, relieved of all duties and responsibilities that might entail unnecessary stress. In Muslim countries, the tradition is that a woman who has given birth is looked after until she has regained her

74 ECFR 2002a, 60–61.

75 ECFR 2002a, 64–66.

health. When the woman lives in a foreign country, on the other hand, she is in a situation where she has to take responsibility for the home and children. Therefore, guests should not expect more than the woman can stand. The Council concludes with a reminder that this is a matter of etiquette and good manners.

But not all pregnancies end with childbirth. It is probably a husband who writes the Council to ask how much he should pay for an unborn child who was aborted before 120 days of pregnancy had passed.[76] The woman who had the abortion thought she would not be able to combine her life as a student of medicine with being a mother of small children. Having an abortion is forbidden, no matter at what point in the pregnancy, says the Council. However, the gravity of the sin increases with the progress of the pregnancy. From the fetus is 120 days old, abortion is entirely forbidden and considered a form of murder, and one is obliged to pay *diya* ("blood money," compensation for killing or physical harm) worth 213 grammes of gold to heirs not party to the abortion. In the matter at hand, the abortion was carried out before the fetus had reached 120 days, and compensation is therefore not required. However, declares the Council, this is a sin for which one must seek forgiveness, and it is not to be repeated.

On the other hand, contraception e.g. by means of pills is permitted in order to temporarily prevent pregnancy. Sterilization is forbidden, save on grounds of medical necessity.[77]

What if one cannot get pregnant the natural way? The medical technology of our time creates new opportunities and poses new questions, large and small, for the scholars. One central principle in the answers is that progeny is tied to married biological parents. The Council declares surrogacy prohibited, whether it is for free or for pay, because it involves having the embryo of strangers implanted in the womb.[78] This creates uncertainty as to the lineage of the child, one of the five vital necessities (*ḍarūriyyāt*) to be protected. The Quran is cited: "… None can be their mothers except those who gave them birth …" (58:2). In this case, the embryo has nothing to do either with the surrogate mother or her husband. Even if the woman is poor, and does it for financial reasons, she should find a legal way to earn her *rizq* (livelihood). The exhortation quotes the Quran: "… And if ye fear poverty, soon will Allah enrich you, if He wills, out of His bounty …" (9:28)

76 ECFR 2002a, 63–64.

77 *Al-Majalla al-ʿilmiyya* 3: 361.

78 *Al-Majalla al-ʿilmiyya* 3: 360.

A somewhat less dramatic variation on the theme is a question on the use of frozen embryos.[79] A married couple temporarily residing in the UK had difficulties having children, and started the process of artificial fertilization. When the woman came to have some of the embryos implanted, it was discovered that she had become pregnant the natural way. The embryos were therefore not used, and were kept frozen. The question is: What should the lady do with these embryos? The Council answers that she may have them implanted as long as she is married to the husband, that is, as long as the marriage is not dissolved either by divorce or death. If she leaves the country and is certain that she will not return, it would be forbidden not to destroy them. In any case, the Council finds no impediment to destroying them. The answer is left open, and the responsibility is left to the woman concerned.

Divorce

The Council has concerned itself with supporting the objectives of marriage and protecting the family. How should divorce be prevented? In one resolution, a number of measures are listed.[80] All people should grow stronger in faith and piety and make sure not to treat each other injustly, should have patience with the qualities one dislikes in others, and treat each other with dignity and respect. Furthermore, one should choose one's partner with care, and lay the foundations for a relationship where the Sharia will be followed. A culture of dialogue and consultation should be developed to solve problems that might arise. Each party should endeavour to satisfy the other. Telling each other nice things that might not be entirely true is not considered lying. If problems arise, one should use all means to find a solution, including persons who can mediate between the parties.

Still, one may be considering divorce not long after getting married. Can a newly-wed man get divorced if he discovers that his wife has lost her hymen, but the wife swears that she has lost it in some other way than by sexual intercourse?[81] Divorce is the most odious to God of all that is permitted, goes the answer, and it is wrong for a Muslim to resort to such a solution for the slightest reason. A divorce will break the woman's heart and destroy a whole family. It will also harm the woman and her reputation. If the wife swears it, the husband must believe her. The burden of evidence in this case lies on the husband. In the case at hand he has no evidence, however, so the wife must be believed.

---

79 ECFR 2002a, 127–128.

80 *Al-Majalla al-ʿilmiyya* 7: 420–421.

81 ECFR 2002a, 58–59.

In any case, the Council states, Islam is based on trust and goodwill. Being suspicious is truly a sin. If it is the case that the wife has had sex before marriage, but has repented, God will have forgiven her, and it is as if she had not sinned. The moral lesson drawn is that it is incumbent on us to adopt the attributes of God and forgive those who err.

What options does the woman have for getting a divorce?[82] In a resolution, the Council states that Islam has given the man the right to unilateral repudiation (*ṭalāq*). The woman, too, may have this right, if she has had it written into the marriage contract. She may also request a divorce from a judge, who for his part should do everything in his power to reconcile the spouses. If this is not possible, he should grant her *khulʿ* (wife-initiated divorce against compensation). The wife may also agree with the husband that they should get divorced if it does not conflict with Islamic principles. In case the husband has caused her harm, the woman may ask a judge to divorce her from her husband (*tafrīq*). The judge may grant her request if she can prove her accusations against her husband, but only after having done everything to reconcile them, which includes getting two mediators to assist.

In questions of divorce, no topic is too narrow or too wide. What is the norm when a woman asks to be divorced from her husband because he has strayed from the right path?[83] The Council begins its argument with the tradition of the Prophet that a wife who asks her husband for divorce without a valid reason shall never know the taste of Paradise. Conversely: if she has a valid reason, her request for divorce is acceptable. On this premise, the question is rephrased: Does the dissolute behaviour of the husband constitute a valid reason to ask for divorce? A number of scenarios are listed. If a man forces his wife to take part in something sinful, such as serving him alcohol, she has the right to request a divorce to avoid doing something forbidden and incurring divine punishment. There is also a right to divorce in case of physical abuse. But sinning husbands who neither force their wives to participate, nor abuse them, are a different matter, the Council says. A husband's drinking, for example, or his failure to perform the ritual prayers out of laziness, is not sufficient grounds for granting his wife a divorce. To the contrary, if the wife hopes that he will repent, and that she can play a role in improving him, she should be tolerant, particularly if there are children involved. This does not apply, however, if the husband holds that drinking alcohol is *permitted* or that he is not *required* to pray.

82 ECFR 2002a, 144.
83 ECFR 2002a, 146–148.

It is frequently asked whether a husband's *ṭalāq* is valid.[84] Two related questions are the subject of ECFR fatwas.[85] The first concerns conditional *ṭalāq*: "If you do so and so, you are divorced." The Council states that intent is crucial. If the *ṭalāq* is pronounced with the intent to divorce, it is valid. If the conditions are made in order to make the wife do certain things, the divorce is not valid. A *ṭalāq* prounounced while intoxicated is not valid. Rage, however, does not detract from its validity.

The other question concerns the triple pronunciation of *ṭalāq* at once. The Council notes that the four schools of law all consider it an irrevocable divorce, but joins the opinion of Ibn Taymiyya that it is considered a single divorce.[86]

The woman may ask for divorce against compensation (*khulʿ*). A Council resolution concludes that this is legitimate in Islam, except if the husband is tormenting the wife into giving up her bride-gift in whole or in part. *Khulʿ* is valid if the parties reach agreement. No judge is required. It is not particularly important whether it should be considered divorce or annulment of the marriage. A new marriage contract, with a bride-gift for the woman, is a condition if they are to cohabit again. If the wife has "harm inflicted upon her," as the Council puts it, she also has the option of asking a judge for a divorce.[87] What about a written divorce certificate?[88] The Council sides with Ibn Hazm (d. 1064), who held that divorce must be witnessed in writing. It also urges Muslims to obtain such certificates, be it from the embassies and consulates of Muslim countries, or from Western public authorities.

Religious norms and national legislations encounter each other in the topic of divorce issued by a non-Muslim judge. The Council states that a Muslim should bring his case before a Muslim judge. In a non-Muslim country without an Islamic judicial system, however, a Muslim who has married according to the laws of the land should abide by the decision of a non-Muslim judge with regard to divorce. Since he accepted the laws governing the marriage contract, he has also implicitly accepted the consequences, e.g. that only a judge

84 Conversations with Council members; my own experience and observations made when present at answer-giving.

85 *Al-Majalla al-ʿilmiyya* 6: 269–270.

86 In Islamic jurisprudence there are two types of divorce, revocable (*rajʿī*) og irrevocable (*bāʾin*). One may divorce revocably twice. The third time, the divorce is irrevocable, and the parties cannot remarry except if the woman has been married to another man in the interim.

87 ECFR 2002a, 144.

88 *Al-Majalla al-ʿilmiyya* 8–9: 362–363.

may dissolve the marriage. This case, the Council says, may be compared with a husband delegating his power of *ṭalāq* to a judge, even if he does so implicitly, which is accepted by the majority of the scholars. The underlying legal principle is that what is considered accepted according to custom counts as a condition (*al-maʿrūf ʿurfan kal-mashrūṭ sharṭan*) for the contract. A non-Muslim judge is also accepted based on the principle of promoting general utility and preventing chaos. If the divorce is granted by public authorities in a Western country, the woman must wait to get married again until she is divorced according to the laws of the country, even if her *ʿidda* period is over.[89]

If there are children in the marriage, the question of custody comes up, and the Council has a relevant resolution.[90] Daily custody is defined as looking after the child in the home and outside it, and includes food, clothing and hygiene. Custody shall be awarded to the person best suited for it, most often the mother—as long as she does not remarry. The person awarded custody has to be able to fulfill the duties entailed, though. The child should not be moved from the mother's residence, as mothers and children should not be separated. The father may not wait long after the mother has remarried before he requests custody, since by allowing a long time to pass, he gives the impression of accepting that the child remains with the remarried mother. It is forbidden to prevent a parent from visiting his or her child. The parents should work out between themselves an agreement on visitation, according to the custom (*ʿurf*) where they live. There is a clear focus on the best interests of the child. The Council makes it clear, however, that it has not exhausted the topic. Other issues tied to custody and custody rights were put on hold pending further study and information gathering on the practice in European countries. As with divorce, custody is regulated by European national legislations, and the ECFR's prescriptions raise questions of legal pluralism.

Social Relations

The regulation of gender relations is also the main topic of the fatwas and resolutions the Council has given in the category of social relations. It is natural for men and women to meet and cooperate, and it cannot be prevented. The Council stresses that the following rules apply in shared arenas:[91] Men and women must not be alone together, they must avoid physical contact that could pro-

89 ECFR 2002a, 145.

90 *Al-Majalla al-ʿilmiyya* 8–9: 361–362.

91 ECFR 2002a, 184–186.

voke lust, and they must avoid revealing parts of the body that are to be covered. The woman must not talk or behave in a way that arouses male desires. Both men and women, however, are responsible for following the rules.

The gendered organization of space also applies to weddings.[92] The Council holds that the Sharia does not ban men and women from being in the same place, on the same three conditions mentioned above. They elaborate on the third point: Women should not let anything show that ought to be covered, should not use perfume or gold, or move in a way that attracts attention. There is a caveat: "However, we see that people often do not abide by these conditions in weddings, and thus the presence of men and women in one place becomes unlawful."[93]

Another question raises the issue that many Muslim women are not allowed to talk to other men, while their husbands permit themselves to talk to other women. Is there a double standard in communications between men and women? What is the norm, then?[94] In some countries, says the Council, women are so strictly treated that they are like prisoners in their own home until death sets them free. Communication between men and women is permitted, but it should be honourable and reasonable, and limited to what is necessary. Shyness is stressed as a beautiful quality for both sexes, but especially for women, as it suits their feminine nature, which does not let them start conversations with male strangers.

Cyberspace offers new opportunities for communication among men and women. What norms apply to chatting with potential marriage partners?[95] The woman should wear the hijab if she can be seen. The conversation must further be decent, and should be restricted to marriage, not deteriorate into pure entertainment, goes the answer.

Several fatwas and declarations deal with the (un)covering of women. What should a female recent convert do if it is difficult to cover her hair?[96] Citing the Quran (24:31), the Council stresses that covering her hair is a duty laid down by God Himself that she may distinguish herself from non-Muslim women. She should keep company with other Muslim sisters who can help and support her. Still, the Council recalls that *khimar*, covering the hair, or hijab—whatever one chooses to call it—is one of the branches of religion, not one of its roots (that is, it is secondary to fundamental religious matters). If being forced to use the

92 ECFR 2002a, 91–92.
93 ECFR 2002a, 92.
94 ECFR 2002a, 92–94.
95 *Al-Majalla al-ʿilmiyya* 12–13: 33–34.
96 ECFR 2002a, 34–36.

hijab could lead one to leave Islam, it is wrong. The Council describes it in terms of abandoning a fundamental principle for the sake of a secondary one. The fiqh of balances (*fiqh al-muwāzanāt*) is invoked.[97] But the Council exhorts her sisters to keep trying to get her on the right path.

In December 2003, the Council issued a fatwa about hijab on IslamOnline.net. Here, not only the duty but also the *right* to bear the hijab is stressed.[98] The background was a French bill banning religious symbols in schools, which was meant to enter into force from the start of the school year in 2004.[99] It is argued that wearing the hijab is part of women's freedom of religion and personal liberty, as guaranteed in modern constitutions, international agreements, and the Universal Declaration of Human Rights. The fatwa also addresses France: "We call upon France, which takes pride in being the mother country of freedom, to respect Muslims' beliefs and feelings all over the world and to accept the religious and cultural variety in its society." In 2004, the Council dealt with the hijab topic again, "… because of the ramifications of the tendency of the French government to prohibit so-called 'religious symbols' that touch the women in France."[100] The head of the Council, Yusuf al-Qaradawi, gave a speech describing the French bill as one of the most important and surprising topics that had arisen over the past year. The Council's statement announced the establishment of a committee for further dialogue on the issue, headed by Council member and former Mauritanian minister of justice Abdullah bin Bayyah.[101]

But covering oneself is not only about wearing the hijab. What should a Muslim woman cover up in the swimming pool with non-Muslim women?[102] Nothing prevents women from swimming in a pool together with non-Muslim women—as long as only women are present. The area that must be covered, from the belly button to the knee, according to the four schools of law, is the

---

97 Tariq Ramadan describes *fiqh al-muwāzanāt* as follows in the book *Western Muslims and the Future of Islam*: "[It] relies on studying and weighing the options on the basis of their faithfulness to the sources, their adaptability to the situation, and so on." (Ramadan 2004, 161)

98 IslamOnline.net. The page is now defunct, but is archived at http://web.archive.org/web/20100105081146/http://www.islamonline.net/servlet/Satellite?pagename=IslamOnline-English-Ask_Scholar/FatwaE/FatwaE&cid=1119503547428, (accessed 5 Jan 2010).

99 Tucker 2008, 206.

100 Resolution 12/1, 5 Jan 2004 (previously accessible at http://www.e-cfr.org/en/index.php?ArticleID=291, now defunct; hard copy on file with author).

101 Resolution 12/1, 5 Jan 2004.

102 ECFR 2002a, 176.

same as vis-à-vis Muslim women. The Council takes the opportunity to encourage good Muslim sisters to introduce the noble values and ethics of Islam to the non-Muslim women.

The principle of covering oneself is not only about clothing, but also about movement. May women take part in children's games that include dance moves? Yes, is the answer, as long as it does not arouse lust and desire, especially if men are present.[103]

All these rules, however, do not prevent the woman from participating in activities and work outside the home (*ʿamal ʿām*). This is not only a liberty, but sometimes even a duty, e.g. when it comes to establishing and directing Islamic centres and humanitarian organizations, which play a role in improving the social status of Muslims, and not least of women. Women may also stand for political office. In all of this, Islamic ethical rules must be followed.[104]

Social relations are not all about gender, but also about relations with non-Muslim relatives, an issue for many converts to Islam in Western Europe. May a husband deny his wife a visit to her non-Muslim parents?[105] The answer is no. A husband must never keep his wife from visiting her parents. On the contrary, he should encourage her to visit them, come along with her, and invite them to his home. This is required behaviour towards relatives. Islam recognizes two kinds of natural relationships, by blood and by marriage. The husband is therefore exhorted to strengthen ties with his in-laws, and do his best for them, not least by trying to bring them to Islam. The Council describes this as promoting good and preventing evil, which results in a reward with God.

Inheritance

Very few questions deal with inheritance. This contrasts with a collection of Muhammad Abduh's fatwas, where questions of inheritance are a major topic.[106] The Council has answered two such questions. The first is a hypothet-

103 ECFR 2002a, 96.

104 ECFR 2002a, 108–109.

105 ECFR 2002a, 81–84.

106 In the edition of Muhammad Abduh's fatwas published at the centennial anniversary of his death (Jumʿa 2005), 53 out of 191 questions dealt with inheritance-related matters. The observation that the topic of inheritance is rarely raised in Europe today was confirmed by Zaki Badawi, the then head of the British Muslim Law (Shariah) Council, in my conversation with him at the Muslim College in London. Jørgen Nielsen, too, refers to Badawi, who in 1975 developed a form that could be used as a testament for Muslims who wished to distribute the inheritance according to Islamic rules. His offer met with no response, a fact Nielsen ascribed to the age of the Muslims. They were still young, so

ical: If a mother dies, is everything she has gathered in life considered hers, including presents she has received, even if they are not registered as hers? Yes, says the answer, this is considered her property to be distributed among the heirs.[107]

But what happens to the mother's estate if she has deposited parts of it in an interest-bearing bank account, given that interest is forbidden, asks one of seven sisters whose mother recently died. The interest accrued on the deposit becomes *ḥalāl*, because there is a change of ownership. The Council here refers to the principle that the responsibility for a violation of the prohibition does not attach to the object of a transfer of ownership if the object transferred is not forbidden in itself to begin with, unlike e.g. alcohol. Thereafter, however, the money must be withdrawn from the interest-bearing account if it is not to be *ḥarām*. However, the questioner is encouraged to donate the accrued interest to the poor. The lady further asks whether maternal uncles have a right to inherit her mother. The answer is yes; the sisters (i.e., the daughters of the deceased) have a claim to two thirds of the inheritance, and their uncles to one third.[108]

ʿIbādāt

Only two of the questions fall under *ʿibādāt* (ritual acts). One asks whether a husband can ban his wife from attending women's meetings in the mosque.[109] The problem, declares the Council, is that many Muslim men aggressively present their own whims and personal opinions as if they were Islam itself. This goes for many men's view of women, too. They look down on women and think they were created merely to serve the husband and satisfy his sexual needs. It is unfortunate that many such men are highly educated and still have made no progress in this area. The Prophet is cited as saying that women may not be denied access to the mosque, as in the Prophet's time, the mosque was the only place for women to learn and increase their knowledge of Islam, as well as to take part in the congregational prayer and Friday prayer and to get to know good Muslim sisters. These are mandatory activities for both women and men. However, the Council clarifies that they must not be at the expense of the rights of the husband and the children. The husband, in his turn, must not abuse his authority.

matters of death and inheritance were probably not considered pressing (Nielsen 1999, 81).

107 ECFR 2002a, 126.

108 *Al-Majalla al-ʿilmiyya* 6: 271–272.

109 ECFR 2002a, 68–71.

Men running mosques and Islamic centres may not deny women entry to the mosque, either. This is stated in a fatwa to a group of women from Århus, Denmark, who face resistance to setting up facilities for women to participate in the *tarāwīḥ* prayer (the prayer of "rest" prayed each night in the month of Ramadan). The question describes the attitudes of the men in the mosque: "Some brothers protested, arguing that we should not burden ourselves with this responsibility as women are not commanded to pray in the mosque and their prayer at home is better."[110] The Council's fatwa stresses that women in Europe need to replenish their spirituality and knowledge, and that they play an important role in the Muslim community. The mosque is the only place for this, and the month of Ramadan is a good opportunity.

Characterizing the Fatwas

The fatwas are given under two designations, *fatwā* and *qarār* (resolution). The fatwas state and elaborate on a norm, and give guidance on right practice. The norm is often stated in the beginning of the text. Next, it is discussed and explained, and justified with the references on which it is based. Then follows an answer to the question posed. Ethical guidance is given at the end. The question on paying compensation (*diya*) after abortion may serve as an example. "Indeed, abortion is forbidden in Islam whether it be in the earlier stage of the pregnancy or otherwise."[111] The elaboration follows: "The extent of sin incurred varies according to the stage of pregnancy ..."[112] Next, terms are defined, and the norms of compensation and the cases in which abortion might be permitted are presented. This reflection is then adapted to the case at hand, and advice is given on how to act:

> However, it remains a sin which one should ask forgiveness for and promise never to commit again. If the mother wishes to give in charity besides all this, then it is even better. Allah, Most High, says in the Holy Qur'an: Verily, the good deeds omit the bad deeds ...[113]

110 *Al-Majalla al-ʿilmiyya* 10–11: 327.

111 ECFR 2002a, 63.

112 ECFR 2002a, 63.

113 ECFR 2002a, 64. The reference is to the Quran 11:114.

Resolutions take a different form. They begin with a more or less fixed formula:[114] *Istiʿaraḍ al-majlis mawḍūʿ* [topic] *wal-abḥāth allatī tanāwalahu, wa baʿd al-mudāwala wal-naẓar qarara mā yalī* ("The Council has considered [topic] and the studies dealing with this [topic], and after discussion and consideration, has decided as follows ...").[115] The text that follows often begins with a definition of the topic. There follow descriptions of causes, consequences, and ethical ideals. The resolution concludes with the giving of advice. The resolution on violence in the family and advice on help (*al-ʿunf al-usarī wa-ʿilājuhu*), for example, follows this pattern.

The language of the fatwas and resolutions is impersonal and formal. They are often given in the third person, and the text is patently a result of discussions among the members. The formal tone may be natural since the fatwas and resolutions are public and meant for publication. The language is also solemn, and characterized by theological formulae such as *Allah taʿalā* (God, the Exalted)[116] and *taqwa Allāh fil-sirr wal-ʿalin* (fear of God in private and public).[117] The stated norms are often followed by conditions, as in the following examples concerning marriage and the validity of the marriage contract: "... her marriage would be correct provided that all other conditions are fulfilled";[118] "... the marriage contract is valid provided the pillars and conditions are fulfilled";[119] and "... any obedience must be within the boundaries of Maʿrūf."[120] These conditions are not concretized, however, and precise knowledge is needed to make out their full meaning. The fatwa may thus appear to address people with knowledge of *fiqh* rather than ordinary lay Muslims.

There may also be other reasons for the lack of clarification. When the Council discusses marriageability, for instance, it makes do with the terms *bāligha* ("mature") and *bāligha ʿāqila* ("mature and of sound mind") without specifying the age of the girl. One might speculate about a link with the Council's ambition to be an authority to Muslims in Europe, who belong to different schools of law and hail from countries with different family codes, and hence have different views on when a girl is ripe for marriage. The age of majority, too, varies from

---

114 Except those fatwas that are also described as resolutions. See e.g. http://www.e-cfr.org/ar/index.php?ArticleID=241 and ECFR 2002a, 128, where the issue is whether the woman may conclude a marriage contract without a *wālī* (guardian).

115 One example is in *Al-Majalla al-ʿilmiyya* 7: 418.

116 *Al-Majalla al-ʿilmiyya* 3: 361.

117 *Al-Majalla al-ʿilmiyya* 8–9: 330.

118 ECFR 2002a, 131.

119 *Al-Majalla al-ʿilmiyya* 8–9: 355.

120 ECFR 2002a, 143.

country to country in Europe. The Council would seem to have taken strategic considerations into account as a transnational body.

A lack of precision is also found in the translations of the fatwas and resolutions. In the case of marriage to a Christian or Jewish woman, the fatwa ends with a literal translation of "*wal-taṣarruf bi-badanihi wa-tarakathu baʿd al-mawtihi*": "Muslim husband may [...] being affected by his wife's non-Islamic way, and after death in terms of issues relating to corpse and inheritance." The translation does not convey the content clearly.

As described above, the legitimacy of the Council is tied to its function in the European context. It is noteworthy, however, that many of the fatwas could have been given anywhere, e.g. those on inheritance, violence in the family, mixed weddings and premarital health checks. Do they, then, play any role with regard to the challenges Muslims face in Europe? One might think that all answers and resolutions ought to relate to the new context, and that timeless questions do not belong to the Council's field of work. Perhaps the anthropologist Hussein Ali Agrama's observation on the authority of fatwas may suggest an answer: "[... T]he vitality and authority of the fatwa lies not in its reforming of doctrine to fit novel circumstances but, instead, in the way it connects and advances the self to and within the practices and goals that constitute Islamic tradition more broadly."[121] In other words, it is not just about deriving relevant norms, but also about creating a sense of belonging to the tradition.[122]

View of Women and Gender Relations

Despite half of all fatwas and *qarārāt* (resolutions) being marriage-related, another issue entirely predominates: the upholding of sexual morality and the organization of gender relations. Sexual relations are to be restricted to marriage as their only acceptable framework. This is linked to the protection of progeny (*nasl*), one of the five *ḍarūriyyāt* (vital needs). This principle is taken to its ultimate conclusion in the resolution on surrogate mothers.

Sexual relations outside marriage are considered a sin, and the fatwas and *qarārāt* present a number of options. A couple who have had extramarital sex should get married—opinions differ, however, on whether they must first do *tawba* (repent and do penance). In the case of the woman without an intact hymen, it is stated that God has forgiven her if she has asked for forgiveness.

121 Agrama 2010, 10.

122 On the authority of the fatwa, see chapter 5.

One fatwa expresses concern over the impact on the morality of Muslim girls if it becomes a widespread practice to marry Jewish or Christian women, who are considered to have less strict norms on premarital chastity. In the fatwa on whether falling in love is a sin, it is once again stressed that a man and a woman must not indulge in acts that will rouse passions and might lead to sin. In the fatwas on men and women together in the workplace and on mixed weddings, conditions for avoiding temptation are listed: A man may not be alone with a woman, women should be covered and should not move in such a way as to attract attention, and they should not come into physical contact with one another. Since people often disregard these rules at mixed weddings, the latter are considered forbidden. A woman accused of having wanted to marry a disreputable co-worker, rather than the man she has since married, is urged to change her workplace in order to restore confidence between the spouses.

Communications between men and women should be restricted to necessary discussions of matters at hand. Shyness is a nice quality in both sexes, but it is better suited to the woman, on account of her feminine character. Chatting on the Internet is not exempt from the rules. Chats should be kept decent and should not degenerate into mere entertainment.

Important rules for upholding sexual morality are tied to the female body. A righteous and moral woman covers herself and uses the hijab. She does not move in a way that excites strong feelings in men. She has the liberty to work outside the home, as long as she follows the ethical rules of Islam. The rules for the organization of communications and mixing between the sexes evidently apply to both sexes, but the woman has an additional responsibility for maintaining the moral order.

This accords with findings from historian Judith Tucker's studies on the organization of men and women in gendered space in historical perspective. "We do see some convergence in the tendency of the jurists to discuss these issues more in relation to women than men. Even though sexual desire affected both sexes, the burden of minimizing sexual contact fell on women and on controlling their bodies."[123] Tucker adds that in historical perspective, ideas of gendering of space, dress requirements, and the gravity of sexual transgressions were developed on the margins of the legal discourse, and that judges and courts do not seem to have been particularly active in their enforcement. Things have changed considerably from the 1970s on, however, and today it is a central topic, tied to Islamic identity. This, Tucker says, is a modern phenomenon. "At present, most discussions of Islamic law, women, and gender gravitate toward a set of

123 Tucker 2008, 215.

issues assumed to lie at the heart of gendered Islamic discourse: gender segregation and/or female seclusion and veiling, and strict rules and sanctions for sexual behavior are the hot topics of the day ..."[124] My own findings demonstrate the same trend described by Tucker. The hijab is dealt with as a subject of fatwas and resolutions, and is described as both a duty and a right. Interestingly, however, the situation in France prompted a resolution that described the use of hijab as secondary to fundamental Islamic principles.

Marriage is *the* arena for intimacy and expressions of sexuality. This view is mirroried in legal discussions of the classical age, Tucker says. She points to how the jurists stressed different aspects of sexual relations. For instance, the Maliki jurist Khalil ibn Ishaq (d. 1374) focused on the husband's enjoyment of his wife's body, and al-Marghinani (d. 1197), the author of *al-Hidāya* (one of the principal works of the Hanafi school), defined marriage as the establishment of ownership rights to sexual pleasure with a person. In the fatwas and *qarārāt* of the ECFR, however, the intimate aspect is highlighted only in one case—with reference to a tradition about how the Prophet and A'isha, one of his wives, took a bath together.

The Council stresses the equality of male and female in a resolution on sex education and gender equality. The resolution is a response to the CEDAW committee's treatment of this topic at its 49th session in New York in 2005. The Council stresses the call for gender equality with regard both to human rights and to duties. Women are legal persons in their own right and have the right to education, work and health services, and to participate in public life.[125]

Nonetheless, there are rules on permissible marriage partners, on making the marriage contract, on the importance of the *wālī* for the validity of the contract, on the right of the man to marry up to four women, and on the right of the man to unilateral repudiation—unlike the woman, who may ask for divorce against payment of compensation. These rules, which have all been considered by the Council, show that the parties are not equal. We do find a certain approximation to equality—in the question of a divorce issued by a non-Muslim judge. In such cases, what applies is national legislation based on equal rights, not Islamic jurisprudence. This implies that the authorities have the power to grant divorce, and that the husband has delegated the right to *ṭalāq* (unilateral repudiation of the wife) to the judiciary. This is in line with Muhammad Abduh's reform proposals in Egypt in the late 1800s.[126]

124 Tucker 2008, 175.

125 *Al-Majalla al-ʿilmiyya* 7: 422–425.

126 See chapter 1.

The Council formulates the relationship between ideals and specific norms in such a way that equality in principle is not opposed to different roles. The husband is the head of the family with maintenance obligations. The woman takes care of the home. Consultation is recommended, but the husband has the last word. The woman may provide for the household, but this is considered a generous act on her part, for which she will be praised in this life and rewarded in the next. The Council does not call the wife's contribution *nafaqa* and thus avoids raising the question of women's inheritance rights. The fatwas on inheritance relate to general problems and do not challenge the currently applicable rules of Islamic jurisprudence.[127]

The two fatwas in the *ʿibādāt* category concern women and the mosque, one on whether the man may refuse his wife going to the mosque, and the other on women's access. Here, gender equality applies. The Council does not mince words when describing how men exalt their own whims as Islam itself. The right to go to mosque and find a space there is described as an important need for women. However, it must not come at the expense of husband and children, and this is where the circle closes for women. Their primary function is that of wife and mother, in a marriage based on equality in principle, but division of roles and inequality in practice—even if qualified by norms that the husband should help his wife, and that everyday life should be governed by mutual support and good manners.

Through the fatwas, a picture emerges of the ideal woman as a moral person: She wears the hijab, seeks knowledge of Islam, practices Islam herself, and supports her husband's practice of Islam. Her femininity keeps her from starting conversations with male strangers, and from dressing or moving in a provocative way. Her emotional strength makes her suited to assume her role in marriage and her responsibility for house, home, and children. This view matches the image of the righteous woman (*al-marʾa al-ṣāliḥa*) constructed by Egyptian Islamists.[128]

The fatwas are given for Muslims in Europe, and two different tendencies may be distinguished in how the Council relates to non-Muslims and to European realities. One tendency is suggested in the fatwa on marrying a *kitābiya*,

127 At the Council session in Dublin in February 2005, I presented the problem that the living costs in Europe require women to contribute to the household with means from salaried work, which might shake the view that half-shares of inheritance for women are just. The head of the Council, Yusuf al-Qaradawi, rejected the point as irrelevant, asserting that it *is* the husband's duty to provide. I understood his statement as that of a "benevolent patriarch" chiefly concerned that the husband should not shirk his responsibility.

128 See Sherifa Zuhur's description of the Islamist ideal woman (Zuhur 1992).

which expresses concern that righteous and moral Muslim women will not get married and that their morals may be corrupted by seeing that Western women can get married without staying chaste before marriage. At heart, there is an "us vs. them" attitude, and an assumption that dangerous moral dissolution will ensue if sex is not restricted to marriage. On this point, the Council is not out of step with its public; the notion of Western immorality is very much alive among many Muslims, also in Europe.[129]

On the other hand, the Council places civil marriage on a par with the Islamic marriage contract, and accepts divorce granted by a non-Muslim judge. This shows that the Council's fatwas in actual fact also imply a rapprochement with the European legal systems, in which the principle is equality before the law, regardless of gender. The view that both marriage and divorce must be publicly registered helps secure women's rights through the legal systems of European states. Such a rapprochement is also implied by the position that one may not enter into a new marriage before one has been granted divorce from a former spouse by domestic authorities, even if the parties are divorced in Islamic terms and the *ʿidda* period is over.

Conclusion

The fatwas and resolutions (*qarārāt*) of the ECFR chiefly reflect the paradigm of equal worth and complementarity with a stress on the duties and subordination of women. They can only to a limited extent be said to promote gender equality with a stress on women's rights. Indirectly, however, we may distinguish cautious steps toward equality before the law, in that the Council urges people to abide by the national legal systems in certain matters, as part of abiding by Islamic norms. Still, the main tendency is clear, and it groups the Council with neo-traditionalists, as described by Ziba Mir-Hosseini.[130]

In this perspective, the fatwas and resolutions do not represent a principled approach to resolving the dilemma by harmonizing the two competing sets of norms. If the norm of relating to the Western legal system is followed, however, it may be an important contribution to solving conflicts over divorce.

129 The author's personal observations.

130 Mir-Hosseini 2000a, 83.

CHAPTER 5

Fatwa, Legitimacy, and Authority

Introduction

Syed Darsh is an example of a mufti working in the local community. He answered questions and gave advice after the Friday prayer and by telephone. This entailed a direct communication with the questioner that was evident in the answers he gave in his *Q-News* column.

The ECFR claims to be a European authority. All Europe is treated as a single region with regard to coordinating the various fundamental differences of opinion within *fiqh*, giving collective answers (fatwas) to satisfy the needs of Muslims in Europe, publishing legal studies on new topics in the European arena, and guiding Muslims in general and Muslim youth in particular by spreading an "authentic Islam".[1] The general European focus of the council also accords with the thought of its head, al-Qaradawi, who considers "Europe" a unit. As Caeiro and al-Saify put it: "… Qaraḍāwī's own thinking de-emphasises the importance of nation-specific structures and speaks of Europe—and indeed of the West—as a whole."[2]

Our survey of fatwas from Syed Darsh and fatwas and resolutions (*qarārāt*) from the ECFR in the preceding chapters shows that both promote the neo-traditional Islamic principle of complementarity, stressing women's duties and subordination, and that they only to a limited extent advocate gender equality with a stress on women's rights. Does this make the fatwas similar, or are there differences between them? Do fatwas and resolutions reflect the fact that Darsh and the ECFR address different readerships, and that they represent different institutional arrangements and processes of fatwa-giving—Darsh as an individual mufti, the ECFR as a collegial body?

To answer these questions, I will seek answers to a number of sub-questions. How do Darsh and the ECFR express their stance on the issues of their fatwas and resolutions? What is their understanding of reality? What relationship do they establish with the reader?[3] To shed light on these questions,

1 According to the Council's presentation of itself on its website (http://www.e-cfr.org/).

2 Caeiro and al-Saify 2009, 110.

3 These three questions follow Svennevig's division of the communicative functions of language into expressive, referential and interpersonal functions (Svennevig 2009).

 | DOI: 10.1163/9789004367852_007

yet more detailed questions may help. What levels are found in the text? A single level, or several discourses intertwined?

The answers to these questions will be examined with regard to the construction, justification and defence of authority, which is an interesting topic, as adherence to a fatwa is not mandatory.

I will compare four fatwas, two on haircuts and two on women in the mosque, as well as a resolution (*qarār*) on the status of the marriage when the wife converts but the husband does not. The fatwas and *qarār* will be presented at full length, including the questions that they answer, to give the reader a glimpse of the format, argumentation and linguistic style.

Implicit in questions for fatwas is the assumption that muftis possess the knowledge to give the "right" answer and are capable of guiding people to do what is morally right. In other words, the questions imply an asymmetric power relation in which the questioner ascribes authority to the questioned.

In the communicative situation between the mufti and the questioner, the mufti figures as the *sender* of the fatwa, and thus holds the power of definition over its design. According to Rolv Mikkel Blakar, the sender is actively creative and structuring with respect to his topic, to the language or medium, to himself, and to the social situation in which the communication takes place.[4] However, the receiver, too, is essential to the process of communication. The identity of the addressee will necessarily be an important premise for the mufti when shaping the text of the fatwa, with regard to the arguments presented, how they are put, what grounds they are based on, and what relationship he establishes with the reader and in what way. The mufti will not speak and argue the same way with the young and the old, with the uneducated and the specialists. According to Svennevig, an utterance will in various ways be adapted to the addressee and tell something about our relationship to her—whether we are close or distant, equals or different in status.[5]

Concerning Haircuts

To the outside observer, haircuts may seem a trivial topic, but to a woman encountering this problematic in her project of living as a "righteous" Muslim, it may be a grave matter to clarify whether they are permitted, or to ask per-

4 Blakar 2006, 64.

5 Svennevig 2009, 24.

mission to get her hair cut. No topic is too small, no topic too big where the implications of "correct" Muslim practice are at issue.

A Fatwa from Syed Darsh

The question goes as follows: "I was brought up with the idea that as a Muslim woman, I should not trim my hair. Is it permissible for Muslim women to have their hair cut?"[6] Darsh replies:

> Yes, it is allowed for a Muslim woman to trim her hair. What is prohibited is to shave as a sign of sorrow for a death of a person, or imitating young men. These are the only two instances where it is prohibited to indulge in this. Apart from that it is reported by Imam Muslim that the wives of the Prophet (peace be upon him) used to cut their hair short until the hair reached the lobe of their ears without leaving it to a long stretch. Two of the great sheikhs, Al Qadi Iyad and Imam Nawawi said this was the manner of the wives of the Prophet (peace be upon him) after his death because they had abandoned looking attractive and beautifying themselves, and they were not in need of having long hair, and wanted to reduce the task of caring for their hair. Imam Nawawi commented on this Hadith by saying that it shows that it is allowed for women to cut short their hair as the wives of the Prophet (peace be upon him).
>
> But there are some scholars, particularly in the Hanafi school, who do not feel happy about shortening the hair—to the extent that the translator of the book of Sahih Muslim tried to avoid that clear meaning of the Fiqh of the Hadith which allowed women to cut short their hair, and he claimed from the source he had already quoted that the wives were not cutting their hair, they were just gathering their hair on top of their head and they did not allow their long hair to be dangling behind them. That is exactly the sectarian point of view which he warned against—but in his translation, at the same time, his explanation goes contrary to the clear meaning of the Hadith regarding the wives of the Prophet (peace be upon him) which allowed them to shorten their hair.
>
> Considering what is happening with so many Muslim girls, who want to study or to work and wear hijab, they do not have the luxury or availability of so much time to sit and comb their hair, they are allowed to shorten their hair on condition that they do not imitate men and do not shave their heads.

6 http://www.iol.ie/~afifi/Ad-Darsh/darsh.htm, 13 Dec 1996.

Darsh opens his fatwa by stating the norm ("Yes, it is allowed ..." and "What is prohibited ..."). He goes on to present the references he uses to argue for the fatwa.[7] Darsh confidently guides the reader into a universe of references and arguments, the significance of which can only be grasped through knowledge: He refers to the wives of the Prophet and their practice as described by Imam Muslim (d. 875), the editor of *Ṣaḥīḥ Muslim*, which is regarded as one of the most authentic collections of hadith in the Sunni Muslim tradition. He then presents the comments of Muslim scholars on this hadith—not just any scholars, but key persons in two of the schools of law, Qadi Iyad (1088–1149) of the Maliki school and al-Nawawi of the Shafiʿi school. Referring to al-Nawawi, Darsh stresses his explicit claim that women may get their hair cut. The reader may not be familiar with all the arguments. By styling Muslim bin Hajjaj as "Imam" and Qadi Iyad and al-Nawawi as "two of the great sheikhs," Darsh signals the authority of these sources. "Imam" and "sheikh" are both titles of authority that will be familiar to any Muslim, young or old. This balance between the informal and the formal helps bring the reader closer to the arguments and references. The reader gets to take part in the justification. Implicitly, Darsh has thus established a close relation with the reader by giving the impression that they now share this universe, which helps to reinforce Darsh's argument.

Darsh also presents references that go against his position: "But there are some scholars, particularly in the Hanafi school ..." Here, the authorities are not presented by name, but in the indefinite plural. This gives an impersonal impression, and the distancing is enhanced by the claim that "the translator of *Ṣaḥīḥ Muslim*" is trying to evade the "clear" meaning of the hadith and instead promoting a "sectarian" position. Darsh here ties his own position to the majority of the Muslim community, and casts the opposite view as marginal. He accuses opponents of having distorted a textual source in translation, but without stating who the translator is, or what language the translation is in. The woolly description of authorities and sources, however, does not prevent Darsh from placing them ("... in the Hanafi school"). This is no coincidence, but an important premise for the fatwa as a whole. The largest Muslim community in the UK originates from the Indian sub-continent, where the Hanafi school is dominant, and there is a widespread view that women are not allowed to get their hair cut.[8]

7 I here use "fatwa" in two senses, (i) the full text and (ii) the statement of the norm itself.

8 See e.g. the Institute of Islamic Jurisprudence's website at http://daruliftaa.com/node/4672, where the UK-based Mufti Muhammad ibn Adam al-Kawthari, educated at Darul Uloom in India, gives a fatwa on the topic.

The last paragraph of the fatwa addresses the everyday life of Muslim girls, whom the fatwa appears to address. Darsh offers his own view that it is time-consuming and difficult to combine long hair with study and work. This may also be read as a practical tip for daily life. Young women who are getting an education or working and using the hijab are presented as a reality, but indirectly also as a model to be emulated; in Geertz's expression, the representation is a model *of* as well as *for* reality.[9] At the end, the norm given at the beginning of the fatwa is given concrete content related to its target group.

As we have seen before, Darsh, a scholar from al-Azhar, had a range of functions. His work also entailed differences of opinion with other scholars taking different views of what norm was right in particular cases, as is evident in the text. Besides the independent reasoning for the norm he states, which I will call the explicit layer of the text, we may also discern an underlying argument addressed to other scholars. The latter argument rises to the explicit layer as information to the reader about the landscape of different interpretations co-existing side by side. Still, the use of linguistic devices leaves no doubt as to which interpretation is right.

A Fatwa from the ECFR

Question: "If a woman wanted to cut her hair, should she seek the permission of the husband?"[10]

Answer:

> There are types of hair trimming which the woman does from time to time and which a husband may not even notice due to the very slight alteration being made. Women usually do this so that their hair does [not] become so lengthy as to become difficult to manage. This form of hair shortening does not usually require the permission of the husband. However there are forms of hair shortening and alteration, which completely change the appearance of the woman, which may surprise the husband if he was not consulted. This form of alteration requires the agreement of the husband and wife so that their relationship is not affected by this radical change in the woman's appearance. Due to the fact that a Muslim woman does not show her hair in public nor in front of foreign [sic!] men, it becomes true that the husband has the foremost right to enjoy his wife's hair. A wise woman would make sure to pursue all means of maintaining love and

9 Geertz 1993, 95.

10 ECFR 2002a, 62.

affection between herself and her husband, ultimately leading to good Muslim households becoming the real basis of good Muslim societies.

According to Yusuf al-Qaradawi, head of the European Council for Fatwa and Research, Muslims around the world face both common challenges and specific local ones.[11] Haircuts may well be said to be a shared human concern without regard to time and place. This fatwa could have been given anywhere in the world, and as it turns out, it was not originally given in a European context. The fatwa was first given by al-Qaradawi and published in *Fatāwā muʿāṣira*,[12] and it is one of 19 fatwas by al-Qaradawi that the Council has considered and given its assent. The question indicates an understanding of the male/female relationship with roots elsewhere than Western Europe in the 2000s, and this impression is reinforced by the description of how a wise woman manoeuvers. The woman's responsibility for the stability and happiness of the family is a frequent topic of the Islamic apologetic literature. It is based on alleged biological differences between men and women, not least in terms of sexuality. The woman is responsible for giving the husband sexual pleasure and enjoyment. This feminine ideal, however, ought not to be unfamiliar to Western readers, as it is rather similar to feminine ideals in the 1950s West.[13]

It should be noted that the fatwa is not supported by legal arguments, but appears purely as an expression of personal taste. The arguments appeal to emotion, by playing on women's supposed experiences ("long hair that could be difficult to manage," "the husband not noticing …"). It offers tips on pleasing the husband by covering the hair in public and letting him alone enjoy the sight. Confidence is established between questioner and mufti, framing the fatwa. When the mufti gives the impression of understanding the woman's situation, unlike her husband, it is easier for the woman to accept the mufti as an authority. Also helping to create acceptance is the kindness expressed toward the woman, which is a traditional way for Muslim scholars to relate to women. They strive to be kind and generous, and take the woman's feelings into account.[14]

---

11 Al-Qaradawi 2001, 5.

12 Al-Qaradawi 2003b, 3:589.

13 Sarromaa 2009, for example, analysed questions and answers in the advice column "Confide in Beate" in the Norwegian weekly magazine *Det Nye* from 1957, 1968 and 1977. In the 1950s, answers stated that men and women had different sexualities, and that the woman was responsible for using her femininity to change her husband so that he would not be unfaithful (cf. http://kilden.forskningsradet.no/c16880/artikkel/vis.html?tid=62029).

14 This Muslim masculine ideal, as I would call it, was something I encountered many times in the course of my fieldwork for this book.

Women in Mosques

The other question concerns women's access to mosques. The mosque is the framework for ritual prayer, Friday prayer, education, and other social activities. For Muslims as minorities in Western Europe, the mosque, as a meeting-place, plays a central role in the life of the community and in the continuity of tradition. The mosque has become the place "where Islam is," and one gets the impression that this is the case for all Muslims, regardless of gender. Most mosques, however, are characterized by restrictions on women. There may be physical divides: women praying in the gallery, in separate prayer rooms, or at the back of the prayer room, separated from the men by a curtain. There are also mosques to which women have no access at all. Compared with the rest of Europe, the UK in particular has many mosques to which women do not have access.

Many Muslim women are themselves dissatisfied with the state of affairs.[15] A statement by Khalida Khan, the founder of An-Nisa Society in London, may illustrate the experiences and aspirations of many Muslim women: "We women do not always feel equally welcome—to put it mildly. When we enter the women's entrance, we first have to pass the toilets; then we have to drag the small children up a staircase [...] before we get to the women's part of the mosque. When I go to the mosque, I want to see something beautiful, and I want to be able to enter through the main entrance, like everybody else! Why should women be segregated in this way?"[16]

A Fatwa from Syed Darsh

However, it is not the case that all men oppose women's presence in the mosques. One man asks:

> My question concerns the admission of women to mosques for prayers, lectures and other events. Until recently, I lived in London where my wife was able to attend the Islamic Cultural Centre as well as our local mosque. I am now in a provincial town. It has a fine mosque with ample capacity for women—only they are not allowed inside. How can that be justified?[17]

Darsh replies:

15 The author's personal observations among Muslim women.

16 Vogt 1995, 214 (retranslated from Norwegian).

17 Darsh 1997, 77.

There is no justification, whatsoever, for harbouring such a narrow-minded and, frankly, anti-Islamic attitude. I am saddened to acknowledge that the majority of prayer facilities in this country lack adequate provision for women. I am often left wondering whether this really is because of shortage of money, as is often suggested, or whether it is the men's lame excuse to exclude the other half of the Muslim population. Whatever its origins, the decision by so many *Imams*, Presidents and mosque committees to shut the mosque doors on women is certainly not rooted in Islam. Even a cursory reading of the numerous *Ahadith* from the life of the prophet and his Companions, blessings and peace be on him and them, should demolish forever this myth that mosques are meant to be 'men only' clubs.

'Do not stop the female servants of Allah from entering the houses of Allah, but ensure that they are decently dressed,' urges one *Hadith*. In another tradition, the second *Khalifah*, 'Umar, may Allah be pleased with him, was publicly challenged in the mosque by a lady to justify, in accordance with the *Qur'an*, his call for dowries to be reduced. Unable to do so, 'Umar had no choice but to back down and concede in public that he was wrong and the lady was right. Mosques were not only just places for men and women, but young children too, according to yet another *Hadith*.

The Prophet, blessings and peace be on him, is reported to have cut short a long recitation during prayer one day when he heard the shrill screams of a baby from somewhere in the midst of congregation. 'The mother must be praying behind me,' the Prophet is said to have thought, as he promptly cut short his *Surah*. The final tradition—but by no means the last—refers to a *Sahabiyyah* who memorized the whole of *Surah Qaf* just by listening to the Prophet during the Friday *Khutbah* in the mosque.

In the light of such insurmountable evidence, how can anyone even try to prove from Islamic history that women are not allowed to attend mosques? Unfortunately, people have tried to just do that. Challenged to find evidence to support their ban on women in mosques, *Imams* and local community leaders have been known to reach out for a line taken from the teachings of *Imam* Abu Hanifa: According to certain community leaders, *Imam* Abu Hanifa is alleged to have discouraged women from attending mosques on the strength of the following saying of 'A'isha, the wife of the Prophet, blessings and peace be upon him: 'If the Prophet knew what women were to invent after him, he would not have allowed them to go to the mosque.'

Such a sloppy attitude has been responsible, to a large extent, for the absence of deep Islamic knowledge in many of our wives and mothers—

> who are charged with the responsibility of bringing up the young: teaching them, playing with them, acting as a role model. Recently, a man from a city in West England approached me with a view to opening up for women one of the city's two magnificent mosques. Nine ladies had just converted to Islam, he told me, and were keen to pray in the mosque. But when I approached the *Imam*, he threatened to resign if a woman ever set foot inside his mosque. Faced with overwhelming evidence to the contrary, the *Imam* insisted he could do nothing until he received a *fatwah* from his *Dar'ul-Uloom* in India. We are still waiting.
>
> I remember being asked to intervene in a mosque dispute almost 20 years ago between members of the Pakistani/Bengali community and their English *Imam* who wanted to open up the mosque for women. What an irony! The two communities, which, up until the appointment of the *Imam* had been at war with each other, actually joined forces to kick him out.[18]

Darsh begins by stating the norm: Women have the right to come to the mosque. Darsh takes a forceful stand in his answer, attacking the attitudes ("harbouring such a narrowminded and, frankly, anti-Islamic attitude") and justifications ("men's lame excuse") of those who deny women access. Through such devices, Darsh appears to position himself, and identify himself with the questioner, in opposition to the "*Imams*, Presidents and mosque committees" running mosques. He accuses them of promoting a practice that, he claims, is not rooted in Islam, and that may be ascribed to inadequate reading of the normative sources.

Over the next two paragraphs, Darsh presents the arguments for his view, one after the other. The intensity of the text matches the strong language in the first paragraph. Six hadiths are recounted in the space of eleven lines. Darsh manages this by rewriting and simplifying the wording of the hadiths, and by describing their actors in an informal way. We recognize this technique from the fatwa on haircuts. The target group may be discerned from Darsh's handling of the source materials; he simplifies them and makes them accessible to the non-expert reader.

The fourth paragraph starts with the claim that these hadiths are "insurmountable" evidence, and a rhetorical question how one can "even try to prove" that women do not have access to mosques. This is a turning point in the text. Darsh now switches to a polemic against his opponents, based on his own

---

18 Darsh 1997, 77–79.

experience with them. He accuses them of having tried, unsuccessfully, to find evidence for denying women access, and points to two concrete cases in which he himself has championed women's right to attend the mosque. He comes close to making fun of his opponents, who make themselves dependent on a faraway, ineffective authority ("We are still waiting"), or close ranks against women's access to mosques even though they are otherwise divided by deep communal conflicts ("What an irony!").

This fatwa, too, contains multiple layers. In addition to the two layers mentioned in connection with the fatwa on haircuts—the explicit layer with statements of norms and independent reasoning, and the implicit layer polemicizing against opponents—we find in this fatwa a third layer: The person of the mufti as an actor in his own right championing women's access to the mosque in concrete cases.

The fatwa conveys a normative message in addition to the statement of the norm itself, what I would describe as a fourth implicit layer. Access to mosques is not a value *per se*, but is tied to "Islamic knowledge" on the part of wives and mothers responsible for bringing up the young. In the end, what is being promoted is the ideal of the righteous Muslim woman (*al-mar'a al-ṣāliḥa*): She possesses Islamic knowledge, and in Darsh's view, she will do what is morally "right" in her role as mother. As in the preceding fatwa, we are again presented with the ideal and the expectation, in Geertz' terms, a model both *of* and *for* reality.

A Fatwa from the ECFR

Question:

> We, the Cultural Arab Association in Argus [*sic—Arabisk Kulturforening, Aarhus*], Denmark, have a small mosque. The month of Ramadan, during which the young and the old men and women frequent the mosque, will commence soon. As a result of this situation we resorted to pitching tents and hiring WC facilities for women to encourage them to come to the mosque. Some brothers protested, arguing that we should not burden ourselves with this responsibility as women are not commanded to pray in the mosque and their prayer at home is better.[19]

Answer:

---

19 *Al-Majalla al-ʿilmiyya* 10–11: 327–326.

> The association should facilitate a place for women as long as this is attainable since they have the right to attend the congregational prayers and the Fridays' [*sic*] prayer and the Taraweeh prayers (A voluntary prayer observed by Muslims during the nights of Ramadan). They also have the right to take part in the lectures delivered at the mosque. That is for the following reasons:
>
> First: The prophet—peace be upon him—said: "Prevent not Allah's female servants from attending the mosque." Agreed upon. This hadith proves women's right to share the mosque with men. Moreover, originally the Islamic obligations usually apply for both men and women unless one sex is exempted due to its nature.
>
> Second: During the lifetime of the Prophet—peace be upon him—and during the era of the [rightly] guided Caliphs women used to go to mosques and perform the congregational prayers and the Fridays' prayers and attend other activities.
>
> Third: The need of women living in Europe for a spiritual and educational provision and to have their positive role in the Muslim community. This can be achieved in no place other than the mosque and the month of Ramadan is a great opportunity for that.

The Council states that women have the right to participate in communal prayer, Friday prayer and *tarāwīḥ* prayer. Reference is made to a tradition that in the view of the Council proves the right of women to share the mosque with men. This is further referred to as the practice at the time of the Prophet, as well as under the first four caliphs.[20] This period is presented as an ideal and a model to be followed. The Council then turns to justifying women's right to attend the mosque in terms of their living in Europe. They need "spiritual and educational provision" that they can only get in the mosque.

The reply to the Arab Cultural Association in Aarhus is rather mildly worded, even though the references and grounds for women's right are clearly stated. Might it be the case that the Council does not, in practice, support women's rights to attend the mosque? This is unlikely. A more plausible explanation relates to the concern with unity and human relations in the mosque.

The question offers three pieces of information: The mosque is small, and they are seeking to create a space for women by putting up a tent and renting toilets. The given physical conditions, thus, do not make it easy to fulfil such a requirement. Second, there are two opinions in the mosque. Some think

20 Abu Bakr, Umar, Uthman and Ali.

that women have the right to come to the mosque, and others think that the mosque should not take responsibility for erecting facilities for women, since women are not required to pray in the mosque, and that prayer at home is better for women. It is thus reasonable to interpret the answer as diplomatic mediation between the representatives of these two views. Full assent is not given to either party, neither to those who do not wish to create space for women in the month of Ramadan (their argument is wrong), nor to those who seek to encourage women to attend the mosque ("The association *should facilitate* a place for women *as long as this is attainable*," emphasis mine). The Council does not go into the details of the case (the tent, the rented toilets), but focuses instead on the norm, with reservations and without being categorical: what one "should" do "as long as this is attainable". They thus look beyond the conflict to the ideals, in a tone of reconciliation, which is stressed at the end of the fatwa: "... Ramadan is a great opportunity for that." Having given guidance on doing what is right and getting along with one another, they put the ball back in the court of the members of the Arab Cultural Association in Aarhus.[21]

A *qarār* from the ECFR

Subject: "A Woman embraces Islam and her Husband does not".[22]

On this issue, the Council issued the following resolution:

> Having considered the numerous papers and studies submitted for its attention over three consecutive sessions, and which carried a variety of perspectives and opinions all dealing with this problem in detail and length, observing the objectives of Sharia and relating those to principles of Fiqh. The Council also recognises and acknowledges the conditions in which the new Muslim sisters in the West find themselves when their husbands choose to remain on their religion.
>
> The Council affirms and repeats that it is forbidden for a Muslim female to establish marriage to a non-Muslim male. This has been an issue of consensus throughout the history of this nation. However, in the case of marriage being established prior to the female entering Islam, the Council has decided the following:

21 The Arab Cultural Association is working to improve facilities. In cooperation with other Islamic organizations in Aarhus, they are behind plans for the building of a mosque. Prospectus for "Mosque and Islamic Centre in Aarhus", 2007, PDF on file with author.

22 ECFR 2013.

First: If both husband and wife revert to Islam and there is no Sharia objection to their marriage in the first place, such as particular blood relations or relations established as a result of breast-feeding, which deems the very establishment of marriage unlawful, the marriage shall be deemed valid and correct.

Second: If the husband reverts to Islam alone, and no object to the establishment of marriage exists and the woman is a Jew or a Christian, then the marriage shall be deemed valid and correct.

Third: If the wife reverts to Islam and her husband remains on his religion, the Council sees the following:

One) If her reversion to Islam occurred and the marriage is yet to be consummated, then they must immediately separate.

Two) If her reversion to Islam occurred after the consummation of marriage, and the husband also embraced Islam before the expiry of her period of waiting, then the marriage is deemed valid and correct.

Three) If her reversion to Islam occurred after the consummation of marriage, and the period of waiting expired, she is allowed to wait for him to embrace Islam even if that period was a lengthy one. Once he does so and reverts to Islam, then their marriage is deemed valid and correct.

Four) If the wife chose to marry another man after the expiration of the period of waiting, she must first request a dissolution of marriage through legal channels.

Fourth: According to the four main schools of jurisprudence, it is forbidden for the wife to remain with her husband, or indeed to allow him conjugal rights, once her period of waiting has expired. However, some scholars see that it is for her to remain with him, allowing him and enjoying full conjugal rights, if he does not prevent her from exercising her religion and she has hope in him reverting in Islam. The reason for this is for women not to reject entering into Islam if they realise that they are to separate from their husbands and desert their families by doing so. Those scholars based their view upon the ruling of Omar ibn Al-Khattab, may Allah be pleased with him, in the case of the women from Al-Heera who reverted to Islam while her husband remained on his religion. According to the authentic narration of Yazeed ibn Abdullah Al-Khatmi, Omar ibn Al-Khattab gave the woman the choice: "If she wishes to leave him, or if she wishes to stay with him." These scholars also base their opinion upon the view of Ali ibn Abi Talib concerning the Christian woman who reverts to Islam and is married to a Christian or a Jew; that her husband is more deserving of his conjugal rights, as he has a contract. This is also an

> authentic narration. It is also known that Ibraheem Al-Nakha'i, Al-Shi'bi and Hammad ibn Abi Sulayman had the same views.

This resolution is controversial, since it is held that a Muslim woman is forbidden from being married to a non-Muslim man.

The process behind the resolution is interesting. Normally, a resolution stems from the fact that a topic is considered significant, not from the question of a *mustaftī*. In this case, however, the resolution is the result of a question held to be significant. The question was posed by a lady who had converted, while her husband had not. The woman thus found herself in a situation that might require her to get divorced. This meant breaking up a family and deserting her husband. The woman faced an ethical dilemma.[23]

The resolution differs considerably from the Council's fatwas, as it primarily argues for references and perspectives that support the argument for the derived norm. It is also stressed that the topic has been thoroughly discussed at three sessions in a row, in recognition of the special challenges facing new Muslim "sisters" in the West. The painstaking work is exemplified: A number of detailed and careful studies with various perspectives have been presented and studied. They include legal views (*ārā' fiqhiyya*) with concomitant evidence with regard to jurisprudential principles and sources, in the light of *maqāṣid al-sharīʿa* (the objectives of Sharia). The introduction ends by stressing the ban on Muslim women marrying non-Muslim men. The target audience of the resolution would seem to be other Islamic scholars, with the detailed argument serving to make authority claims in a scholarly discourse.

First, the Council declares agreement with the consensus view among Islamic scholars that a Muslim woman is forbidden from marrying a non-Muslim man. Then, a new element is introduced. What about marriages contracted before a spouse converts to Islam? Three scenarios are described: the conversion to Islam of both spouses, of the husband alone, or of the wife alone. The third scenario is the most interesting one, and is discussed in detail. The relevant point for the questioner is that she may remain in the marriage while she waits for her husband to convert, even for a prolonged period. This opinion is argued in terms of the concepts and methods presented in the Council's statutes. The Council bypasses the four schools of law. In my interpretation, the argument entails the use of *maqāṣid al-sharīʿa*, where preservation of religion ("if he does not prevent her from exercising her religion") tops the hierarchy

23 Caeiro 2002, 121.

of objectives along with other *ḍarūriyyāt* (vital necessities) such as preservation of life, property, mind, and progeny.[24] Further, a missionary argument is presented. Family and marriage entered into before the conversion should not form any obstacle to conversion. Two references are given in support of the Council's position: Umar ibn al-Khattab and Ali ibn Abi Talib, two of the Prophet's Companions, who are declared to be the sources of the Council's *ijtihād*.

The resolution is nearly identical with the fatwa on the same subject in Yusuf al-Qaradawi's book on *fiqh al-aqalliyyāt*.[25] This fact may be ascribed to al-Qaradawi's charisma and position, and the fact that he is the head of the Council. Al-Qaradawi's text is longer and more detailed, and includes a section on whether one may give fatwas based on normative statements by the *ṣaḥāba* (Companions of the Prophet) and *tābiʿīn* (the following generation), concluding in the affirmative. He also refers to a study by hadith scholar and ECFR member Abdullah al-Judai that was written for the Jordanian Council on Fatwa and Research.[26] According to al-Qaradawi, al-Judai's argument follows the same lines as his own. This adds weight to the assumption that Islamic scholars are the target audience.

It may be worth mentioning that the woman who posed the question was happy with the resolution and gave the Council her thanks.[27]

Comparison of the Fatwas and the Resolution

Although the haircut fatwas are primarily concerned with clarifying the norm, the muftis themselves, Darsh and al-Qaradawi, figure in their own fatwas in different ways. Darsh figures in his fatwa as an actor in a debate, polemicizing against scholars in the UK who hold that getting a haircut is forbidden. In his argument, he uses his authority as an *ʿālim*, Islamic scholar, with all the knowledge of the Islamic sources that it entails. Al-Qaradawi is also visible in his own fatwa on the topic, but not in a polemic with other scholars. He figures as an

---

24 Hallaq 2003, 112.

25 Al-Qaradawi 2001, 105–122.

26 Al-Qaradawi 2001, 124–125. Judai's study would seem to be the result of a question from Batool al-Toma, who is in charge of the New Muslim Project at the Islamic Foundation, Leicester, UK. In a conversation with the author, she disclosed that she had encouraged Judai to address this question, because it was a problem she had encountered many times in her work. (Conversation with Batool al-Toma, Brussels, 1 Nov 2009).

27 Caeiro 2002, 12.

understanding man, who offers guidance on securing the relationship with the husband with emotional arguments. This fatwa lacks the reference to a local environment found in Darsh's fatwa.

The same tendency is found in the two fatwas on women's access to the mosque. The derivation of the norms nearly becomes but a minor detail in these fatwas. Whereas Darsh figures as an independent actor promoting women's access to the mosque, the ECFR's fatwa is at least equally concerned with reconciling active Muslims with opposing views.

The resolution (about a woman converting when her husband does not) differs quite a bit from the fatwas, as the primary intent seems to be to argue vis-à-vis other Islamic scholars for the authority of a norm given for Muslims in the West. It argues not only that given references and concepts support the conclusion, but also *which* references and concepts are relevant and should form the jurisprudential canon in this matter.

I would claim that the argumentation in these five examples serves two main objectives, albeit to varying extent. One is to legitimate the authority of the mufti vis-à-vis other scholars. The mufti's authority depends not least on the legal sources he uses in his derivation of norms being accepted as part of a canon of sources. Whether the mufti has the "right" education (from an Islamic system of education), however, is an important precondition for his argument on sources to be taken into consideration and perhaps accepted. Certain educational institutions are also more prestigious than others, lending extra weight to the arguments of their graduates. The other main objective is authority vis-à-vis the lay Muslim. The muftis are traditional scholars, and Darsh and al-Qaradawi, the latter as the head and symbol of the ECFR, both represent the *tradition*. Both studied at Al-Azhar University in Cairo, one of the oldest and most prestigious Islamic educational institutions in the Muslim world. Their use of the *kākūlā* (long coat) and *ʿimāma* (a fez wound about with a white cloth), the dress of Azhar-trained scholars, also gives them a visible sign of authority. This authority plays an important role when they give guidance and propose solutions, whether on haircuts, access to mosques, or the legality of converts' marriages. When the believer follows their advice and guidance, he or she is drawn into the *universe of tradition*, and becomes part of something greater than him- or herself.

Boundaries and the Borderless

Although the fatwas and the resolution have been given for local circumstances,[28] they frequently show signs of being borderless. This is the case with the references used, the scholars appearing as opponents in polemics, the target audience, and the source of authority. Both Darsh and the ECFR are clearly actors in what the anthropologist John R. Bowen terms "a transnational public space".[29] Transnational Islam, according to Bowen, can be used to describe a number of phenomena, of which he stresses three: demographic movements, transnational religious institutions, and the Islamic field of reference and debate. The latter phenomenon in particular, he claims, has been overshadowed in research by the other two.[30]

This third form of transnational Islam is described as the development of debates and discussions among Muslims on the nature and role of Islam in Europe and North America, and the development of institutions for systematic reflection among scholars. The point of departure for transnational Islam as a field of debate and reference, Bowen argues, is the historical development, communications, and institutional innovations of Islam. Besides, Islam is inherently universal as regards the message, the global faith community, and religious ritual. He describes transnational Islam as follows: "This sense of Islam's transnational character is diffuse but powerful, and it derives its power from the ways in which rituals reproduce, and histories remind Muslims of, the shared duties and practices of Muslims across political boundaries."[31] Their awareness of the transnational character of Islam leads Muslims to seek across the world for the highest—that is, the most learned—authority in Islam-related matters, Bowen says.[32]

As we have seen, Syed Darsh and the European Council for Fatwa and Research argue within the frame of Islamic references, and seek to legitimate their arguments vis-à-vis other scholars, regardless of national boundaries. The thinking is predominantly guild-like, requiring a certain kind of knowledge to be accepted as a scholar.[33] One addresses one's arguments to one's peers. The

---

28 I choose to use the word "local" even about fatwas from the ECFR, which is a transnational actor both in its structure and its area of influence.

29 Bowen 2004, 879.

30 Bowen 2004, 880. I would suggest that this is not least true in Europe, where research on Muslims for years focused precisely on immigration patterns and institutions.

31 Bowen 2004, 882.

32 Bowen 2004, 883.

33 One example is the criteria for membership of the ECFR.

fatwas and resolutions therefore have a horizontal dimension, between scholars, a fact reflected in the justification of the norms.

Al-mustaftī and the Authority of the Fatwa

The lay Muslim, too, has become part of this space of debates and references, and has thus acquired a certain ownership of the tradition. This may be seen as an outcome of the democratization of knowledge that some researchers claim began with *al-Manār*, and that has accelerated over the 20th century.[34] Cassette tapes were popular in the last decades of that century. The most recent media are Islamic satellite channels and innumerable Islamic websites. Anarchy reigns. The lay Muslim has become familiar with concepts and arguments used by the scholars, and he has his own opinions as to which one is right; thus, he has been drawn into the Islamic field of reference and debate.[35] In particular, Syed Darsh's simplified references to the sources help make ordinary Muslims experience a shared ownership of tradition with the scholar.

One characteristic of the fatwa is that it is not enforced by any authority, nor does it require adherence. In what, then, does the fatwa's authority over the believer consist? Or to put it differently: What is its appeal? In the fatwas I have presented, there is a clear tendency to promote gender balance and complementarity, with unequal rights when entering into and dissolving marriage.[36] They thus fail to contribute to solving the women's dilemma of being torn between the ideal of duties and subordination, and the ideal of equality and rights. Why would women and men adhere to the fatwas that are given if it conflicts with their own views and interests?

---

34 See Masud, Messick, and Powers 1996, 30–31. In *Defining Islam for the Egyptian State*, Skovgaard Petersen describes how the press became a new medium for spreading the message of Islam from the end of the 19th century (Skovgaard-Petersen 1997, 78–79).

35 Hirschkind 2005 gives an example of an arena of discourse where lay Muslims prove themselves: a conversation overheard among passengers during a taxi ride in Cairo. The conversation, between a young man, a lady with hijab, and a bearded taxi driver with jalabiyya, had every ingredient: a lesson with the well-known preacher Umar Abd al-Kafi, a discussion of whether music is forbidden or permitted, the argument of faith or lack of faith in the Quran and Sunna, questions over the authenticity of hadith, the ban on alcohol, the corrupting influence of love songs, the use of Quranic verses as proof, and objections to such use. They concluded that music was *ḥarām*, but love was not.

36 See chapters 3 and 4.

I will seek to shed light on these questions with the aid of anthropologist Hussein Ali Agrama, whose article "Ethics, Tradition, Authority" examines the authority of fatwas and their ethical dimension.[37] Because fatwas are answers to questions about what is the right action, they are "necessarily part of an ethical practice," Agrama claims.[38] Agrama seeks to answer, not *why*, but *how* fatwas have authority, defined as "a form of willing obedience to another that is irreducible to either coercion or persuasion".[39]

Agrama claims that the literature has placed emphasis on analysing fatwas as an instrument and expression of change in Islamic jurisprudence, rather than on the capacity of fatwas to secure authority in the light of shifting circumstances.[40] This has undermined the understanding of the ethical dimension of the fatwa. "… [T]he vitality and authority of the fatwa lies not in its reforming of doctrine to fit novel circumstances, but instead, in the ways that it connects and advances the self to and within the practices and goals that constitute Islamic tradition more broadly," he claims.[41]

The muftis Agrama interviewed about their work clearly stated that they gave fatwas in order to help people with their affairs and find solutions. In the interaction between questioner and mufti there was also an element of *tarbiyya*, education to become a better Muslim. The muftis give fatwas based on the information provided by the questioner, without suspicion. According to Agrama, a fatwa is thus about what a mufti is able to say, in good faith, to questioners that they ought to do—within the frame of doctrine, as well as in light of the ideal of being a good Muslim. Through the fatwa process, questioner and mufti are tied together in a relationship marked by uncertainty and responsibility on both sides—regarding what to do, on the one side, and what to say, on the other. Agrama comments: "Here it is not the creativity of the fatwa that matters but, rather, its capacity to enable a self to stay and advance on an already defined path toward an ideal Muslim self."[42]

How, then, does the fatwa have authority? In Agrama's formulation, "It is the promise intrinsic to this capacity to guide, the mutual uncertainty and respon-

---

37 Agrama's article is based on fieldwork at the Fatwa Council of al-Azhar in Cairo, where he audited sessions of oral fatwa-giving for people who came to ask questions of the muftis available during the opening hours of the fatwa service.

38 Agrama 2010, 2.

39 Agrama 2010, 6. Citing political philosopher Hannah Arendt, Agrama points out the problem of an inability to distinguish coercion from authority.

40 Agrama 2010, 7.

41 Agrama 2010, 10.

42 Agrama 2010, 14.

sibilities involved in it, the range of emotion and the temporalities it mediates, and the future(s) that it aims to facilitate and secure, that structures the fatwa's authority."[43]

"Doing what is (morally) right" entails becoming a better Muslim, which in turn engenders a belonging to tradition and to the community of the faithful, the Muslim *umma*. It is in this perspective that every detail of Islamic practice gains significance, from haircuts to mosque attendance, gender relations, and ritual duties.

Agrama's materials are oral fatwas, based on the observation of communications between mufti and questioner(s). My fatwas are written, and the face-to-face dimension is absent. How is the mufti's authority reflected in written fatwas; specifically, in my own materials?

Darsh's fatwa on haircuts might be said to have three main elements: the statement of the norm; the reference to the sources, where the reader is drawn in and given ownership to the tradition; and finally, practical advice to busy girls that they cannot be expected to spend their time taking care of long hair, but need something more low-maintenance. The statement of the norm thus becomes an aid to being *al-mar'a al-ṣāliḥa*, the righteous Muslim woman, as seen by Darsh.

In al-Qaradawi's and the ECFR's fatwa on whether a woman needs her husband's permission to cut her hair, a relationship is established with female readers based on emotional arguments. The ideal woman is presented: she covers her hair when with non-*maḥram* men. Only her husband should have the pleasure of seeing her hair. She is wise, using every means to maintain love and devotion between herself and the husband, and thus becomes a partner in the enterprise of building the family and, through it, the righteous Muslim community.

In Darsh's fatwa on women's access to the mosque, the norm is emphatically stated, but it is only one of several elements. The reader is included and given ownership to the tradition. The ethical ideal of *al-mar'a al-ṣāliḥa* is highlighted: women are described as "female servants of Allah," with "Islamic knowledge" that comes in useful in raising children and fits the mother for teaching them, playing with them and being their role model.

In the ECFR's fatwa on access to the Aarhus mosque, the norm itself plays a minor role compared to the attempt to reconcile the differing opinions among male members of the mosque, and get them to agree to do "what is right"—but only as far as they are able. The fatwa is markedly solution-oriented. What

43 Agrama 2010, 14.

matters most is not being right and pushing one's opinion through at others' expense, but agreeing on how to proceed to realize the norm of women's access to the mosque—even if this may mean a long wait before the women are truly able to attend the mosque.

The resolution on whether a female convert may remain married to her non-convert husband offers support and comfort for the questioner, who had already received the opposite opinion from other scholars.

We see that the elements listed by Agrama, the mufti's attempt to help people and find solutions, as well as his *tarbiyya* or Islamic educational work, are also found in the fatwas presented in this chapter, whether as information, diplomacy, reprimand, personal opinion, or emotional argument. The aim is guidance to become a better Muslim, and the mufti is a helper in this regard. Yusuf al-Qaradawi describes the focus of fatwa-giving as supplying practical solutions, without any exaggerated stress on hypotheses.[44]

Conclusion

This chapter has taken its cues from John Bowen's use of the concept "field of reference and debate" as part of "a transnational public space," and from Hussein Ali Agrama's exploration of how the authority of a fatwa is created. The discussion has shown that the fatwa has two axes of authority: a horizontal axis among scholars, where the use of concepts and methods as well as the scholar's references and personal qualities are important determinants of whether a fatwa will gain recognition; and a vertical axis between the learned and lay Muslim, where the authority of the fatwa consists in its being a guidance to becoming a better Muslim and feeling that one belongs to the tradition—in other words, to something greater than oneself. The same elements that Agrama found by listening to oral fatwas may be traced in the written fatwas I have studied.

The fatwas discussed in this chapter were given for the local, European context, but in different ways. Darsh was a typical "grassroots mufti" belonging to a local setting. The ECFR is a transnational body that claims Europe as its area of authority. They both exemplify the fatwa as an element in transnational Islam as a global field of reference and debate. *Al-mustaftī*, the questioner, provides a description of his or her situation as one item of knowledge referenced in the mufti's answer. The fatwas may be read as answers to a question, or as a source

44 Statement during the ECFR's session in London, July 2004.

of knowledge that may in turn be used in discussions with other Muslims, be they laypeople or scholars. In this way, the lay Muslim, too, situates himself in this global field.

From the perspective of the vertical authority of the fatwa, as I have described it here, fatwas may have relevance for Muslim women even if they do not solve the dilemma of facing contradictory expectations tied to, respectively, the traditional Islamic principle of inequality with a stress on women's duties and subordination, and gender equality with a stress on women's rights and equality before the law. Adhering to a fatwa means being a part of Islam, understood as a tradition. It may give women a sense of a meaningful life, in relation both to the past, the present, and the future, and not least a sense of belonging to an imagined community of faith. A fatwa thus represents a dialectics that can reconcile conflicting views of what constitutes "Islamic standards". The *mustaftī*'s participation in the fatwa-making enterprise helps to cushion contradictions, as does the overriding concern with meaning and belonging. This entails both an opportunity for and a constraint on change. The notion of an "Islamic standard" is seen as an immutable yardstick, while its content is debated and changing. I submit that the fatwas may be seen as contributing to determining the contents of one view of the notion of an "Islamic standard".

As regards the horizontal axis among the scholars, the resolution (*qarār*) in particular exemplifies, to use the words of Muhammad Qasim Zaman, "how that authority is constructed, argued, put on display, and constantly defended."[45] In this case it means that the use of concepts and method, defended and argued for in the independent reasoning for the resolution, are to be part of a canon for the derivation of norms. As the intended readers of the resolution, other scholars figure as the significant other of the mufti. They act as "guarantors" for the orthodoxy of the norms, which requires the use of concepts and methods from within a certain canon. But the ECFR also views itself as a guardian of "correct" use of concepts and methods, even when this entails the change of a norm in a sensitive matter. Based on the materials I have presented, the scholars may be described both as "guardians of tradition" and "custodians of change."[46] This is one possible explanation why the method and concepts used in the argumentation are as important as the statement of the norm itself.

Regardless of axis, it is the principle of complementarity and not the principle of equality that is argued for in these fatwas. The resolution that a female convert may remain married to her non-Muslim husband on certain conditions

45 Zaman 2002, x.

46 The terms are borrowed from Zaman 2002, ix.

may nevertheless be read as a very cautious step toward unsettling a prohibition that is considered just about untouchable in Islamic tradition.

The fatwas and resolutions seek to answer two issues. One issue is how Muslims in Western Europe are to abide by God's commands and prohibitions. Here, the fatwas in my view seek to construct an Islam that can be practiced in a European context.[47] The other issue concerns external aspects, or how religious commands should be interpreted so that Muslims are not torn between religious commands and the demands of their surroundings. How do the muftis argue for statements of norms in cases that entail possible conflicts of norms?[48] This will be one theme of the next chapter, which deals with fatwas on the making of a marriage contract.

---

47 I here refer to Leila Babès' argument about a shift from the first generation's focus on a lived Islam (*islam vécu*) to later Muslim generations' focus on a constructed Islam (*islam construit*) (Babès 2004, 199).

48 Rohe 2007, 65 uses the terms *forum internum* and *forum externum* in describing the challenges with regard to developing a European Sharia.

PART 3

The Muftis' Reasoning in Local Context

CHAPTER 6

Fatwas in Context: Muftis and Local Challenges

Introduction

As we have seen, marriage-related topics predominate in the questions that are being asked. In these questions, conclusion of marriage holds a special position,[1] since this field is regulated by the national legislations where Muslims live. The ECFR has stated that Muslims should follow the law of their country of residence.[2]

Islamic legal thought and practice is transnational in character. It has not been adopted into the legal systems of European countries.[3] In most European countries, an "Islamic" marriage is therefore not considered legally valid.[4] At the same time, the marriage issue affects many Muslims in Europe—and raises many other questions besides the requirement of validity. It is a complex topic, where Islamic jurisprudence, European national legislations, and the legislations of Muslim countries all play a role. To Muslims, it matters that the marriage be correct according to Islam, as they see it. What may be said to be correct according to Islam, however, is a matter of some confusion and disagreement, as Muslims in Europe hail from many different countries, with different family laws, schools of law, religious traditions, interpretations of Islam, and cultural practices. No question has an unambiguous answer.

In this chapter, I will explore fatwas from Syed Darsh, the ECFR, Larabi Becheri (Dar al-Fatwa/ECFR), and Barkatullah Abdulkadir regarding various aspects of entry into marriage, which quantitatively dominate my materials.[5]

1 The dissolution of marriage is also an important topic.

2 The ECFR recalls this in the concluding declaration after every session.

3 In the Muslim world, provisions concerning the conclusion and dissolution of marriage are codified in national legislation on the family. Islamic jurisprudence is not applicable in itself. See e.g. Mir-Hosseini 2000b on the relationship between Islamic rules and national legislation in Iran and Morocco respectively.

4 This also holds for the Muslim world. For example, Mir-Hosseini notes that women married in a non-registered marriage make up a category of their own in paternity cases in the Moroccan justice system. Their suits are always rejected, as Mir-Hosseini explains: "The court's rejection of cases involving *fātiḥa* marriages is due to an amalgam of the classical Maliki interpretation of the concept of *nasab* [offspring] and the modern definition of a valid marriage" (Mir-Hosseini 2000b, 145).

5 See chapters 3 and 4.

 | DOI: 10.1163/9789004367852_008

The questions I seek to answer are: What concepts and methods are used in the argument on which the fatwas are based? What is similar and what is different? Are the muftis' arguments affected by local circumstances? Can a development over time be traced in these fatwas given from 1992 to 2008? And finally, do the fatwas help to reconcile the two competing sets of norms: equal worth and complementarity with a stress on obedience, versus equality and rights with a stress on equality before the law?

Syed Darsh

In 1975, the Union of Muslim Organizations in UK and Eire (UMO) launched a conference in Birmingham. The theme, as Jørgen Nielsen describes it, was "recognition of Shariʿah family law".[6] The matter was raised by Syed Darsh, the then imam of the Regent's Park mosque in London. Darsh's document includes the following arguments among others:

> When a Muslim is prevented from obeying this [Islamic family] law he feels that he is failing a religious duty. He will not feel at peace with the conscience or the environment in which he lives and this will lead to disenchantment. [...] When we request the host society to recognise our point of view we are appealing to a tradition of justice and equity well established in this country [Britain]. The scope of family law is not wide and does not contradict, in essence, the law here in this country. Both aim at the fulfillment of justice and happiness of the members of the family. Still, there are certain Islamic points which, with understanding and the spirit of accommodation, would not go so far as to create difficulties in the judiciary system. After all, we are asking for their applications among ourselves ...[7]

It is interesting that Darsh claims a religious obligation to obey Islamic family law, and uses the feelings of Muslims as an argument. He does not define "Islamic family law," however, nor does he explain who would be responsible for its introduction and enforcement.[8] He asserts the principle of legal pluralism: a separate law should apply to Muslims within the borders of Britain.

---

6 Nielsen 1999, 79.

7 Nielsen 1999, 79–80.

8 Nielsen 1999, 80.

The argument is not irrelevant, given how the British collected and put in writing the "native norms" of Muslims in colonial India, resulting in the "Anglo-Muhammadan law" that applied to Muslims in colonial courts.[9]

Still, the point of view has been stated: obeying the commands and prohibitions of God has priority, even if Darsh's document does not specify the implications. The concrete challenges of practicing what I choose to call the *idea* of an Islamic family law (since the Islamic principles are neither codified nor backed by a sanctioning authority) can, however, be found in the fatwa literature.[10]

Seventeen years after this document on Islamic family law, Darsh has become a *Q-News* columnist. Marriage is one of the most important topics he deals with, and one question is precisely about the relationship between Islamic jurisprudence and national law: "Is it necessary to also have a civil marriage?" Darsh replies:

> It is important to have a marriage registered with a civil authority so that it may be recognised. There are many implications as a result of such a registration. Firstly, it is a recognised form of marriage in this country. An Islamic marriage, in the narrow sense, is not recognised in this country. A civil marriage—if it is attended by the guardian of the girl and at least two male Muslim witnesses—amounts to a correct Islamic marriage. It is only the social aspect which leads to another ceremony in the mosque with an Imam officiating, although these things are not required Islamically.
>
> Secondly, without the civil marriage, the spouses' entitlement to inheritance, pension and legal documentation are not accepted by the present authorities—so for the sake of legality it must be registered. Even in Muslim countries nowadays they have made it an administrative obligation to register marriages. This is to validate and recognise all rights and duties that arise from marital relationship. So, if for nothing else, it is a must for the sake of the children.[11]

The answer focuses not on form, but on substance. Three topics are dealt with: public recognition of the marriage, Islamic recognition, and securing the legal rights of the spouses and their children. The message is that civil marriage real-

9 M.R. Anderson 1996, 12.

10 So-called "Islamic family law" is not recognized in the Muslim world, either, with the exception of Saudi Arabia, which has no codified family law (Welchman 2007, 16).

11 Darsh 1997, 99.

izes Islamic principles. The tone, however, is influenced by the fact that Darsh has no sanctioning power to back up this statement of the norm. He cannot make demands, he can only point out its importance. Darsh also seems to have gone further than in 1975, when he used the feelings of Muslims as an argument when advocating an Islamic family law. Now, he puts civil marriage on a par with a marriage contract made the Islamic way, as long as the same conditions are met, that is, the presence of at least two Muslim witnesses and the girl's guardian. The mosque ceremony is just a social occasion. He deals with the question of the guardian as a separate matter in another fatwa.

Guardianship (*wilāya*)[12]

Darsh starts from the observation that the majority of British Muslims belong to the Hanafi school, so he chooses to expose the position of the Hanafi school on marriage guardianship.

The Hanafi school divides this matter into two categories, which Darsh describes as follows:[13]

a) *Limited or confined guardianship:* This concerns the right of a person who is legally entitled to enter into contracts. Muslim jurists of all schools of thought agree that a mature sane man has the right to enter into a contract of marriage with any woman who accepts to marry him, and that he is free to offer her the dowry which she demands and is prepared to accept. No one has the right to object to the man's contractual obligation, whether father, mother, son or uncle.

b) *Shared or recommended guardianship:* This is where the Hanafi school is unique. The two Shaikhs, Abu Hanifa [d. 767] and Abu Yusuf [d. 798] say: The sane, mature girl enjoys the right of limited contract; limited in the sense that it affects her. She is free to enter into a marriage contract on her own, without the need of any male relative guardian[,] father or otherwise.

Such a contract, however, is valid on the condition that:

12 *Q-News*, 9 Oct 1992.

13 I reproduce the fatwa without the introduction.

> *i*) The man is equal to her in social outlook, education, age, wealth, or the ability to provide for her one month[']s maintenance at the most.
> *ii*) The dowry is equal to that which is given to the girl of her position.
>
> Once these two conditions are fulfilled the contract of marriage is valid and no-one has the right of objection.
>
> However, shared guardianship means that the girl in that position may give the right to the father to contract marriage on her behalf. This is recommended. In the view of the two Shaikhs the father has no right to force a mature and sane girl into a marriage without her consent. For evidence they refer to the hadith of the Prophet (pbuh) saying that: "the virgin is to be consulted in her marriage." Hence to marry a person against her will, i.e. forcing her, is a negation of that right. [...] Relatively speaking this is the most liberal view on the crucial issue and it is to the credit of the two Shaikhs. For their opinions both protects [*sic*] and free mature Muslim girls from the yoke of forced marriages.

Wilāya has a number of different meanings.[14] A suitable definition in connection with marriage could be "authority to contract marriage on behalf of ..." In most cases it applies to girls or women.[15] In the *fiqh* literature, *wilāya* is primarily discussed in terms of the conditions for the validity of the marriage contract, and the legal role of the guardian and its limits.[16]

> Maliki, Shafiʿi and Hanbali schools insist that a female must always be married off by a guardian; though a woman can conclude other contracts, she may not conclude a marriage contract. The dominant Hanafi view is that a guardian is required for the marriage of a minor female but merely recommended for a female past majority [...] though dissenting opinions [...] hold that such a marriage contracted by a woman without the intervention of her walī is altogether void or suspended until he approves it or a judge does so.[17]

---

14 "Wilāya" in EI2 (Dien and Walker 2010): "a noun form from the root *w-l-y* 'to be near, adjacent, contiguous to' [someone or something] and a term with a range of meaning in the political, religious and legal spheres."

15 In the classical legal literature, *wilāya* also applies to males, though only to minors. In practice, it mainly affects females.

16 See e.g. Ibn Rushd 2000, 2:8f.; al-Marghinani 1989, 1:95ff.

17 Ali 2008, 14.

Ibn Rushd discusses their difference in his *Distinguished Jurist's Primer*:

> The reason for their disagreement is the absence of a verse or tradition that is apparent (*zāhir*), not to say explicit, about the stipulation of guardianship as a condition in marriage. In fact the verses and traditions that are quoted in practice, by those who stipulate it as a condition, are all subject to interpretation. Similarly, the verses and traditions that are quoted in support of its absence as a condition are also not so clear on the issue.[18]

There are differences over the *walī* requirement within as well as between the schools of law. For instance, consider the Hanafi school.[19] Its eponym Abu Hanifa held that a mature woman (*bāligha*) is not dependent on a *walī*, whether for permission to marry or to make a marriage contract, just as she can enter into other kinds of contract without a *walī*. There are some restrictions, though: A *walī* may have the marriage annulled through the judicial system if the woman marries a husband who is "unsuitable" for someone of her status.[20]

This fatwa enters directly into the debate on the wishes and interests of daughters and their parents. To what extent should parents decide whom their daughter should marry? And to what extent may she decide for herself? Daughters cannot be forced to marry, but must themselves accept their spouse to be. Darsh here appears to argue against the practice of forced marriages, of which he was likely aware at the time (1992), and which has since come ever more in the media spotlight. The fatwa is about young women with the capacity to conclude contracts on their own behalf; that is, women of age. It is stressed that the woman must be "sane, mature," presumably corresponding to *ʿāqila* (of sound mind) and *bāligha* (mature). Darsh presents her legal options: she requires no *walī* to make a marriage contract; and ethical advice: she is recommended to let the father make the contract on her behalf. He also argues why his statement of the norm should be relevant for British Muslims, even though it represents the most liberal view among the schools of law (most of them belong to the Hanafi school). Allowing that young women might marry without a *walī* will naturally shake the traditional authority of the parents over their daughter's marriage, since she will no longer need their approval and blessing.

18 Ibn Rushd 2000, 2:9.

19 The majority of British Muslims originate from the Indian sub-continent, where the majority belongs to the Hanafi school.

20 Ali 2008, 15.

When Darsh points to equality of status (*kafāʾa*) as a condition for the marriage, and to the size of the bride-gift as a condition for the validity of the contract, he places himself squarely within an Islamic legal universe. These conditions will not hold before a British court.[21] Whether this rule is obeyed, depends on whether those concerned feel obliged to follow it. This fatwa, seen in connection with the previous one on registration of marriages, entails giving precedence to the rules of civil law, with the possible result of a power shift in the parent-daughter relationship. Daughters are given the Islam-approved opportunity to seek their happiness, even if against the wishes of their parents.

Polygamy

If followed, Darsh's fatwa on the registration of marriage would place restrictions on polygamy, as polygamy is banned under British law. Darsh, however, appears to disregard this implication in his fatwas on polygamy. He gave two such fatwas in *Q-News*, one on the woman's formal right to prevent her husband from taking a second wife, and one on circumstances in which a man may marry more than one woman.

This brings us back to the marriage contract. The question on preventing the husband from taking more wives goes: "As marriage in Islam is a contract between two people, can a wife stop her husband from taking a second wife, during their marriage, by having a prohibition clause written into the marriage contract?"

Darsh replies:[22]

> Muslim jurists are in two camps on this issue. But unlike other instances of disagreement that have appeared in these columns, this time it is the Hanafi school which emerges as the most strict. According to this opinion, a marriage contract should not contain clauses outlawing any tradition which Islam has allowed. The Hanbali opinion, on the other hand, is more liberal. When a marriage contract is drawn up, according to this school of Islamic jurisprudence, women are allowed to stipulate terms and conditions which protect and reinforce their rights in marriage. Under Hanbali fiqh, a newly married woman has the right to live in her own house or

21 Conversation with Barkatullah Abdulkadir, London, 23 Feb 2009.

22 *Q-News*, 18–25 Mar 1994. I quote excerpts from the fatwa.

> locality and she is also allowed to stop her husband from taking another wife. As such there is no opposition to her writing such prohibitions into the marriage contract.

The other fatwa is an answer to the following question: "In what circumstances are Muslim men permitted to marry more than one wife? I am interested in taking on another wife—my first wife has given her consent—but I am unsure if it is a good idea since polygamy is officially prohibited under British law."[23]

Darsh replies:

> If you are asking my advice, I would say that one wife is more than enough. One is quite a handful for any husband, let alone two.
>
> But if you feel that you can provide for both wives, then there is nothing stopping you from taking a second wife—least of all the law of this country. Marriage in Islam does not depend upon the registry office, that is just a civil record. One extra wife is no extra burden on a legal system that allows you to have 10 girl friends and 15 common-law spouses. [...] Generally speaking, the ability to marry more than once at the time acts as a useful vent for society to keep a check on infidelity and creeping immorality. And, unlike the thousands of children born as a result of casual relationships, today children born to second and subsequent wives in Muslim families are guaranteed full inheritance and do not need elaborate multi-million-pound State institutions.
>
> But whatever your reasons to marry twice, Islam makes it clear that you must be able to provide for both women and children. The Qur'an, in two instances in chapter four, *The Women*, clearly says that men should refrain from marrying more than one wife "if ye fear that ye shall not be able to deal justly (with them) ..." (4:3).

Both fatwas argue from within the universe of Islamic law. In the first case, this is natural, since the question is posed in terms of "the marriage contract". In his answer, Darsh allows the woman to limit her husband's access to marrying a second wife. He does so by using *takhayyur*, the option of choosing between the schools of law. The woman's right to live in a non-polygamous marriage is the focus of the fatwa.

23 *Q-News*, 18–25 Mar 1994.

The other fatwa begins and ends with a moral argument as a possible barrier to polygamy. The legal aspects, however, are not only discussed in a *fiqh* perspective, but also with regard to—and in opposition to—domestic legislation. If a Muslim wishes to marry more than one woman, the law and the authorities cannot stop him, since marriage in Islam does not depend on registration. Moreover, Darsh presents arguments why one might marry more than one woman: Living in a *de facto* marriage, without registering it, is not a crime. He even considers polygamous marriages as a solution to infidelity and immorality, and to the many children who are born without rights. Children of polygamous marriages, on the other hand, will be guaranteed inheritance rights, according to Darsh.

This fatwa not only weakens the first fatwa on registering marriages and abiding by the law of the country. Even though civil marriage is advocated from an Islamic position and with Islamic motives, and would entail an orderly practice of entering into and dissolving marriages, the second fatwa, on polygamy, does not follow up. Darsh also sows confusion as to what makes up a marriage. Is it the content of the marriage, is it the Islamic ceremony, or is it the substance of the conditions for a valid marriage contract? And what about registration? When Darsh argued for the introduction of the Sharia for UK Muslims in 1975, he claimed that Muslims would be able to feel at peace with their conscience and their surroundings if they were able to practise Islamic family law. Perhaps this is a clue: What is at stake are religious feelings, rather than a systematic stance on questions of marriage and on the relationship between the norms.

Polygamy has also come to play a role as a marker of identity. In non-Muslim Europe, it is not only considered immoral and prohibited by law, but also as symbolizing the backwardness of Islam. Muslims, in turn, have turned the right to polygamy into an identity marker vis-à-vis the West. This right is held to have been given by God Himself in the Quran. Arguing against polygamy may expose one to accusations of questioning the Quran as revelation. Roald comments as follows on polygamy: "The question of polygyny in Islam is a matter of great concern, not only as an argument *against* Islam for non-Muslims, but also for many Muslim women who dread the prospect of their husbands taking a second wife.[24] [...] It seems that the issue of polygyny raises the emotions of Muslims in general ..."[25] My survey of Darsh's fatwas[26] showed that he often gave fatwas based on his own experience with the Muslims where he worked,

24 Roald 2001a, 201.

25 Roald 2001a, 210.

26 See chapter 3.

whether with regard to marriage, personal care, or social relationships. The advice is frequently given, not in a vacuum, but in a social setting: that of Muslims as a minority within a society with a non-Muslim majority, and of possible intergenerational conflicts between the parents with their foreign cultural baggage and interpretations of Islam, and the young who have grown up in the UK.

This insight, however, does not seem to extend to his view of the relations between *fiqh* and national marriage laws, whether the topic at hand is equality of status as a condition for marriage (*kafāʾa*), the role of the guardian and its limits (*wilāya*), or polygamy. The fatwas reproduced above appear as isolated pictures lacking inner coherence. In this regard, the fatwas do not contribute to securing the rule of law for women in matters of marriage. The lack of coherence may be due to the fact that the local contextualization of Islam had barely begun, as confirmed by Ataullah Siddiqui, academic director of the Markfield Institute of Higher Education (MIHE), Leicester: "The heritage of Darsh is that his fatwas brought out a kind of a level of understanding, where contextualisation began."[27]

The ECFR

The explicit aim of the European Council for Fatwa and Research is to promote unified fatwas (*tawḥīd al-fatwā*) in Europe in order to solve the problems of Muslims in the light of the Sharia.[28] The Council also sees itself as guiding and correcting the development of Islam in the West. Further, it has ambitions on the local level: "The Council is also designed to become an approved religious authority before local governments and private establishments ..."[29] It is safe to assume that the Council has set its sights on becoming the European authority and representative of Sunni Muslims. By promoting the message of *taysīr* ("easing") and taking into account *al-wāqiʿ* ("reality"),[30] they seek to reach as many

27 Conversation with Ataullah Siddiqui, Oslo, 25 Nov 2008.

28 The fatwas in question pertain to Sunni Islam.

29 The references in this paragraph are taken from ECFR 2002a, ix–xii.

30 The concept of "reality" can be problematic. As Caeiro comments, in connection with the Council: "The ambiguity stems from the notion of 'reality' itself. In the fatwas of the ECFR, reality sometimes refers to a naturalized condition—for example, the reality of men's sexual appetites, used to justify polygamy—and sometimes to a more or less pressing social constraint (such as that which justifies the presence of women and men in shared spaces). As many sociologists have shown, reality is always in part socially constructed, and clearly

Muslims as possible and include them in their following, "even if they practiced no more than the absolute minimum of obligations."[31] There is a clear orientation toward mission and revival.

The concluding declaration (*bayān al-khitāmī*) that is read aloud and adopted at the end of each session always contains a section titled "recommendations" (*tawṣiyāt*), each time repeating the same points with minor changes. Muslims are exhorted to work for the recognition of Islam and the rights of other minorities in the European context. In the concluding declaration after the Council's seventh session, the right to manage one's own affairs concerning marriage and divorce is mentioned:

> The Council calls upon Muslims in Europe to seek the recognition of their respective countries of Islam as a religion, and Muslims as a religious minority similar to other religious minorities who enjoy full rights and dues, including administrating their own personal status regulations, concerning marriage, divorce and the such. Therefore, the Council advises Muslims to establish Shari'a entities which would be capable of organising their personal status affairs according to Islamic Shari'a and in accordance with the laws of the land.[32]

At the same time, it is stressed that Muslims should obey the laws of the land: "To respect and abide by the laws of these lands which have welcomed them, given them shelter, granted them protection and allowed them to prosper and enjoy all means of good living. Allah Almighty stated in the Holy Quran: '[T]he reward of good [is] but good.' "[33]

How is this apparently contradictory call reflected in fatwas and resolutions on marriage? What is the Council's message with regard to national legislations? In the following, I present three resolutions (*qarārāt*) and one fatwa that suggest a possible answer to these questions. The first resolution is on whether a woman needs a guardian (*walī*) to get married.

not enough research has been done on what counts as reality in Muslim and non-Muslim engagements with the 'Muslim question' in Europe." (Caeiro 2010, 446 n. 8)

31 ECFR 2002a, x.

32 http://www.e-cfr.org/en/index.php?ArticleID=280 (accessed 24 Jun 2010, now defunct).

33 http://www.e-cfr.org/en/index.php?ArticleID=281 (accessed 24 Jun 2010, now defunct), citing the Quran 55:60.

Guardianship (wilāya)

The resolution goes:

> Upon deliberation of the research submitted regarding "Guardianship in Marriage" the ECFR reached the following resolution:
>
> The Muslim scholars have two opinions in this regard:
>
> The first view is [that] to have a guardian is a prerequisite to enter into a marriage contract. This opinion is based on the hadith narrated by Abu Musa Al-Ashari in which prophet Muhammad—peace be upon him—said: "There can be no marriage without a guardian." This opinion is held by the majority of Muslim scholars of Fiqh and hadith. Some of them categorized it as a pillar of the contract.
>
> The second view states that a guardian is not a prerequisite of marriage. If a woman marries a fit [*kufʾ*] man this marriage is valid. This opinion is held by some Muslim scholars of Fiqh e.g. Hanafi School who support their opinion with other proofs.
>
> These two opinions are highly respected. Upon deliberation the ECFR confirms the religious and social importance of the guardian's consent when entering into a marriage contract. But in certain cases e.g. difficulty of getting the guardian's consent or his continuous prevention of marriage, there is no harm in entering into the marriage contract without a guardian. If the contract is made without a guardian, it is valid according to the second opinion.
>
> The ECFR clarifies that not every relative is fit to be the bride's guardian in marriage. He has to fulfill certain conditions the most important of which is that what he does should be beneficial to her and not causing any harm to her.[34]

In this resolution, the Council first presents the two positions on guardianship taken by the scholars, with references. The Council expresses its respect for both views, and gives reasons for choosing one of them. The importance of the guardian's consent is stressed, but it is acknowledged that the guardian can be an obstacle if he exceeds his mandate. The wording ("… there is no harm …") might be interpreted to mean that, while the Council does not recommend that women marry without a guardian, it is possible in certain cases.

---

34 Resolution 14/3, Dublin, 2005. English version at http://www.e-cfr.org/en/index.php?ArticleID=294 (accessed 21 Apr 2010, now defunct). Arabic version in *al-Majalla al-ʿilmiyya* 7: 415.

This resolution implies a possible solution for women who, as the Council sees it, are prevented from marrying by their guardian on unjustifiable grounds. It exemplifies the use of the notion of *taysīr* ("easing") as a basis for resolutions. Guardians who exceed their mandate may be seen as the "reality" (*al-wāqiʿ*) on the grounds of which the Council makes this statement.

The resolution does not, however, discuss whether Abu Hanifa's suitability requirement as a condition for marriage (*kafāʾa*), as defined by the Council, should be implemented, since the requirement is not backed by legal sanctions. Still, the resolution may serve as an argument for women who face their guardian's opposition to their choice of husband.

When the Guardian Prevents a Marriage

The guardian who prevents a marriage is the subject of a separate resolution:[35]

> Upon deliberation on the issue of "Guardian's Prevention of marriage" and the research submitted in this regard, the ECFR reached the following resolution: The guardian is not allowed to prevent a woman from marrying a man fit to her on the basis of dowry of her peeresses and if he does guardianship will be transferred to the one next to him or to the judge or whosoever represents the Muslims e.g. officials running Islamic centers and Imams in the West. Actually postponing marriage and guardian's prevention of marriage have profound negative impact on the individual and society level. The phenomenon of guardian's prevention of marriage is widely spread. Hence in Muslim society it is to be tackled in a way that would terminate it. In this regard it is vitally important to distinguish between the Islamic rules and customs and cultural aspects. It is also important to raise awareness of Islamic rules among Muslims via leaflets and courses and forming arbitrary [*sic*] councils to refer thereto.

This resolution would seem to confirm that the Council considers guardians overstepping their bounds a part of "reality" (*al-wāqiʿ*); indeed, their prevention of marriage is a widespread phenomenon. In this resolution, however, the Council does not support the woman's marrying without a guardian. If the guardian denies the woman marriage, the guardianship should pass to the next person in line, or ultimately to imams or those in charge of Islamic centres

35 Resolution 14/5, Dublin, 2005. English version at http://www.e-cfr.org/en/index.php?ArticleID=294 (accessed 22 Apr 2010, now defunct). Arabic version in *al-Majalla al-ʿilmiyya* 7: 415 f.

in the West. We see a balancing act between the two views presented in the previous resolution, which concluded that there was "no harm" in marrying without a guardian. In this case, though, the Council follows the majority of scholars who think marriage should be done with a guardian. The resolution concludes by declaring that this phenomenon of guardians keeping women from marrying must come to an end, and offering guidance on how to achieve this aim.

The resolution clearly expresses the Council's view of its own authority: "The guardian is not allowed to [...] and if he does guardianship will be transferred to [...]." Equally authoritative in tone is the statement on doing away with the phenomenon: "Hence in Muslim society it is to be tackled in a way that would terminate it." The Council, however, has no power of sanctions, and one is not obliged to obey a fatwa. The guidance offered at the end of the text may give a clue to the appeal of their authority.[36]

Neither this resolution nor the previous one relates to national legislation. The argument is based on Islamic norms and what the Council holds to be "reality".

Forced Marriage

A guardian may also abuse his role by forcing a woman to marry. In another fatwa on guardianship, the Council states that a woman cannot be forced to marry:

> ... Allah did not allow for the guardianship of the father of the bride or any one else to become one by which the guardian forces or compels the woman to marry to a man who she does not want. Indeed Islam granted the woman full rights to accept or reject whomever proposes to her in marriage.[37]

Forced marriage is also the topic of a resolution (*qarār*), which signals the importance placed on this issue. The resolution goes:

> Upon deliberation on the issue of "Forced marriage" the ECFR reached the following resolution:
>
> The parents and the guardians have to marry their daughters with their consent. If a daughter approves of marriage it will be valid and [vice

36 On the vertical authority of the fatwa, see chapter 5.

37 ECFR 2002a, 128–129.

> versa]. Prophet Muhammad—peace be upon him—said: "A deflowered [previously married woman] cannot be married unless she expresses her approval and a virgin cannot be married unless with her permission." They said: 'O messenger of Allah! How does she express her permission?' He—peace be upon him—said: "Her permission is expressed by her silence." Reported by Al-Bukhari.
>
> Ibn Abbas narrated that a virgin woman came to Prophet Muhammad—peace be upon him—and stated that her father married her without her consent. Prophet Muhammad—peace be upon him—gave her the choice of either terminating or continuing that marriage. In another narration it is stated that Prophet Muhammad—peace be upon him—nullified this marriage.[38]

The resolution addresses the parents as well as the guardian. The Council notes that marriage requires the consent of the daughter. Without consent, the marriage is not valid. The norm is justified by traditions from the Prophet Muhammad. The view of voluntary consent as a condition for the validity of the marriage is not argued with reference to national legislation, but wholly in terms of Islamic references.

Valid Marriage

The definition of a valid marriage is about more than the condition of voluntary consent, as we see in a fatwa on the relationship between civil and Islamic marriage:[39]

> A man used to have a sexual relationship with a woman (either Christian or Jew) without being bound by an Islamic marriage contract. He later entered into marriage with her by virtue of a civil marriage contract, after which they had a baby daughter. He now wishes to ratify an Islamically legal marriage contract. May we write such a contract for this couple? If the answer is yes, what must we do prior to the ratification of the contract?

The Council answers:

38 Resolution 14/4, English version at http://www.e-cfr.org/en/index.php?ArticleID=294 (accessed 22 Apr 2010, now defunct). Arabic version in *al-Majalla al-ʿilmiyya* 7: 415.

39 ECFR 2002a, 57–58.

> Yes, you may write such a contract that will act as an accreditation to the civil contract which was previously ratified, on condition that the civil contract has fulfilled all legal requirements. The contract that you write, must be dated similarly to the civil contract. It is preferable to have witnesses to testify to the correctness and authenticity of the contract. There is no need to renew the civil contract if it has fulfilled all legal requirements. Before the contract is made, you only have to remind the couple of Allah (Glorified and Exalted be He) and to ask for his forgiveness for what they committed prior to the civil marriage contract being ratified.

The Council establishes that a civil marriage contract is valid as long as all legal requirements are met.[40] An Islamic marriage contract may also be drawn up, but only to confirm the civil contract, and it is not necessary. However, the matter is then brought back to the Islamic moral universe. The couple have had extramarital relations, and must ask forgiveness before the Islamic marriage contract can be made.

The Council equates civil and Islamic marriage on the condition that all legal requirements are met. In the final analysis, though, it is the intent of the two parties that determines the validity of their marriage. In a resolution, the Council says that the contract's validity depends on the intention being genuine. Consequently, marriage and divorce entered into by mistake, under compulsion, or in anger is not valid.[41]

The Council shows that national legislation is taken into account with regard to marriage. However, legal requirements (which the fatwa fails to specify) are subordinated to the moral rules of Islam. For the definition of a valid marriage, the core question is the underlying intent (*niyya*). The Council's rejection of forced marriage with reference to voluntary consent as a condition for the validity of marriage is one aspect of this theme.

Valid Marriage in a New Context

An important part of the Council's activities is carrying out studies on topics slated for discussion.[42] Resolutions are made after one or more studies on the

40 The Council's tendency not to concretize the concepts in its fatwas is discussed in chapter 4.

41 Resolution 15/2, Dublin, 2005. English version at http://www.e-cfr.org/en/index.php?ArticleID=295 (accessed 22 Apr 2010). Arabic original in ECFR 2013, 141f.

42 The so-called *amāna al-ʿamma* ("general secretariat") decides what topics shall be dealt with at the upcoming session, and asks the members to prepare studies for presentation. In 2008, the secretariat consisted of Hussein Halawa, Abdulmajid Najjar, Ahmed Jaballah,

topic have been presented and discussed. Sometimes, it is concluded that more studies are needed before a resolution can be made. A study, then, is a step on the way to a resolution.

Ounis Guergah's study *al-Ḥukm al-zawāj bayna al-ʿaqd al-ʿurfī wal-ʿaqd al-madanī*, on the relationship between civil and non-registered Islamic marriage, was presented at the Council's session in London in 2004.[43] The study's point of departure is the challenge to imams and Islamic institutions posed by *ʿurfī* (non-registered) marriages.[44] When a marriage goes unregistered, the interests of the parties and of any children are not secured. In particular, this has turned out to the detriment of women in divorce matters.[45] Guergah compares civil and unregistered marriage contracts in the French context, and concludes by declaring the marriage contract to basically be a civil contract like other contracts. Muslims should get a civil marriage and then the *ʿurfī* one, in order to follow the law of their country of residence.[46] This study would seem to be connected with the Council's later resolution on the importance of official registration: "… it is essential to register marriage contracts in a registrar's office while observing marriage procedures at Islamic centres as a means to preserve the rights pertaining to the husband, wife and children."[47]

The registration of marriage limits the opportunities for polygamous marriages, and there is a wide gap between this resolution and the fatwa adopted by the Council at the fourth session in 1999, which defended the right to polygamy without regard to European national legislations. The explanation may be that the authors of these two decisions hail from different contexts. Whereas Ounis Guergah lives and works in France, Yusuf al-Qaradawi is based in Qatar, and has an outsider's perspective on Muslims in Europe. Alexandre Caeiro, too, has observed this tension in the fatwas, commenting and explaining:

> A close reading of the ECFR's fatwas suggests an underlying tension between, on the one hand, the attempt to reconcile traditional Islamic norms with the dominant practices of the mainstream host society and,

Mohammed Hawari, and Salem Shaykhi. (Conversation with Ounis Guergah, Paris, 12 May 2008).

43 Guergah 2004.

44 Guergah 2004, 1.

45 Guergah 2004, 6.

46 Guergah 2004, 7.

47 *Al-Majalla al-ʿilmiyya* 12–13: 36. The resolution concerned was no. 4 of the 15th session. The Arabic original is titled *al-Ishhād ʿalā al-ṭalāq* ("Attestation of divorce"), whereas the English translation is titled "Attestation of marriage".

> on the other hand, a reiteration of the Islamic tradition's contemporary relevance. [...] The tension sketched above can be partly traced to the membership of the ECFR. Although most of the members are Europe based, and many have been directly involved in national processes of state institutionalization of Islam across Europe, the Middle Eastern leadership provided by Yusuf al-Qaradawi and Faysal Mawlawi (the ECFR's chairman and vice-chairman, respectively) give the council a distinctively diasporic flavor. Although they "carry the worries and anxieties of their fellow Muslims in Europe, visit them on a frequent basis, and appreciate their condition," the charismatic scholars based in the Middle East work within a discursive field primarily shaped by conditions in the Muslim world—and in particular by the problematics of the Islamic Revival. Both Qaradawi and Mawlawi have accordingly striven to place the European fatwa council squarely within the revivalist movement. By contrast, the muftis based in Europe (particularly those affiliated with the FIOE) have been preoccupied with national discourses about the "integration of Muslims" and the fear of "Islamic radicalization."[48]

The differing geographic backgrounds of the members, however, are not a sufficient explanation for the gap between the polygamy fatwa and the marriage-registration resolution. Temporal distance, too, may help explain how the Council has managed to give such contradictory fatwas. The polygamy fatwa was given at the fourth session of the Council, in October 1999, that is, at a fairly early stage of the Council's history. The marriage-registration resolution was given at the 15th session, in June 2005, nearly six years later. In the meantime, a number of issues had been studied and been the subject of resolutions, not least relating to marriage and the family. The marriage-registration resolution suggests that the Council has become more aware of issues affecting Muslims in Europe than was the case at the time of the polygamy fatwa. Indeed, the polygamy facta is not being actively promoted, and the French fatwa-collection affair in 2005 suggests that this fatwa is rather seen as an obstacle to integration and recognition in the local European context.[49]

Women's Rights

The fatwas and resolutions presented above show that women's rights are promoted within well-defined Islamic limits, both with regard to getting married

48 Caeiro 2010, 436–437.

49 See chapter 2.

without a guardian, forced marriage, and registration of marriages. The Council promotes the civil registration of marriages as a matter of utmost importance, and such registration may act as an obstacle to polygamy. Civil marriage will also help secure equal rights to divorce, as the terms are set by national legislation. The Council has given a fatwa declaring that the judicial dissolution of marriage is valid according to Islamic norms if the marriage was concluded according to national legislation, even if the judge is a non-Muslim.[50] In this way, the fatwas and resolutions provide indirect support for the principle of equality before the law, on Islamic grounds, and serve as a contribution to solving the dilemma of Muslim women faced with two competing sets of norms, equal worth and complementarity versus equality and rights.

But how does this view reach Muslims in Europe? The Council and its resolutions are at a long remove from Muslims in local communities around Europe. Mohamed al-Mansoori, a Council member, said that the fatwas and resolutions easily end up in a drawer in an Islamic centre. The Council's publishing channels may not be the most effective at reaching ordinary Muslims. The Council published fatwas and resolutions in book form in 2002, and again a decade later, in 2013, covering a period from its establishment to 2010. The *al-Majalla al-ʿilmiyya* journal mainly targets Muslim leaders and scholars. The ECFR's website is far more difficult to use than, say, the fatwa bank that IslamOnline.net used to have before it was closed in 2010. Nor did the latter systematically publish all fatwas and resolutions from the Council.

Another possible challenge lies in the general nature of the texts. Are they precise enough to be meaningful in a local context? There is a difference between the fatwas and resolutions of the ECFR and fatwas given for a limited local context. Whereas the ECFR's fatwas are general (intended to apply in more than one European country), fatwas given by a local mufti or fatwa council are more precise. Ahmed Jaballah, who was the rector of the Institut Européen des Sciences Humaines (IESH) in Paris at the time I interviewed him, mentioned the Dar al-Fatwa of the UOIF as an example, noting that the latter's fatwas were characterized by more specific language and clearer conclusions.[51] In the following, I will present a fatwa on unregistered Islamic marriages, given for the local French context. The fatwa and its justification may be read as giving substance to the general resolution of the ECFR on the importance of registering marriages.

50 ECFR 2002a, 145.

51 Conversation with Ahmed Jaballah, Paris, 30 Mar 2007.

Larabi Becheri

The occasion is the annual mass gathering of the UOIF in Le Bourget outside Paris in 2008. The hall, which seats thousands, is nearly full (it is hard to give a more precise estimate). At the podium stands Larabi Becheri, a teacher at the IESH in Chateau Chinon and member of the ECFR, who will later be in charge of the Dar al-Fatwa. In his talk, *Le mariage musulman en France: lecture théologique et canonique*, Becheri describes marriage both as a means to procreation, and as an aim in itself (having a strong family). Without witnesses, the marriage contract is not valid, and based on a certain interpretation of this requirement, Becheri declares unregistered marriage (*ʿurfī* marriage) to be forbidden (*interdit*).[52] In a conversation with Becheri, I ask him to explain just what *interdit* means.[53] *Ḥarām*, he answers. But how can a marriage be both valid and *ḥarām* at the same time? Becheri replies with an analogy: sales during Friday prayers are valid, but forbidden.

The reason he declares unregistered marriages *ḥarām*, Becheri says, is all the problems people have with *ʿurfī* marriages. The witnesses to an *ʿurfī* marriage are not recognized by the court as valid witnesses, whether in France or in a Muslim country. This causes problems, particularly in divorce cases. One divorce case mentioned by Becheri during a panel discussion may serve as an example. The question came from a convert who had married a man from Algeria after an *ʿaqd fātiḥa* (concluding an unwritten contract, with a reading of the first Sura of the Quran). The man is gone, and the woman wants a divorce. But how can she get divorced when there is no written contract, Becheri asks rhetorically. Such a case can only be solved by finding the imam who married them; it will be his task to search for the man who vanished.

John Bowen, too, comments on this problem:

> How do you break a halāl marriage if there was no written contract or certificate? [...] Many Muslims are concerned about this problem. Although a Muslim husband may divorce his wife on his own, a Muslim wife has no corresponding way of ending the marriage by herself. In countries of Muslim judges, she may ask that the marriage be annulled or the husband be asked to grant a divorce, but France has neither Islamic judges nor Islamic arbitration panels.[54]

---

52 Le Bourget, 9 May 2008.

53 The text that follows stems from a conversation with Larabi Becheri at Le Bourget, 10 May 2008, and at Chateau Chinon, 14 May 2008.

54 Bowen 2010, 161.

Becheri later told me that the fatwa he gave during the Le Bourget gathering was the result of an *ijtihād* in the form of a study titled *Al-muslimūn fī ūrūbā bayna al-zawāj al-ʿurfī wal-zawāj fil-qānūn al-madanī* (The Muslims in Europe between informal marriage and civil marriage).[55] In the following I will give the gist of this study as I have read it in manuscript.[56]

Becheri poses three questions. (i) Is it sufficient for Muslims to marry according to (French) civil law? (ii) Is it sufficient to make an *ʿurfī* contract?[57] (iii) Or is it necessary to enter into both contracts at the same time? He seeks to answer these questions by disclosing the content of *ʿurfī* marriage, and then showing the differences between *ʿurfī* marriage and the French civil-law marriage contract.

ʿUrfī marriage, that is, unregistered Islamic marriage, is a marriage that apparently satisfies all the formal basic elements (*arkān*) and conditions (*shurūṭ*), but which is not registered with the authorities. Becheri follows up this definition with the question: Is registration necessary if the basic elements and conditions are satisfied? The question cannot be answered without knowing the relationship between contracts and documentation of contracts in Islamic teachings, Becheri states.

Becheri's Argument

Becheri's point of entry, and the framework of the study, is the rules for documenting contracts. He shows that the Sharia has taken precautions *before* the transaction takes place, by banning the reasons why things might go wrong, and *after* the transaction, by requiring documentation whether in the form of witnesses, written documents, or security.

The marriage contract is a contract like other contracts, but it holds a special position because it is not about economic transactions, but about establishing a religiously and legally recognized relationship between the parties living together. The Sharia therefore takes precautions with the marriage contract that do not apply to other types of contract. It requires witnesses and public notice as documentation: in case one of the parties comes to deny having

55 14 May 2008.

56 Becheri stressed that this was a work in progress, not finished. There might be changes and additions at a later date. The study must therefore be read as reflecting a stage of Becheri's process of reflection on the topic. The study has not been published, and may have changed since May 2008.

57 Becheri defines *ʿurfī* marriage as an "Islamic marriage that has not been publicly registered" (Becheri 2008, 2).

entered into the contract, to prevent suspicions, and to protect honour and reputations. This holds whether the witnessing takes place at the entry into marriage, as required by the majority of the scholars, or at the consummation of marriage, as held by the Maliki school.

The marriage contract falls under the category of *muʿāmalāt*, social transactions, which have been defined as follows: "… they define juridico-human relations and ensure that the Muslim's behaviour conforms to juridico-moral theories."[58] An important aspect of this category is the possibility of changing the law. As the *Oxford Dictionary of Islam* puts it, "In muamalat […] there is considerable […] room to develop and change the law to facilitate human interaction and promote justice."[59]

Becheri's study discusses witnessing as documentation of a marriage contract. Witnessing is considered a basic element (*rukn*) of the validity of marriage in three out of four schools of law (by Hanafis, Shafiʿis and Hanbalis), whereas the Maliki school accepts marriage without witnesses, but requires witnessing of *dukhūl* (the husband's going in to the bride, i.e. consummation of the marriage).

With reference to Ibn Taymiyya and Sarakhsi (d. 1090), Becheri notes two purposes of witnessing: as a safety against denial of the marriage, and to distinguish the relationship from adultery. However, a valid marriage contract is also important in relation to the national authorities, who guarantee the safeguarding of the interests of the parties.[60] These examples make it clear that witnessing is not an aim in itself, as Becheri also stresses. He relies on Ibn Ashur's (d. 1973) definition of "means" as a norm established in order to realize other norms.

With reference to Ibn Abidin's recommendation that the emancipation of slaves should be documented by a written contract, Becheri goes on to argue that the witnessing of a marriage should follow the same norm. He calls this an upgrading of the means, and ties it to the notion of *fasād al-zamān*, citing

58 R. Brunschvig, quoted in "Muʿāmalāt" in *EI2* (Bernand 2010).

59 Esposito 2003, 209.

60 Becheri's explanation goes as follows: An *ʿurfī* marriage contract is based on religious obligations, not on obligations to the authorities. Even if an *ʿurfī* marriage contract is based on witnesses, it is outside the law. The Sharia raises two bars to protect contracts: one is religion, the other is the authorities. Marriage contracts require the protection of the authorities. They cannot be left to the protection of religion alone now that faith and morals have declined. Therefore, we find the majority of the scholars in agreement that documentation takes place in writing, by witnessing, or by security. This is encouraged in most types of transactions.

what he calls the famous statement of Umar ibn Abdulaziz (d. 720) that new cases and methods arise depending on how sinfully people act.[61]

The French law on marrying, marriage, and divorce contains elements similar to Islamic norms (parental approval if the person is a minor, the right of others to oppose the marriage); elements at the same time similar and dissimilar (noone can marry before the first marriage is dissolved); and distinctive elements (the family as an economic unit, mutual obligation to support, only the judge can grant divorce). Given that several elements do not agree with Islamic norms, is civil marriage allowed?

Becheri starts by comparing the French civil marriage contract with an *ʿurfī* marriage contract. Muslims in France have to relate to two types of contract, one might say: (i) A legal contract that is not sufficient in an Islamic perspective, because it is deficient with regard to basic elements (requirements) and because of those consequences that differ from the Islamic contract. (ii) The *ʿurfī* marriage contract, which, as explained above, is meaningless, lacks documentation for the case that one of the parties denies having entered into it, and should be administratively registered in order to be valid according to the Sharia.

According to Becheri, we face a dilemma if we have to accept one of them, as neither one realizes the objective, one due to its consequences and to its lack of basic elements (*arkān*) and conditions (*shurūṭ*), and the other due to a lack of documentation.

Rather than accept the differing consequences, one might combine the contracts, but this is difficult because the Sharia does not allow two contracts for the same agreement. In the case of conflict, each party would approach the authority that would best protect their own interests. Combining the two contracts is a precondition for keeping the purpose of the marriage contract. It may be said, then, that it is not right to consider two separate contracts as having equal weight, but that the *ʿurfī* marriage contract is considered the fundamental one, and the legal contract as its supplement and as a remedy for its inadequate documentation, meeting the requirement of witnessing.

61 Schacht translates *fasād al-zamān* as "the ever-increasing corruption of contemporary conditions" (Schacht 1991, 84). Marion Holmes Katz renders it as "the ongoing deterioration of social morality until the advent of the end of times"; she cites Haim Gerbner on the point that the concept is not a legal one, but is significant for connecting law and the wider culture (Katz 2006, 174). It should also be understood in eschatological perspective. As Hallaq writes, belief in a history of progressive degeneration from the Golden Age of the Prophet was consistent with the belief in the Day of Judgment (Hallaq 1986, p. 138).

Therefore, Becheri concludes, it is possible to enter into two marriage contracts at the same time, civil and Islamic. Citing Shatibi, he defines marriage as *ḍarūra* (a vital necessity). One may seek a solution that is not in accordance with Islamic norms, but try to take one's precautions as best one may. The solution is to define *ʿurfī* marriage as marriage without witnesses, in accordance with the Maliki school, which only requires witnesses at the consummation, a requirement fulfilled through civil marriage by means of written documentation.

Becheri stresses that this is a temporary solution, and that a better solution would be for Muslims to take charge of their affairs themselves. I would interpret this as a strategic utterance meant for Muslims who do not accept bowing to non-Muslim laws.[62]

The Context

John Bowen distinguishes three categories of Muslims in France: those who would let French norms govern their lives, those who would have Islamic norms apply, and those who find both French and Islamic norms relevant to live by. For the latter, life can be complicated. Bowen raises the question how they "combine or accommodate or broker among these competing sets of norms".[63] The dilemma pertains not least to getting married. French law requires marriage to take place in *la mairie*, city hall. Under French law, marriages performed by imams are not only invalid, they are also illegal if performed before the city-hall marriage takes place. The maximum sentence for a religious leader who marries someone before their civil marriage is six months of prison and a fine of 7,500 euros. In 2008, an imam in Orleans was convicted of violating this law, according to Ounis Guergah, the head of Dar al-Fatwa.[64] As a newcomer to the country, unaware of the rules, he was sentenced to three months of prison (suspended) and fined 1,000 euros.[65]

Nonetheless, there is much confusion among Muslims as to what is a so-called *ḥalāl* (permitted) marriage. These questions are discussed, for example,

---

62 A similar case of offering a temporary solution is Tariq Ramadan's call for a moratorium on *ḥudūd* punishments, which argues within the framework of the Islamic tradition for an end to these punishments: http://tariqramadan.com/english/2005/04/05/an-international-call-for-moratorium-on-corporal-punishment-stoning-and-the-death-penalty-in-the-islamic-world/, see also Ramadan 2009b.

63 Bowen 2010, 157.

64 Conversation with Ounis Guergah, Le Bourget, 11 May 2008.

65 According to Ounis Guergah. John Bowen says that two imams were convicted of violating this law in 2008 (Bowen 2010, 157, 165).

in forums on the Internet.[66] By following such discussions, one can get an idea what the participants see as the challenges related to getting married. Against this background, Bowen poses the question:

> Is a marriage halāl if the couple follows the religious steps helpfully outlined by the respondents on the Internet sites mentioned above, regardless of whether they also marry at the city hall? Or does the phrase "halāl" marriage indicate that the man and woman have made a binding promise before God and *refuse* to travel to the city hall? Or does it mean the opposite: *requiring* that the couple marry in the city hall, so that the state may ensure that both parties adhere to their promises?[67]

According to Bowen, all these views are expressed, but all agree that "the real marriage" is the religious marriage, which is the one that is lawful, *ḥalāl*. We recognize the emotional aspect of Muslims' wish to live in accordance with Islamic law, as described by Syed Darsh in his argument for introducing Islamic family law in the British context.

The fact that religious leaders have many different views of the definition of valid marriage does not make matters easier. Bowen presents some of them. Najjar Mondher, the imam of the grand mosque of Lyon, refuses to carry out so-called *ḥalāl* marriages, on the grounds that France lacks institutions for dissolving religious marriages. A woman should therefore secure the option of a future divorce by entering into civil marriage.[68] Dhaou Meskine, the imam of a mosque in Clichy-sous-Bois (a suburb of Paris) and the rector of Collège Réussite ("Success High School") is basically negative to *ḥalāl* marriage for the same reason. On the other hand, he thinks it better for Muslims to marry young through *ḥalāl* marriages. This can be compared to the French *concubinage* or domestic partnership, and can be officially registered, though it provides no financial rights in case of divorce.[69]

66 Bowen says about the use of Internet forums by young Muslims: "Many young Muslims look for horizontal forms of exchange rather than authoritative replies. They also wish to explain their particular situation in detail and to have it taken into account, and to encourage others to ask relevant questions, something not possible on the other types of sites. Many Muslims in Europe have made shari'a into a set of individual commitments, and seek to compare opinions with others. The forums are well-suited to this sort of communication and knowledge seeking, and may be attractive for these reasons, even if the participants may not be well versed in religious matters." (Bowen 2010, 160)

67 Bowen 2010, 160.

68 Bowen 2010, 163.

69 Bowen 2010, 163–164.

Hishem El-Arafa, founder and teacher at CERSI, Centre d'Études et de Recherches sur l'Islam in Saint Denis, Paris, holds that civil marriage is an Islamic requirement. The experience with people who only get married *ḥalāl* is that they fail to take it seriously. Getting married at city hall makes people take the whole thing more seriously, and thus contributes to the stable marriage intended by Islam.[70] Bowen puts El-Arafa's view as follows: "… the more damaging the consequence of avoiding city hall, the more justified is proclaiming civil marriage to be Islamic in nature."[71] Larbi Kechat, director of the al-Daʿwa Mosque in rue de Tanger, Paris, claims that a civil marriage should be considered an Islamic marriage, because all conditions for Islamic marriage are satisfied: both parties accept it, there are two witnesses, and the ring counts as *mahr* or bride-gift. The mosque ceremony may be considered a solemn blessing of the marriage. Public registration contributes to the stability of marriage, and hence to realizing a *maqṣid* (objective).[72]

Tareq Oubrou, imam of the Mosque of Bordeaux and a member of the UOIF's Dar al-Fatwa, goes one step further. Based on his project of *sharia de minorité*, Oubrou argues that one should first look to the norms and requirements of French law, and then select those Islamic viewpoints that best fit with those premises. Regarding polygamy, he refers to the Hanbali view. If the local culture practices monogamous marriage, then that is also the applicable Sharia.[73]

We may now situate Larabi Becheri's study among the views surveyed above. Becheri takes a radical position in claiming that civil marriage satisfies the Islamic requirement of documentation, whereas *ʿurfī* marriage does not. Amid the confusion on what makes a marriage in the Islamic perspective, Becheri's may be said to be the clearest fatwa that has been given on the definition of a validly contracted marriage. The independent reasoning (*ijtihād*) involved is also a novelty in that it does not regard Islamic marriage through emotional glasses, but analyses principles and practices with respect to the basic elements and conditions for a valid marriage contract. It is interesting that a Muslim jurist declares a so-called Islamic marriage *ḥarām* based on an evaluation of

70 Bowen 2010, 166–167.

71 Bowen 2010, 167.

72 Bowen 2010, 167–168.

73 Bowen 2010, 168–169. Bowen mistakenly says that Tareq Oubrou, with his *sharia de minorité* project, follows Yusuf al-Qaradawi as an advocate for a Sharia for minorities. Obrou's project does have minority Muslims as its target group, but it stands in opposition to al-Qaradawi's project, hence the term *sharia de minorité* to contrast with al-Qaradawi's *fiqh al-aqalliyyāt*. See chapter 2.

the consequences of the practice, and insists that civil marriage satisfies Islamic requirements of documentation.

Becheri's fatwa may also impact the practice of polygamy. His text notes that French law restricts the man's right to enter into more than one marriage at the same time. In conversation, however, he elaborates on his view of polygamous practices in France: Polygamy is prohibited on French territory by French law, and men should therefore renounce this right. "We don't want clandestine families," he adds. Besides, a second marriage is often built on the ruins of the first.

It should be noted that if translated into practice, this fatwa, the most radical to date, would also mean relating to the French *ordre public*. In other words, the fatwa agrees with what Bowen[74] calls "the morality and values of the French tribunal," both with regard to entry into marriage, and possible impacts on the practice of polygamy.[75] The fatwa may thus be described as a significant contribution to the legal integration of Muslims in France. The fatwa would also seem to agree with the UOIF's self-understanding as *de France* (French) rather than *en France* (in France), and their ambitions to be citizens of the Republic.

Becheri's fatwa also forms part of a trend that Bowen describes with reference to Olivier Roy: "Muslim political demands are for the even-handed application of *French* laws (on schooling, religious freedom, houses of worship) and not for the development of shari'a based laws."[76]

The fatwa may also fit in with the French context and French identity. On 19 June 1997, the then new prime minister Lionel Jospin opened his political declaration to the national assembly with the following words: *"La France, ce n'est pas seulement le bonheur des paysages, une langue enrichie des oeuvres de l'esprit: c'est d'abord une histoire.* [...] *Avant même de s'enscrire dans des institutions, la République, c'est un état d'esprit."*[77]

Part of this idea of the Republic is the notion of being a *citoyen* of French society, and the expectation that all should assent to shared values in the public sphere. Bowen illustrates the point with a 2003 statement by the then minister of the interior Nicolas Sarkozy: "[F]reedom is the rule in the private sphere; republican conformity is the rule in the public sphere."[78] The very identity marker of French public space is the principle of *laïcité*, the French version of

74 Bowen 2010, 173.

75 This also implies a change with regard to divorce, but that topic falls outside the discussion in this chapter.

76 Bowen 2010, 191.

77 Sfeir and Andrau 2005, 173.

78 Bowen 2007, 157–158.

secularism.[79] Olivier Roy distinguishes between a legal interpretation of *laïcité*, based on the 1905 law that restricted religion in public space, and an ideological interpretation, which "claims to provide a value system common to all citizens by expelling religion into the private sphere."[80] The principle of *laïcité* plays a role as social glue, as described by Roy: "*Laïcité* therefore defines national cohesion by asserting a purely political identity that confines to the private sphere any specific religious or cultural identities."[81] Defending the principle of *laïcité* therefore becomes a matter of the encounter of French identity with Muslims—in the country with the largest Muslim minority in Europe.

It seems not so much a matter of defending *laïcité*, though, as of defense against *communautarisme* as a threat to the French national project.[82] Bowen comments: "Communalism threatens the processes of direct communication between the state and the citizens that underlie French political philosophy. It separates citizens by valuing their affiliation to communities over their collective participation in the nation."[83]

After the ban on wearing religious symbols in French schools was introduced in 2004, targeting girls with hijab in particular, and the riots in the banlieus in 2005, Muslims in France did not make newspaper headlines until 2009, when the question was raised whether dress that covers the face is a threat to the French principle of *laïcité*. A commission of jurists was set up in 2009 to study the question.[84] The French parliament passed a ban the following year.

Roy calls what is going on with Muslims a process of *formatage*: Islam is being "formatted" to fit in with the dominant social norms. "Formatage can be done from below, or imposed from above," he says. Citing Roy, Simon Kuper says the purpose is to define a French Islam:

---

79 The Larousse dictionary defines *laïcité* as: "Conception et organisation de la société fondée sur la séparation de l'Église et de l'État et qui exclut les Églises de l'exercice de tout pouvoir politique ou administratif, et, en particulier, de l'organisation de l'enseignement. (Le principe de la laïcité de l'État est posé par l'article 2 de la Constitution française de 1958.)" http://www.larousse.fr/dictionnaires/francais/laicite.

80 Roy 2007, xii.

81 Roy 2007, xiii.

82 The Larousse dictionnary defines *communautarisme* as: "Tendance du multiculturalisme américain qui met l'accent sur la fonction sociale des organisations communautaires (ethniques, religieuses, sexuelles, etc.)." http://www.larousse.fr/dictionnaires/francais/communautarisme.

83 Bowen 2007, 156.

84 http://edition.cnn.com/2009/WORLD/europe/06/23/france.burkas/index.html, accessed 27 Apr 2010.

> What is happening now is that the Republic is drawing the borders of French Islam. France has accepted the presence of Muslims […] and now it's setting limits. […] It's the same path followed by the Italians, Jews and Poles who have come to France at different times during the past 150 years. All were considered alien. All have since been assimilated.[85]

This forms the context of Becheri's independent reasoning (*ijtihād*) leading to the fatwa that *ʿurfī* marriage is *ḥarām* (prohibited).

Barkatullah Abdulkadir and the Marriage Contract

The *Model Muslim Marriage Contract* (hereafter: the Marriage Contract) was launched on 8 August 2008 in the Muslim forum City Circle in London.[86] It was the British-Muslim think-tank Muslim Institute that took the initiative to draw up such a model contract in 2004.[87] Ghayasuddin Siddiqui, head of the Muslim Institute, was one of three members of the committee that shaped the document. The other two were Barkatullah Abdulkadir and Cassandra Balchin.[88] The Marriage Contract was the outcome of four years of work. A Muslim Institute press release described it as "a consensus effort to protect the right of both parties" providing women with "written proof of their marriage and of the terms and conditions agreed between the spouses."[89]

In the press release for the launch, Siddiqui claimed the contact was "less about divorce than designed to guarantee greater harmony within Muslim mar-

85 Kuper 2009.

86 Archived at http://web.archive.org/web/20090121191727/http://www.thecitycircle.com/events_full_text2.php?id=521.

87 The history of the Muslim Institute goes back to 1974. See http://www.musliminstitute.org/about-us/overview.

88 Cassandra Balchin (1962–2012) was a freelance writer, human rights activist and part of the network Women Living Under Muslim Laws (WLUML, http://www.wluml.org), a Muslim human rights movement with a secular profile. She lived in Pakistan for 17 years (1983–2000), first as a journalist and then as an associate of Shirkat Gah in Lahore, a local chapter of WLUML. She was a board member of Muslim Women's Network UK (http://www.mwnuk.co.uk) and member of the planning committee for the international Musawah network (http://www.musawah.org), which promotes equality before the law in Muslim family law.

89 "Muslim Institute to launch model Muslim Marriage Contract", 8 Aug 2008, http://web.archive.org/web/20170426051401/http://www.muslimparliament.org.uk:80/MuslimMarriageContract.html.

riages in Britain". This may seem a curious statement, both for mentioning divorce at the launch of a marriage contract, and because the stated objective of the contract was not a legal one. Surely, the idea of a marriage contract is the regal regulation of marriage.[90] The contract, however, stresses the "Islamic vision" for marriage, a relationship based on *mawadda* (love, friendship), *raḥma* (mercy) and *sukūn* (peace and tranquility, in the sense of "without external disturbance"). These are values for the individual to adopt and act on so as to accomplish the good life. The background and process behind the contract may explain the statement.

Background and Process

The three members of the committee, each in their way, described their lived experience among British Muslims as their motivation for formulating a marriage contract. Ghayasuddin Siddiqui's experience was that of heading the Muslim Parliament, which he described as a "community forum":

> After dealing with problems of women approaching The Muslim Parliament because of forced marriages, domestic violence and honour killing, we drew the conclusion that 'we have to do something'. According to my opinion there is a relation between the three aspects. Forced marriage is linked to *wilāya* out of proportion, which implies emotional violence, which is a kind of domestic violence, and that could lead to honour killing.[91]

Barkatullah Abdulkadir, member of the Sharia Council and in charge of Freefone Islamic Helpline, describes his motivation as follows:

> After 10,000 cases, one clearly identified the cases and the challenges they represented. The problems were related to *ṭalāq* and *khulʿ*. A main problem is when the husband has gone into a multi-jurisdictional world, in such matters as child custody and finances. Most problems are due to multicultural confusion. I then thought: Let us start from the beginning to avoid these problems.[92]

---

90 This may be related to a 2004 proposal for criminalizing forced marriage, which was later dropped. The Muslim Council of Britain protested against the proposal, claiming it would lead to increased stigmatization of Muslims. *Daily Mail*, 22 May 2009.

91 Interview with Ghayasuddin Siddiqui, London, 25 Feb 2009.

92 Interview with Barkatullah Abdulkadir, London, 24 Feb 2009.

Cassandra Balchin had been working on the conflict between Pakistani and Bangladeshi law and domestic legislation with respect to human rights violations. From 2000, she engaged in work against forced marriages together with Siddiqui. Individuals also contacted her for advice on marital questions. Moreover, she had been doing research on marriage contracts in the Muslim world for fifteen years. She believed she had something to contribute to the process of drawing up a model contract, and so accepted Siddiqui's invitation to join the committee. Through her work on codified laws, she said, she also brought in knowledge of laws in e.g. Morocco or Algeria where *wilāya* was not a requirement. Balchin brought women's rights arguments into the work on the Marriage Contract. This places her in a trend of women's rights activists: "… we find that in widely diverse contexts worldwide activists for women's rights have chosen the marriage contract as a means to pursue their reforms …"[93]

All three gave their full commitment because they saw the status quo as intolerable. Balchin puts it this way: "It was a sense of horror and stress over what is happening to women with unregistered marriages, which was *the* issue." The process was informal. The three of them met at uneven intervals, often to present drafts for the text. Many of the topics had been defined in advance; Cassandra Balchin named "witnesses" as an example when I asked her. A special meeting took place in 2005, Balchin says. Siddiqui had invited a number of scholars, including conservative ones. "Just the fact that such a wide range of scholars were willing to listen was in itself impressive."[94]

The Outcome

The Marriage Contract consists of a cover page listing seven organizations that support it,[95] an introduction titled "A Guide to a Happy Marriage," two pages of explanatory notes, and a certificate of marriage, with a form on the front and "terms and conditions" on the back. A Muslim Institute press release in advance of the launch described the principles and contents of the contract.

The British-Iranian anthropologist Ziba Mir-Hosseini describes the contract as a step in the right direction toward "gender equality," while Usama Hassan, founder of City Circle and imam of the Tawhid Mosque, Leyton, comments: "This new Muslim marriage contract is an excellent development, since

93 Quraishi and Vogel 2008, 1.

94 Telephone interview with Cassandra Balchin, 25 Feb 2009.

95 Council of Imams and Mosques, Utrujj Foundation, Muslim Council of Britain (MCB), Muslim Parliament, City Circle, Muslim Women's Network UK, Fatima Women's Network.

it draws on those traditional Islamic legal opinions that are more in keeping with the spirit of gender equality."[96] The press release focused on *wilāya* (guardianship), witnesses, polygamy and *talaq-e-tafweed* (delegated right to divorce). The background was Abdulkadir's experience as a mufti and member of the Sharia Council, and his wish to make a substantial contribution to *preventing* potential future marriage conflicts. His experience both motivated and formed an element of the independent reasoning (*ijtihād*) he carried out that concluded with the statements of the norms we find in the Marriage Contract.

Guardianship (wilāya)

The sixth point under "Explanatory Notes" reads as follows:

> Parents are responsible for the upbringing of their children. Out of respect and courtesy it is important that young people involve their parents or guardians throughout the process of marriage. However, parental or guardian's legal role finishes when children reach adulthood. Thereafter their role is optional and complementary. Hence the Muslim Marriage Certificate does not require the approval of the parents.

This paragraph contains two fatwas: "… parental or guardian's legal role finishes when children reach adulthood" and "… the Muslim Marriage Certificate does not require the approval of the parents". Barkatullah Abdulkadir bases this on the view of Abu Hanifa: "A woman who is adult, and of sound mind, may be married by virtue of her own consent, although the contract may not have been made or acceded to by her guardians; and this, whether she be a virgin or a Siyeeba [previously married]."[97] This contrasts with Shaybani's view that she may be married but that the validity of the marriage depends on the consent of the guardian, and with Abu Yusuf's view that marriage can only be done through a guardian, though the latter's consent is not required.[98] Barkatullah made a *khiyār* (choice) between these two positions, and opted for Abu Hanifa's, based on the following reasoning: "The girl has full authority and it is her sole decision, but the *walī* also has an interest, and *ḥaqq al-ʿitirāḍ* [right

---

96 Muslim Parliament press release, 8 Aug 2008.

97 al-Marghinani 1989, 1:95.

98 al-Marghinani 1989, 1:95. Abu Yusuf and Shaybani are known in the Islamic literature as followers of Abu Hanifa, whose works played an important role in the establishment of the Hanafi school and are considered the principal references for this school of law.

to contest, i.e. to contest the validity of the marriage]. But the *awliyā* will have to present evidence. This is such a big hurdle, so they should abstain from doing it."[99]

In my conversations with Abdulkadir, however, he was very clear about the significance of the relationship between the woman and her guardian, and that the latter had to play a role when she got married. In other words, he lifted the whole topic out of the strictly legal field into the ethical one. Abdulkadir thought this was a suitable position for two reasons: First, because Muslims were living as a minority in British society, where the *walī* did not play the same role as in Muslim-majority societies. Second, because "half" the Muslims in the UK were from the Indian subcontinent, where the Hanafi school prevailed.[100]

Witnesses

"According to Islamic law, a witness should be sane, adult and reliable. This requirement is gender/faith neutral. Hence, the Muslim Marriage Certificate requires to be witnessed by 'two adult witnesses of good character.'" According to Barkatullah Abdulkadir, he wrote the first and last sentence of this point. The sentence about the requirement being gender/faith-neutral was introduced on the initiative of Cassandra Balchin, backed by Ghayasuddin Siddiqui. This point in particular was explicitly stated at the launch, which led to strong protest.[101]

The Islamic Sharia Council is one actor protesting against the Marriage Contract, and disagrees particularly over the requirement of witnesses. In a statement, the Council stressed that witnesses are required for the contract to be valid and that the witnesses must be Muslims:

> The requirement of witnesses is a condition of marriage according to the majority of the scholars including Abu Hanifa, Shafiʿi, and Ahmad. Imam Malik was of the view that witnesses are not a condition if the marriage was announced or carried out publicly and therefore his opinion is more or less similar to the other schools of thought. However, to claim that the requirement of witnesses is gender/faith neutral is false, which no scholar has recognized. There is no disagreement amongst scholars about the fact that witnesses are a condition of marriage, and that they must be Muslims if the Nikah is taking place between Muslims.[102]

---

99 Conversation with Barkatullah Abdulkadir, London, 23 May 2009.

100 Interview with Barkatullah Abdulkadir, London, 24 Feb 2009.

101 Conversation with Barkatullah Abdulkadir, London, 23 May 2009.

102 The statement could for a while be found on the Sharia Council website (http://www.islamic-sharia.org), but has since been removed.

According to Abdulkadir, the original point had been left intentionally vague. He had started out by choosing the Maliki position that public announcement suffices for the validity of the marriage contract.[103] The registration of the marriage contract serves as public announcment. On this view, the role of the witnesses is only to sign the document. The validity of the marriage does not depend on them. Abdulkadir may seem to have downgraded the role of the witnesses. He may be interpreted as saying that the requirement of witnesses need not be satisfied when registration of the marriage is defined as public announcement, and hence satisfies the Maliki conditions for validity. If so, the parties may decide who they want as witnesses without regard to gender or religion.

The process behind the point on witnesses—from independent reasoning to the launch of the extant formulation—may be interpreted as a clash of two cultures: Abdulkadir's carefully intended unclear formulation, based on the independent reasoning of a person with mufti experience, who was aware of the resistance this point would arouse if it were too clearly formulated; and Balchin's and Siddiqui's non-theological, activist focus on results and clarity.

However, the norm about non-Muslim witnesses had already been stated by Muhammad Abduh in a fatwa on the marriage of a Muslim man to a woman from *ahl al-kitāb*, albeit without a justification.[104] Abduh clearly did not go as far as Abdulkadir, though, as he appeared only to join the view of Abu Hanifa and Abu Yusuf that non-Muslim witnesses are acceptable when a Muslim marries a non-Muslim women. Abduh did, however, accept a civil marriage from a European country.[105] The question was whether marriage contracted with a Christian woman in Germany—according to German law, and with witnesses present—was valid in Egypt. Yes, went the answer, as long as there were two witnesses present, even if they were *dhimmūn* (Jews or Christians).

Polygamy

The marriage contract stipulates that the husband may *not* marry other women as long as he is married: "The husband is not to enter into formal or informal *nikah* (Muslim marriage) contract in the UK or abroad with another woman,

103 Ibn Rushd 2000, 2:20 supports this view: "Abu Thawr and a group of jurists said that attestation by witnesses is not a condition for the validity of marriage, neither a condition of validity nor that of completion. Ḥasan ibn ʿAlī is reported to have done this. It is related about him that he married without witnesses and then proclaimed his marriage."

104 Jumʿa 2005, 196 (question no. 152).

105 Al-Marghinani 1989, 1:75.

as it is unlawful under the laws of England and Wales as well as the Scottish legal system."[106] According to Cassandra Balchin, this was not a "big issue," as polygamy is a lost cause in the British context. Nonetheless, the point on polygamy was the result of independent reasoning (*ijtihād*) by Abdulkadir.

The problems with polygamy are many: "People regard it not as *rukhṣa* [permission], but a privilege to the point of being *wājib* [mandatory]. By exercising a Sharia option, they violate several Sharia commandments. It often leads to cheating and committing fraud in relation to *nafaqa*, hiding one marriage from the other, and breaking justice requirements. Sharia is therefore ruined in the process."[107]

Abdulkadir describes polygamy as "mission impossible" with reference to the Quran: "Ye will not be able to deal equally between (your) wives ..."[108] The negation used, he says, is *lan*, which he would translate as "not nearly," a stronger word than "not." Moreover, he holds that when the practice of polygamy conflicts with tradition and culture, Muslims should take this into account. Personal preferences also play a part, he says, pointing to two traditions included by Ibn Hazm (d. 1064) in his *Jawāmiʿ al-sīra*. One of these concerns the case when women do not accept being co-wives, and the other shows that the Prophet Muhammad did not accept that his own daughters would be co-wives.

> Umara bint Abdurrahman said: It was said to the Messenger of God: O Envoy of God, will you not marry women from the *anṣār*, they are so beautiful? The Messenger of God said: They are very jealous women and will not tolerate co-wives. I am a man with several wives, and I dislike offending their tribe in that [i.e., by marrying *anṣār* women and thus imposing co-wives on them].
>
> Ibn Ishaq said: A trustworthy man told me that the Messenger of God, peace and blessings upon him, was very jealous on behalf of his daughters and did not marry them off to be co-wives.[109]

Abdulkadir's independent reasoning leads him to point out that polygamy is an option, not a duty, and hence is not to be practiced when against the law;

106 See the section "Special Conditions" under "Terms and Conditions of the Muslim marriage contract" (p. 5).

107 Conversation with Barkatullah Abdulkadir, London, 24 Feb 2009.

108 Quran 4:129, Pickthall's translation.

109 Ibn Hazm n.d.

moreover, he develops an Islamic argument based on the sources, with the conclusion that polygamy should not be practised in the UK.[110]

The work on the marriage contract was based on what Abdulkadir termed a "justice- and fairness-based Sharia model" in a "long-term *maṣlaḥa mursala* [interest] perspective." It involved re-thinking the roles and duties of the spouses. Decisions were not to be made by the man alone, but by both jointly, including matters of education and having children. The fact that two incomes were necessary would necessarily also have consequences for inheritance. Having *talaq-e-tafweed* built into the contract would make divorce easier, and Abdulkadir joked that the Sharia Council would have less work to do. The *maṣlaḥa mursala* perspective belongs to the theory of *maqāṣid al-sharīʿa* (objectives of Sharia).[111] Asked how he defines *maqāṣid al-sharīʿa,* he replied: "After reading the Qurʾan and Hadith for half a century, one develops a feeling of what is the overall longterm purpose of the Sharia. It is like a sixth sense of every scholar, and depends on everybody's horizon."[112]

However, there has been harsh criticism of Abdulkadir's method as it emerges through these points, not least from the Islamic Sharia Council:

> It is a well established juristic rule that Muslims are not allowed to deliberately select and choose a concession or irregular opinion attributed to a scholar; to gather all such opinions for the purpose of acting upon them, then, is even more unsightly. Sulayman al-Taymi (d. 760) said, "If you take the concession of every scholar you will combine all your evil in yourself". The scholars consider this action as a sin and regard it as being unlawful. A number of scholars including Ibn Hazm, Ibn ʿAbdul-Barr and al-Shatibi report a consensus on this matter. Imam Ahmad said, "If a man takes the view of the people of Kufa regarding nabidh [a drink that may contain alchohol], the view of the people of Medina on singing and the view of the people of Makkah on mutʾah he will become a fasiq (a heretic)."[113]

Abdulkadir was not perturbed by the criticism, describing it as "a storm in a teacup," even though he said he had been called "a devil" for his work on the

110 In my conversation with Barkatullah Abdulkadir, he was clear that the gender perspective has been little stressed in the biography of the Prophet, perhaps because the authors of such biographies have been male. London, 23 May 2010.

111 See chapter 7.

112 Conversation with Barkatullah Abdulkadir, London, 24 Feb 2009.

113 *ISC Stand on the Marriage Contract*, 1.

Contract. He commented: "It is the stakeholder approach. The scholars do not accept other scholars, so they end up isolated." What matters most to Abdulkadir is that the Contract will serve the young generation of Muslims.

Validity

At the bottom of the Contract form is a note: "For a Muslim marriage to be recognised in British law it must be held at a mosque registered as a place for the solemnisation of marriage, otherwise the civil ceremony must take place at a registry office first before the *nikah* (Muslim marriage) ceremony."[114]

The insistence on public registration of the marriage may relate to the situation of the many women in unregistered marriages, which Balchin, as we have seen, described as "*the* issue".[115] According to Balchin, "traditional Islamic marriage" is practised especially in groups with low education and manual work. Regardless of education levels and career choices, though, convenience may also be a motive. "… [M]any see a *nikah* as some sort of half-way house: sufficiently valid to satisfy or convince parents and moral conscience and 'book' the partner in anticipation of them being married off elsewhere by their parents, but also sufficiently informal to allow for easy undoing at a future date."[116] Warraich and Balchin illustrate how widespread is the practice of unregistered marriage with Shah-Kazemi's figures from one of the Sharia councils: Out of 287 cases in the 1985–1995 period, 27 % concerned unregistered marriages. 37 % had had a civil ceremony before entering into *nikāḥ*.[117] They conclude:

> *Imams* are faced with a dilemma: either they provide (legally irrelevant) "sanctification" for a relationship that is clearly on the verge of becoming sexual, or they refuse knowing that the couple is likely to then commit *zina* (a possibility strongly condemned by religion and custom). Many more liberal *imams* inform the young couple that they ought to have a Registry marriage in order for their partnership to be valid in the eyes of the law but are also willing to give their blessings to young couples in private ceremonies, feeling that at least the religious aspect has been taken

114 The right to solemnize marriages means doing so under English law. The mosque is required to be registered according to the *Places of Worship Registration Act* (1855) and as a "Place of Religious Worship for the solemnization of Marriages" under Section 41 of the *Marriage Act* (1949).

115 See above, this chapter.

116 Warraich and Balchin 2006, 30.

117 Warraich and Balchin 2006, 31.

> care of. This is not just a question of easing consciences but also avoiding the situation where the religious authorities become irrelevant to young people because they ignore their needs.[118]

But apart from noting that civil marriage should precede *nikāḥ*, and encouraging the use of this document, what status does the Marriage Contract have? Balchin replies: "It has no legal value, but a moral one. Two people have signed a piece of paper. Only the registered marriage is valid according to the law. It could be solved by registering mosques for solemnisation of marriages."[119]

The whole question of the Model Muslim Marriage Contract has since been overshadowed by the Muslim Arbitration Tribunal, which was established in 1997 under the Arbitration Act (1996), and which acts as a voluntary arbitration council in a limited range of cases.[120] This has prompted reactions in British public debate,[121] because what is at stake is the relationship between Sharia and British law. As we have already seen in this chapter, this is not a new question.

The Context

In 1983, the Union of Muslim Organisations followed up the 1970s initiative by publishing the paper *Why Muslim Family Law for British Muslims?* The paper is said to have been presented to the government several times, with lukewarm reactions. "The importance of family law to British Muslims was never disputed, but the reasons for demanding a separate system were insufficient to convince the government to take proposals further."[122]

According to Freeland and Lau, the backdrop to this initiative was familiarity with legal pluralism in the countries of origin of the majority of British Muslims: Pakistan, Bangladesh, and India. This was a historical experience: As early as 1772, a so-called "dual law system" was officially approved by the

118 Warraich and Balchin 2006, 30.

119 Telephone conversation with Cassandra Balchin, 25 Mar 2009.

120 Women-related topics mentioned are forced marriage, domestic violence, and family conflicts, including questions of *ṭalāq* and inheritance. http://www.matribunal.com/cases_faimly.html (sic).

121 As an example of the press reactions, the *Daily Mail* (15 Sep 2008) reported that "Islamic sharia courts in Britain are now 'legally binding'". The headline was an exaggeration, since it is up to the parties whether the MAT's rulings are to be binding (as the article did in fact note). http://www.dailymail.co.uk/news/article-1055764/Islamic-sharia-courts-Britain-legally-binding.html.

122 Freeland and Lau 2008, 340.

British in India. "Regulation II provided that 'in all suits regarding inheritance, succession, marriage and caste and other usages and institutions, the laws of the Koran [Quran] with respect to Mahomedans [Muslims], and those of the Shaster with regards to the Gentoos [Hindus], shall be invariably adhered to.'"[123] Legal pluralism may also be found in English law, however. In the 1753 Marriage Act, the Anglican Church was given the sole right to solemnize and register marriages, but exemptions were made for Jews and Quakers, who have been allowed to marry according to their own laws and traditions up to the present.[124]

The demand for a parallel Islamic legal system should also be understood in terms of the idea that different cultures can co-exist peacefully and on an equal footing within a country, and that some kind of policy should be conducted to look after this diversity, that is, the idea of multiculturalism, of which the UK has been an exponent. The ideal of multiculturalism, according to Cora Alexa Døving, is "a society where minority groups participate with equal rights and duties without having to relinquish their specific national, cultural, or religious features," and the aim is an integrated society.[125] Its critics, she notes, believe that multiculturalism as a political strategy reinforces cultural boundaries, turning multicultural society into a tribal society.

The anthropologist Stephen Vertovec comes across as one of these critics. In the article "Multiculturalism, Culturalism and Public Incorporation," Vertovec claims that political initiatives towards minorities have often resulted in their exclusion from participation in the field of majority politics. This has to do with interpretations of the concept of "culture" that, when operationalized, function to create social and political distance to minorities.[126] Many of the ways in which "multiculturalism" is used, Vertovec says, seem to share an implicit view of "culture" as

> … a kind of package (often talked of as migrants' 'cultural baggage') of collective behavioral-moral-aesthetic traits and 'customs', rather mysteriously transmitted between the generations, best suited to particular geographical origins yet largely unaffected by history or a change of context, which instils a discrete quality into the feelings, values, practices, social relationships, predilections and intrinsic nature of all who 'belong to (a

123 Freeland and Lau 2008, 340.
124 Freeland and Lau 2008, 338.
125 Døving 2009, 44.
126 Vertovec 1996, 49.

> particular) it'. Populations and population segments, it follows, are categorized culturally according to cultural essences which are presumed to be imparted at birth.[127]

Such a view would seem to underlie British policies on minorities in local communities around the country. As Vertovec describes it: "Since the early 1960s the highly decentralized local authorities throughout Britain (metropolitan, county, and district councils, London boroughs) have undertaken a variety of measures to recognize and to assist various minority groups."[128] One problem with this way of organizing and relating to minorities, according to Vertovec, is that the authorities have related to "representatives" of these groups, which were mistakenly viewed as cultural corporations.[129] As a result, the few might speak on behalf of the group or groups without following democratic principles, and without regard for within-group variation (not least in a gender perspective). In this process the notion of "community" emerged and was operationalized politically.[130]

Muslim demands for a family law of their own may be seen to mirror all these circumstances, not least the argument that a separate law was the only way British Muslims could establish a stable "community".[131]

Multiculturalism, however, did not to the same degree extend to legislation. Poulter comments as follows on the rejection of a separate Muslim legal system:

> First, it seems to have been argued that the proposal ran counter to the English tradition of a unified system in family matters in terms of which a uniform set of rules is applied to all, regardless of their origins, race or creed. This would not seem to be an adequate reason in itself, especially since [...] it is not wholly accurate. However, this argument is perhaps rather more convincing if it asserts that a basically uniform system has helped in the past to create a more cohesive society and that it is still needed today, more especially as a part of the process of nation-building required to integrate the newer minorities into the general framework of English life and some of its most important values.[132]

---

127 Vertovec 1996, 51.
128 Vertovec 1996, 52.
129 Vertovec 1996, 53.
130 Vertovec 1996, 55.
131 Freeland and Lau 2008, 341.
132 Poulter 1990, 157–158.

In the scholarly literature, Islamic marital norms are also contrasted with English law to show that the two systems are not compatible.[133] Among the points highlighted are men's right to marry up to four women, the different rights of men and women to divorce, and the prohibition on women marrying non-Muslim men.

Muslims reacted to the rejection of their demand for their own family law by setting up a number of voluntary bodies that act as authorities in family matters, so-called Sharia councils. English law enables this by allowing arbitration outside the judicial system in family conflicts. "… English law generally approves of the settlement of family disputes outside the courts (save for the actual obtaining of a divorce). This means that there is an opportunity for family, religious and community values to come to the fore through the process of negotiation, conciliation and mediation."[134] The Islamic Sharia Council, where Syed Darsh was one of the founders and Barkatullah Abdulkadir is a member, is the best-known body of this sort. It is not organized according to the 1996 Arbitration Act, however, unlike the Muslim Arbitration Tribunal. Though this is a new institution in the Muslim landscape, the same mechanisms are at work as before. The basis for the Tribunal is the opportunity afforded by English law to solve conflicts. They report an increasing workload, and non-Muslims, too, resort to the Tribunal in financial disputes.[135] The British jurist Samia Bano describes Sharia councils as a "semi-autonomous field [that] can generate rules and customs and symbols internally, but that is also vulnerable to rules and decisions and other forces emanating from the larger world by which it is surrounded."[136]

Where does the Marriage Contract belong in this picture? As we have seen, a number of fatwas promote women's rights and equality before the law. In case of conflict, however, the parties should not go to court before they have tried arbitration through a Sharia council: "Before resorting to legal redress through British civil courts parties undertake to seek arbitration/reconciliation through a reputable UK-based Shari'ah panel/body/council whose decision shall be morally binding on both parties."[137] When asked about this clause,

---

133 See Poulter 1990, 149–153 and Freeland and Lau 2008, 341–342.

134 Poulter 1990, 164–165.

135 Afua Hirsch, "Fears over non-Muslim's use of Islamic law to resolve disputes", *Guardian*, 14 Mar 2010, http://www.guardian.co.uk/uk/2010/mar/14/non-muslims-sharia-law-uk.

136 Bano 2007, 8.

137 The Model Muslim Marriage Contract, page 5: Terms and conditions of the Muslim marriage contract.

Abdulkadir replied that the aim was to ease the process in case of marital conflict, since going through the courts took more time, and that this kind of solution had proven successful in financial disputes.[138] Samia Bano's research, however, shows that arbitration processes can go on for up to six months, and that women have mixed experiences with such councils.[139] In other words, the Marriage Contract is the result of fatwas that point towards equality before the law, but research suggests that the clause about arbitration to take place through Sharia councils might weaken women's rights.[140]

Summary and Conclusions

This chapter has dealt with questions about getting married. We have seen fatwas and resolutions (*qarārāt*) and accompanying independent reasoning (*ijtihād*) about guardianship (*wilāya*), restrictions on guardianship, witnesses, and registration of marriage. These have led us to a number of other topics, such as the validity of marriage, forced marriage, polygamy, and the views of muftis about the relationship between Islamic norms and domestic legislation. The independent reasoning clarifies the reasons for the fatwas, as perceived by the muftis. Hence, it may represent social data, not least with regard to the frequency of unregistered marriages, which as we have seen was the main reason for Larabi Becheri's and Barkatullah Abdulkadir's fatwas.

Where guardianship (*wilāya*) is concerned, both Syed Darsh, the European Council for Fatwa and Research and Barkatullah Abdulkadir promote the Hanafi view that a woman who is mature and of sound mind (*bāligha ʿāqila*) can get married without a guardian (*walī*). The marriage contract will still be valid, on two conditions: that the husband is suitable (*kufʾ*) and that the bride-gift is similar to what other women in her position would receive. Darsh stresses this point, but does not reflect on how it could be judicially enforced. The ECFR sets out its view in light of the other three Sunni schools of law, which makes the woman's marriage conditional on her having a guardian. The consent of the guardian matters both in social and religious terms. Marriage without a guardian should therefore only take place in exceptional cases. Abdulkadir's fatwa that the Marriage Contract does not require parental consent implies that the woman can marry without a guardian. All three, however, stress the

138 Conversation with Barkatullah Abdulkadir, London, 23 May 2009.

139 Bano 2007.

140 This pertains mainly to divorce, which falls outside the topic of this chapter.

ethical ideal that the relationship between a woman and her parents should not be ruined in connection with her marriage. The preservation of family relations is a premise for the fatwas. The reminder about the importance of family relations and the woman's responsibility for preserving them may also be read as a realistic acknowledgment that Muslims in Europe lack the authority to enforce these norms as law.

The issue of guardianship also brought up the question of restrictions on the role of the guardian. Both Darsh and the ECFR say outright in their fatwas that a guardian may not force a woman into a marriage she does not want. This was a premise for all the work on the Marriage Contract. *Ijāb* ("offer") and *qubūl* ("acceptance") is a basic element (*rukn*) in the validity of the marriage contract. If the marriage has not been entered into voluntarily, it is not valid. The ECFR, too, is at pains to make clear that the guardian should not prevent daughters from getting married. Getting rid of the *wilāya* institution, however, is not up for discussion. If the father is not suited, the "next in line" should take on the responsibility.

The question of the validity of marriage ranges from the keeping of God's commandments, far beyond the scope of control by others, to the relationship between Islamic and civil marriage contracts. The ECFR considers the *niyya* (intent) constitutive of the validity of marriage. It does not matter that all formal requirements are met if the intent of the parties is not to get married for the sake of marriage. If the intent is to marry to obtain a residence permit, or planning to divorce in a certain while, the marriage is not valid. All actors behind the fatwas in this chapter recognize civil marriage as valid, as long as the basic elements and conditions are present. Darsh gives substance to this point by saying that the woman's guardian and two male Muslim witnesses must attend the ceremony. The ECFR are less precise about the requirements ("… if it has fulfilled all legal requirements"). Becheri goes a long step further, defining civil marriage as a condition for an Islamically defined valid marriage. The same requirement is implied, but not explicitly argued for, by the registration clause of the Marriage Contract. These four positions on registration (i.e., on civil marriage) may be placed on a scale from Darsh at one end ("it is important to have a marriage registered"), followed by the ECFR ("it is essential to register marriage contracts"), the Marriage Contract (the Islamic ceremony must wait until civil marriage has taken place), and at the other end Becheri (who requires civil marriage for the marriage to be valid according to Islam). Becheri and Abdulkadir both argue that registration is required for the marriage contract to be valid. Becheri considers the registration a form of witnessing, whereas Abdulkadir considers it a form of public notice. Both reason within the frame of Maliki requirements for a valid marriage contract. The argument is that the rights of the parties must be secured. As we have seen, the reasoning involved makes subtle use of theological references from Islamic tradition.

It is clear from the fatwas that the Islamic legal institutions have no power of sanctions, but are reduced to a set of ethical rules. Doing the right thing involves obeying the law of the land and registering one's marriage, but one is also encouraged not to disregard the *walī* and his role. This would be a solution, not only with regard to the law, but also for the chaos of unregistered marriages among Muslims in Europe described by the muftis.

This position also has consequences for the possibility of practising polygamy. At one end of the scale, we find the ECFR's entirely context-free fatwa in defence of polygamy, followed by Darsh, who finds it ethically questionable, but legal; Becheri, who finds it undesirable; and at the other end Abdulkadir, who argues against polygamy based on Islamic sources. In any case, the requirement of registering marriage serves as an impediment to marrying more than one person at a time.

Even though the fatwas of these four actors point in the same normative direction, they argue in different ways. This may be for the sake of the target groups of the fatwas. As we have seen, the language and references of Darsh's fatwas were adapted to young people as the target audience of the *Q-News* fatwas. The ECFR's target group is Muslims all over Europe, as well as other scholars with various theological positions. Abstract language can be a way to reach as many as possible and to create the broadest possible agreement. Becheri's and Barkatullah's fatwas bear the marks of French demands for assimilation and British multiculturalism, respectively. The fatwas also tell us something about the muftis themselves: Darsh, who worked in close contact with young people; the ECFR, with the contradictory perspectives of its various members; Becheri, as an actor within French Islam; and the solution-oriented Barkatullah, with his experience from many cases before the Islamic Sharia Council.

We have seen that these muftis use the theory of *maqāṣid al-sharīʿa* as one perspective in their independent reasoning (*ijtihād*). This theory includes the concept of *maʾālāt* ("consequences"). A norm is evaluated for its presumed consequences. The fatwas in this chapter have been given based on the assumption that the norms will prevent forced marriage, that fathers will cease to prevent their daughters from getting married, and that children will no longer be left without legal protection due to unregistered marriages. This perspective entails a tendency to promote women's rights, not least because it is considered to be Sharia to obey the law of the land, which provides equality before the law. In this way, these fatwas may be seen as possible contributions to a European Islamic jurisprudence in the long term, or a solution to problems with developing a European Sharia listed by the German jurist Mathias Rohe. At stake is both the internal aspect or the *forum internum*, how European Muslims can be sure that they are abiding by God's commands and prohibitions; and the outer aspect or the *forum externum*, how religious commands can be interpreted so as not to conflict with the demands of the surroundings.[141]

141 Rohe 2007, 65.

CHAPTER 7

Maqasid al-shariʿa and Modern Common Morality

Introduction

We have gained insight into fatwa-giving as a discursive field, the challenges and dilemmas faced by muftis, and the considerations they seek to take into account and weigh against each other when they give fatwas, whether they have the questioner or other scholars in mind. We have also looked at the place of the fatwa in Islamic tradition. The fatwa's lack of sanctioning power does not preclude the fatwa from having a construction of authority built into it. Everything—from permission for women to cut their hair, access to mosques, marriage and divorce, to playing tennis—is theorized and included in a claim to "correct Islamic practice."

Muslims in Europe live as a minority, and the focus on an Islamic justification for norms raises the question of the relationship between Islamic jurisprudence and national laws in different ways than in the Muslim world. Not least, the question is brought up by political actors in various public debates to clarify if Muslims are law-abiding and loyal citizens.

We have often seen that the statements and attitudes of Muslims have caused consternation, or even disgust. This is probably not because the majority dislikes Muslims in general. More likely, certain statements and attitudes give offence because they appear to ignore or conflict with the *common morality* of society, "the morality of ordinary people," as the Norwegian philosopher Knut Erik Tranøy defines it.[1]

The claim that fundamental European values are incompatible with Islamic ones is often heard in European public debate. "Fundamental European values," however, are not clearly defined, and attempts to define them often turn on what they are not: Of central importance is the European majority society's rejection of an oppression of women that is supposedly based on Sharia and is seen as a threat. Nor does the reasoning behind the fatwas in this book give the impression that there exists a common language or connection between the two sets of values described above, with their diametrically different views of women and gender relations. The term "fatwa," with its negative connotations from the so-called Rushdie affair, does not improve matters.

1 Tranøy 2001, 104.

 | DOI: 10.1163/9789004367852_009

Fatwa discourses on women-related questions could be said to symbolize the supposed incompatibility of "fundamental European values" and "Islamic values". The majority community regards such discourses with hostility. Does this mean there is no common "language" into which the discourses on values can be translated? In an article on how Muslims are accused of "double talk" in French public debate, because the complexity of Islamic discourse is not understood by the majority, Frank Peter concludes: "The questions to be asked now concern the commensurability of Muslim discourses with other discourse systems in France and the conditions under which Muslims realise the translation work incumbent upon them when entering public debates".[2]

In this chapter, I will argue that the muftis' arguments for their fatwas are translatable into a more widely accessible language that allows clarifying fundamental values and their interpretations. I will argue that the *maqāṣid* theory forms one Islamic counterpart to the theory of *modern common morality*, "the morality of ordinary people," as spelled out by the Norwegian philosopher Knut Erik Tranøy.[3] I seek to uncover a possible correspondence between the concepts of the two models. According to these theories, the categories of *ḍarūriyyāt* and what Tranøy calls "bio-moral values," respectively, are fundamental values that serve as a basis for any society. Conflicts may emerge when these fundamental values are to be interpreted. I present Tranøy's theory of competing common moralities, which could help understand the "clash of moralities" and hence the unease of multi-religious societies. It might also shed light on the foundations of diverse understandings of morality among Muslims. It is in the light of Tranøy's theory of change in common morality that I will present Yusuf al-Qaradawi's and Muhammad Khalid Masud's interpretations of the *maqāṣid al-sharīʿa* theory, and point to mechanisms and principles for deriving values and norms and, possibly, for changing them. Masud's theory is used as a source of arguments for Islamic feminism, and as a so-called "new religious intellectual", he is an actor in the discursive field. The exposition of Qaradawi's and Masud's theories of *maqāṣid* will show that the derivation of norms for women-related questions is closely tied to foundational and highly contested questions in Islamic history. As al-Qaradawi put it in Doha in 2011, when I asked him about the notion of justice: "It's a question of *ʿaqīda* (credal doctrine)".

Insight into and recognition of common fundamental values could help enable a meaningful conversation in a common language between non-Muslim

2 Peter 2012, 146.

3 Tranøy 2000.

majorities and Muslim minorities on moral dilemmas and fundamental values of the society in which they live. On an optimistic view, this could build trust between minorities and majorities. However, I end this chapter on a pessimistic note, posing the question whether the opportunity space for such agreement on common values is restricted by today's vociferous dominant political discourse, at the expense of women.

Maqāṣid al-sharīʿa

All fatwa actors in this book have in their various ways referred to *maqāṣid al-sharīʿa* (the objectives of Sharia) in their *ijtihād*. This theory, then, is part of the canon of methods, concepts, and references they use to derive norms. Individual *maqāṣid*, such as protecting the family (originally the "offspring," *nasl*), preserving the *dīn* (religion), and protecting property (*māl*), may serve as premises for a fatwa. Syed Darsh takes stable family relations as a premise for a number of fatwas arguing for women's access to the mosque and pilgrimage. The ECFR bases itself on the same premises, as seen inter alia in the fatwas and resolutions about a woman asking her husband's permission to cut her hair, on a woman's right to go to the mosque, and on a woman who converts to Islam when her husband does not.

The Council also stresses the concept of *taysīr* ("easing"). The norms are not to cause needless harm and suffering. The concept is salient for the theory of *maqāṣid al-sharīʿa* as a maxim of Abdullah bin Bayyah's exposition of *fiqh al-aqalliyyāt*. Bin Bayyah holds that the general situation of Muslims outside the Muslim world can be described as *ḍarūra* (vital necessity), with the implication that *ḍarūra* and *ḥāja* are joined into one category. Matters that are not considered vital necessities in the religio-legal sense are thus nonetheless comprised by the maxim that "necessity renders the forbidden permitted".

Moreover, we have seen that the *maqāṣid* have played an important role in the *ijtihād* of Larabi Becheri and Barkatullah Abdulkadir, in that they placed weight on the possible consequences (*maʾālāt*) of the norms they derived. A stress on outcomes and consequences of the derived norms is characteristic of the *maqāṣid* approach. As the expert on Islamic law, Mohammad Hashim Kamali, puts it: "Another feature of *maqāṣid* which is important to ijtihad is the attention a mujtahid must pay to the end result and consequence of his ruling. For a fatwa or ijtihad would be deficient if it fails to contemplate its own consequences."[4]

---

4 Kamali 2008, 23.

Yusuf al-Qaradawi and his theory of *maqāṣid al-sharīʿa* play an important role in defining the terms of the ECFR's fatwas. In 2006, al-Qaradawi published his *Dirāsa fī-fiqh maqāṣid al-sharīʿa* (Study of Jurisprudence based on the Objectives of Sharia). In this book, al-Qaradawi ties the *maqāṣid* to divine wisdom, which he interprets as the realization of what is good and useful for human beings in this life and the next. He notes that many of his books have taken a *maqāṣid* perspective, among them *al-Ḥalāl wal-ḥarām fil-islām*, *Fatāwā muʿāṣira* and *Fī-fiqh al-aqalliyyāt*. The *maqāṣid* find expression, al-Qaradawi says, in the construction of the righteous person, family, society, *umma* (community of faith), and invitation to the good of humanity. He defines these as five *kulliyyāt*, higher principles of law, in addition to the five we have already met.[5] The subtitle of al-Qaradawi's book on the *maqāṣid*, *bayna al-maqāṣid al-kulliyya wal-nuṣūṣ al-juzʾiyya* (Between Higher Principles and Detailed Texts) signals al-Qaradawi's trademark "middle position" (*al-wasaṭiyya*). So does the structure of the book, which is a study of the relationship between the texts and the *maqāṣid*. The message is that one should follow the middle path between those who stress a literal interpretation of the texts, and those who disregard the texts with reference to *maqāṣid*.

Al-Qaradawi's starting point is that the wisdom of Sharia provides people with everything they need, and sees to it that the norms do not cause them needless suffering.[6] Sharia is mercy, justice, wisdom and *maṣlaḥa*, he writes, citing Ibn al-Qayyim.[7] Al-Qaradawi takes the Quran and the Sunna of the prophet Muhammad as the yardstick for the evaluation of legal norms. This forms the premise for his reference to Ibn al-Qayyim, who saw *maṣlaḥa* as synonymous with *ʿadl*, and promoted the use of *raʾy* (opinion) in Islamic legal thought; as well as his reference to Shatibi's *maqāṣid* theory. Even though Qaradawi affirms an inductive method, he does not in practice break free from what Johnston terms a "literalistic hermeneutic".[8] It is an important premise to al-Qaradawi that the *maqāṣid* cannot go against the *nuṣūṣ al-qaṭʿiyyāt* ("clear and unambiguous texts"). He gives examples of subjects dealt with in such texts, and claims that there is no genuine *maṣlaḥa* in banning polygamy or in giving brothers and sisters equal inheritance rights. This may be seen as a programmatic statement from al-Qaradawi that is likely to be experienced as unjust by Muslim women in Western Europe in the light of the challenges and conflicting expec-

5 Al-Qaradawi 2006, 27.

6 Al-Qaradawi 2006, 147.

7 Al-Qaradawi 2006, 149.

8 Johnston 2014, 50–53.

tations they face from competing sets of norms.[9] This textual approach clearly conflicts with modern understandings of justice and the common good. The dilemma becomes acute as to what should take precedence: Texts, in the sense of the Quran and the practice of the Prophet (*naql*), or reason (*ʿaql*)? This has been a central controversy in Islamic history, not least in classical Islamic legal thought.[10] Abu Hamid al-Ghazali (d. 1111), who as we have seen contributed to developing the theory of *maqāṣid al-sharīʿa*, intentionally tied ethical knowledge to the specific indications (*adilla*) of the sacred text. According to Johnston, this position entails that there is no objective reality in the words "good" or "evil", "justice" and "injustice". It naturally follows that human beings cannot access this knowledge outside divine revelation.[11] Qaradawi situates himself well within the bounds of this position, which is also the dominant position in Sunni Islam, and rejects the Muʿtazalite position that reason overtakes revelation. The Muʿtazilites hold that God is just, and that "the contours of justice are also accessible to human minds", as Johnston puts it: "If God commands his creatures to act justly, they reason, then he must have given them innate knowledge of what a just act looks like apart from what they might learn from revelation. So here we have simultaneously an ontology of objective ethical values and an epistemology that makes them available to human reason."[12]

---

9 I presented a study of the challenges to Muslim women in Western Europe at the ECFR's session in Dublin in February 2005. Polygamy and equal inheritance rights were two of the challenges I defined, the former because it is criminalized in European countries, the latter because of the reality in which women actually live: two salaries being a necessity for most households in Western Europe, many women provide as much for the family as men do. It therefore appears unjust for women to inherit half as much as their brothers, I claimed, and challenged the Council to discuss this situation with regard to matters of Islamic inheritance. Al-Qaradawi dismissed my argument on both counts. For polygamy, there was a clear verse in the Quran; however, living in Europe meant abiding by the law and hence marrying only one woman. He dismissed the inheritance issue by stating that supporting the family is a male responsibility. He appeared to be more concerned with focusing on the male duty to provide than on the reality women had to deal with according to my study.

10 The views of the classical age on the *ʿaql–naql* relationship do not simply fall into two opposite positions, however, but form a more nuanced picture. Bektović, following Hourani's survey of the various theological-philosophical positions, argues that most of the schools sought a compromise between reason and revelation, while differing over their relative priority and over the independence accorded to reason. Bektovic 2012, 50–54.

11 Johnston 2014, 44.

12 Johnston 2014, 44–45.

Muhammad Khalid Masud's interpretation of Shatibi's theory of *maqāṣid* does take reason into account. The objective of the Lawgiver is people's *maṣlaḥa*, which is an independent principle, decoupled from Islamic legal theory. The commands of Sharia are meant to protect the *maqāṣid al-sharīʿa*, which aim to protect people's interests (*maṣāliḥ*). According to Masud, Shatibi divides the *maqāṣid* or *maṣāliḥ* into the *ḍarūrī* (necessary), the *ḥājī* (needed) and the *taḥsinī* (commendable). The first category is called necessary because it is indispensible for defending the *maṣāliḥ* of this life and the beyond. Failure to protect the five *maqāṣid* will cause what Masud terms the "*maṣāliḥ* of the world" to collapse. But *maṣlaḥa* is also tied to *ḥājiyyāt* and *taḥsiniyyāt*, Masud says, citing Shatibi's definitions of these concepts:

> The *ḥājiyyāt* are so called because they are needed in order to expand (*tawassuʿ*) the purpose of the *maqāṣid* and to remove the strictness of literal sense, the application of which may lead to impediments and hardships and eventually to the disruption of the *maqāṣid* (objectives). Thus if *ḥājiyyāt* are not taken into consideration along with the *ḍarūriyyāt* the people on the whole face hardship. [...] *Taḥsīniyyāt* means to adopt what conforms best to the customs (*ʿādāt*) and to avoid those manners which are disliked by wiser people.[13]

These three kinds of *maṣāliḥ* complement and protect each other. The relationship between them can be likened with three concentric circles. Innermost, we find the *ḍarūriyyāt*, next the *ḥājiyyāt* and finally the *taḥsīniyyāt*.[14] Masud's restatement of Shatibi in modern terms has been summarized as follows in the context of family law:

> Al-Shatibi places the family in the first circle as a basic natural need. The legal norms in the second circle, e.g. norms regulating marriage, divorce and inheritance, are required to protect the family. They are not in themselves basic needs. The social preferences (third circle), such as that marriage partners be of equal social standing (*kafaʾa*), or the provision of a proper dower (*mahr al-mithl*), are refinements that help ground legal norms in a local culture. The absence of these social norms and practices, Masud argues, does not violate the legal norms that sustain the institu-

13 Masud 1995, 151–152.

14 Masud 1995, 153.

> tion of the family, i.e. the second circle. Hence these values may change with time, and new cultural values may replace old ones.[15]

It would seem that Ibn al-Qayyim's conception of Sharia as mercy and justice, and his conception of justice (*ʿadl*)[16] as synonymous with *maṣlaḥa*, in conjunction with a conception of *maṣlaḥa* as potentially independent of the texts, may present a solution to the question whether change and modernization can be pursued under the aegis of Islamic law. As argued by Ziba Mir-Hosseini, however, contemporary notions of justice, informed by the ideals of human rights and equality, depart substantially from those that underpin rulings in classical *fiqh* and established understandings of Sharia. For example, Ibn al-Qayyim regarded Sharia in its abstract form as just, but did not see injustice in the *furūʿ* when women were not given equal rights. He regarded the wife as her husband's prisoner and as akin to a slave.[17] The example of Ibn al-Qayyim shows that justice can be understood on two levels: it can be left in the abstract, or it can be interpreted in terms of specific norms. The normative understanding will depend on the common morality of society.

Modern Common Morality

Common morality, "the morality of ordinary people," is defined by Knut Erik Tranøy as "the set of moral values, norms and virtues—and the corresponding practices and institutions—that enjoy broad acceptance and are internalized and respected in a given culture at a certain time."[18] There are many common moralities, according to Tranøy, but this does not preclude all common moralities from having a shared ground.[19] This shared ground of the common-morality system he terms the *bio-moral values*, such as life, procreation, care for offspring, and a minimum quality of life. These values presuppose non-moral values, such as economic, political, social and cultural values. Violations of these values are among the legally and morally gravest crimes in our culture.[20] The bio-moral values are also the foundation of some basal norms—such as

15 Mir-Hosseini et al. 2013b, 24.
16 Discussions of the Islamic concept of justice in the scholarly literature include Khadduri 1984; Kamali 2002; Krämer 2007; and Kadivar 2013.
17 Mir-Hosseini et al. 2013b, 7.
18 Tranøy 2001, 106. All quotations from Tranøy are translated from the Norwegian.
19 Tranøy 2001, 107.
20 Tranøy 2001, 29–30.

not to kill, not to impose needless suffering on others—which belongs to what Tranøy calls the community of common morality.

Common morality consists of a value sector (concerning good and evil) and a norm sector (concerning right and wrong), Tranøy says.[21] The value sector consists of goods and evils, and in particular, of the good and bad consequences of actions and omissions. The distribution of goods raises the question of justice and injustice. In common morality, justice and injustice are central: A sense of justice is embedded in every human being, and it is well known that even small children have strong views on justice and injustice, Tranøy notes. The norm sector comprises duties, prohibitions, rights, laws, rules, guidelines, codes and so forth. Common morality is not constant, but changes in time with other social and cultural changes. Common morality is not the same thing as personal morality. The individual has options to choose from the range of norms and values placed at their disposal by common morality, within the limits set by a common ground, Tranøy says.[22] He explains the continuity and change of common morality by reference to its two levels: a *basic level* where e.g. the prohibitions against killing, stealing and lying are found, characterized by stability and durability; and a *higher level* where change may take place.[23] A change of morality may involve a change of values or a change of norms. It may happen through a change in the contents of common morality, or a change in people's attitudes toward the norms and values that form common morality.

A central question is that of "the good life" and how we ought to live in order to lead a morally good life. According to Tranøy, these are two different questions that confront us with the unclear relationship between the *good* and the *right*. Two concerns are implied: The self-realization of the person who acts, and the duties the person who acts has toward others, or his orientation towards his fellow humans. Self-realization must not come at the cost of other people's rights. The grounds for this claim are found in the idea of human dignity.

Common morality represents the moral order which, together with the legal order, is a precondition for a well-organized society, says Tranøy. Morality and law may overlap, but cannot replace each other. Codifying the common morality would be unnatural, even seemingly meaningless.[24] Tranøy does not consider it a weakness that the common morality lacks precise formulations and definitions of terms, but is satisfied with vague designations such as justice,

21 Tranøy 2001, 167.

22 Tranøy 2001, 132.

23 Tranøy 2001, 165.

24 Tranøy 2001, 188.

mercy, honesty, lies and truth. It is also characterized by what Tranøy calls a free normative space, that is to say, accepted disagreement within certain bounds. Furthermore, the moral order is an open order.[25] Moral decisions do not necessarily mean an end to the matter at hand; rather, they are steps in an ongoing process. And not least: The moral order requires free choice. Moral statements therefore cannot have the force of sanctions, but only of recommendations.[26]

Common Morality and the *maqāṣid*

Based on Tranøy's analysis of common morality, the *maqāṣid al-sharīʿa*, as described above, would appear to be an example of a theory of common morality grounded in Islam. Largely speaking, what Tranøy describes as bio-moral values seems to have a counterpart in the category of *ḍarūriyyāt* (vital necessities). They are not perfect matches: there are commonalities (protection of life and offspring) and differences (Tranøy does not list religion among the basal values).

Tranøy's category "a certain quality of life" appears open and capable of including a number of elements. The two necessities of intellect (*ʿaql*)[27] and property (*māl*) could be described as one way of specifying the quality-of-life concept. Tranøy's open concept might also comprise elements that Muslim scholars have added to the list of *ḍarūriyyāt* throughout history and up to the present. Tranøy ties the bio-moral values to some fundamental norms, such as prohibitions on killing or imposing needless suffering on others, which he calls the community of common morality. Violation of these norms incurs strict punishments. This is familiar from the theory of *maqāṣid al-sharīʿa*. We have also seen that *taysīr* is held up as a fundamental principle for the derivation of norms, with the justification that human beings should not be exposed to needless suffering. Life is also held to be protected inter alia through strict punishments for killing. The *ḍarūriyyāt* category was defined based on the violations of norms that incurred *ḥudūd* punishment, and corresponds to the value sector in Tranøy's theory of common morality.

25 Tranøy 2001, 189.

26 Tranøy 2001, 190–191.

27 The concept of "intellect" (*ʿaql*) as a necessity (*ḍarūra*) and as the basis for a certain quality of life can be explained by Shatibi's definition of *maṣlaḥa*: "I mean by *maṣlaḥa* that which concerns the subsistence of human life, the completion of man's livelihood, and the acquisition of what his emotional and intellectual qualities require of him …" (Masud 1995, 151).

The value sector, being concerned with goods and evils resulting from acts and omissions, has a counterpart in the concept of *maʾālāt* (consequences), which, as we have seen, is a criterion the mufti should take into account in his *ijtihād* as a part of *iftāʾ*. The norm sector in Tranøy's theory comprises duties, prohibitions, rights, laws, rules and guidelines. In *maqāṣid* theory, the norm sector consists of the categories *ḥājiyyāt og taḥsīniyyāt*. We recognize the categories of norms in Islamic jurisprudence: "forbidden" (*ḥarām*), "obligatory" (*wājib*), "reprehensible" (*makrūh*), "recommended" (*mandūb*) and "permissible" (*mubāḥ*). Fatwas might be described as declarations of these norms. Justice, according to Tranøy, is central both to the value sector and the norm sector. Correspondingly, Muslim scholars see the Sharia as justice, with reference to Ibn al-Qayyim's dictum that any norm that leads to injustice is not a part of Sharia.

Common morality belongs to the moral order. It may overlap with the legal order, but does not replace it. The moral order is an open order, Tranøy says. Moral decisions are not the end of the matter, and they have no power of sanctions, but only have the nature of recommendations. This description also fits fatwas and the processes and debates among scholars in the global Islamic field of debate and reference. Tranøy considers it a strength of common morality that it lacks precise formulations and definitions of terms, and makes do with expressions such as justice or mercy. The same might be said for *maqāṣid al-sharīʿa*, where the concepts of *maṣlaḥa* (utility, interest) and *ʿadl* (justice) are central. It affords opportunities to invest these broad concepts with new ideas, as do e.g. Islamic feminists who promote a re-interpretation of the concept of justice in their struggle for women's equality and rights.[28] As we have seen, however, the *maqāsid* theory may also pose an obstacle to reform. The different explanations of the *maqāṣid* illustrate an important difference between views of *maṣlaḥa* and the good: Qaradawi represents the view that *maṣlaḥa* is something discoverable, whereas Masud holds that it is a social construction. We can see that Masud's theory of *maqāṣid* entails an interpretation of the concepts that lies closer to Tranøy's interpretation than Qaradawi's theory does.

Competing Common Moralities

Does that fact that common morality changes in time with other social and cultural changes entail a decline from yesterday's common morality? Some

28 See e.g. http://www.musawah.org. Mir-Hosseini 2009, for example, sides with the Mu'tazili view that the notion of justice is inborn, based in reason, and exists independently of revealed texts.

changes raise concern in various circles, such as legal balancing acts in finance, drug abuse among young people, and nightlife violence. Still, Tranøy says no: The capacity for moral as well as immoral behaviour is inherent to human nature. There is little reason to believe that this nature has changed over the 2,500 years that have passed since the first Greek philosophers entered the Western cultural arena. The view of moral change as decline is often connected with people's disregard for established norms. This does not, however, automatically mean that people lack morality. It could mean a change in their view of the contents of morality. Drug crimes involve disregard for norms; women's right to decide on abortion might involve a change in the view of the contents of morality, even though some would see it as a decline of morality. The fundamental level—corresponding to the bio-moral values of life, procreation, care for offspring, and a minimum quality of life—stays fixed, while change takes place in the *interpretation* of these values. It is change in the interpretation of the contents of the values that implies a potential for social conflict. Let us take "life" as an example. What is a human life? This question is salient with regard to the beginning and end of life, the ethical challenges posed by questions of abortion and euthanasia. How to interpret "procreation"? This brings us to the view of marriage, whether between a man and a woman or between two persons of the same sex; the ethical question of surrogacy; and the rights of the child to know its parents, which is not least a question of caring for offspring. And how to define quality of life? That is a subject of constant discussion. These questions may be some of the most difficult problems in contemporary Western society.

The fatwas in the present book have as their stated purpose the protection of *ḍarūriyyāt*—religion, life, intellect, offspring and property—which form a mirror image of what Tranøy calls bio-moral values. Illustrations include the definition of a valid marriage, choice of spouse, keeping family relationships intact, abortion, divorce, surrogacy, staying married after conversion to Islam, and purchasing a house or apartment with a bank loan instead of paying rent. Existing Islamic norms and customs clearly are not in harmony with surrounding society, and are perceived as problematic by society at large. Muslim women experience this as a dilemma, and are torn between the two competing sets of norms, inequality and subordination versus equality and rights. Through their questions, the questioners (*al-mustaftūn*) in this book show that their purpose in asking is to live good and right lives in which their rights are respected. It seems safe to say, then, that the women's concern is not to avoid dealing with the established Islamic common morality, but to question its contents. Questions connected with finances and gender relations are good examples. The challenge to the muftis is to try to interpret the questions with a view to protecting the bio-moral values in a new light, which might contribute to the emergence of a new Islamic common morality. The different interpretations of the bio-moral values involve competition between common moralities. This causes unease, and it defines "us" vis-à-vis "the others," both within the same religious community and across boundaries of religion and belief. This insight also entails the possibility of an inclusive conversation about fundamental values, in which participants do not experience themselves as immoral or as lacking the right to put forward arguments seen as moral and just.

Situating the *maqāṣid al-sharīʿa* and *iftāʾ* as part of the moral order, which entails flexibility, contributes, in my view, to securing the possibility of different common moralities grounded in Islam existing side by side. These moralities, however, are not static in terms of norms and values; rather, they are in constant flux. Changes in values or norms or both are taking place, not least where the view of women is concerned. It is an open question how Muslim scholars, intellectuals and activists can converse with each other on the *good* and the *right*, particularly with regard to women's issues, which are central to Muslims living in Western Europe.[29] As we have seen, fatwas have their own dynamics of authority, which contributes to the individual's experience of belonging to the tradition. It is partly a matter of the authority that the scholars are seeking to reclaim from the "engineers". According to Eickelman and Piscatori, the ulama and the "new" religious intellectuals compete to gain ascendency as the arbiters of Islamic practice. The political implications of this process, they note, were evident in ninetheenth-century India, where the multiplication of printed texts, at first controlled by the ulama, "struck right at the heart of Islamic authority".[30] I have made the same finding in my own materials. The printed word and new channels of communication in the 20th century democratized the access to knowledge and threatened the authority of scholars to an unprecedented degree. Zaman formulates the challenges as follows: How are the foundational texts to be interpreted, what qualifications are most suitable to interpreting these texts, and what is the scope of legitimate interpretation?[31] And we may add: how do the scholars defend their authority? By presenting the muftis and their fatwas in this book, I have sought to shed light on these questions and offer insight into the complexity of Islamic discourse.

Our comparison of Knut Erik Tranøy's theory of modern common morality with the theory of *maqāṣid al-sharīʿa* opened for the possibility that the Muslim

29 These are concerns shared by Muslim women around the world. See e.g. Mir-Hosseini et al. 2013; Mir-Hosseini, Al-Sharmani and Rumminger 2015.

30 Eickelman and Piscatori 2004: 44.

31 Zaman 2009: 206.

minority and the non-Muslim majority might have shared fundamental values, implying a potential for dialogue and discourse across the borders of religions and life stances, or even for a shared point of view. In my view, this perspective might offer a dialectics that could reconcile, or at least defer the conflict between, the two sets of norms: on the one hand, unequal gender rights, with an emphasis on women's submission and obedience; on the other, equal rights, with an emphasis on women's rights and equality before the law.

Obstacles abound, however. Frank Peter argues that Muslims face the challenge of presenting their concerns in a "language" comprehensible in the public sphere.[32] I hold that the majority faces a challenge of the same magnitude, not in terms of language, but in defining what constitutes "fundamental values". In public and popular discourses, Sharia is described as a monolithic, static law that inherently conflicts with Western values and poses a threat to Europe. If the West is not vigilant, it is argued, future European societies will be dominated by the Sharia. Protecting European and national identities thus becomes an almost existential question. There are many arguments for such a defence strategy. One contribution to the debate is that of William Oddie, an English Catholic writer and editor of The Catholic Herald from 1998–2004.[33] He holds that Christians should be concerned over "recent attempts to give Sharia law a quasi official status alongside the law of the land that governs the rest of us." The encroachment of Sharia poses a threat to English law, founded in Judaeo-Christian morality and Western tradition, which Oddie identifies with equal inheritance rights for women. Muslim women, he argues, need to be protected against the suffering Sharia would inflict on them. He refers to the explanation Baroness Cox gave for the "Arbitration and Mediation Services and Equality Bill" she proposed in the House of Lords in 2012:[34]

32 Peter 2006, 445–446. Communication of theological thought and ethics in the public sphere is not only a challenge for Muslims, but also for actors from other religious traditions. A topical and well-known example from the Christian context is the struggle over same-sex marriage.

33 http://www.catholicherald.co.uk/commentandblogs/2014/03/27/this-is-still-a-christian-culture-but-the-law-society-is-now-encouraging-sharia-principles-that-are-deeply-hostile-to-our-values/.

34 "The Bill seeks to address two interrelated issues: the suffering of women oppressed by religiously sanctioned gender discrimination in the country; and a rapidly developing quasi system which undelines the fundamental principle of one law for all." http://www.publications.parliament.uk/pa/ld201213/ldhansrd/text/121019-0001.htm#12101923000438.

> We live in a country where we have a fundamental commitment to equality under the law and to freedom and that's a very precious commitment to our liberal democracy and our traditions, but there's been growing up in our midst, an alternative system, which affects many citizens, especially women. It's a kind of quasi legal system that goes under the name of Sharia law and obviously it's associated with the Muslim community. It discriminates systematically against women, particularly in matters of family law and testimony evidence before the law and domestic violence. I just don't feel you can have a quasi legal system operating alongside our own historic and traditional legal system, particularly one which discriminates against women and is causing many women real suffering.[35]

French politics and national identity discourses, too, are concerned with the oppression of Muslim women and the need to save them from Islamic practices. This found expression in the hearings about the proposed ban on face coverings that was adopted in 2010. The perception of Muslim women's attire as a threat to the identity of an entire nation can lead to bizarre outcomes, as when four armed policemen, invoking a recent local ban on "burkinis", forced a Muslim woman on a beach in southern France to take off her tunica in August 2016. A photograph of the incident was shared around the world, and seems to have gained an iconic status that might shift the discourse from rescuing Muslim women to recognizing that female autonomy applies to them, too. The burkini ban on French beaches was overturned by the Conseil d'État shortly after the incident.[36]

Are the shared concerns found in Islamic women-related discourses being drowned out by the anti-Islamic rhetoric of the European populist right, though? The appeal of the populist parties, according to Marzouki and McDonnell, is based on "the claim that a homogeneous "good" people is suffering due to the actions, from above, by elites, from below, by a variety of "others"."[37] The "others" are "depicted as depriving (or attempting to deprive) the sovereign people of their rights, values, prosperity, identity and voice."[38] The category of "others" mainly consists of immigrants in general and Muslims in partic-

35 Quoted by Oddie, apparently from an interview with Cox at http://www.crossrhythms.co.uk/articles/life/Baroness_Caroline_Cox_And_The_Sharia_Bill/43747/p1/.

36 http://www.conseil-etat.fr/Actualites/Communiques/Mesure-d-interdiction-des-tenues-regardees-comme-manifestant-de-maniere-ostensible-une-appartenance-religieuse-lors-de-la-baignade-et-sur-les-plages.

37 Marzouki and McDonnell 2016, 2.

38 Marzouki and McDonnell 2016, 3.

ular. Muslims, as Marzouki and McDonnell write, "allegedly want to impose their religious values and traditions on the people as part of a surreptitious 'Islamisation plan'. [...] Ideas of invasion, infiltration, contagion, conspiracy, replacement and impending irreversible crisis represent key compenents of the populist imaginary, and all of these are present in the notion that a deliberate process of Islamisation is occurring under our noses in many Western democracies."[39] This must be fought, and religion, in the sense of "belonging" rather than of "belief," becomes a useful tool in this struggle to define "us" and "them" and combat the "Islamic threat". For the populists, the struggle is about protecting "our" religious identity, traditions and values, rather than about theological dogma.[40] Religion is not the only resource in this struggle, though; a national secular identity can also play a part. To the Front National party in France, according to Olivier Roy, *la laïcité* offers "a more appealing and fruitful tool with which to fight 'Islam' than a Christian religion whose practice is in steady decline."[41] Common to both religious and secular arguments is the "concern" for Muslim women and their emancipation from oppression under Muslim men. Banning women from using headscarves, niqab or burkini is presented as promoting the rights of Muslim women, but has become part of the right-wing populist struggle to "protect" public space from "Islam". Has the space of opportunity for agreeing on values common to the non-Muslim majority and the Muslim minority, then, become restricted by the vociferous political discourse that dominates today? In this picture, it is ultimately women that seem to be marginalized and rendered suspect.

39 Marzouki and McDonnell 2016, 5.

40 Marzouki and McDonnell 2016, 2 ff.

41 Roy 2016, 80.

CHAPTER 8

Concluding Reflections

This book has examined fatwas as proposed solutions for the challenges faced by Muslim women in Western Europe. Muslim women are torn between two competing sets of norms: the traditional principle of inequality (or the neo-traditional principle of complementarity), with a stress on women's duties and subordination; and gender equality, with a stress on women's rights and equality before the law. I have explored whether Islamic scholars contribute, through their fatwas, to reconciling adherence to the Islamic tradition with the Western European ideal of equality. In the process, I have uncovered potential contributions to a dialectics that reconciles these sets of norms or defers the conflict between them.

I have used the concept *women-related fatwas* to render women's issues visible, which they often are not in descriptions of religion. From this starting point, it was natural to explore where women-related fatwas are found. What documentation is there to shed light on women-related fatwas? The scholarly literature on fatwas covers everything from the formative period of Islam until the present. My materials are from the recent period, fatwas given after 1992, but as a background, I have also briefly discussed women-related fatwas in historical perspective. One work from the formative period, *Muwaṭṭa'*, ascribed to Malik bin Anas, provided directions for future *fiqh* manuals and, in part, for fatwa collections, up until the modern period. The fatwa from the *Muwaṭṭa'* presented in chapter 1 well illustrates the point of defining Islam as "a discursive tradition".[1] It is not just a matter of the arguments, but also of the contexts that help to shape them.

In late 19th-century Egypt, a change took place with regard to women as a topic of Islamic discourse. The idea of social reform had taken root, and women's questions in particular were vigorously debated. The modernist project consisted in bridging the gap between traditional Muslim culture and modern Western influence, without going against central Islamic dogma. An important concern for Muhammad Abduh, and for the line of subsequent fatwa actors I have presented, was doing *ijtihād* and arguing for concepts and methods for the derivation of norms. Since the use of concepts and methods is as important in the eyes of the scholars as the norms themselves, Abduh's

1 Masud 1995.

 | DOI: 10.1163/9789004367852_010

way of arguing may also be interpreted as a strategy for gaining legitimacy and authority among other scholars.

I have described the 20th-century actors Muhammad Abduh, Muhammad Rashid Rida, Muhammad al-Ghazali and Yusuf al-Qaradawi, as background and explanatory lens for the actors and fatwas I have studied. They form a continuous line that ends in Western Europe with al-Qaradawi, and they represent one trend among fatwa actors, namely those who claim to take the existence of Muslims as minorities into account in fatwa-giving. The views of the above-mentioned persons all exemplify how the social and cultural context and historical developments impinge on the performance of *ijtihād*, which in turn underlines how suitable is the description of Islam as a "discursive tradition," a concept that manages to capture the complexity of the context.

The overwhelming modern-day Muslim interest in women finds expression inter alia in the structuring of fatwa collections. Yusuf al-Qaradawi's books *al-Ḥalāl wal-ḥarām fil-islām* and *Min hadī al-islām* have been presented as examples. The headings of "Woman" and "Family" organize the women-related fatwas. The use of these two concepts places al-Qaradawi within Islamic modernism. The former reflects the modernist focus on women, while the latter, "Family," is a concept that was adopted by the modernists and that represented a re-articulation of kinship ties.

Rashid Rida was the publisher-in-chief of the *al-Manār* magazine. This was a new channel for spreading the Islamic message, which had traditionally taken the form of sermons and private fatwas, and an important step in the democratization of access to knowledge about Islam. This has been a steeply growing trend over the 20th century, in an ever-increasing number of media. The new medium of the printing press also played a significant part in building the charisma and authority of new actors in the fatwa field. It seems to have given rise to a debate on who is entitled to give fatwas. I have sketched two responses: The first is al-Qaradawi's book *al-Fatwā bayna l-inḍibāṭ wal-tasayyub*, which falls into the *ādāb al-fatwā* genre, and is intended as a remedy against every Tom, Dick and Harry declaring matters and actions "forbidden" or "permitted". The second is a declaration that the time has come for the scholars to "take back Islam" from the so-called "engineers," who the scholars think lack the necessary schooling, and to take on the task of leading the believers through Islamic jurisprudence in Western Europe. I think these two concerns are part of the motivation behind the founding of the European Council for Fatwa and Research (ECFR) in 1997.

Chapter two presented selected fatwa actors in Europe: two local muftis, Syed Darsh and Barkatullah Abdulkadir; one national collegial body of muftis, the Paris-based Dar al-Fatwa; and one transnational council, the ECFR. I have given an account of their profiles, work, and use of concepts and methods. The French Dar al-Fatwa turned out to be part of a whole network of committees and activities in one of the nationwide French Islamic organizations, *Union des organisations islamiques de France* (UOIF). The network includes institutions of learning that aim to educate future muftis. The members of Dar al-Fatwa argue for different sets of concepts and methods. One of these is similar to the canon of the ECFR. Tareq Oubrou has advanced his own theory of *sharia de minorité* in which the fatwa is understood as a key to the integration of Muslims in Europe.

When the UOIF is discussed in the scholarly literature, one cannot ignore claims about whether the UOIF represents the Muslim Brotherhood on French soil, and forms a potential political threat. I have presented an analysis of the dominant media discourse on "Islam in France" in order to understand the dynamics of evolving views of the UOIF. At the end of the 1970s and in the 1980s, they were tied to the revolution in Iran and the settlement of immigrants in France. In the 1990s, they were mainly about the establishment of an *islam de France* and the media's division of Muslims into "moderates," who should be defended, and "Islamists," who should be fought. After 11 September 2001, the media discourse on Islam has been characterized by a focus on national security, closely tied to national identity. In my view the scholarly literature has a rather limited focus where the UOIF is concerned, and that the materials I have presented here represent new knowledge.

The London-based Syed Darsh, the Paris-based Dar al-Fatwa and the Dublin-based European Council for Fatwa and Research all relate in their work to a certain canon of concepts, methods and references. This places them within what John Bowen calls "the global field of reference and debate," one dimension of transnational Islam. The acceptance of the same canon by other scholars secures the legitimacy and authority of the individual mufti. The use of concepts and methods, therefore, has proven to serve as a canon in the sense of "a rule, standard, ideal, norm, or auhoritative office".[2]

The fatwa actors I have looked at use different words for "fatwa," such as "questions and answers," *fatwā* and *qarār*. While the use of "questions and answers" was an expression of Darsh's modesty—he claimed he was not doing *ijtihād*, just trying to help—the ECFR's use of *qarār* entails a claim to authority. As a "collective mufti," the Council has itself raised issues it thinks important for Muslims in Western Europe, and has given what it calls resolutions (*qarārāt*)

2 Masud 1995, 153.

in the framework of *fiqh al-aqalliyyāt*. The concept of *fiqh al-aqalliyyāt* represents the ECFR's claim to legitimacy vis-à-vis other fatwa councils, and its claim to European soil as its own "jurisdiction". The use of the term *qarār* would seem to be meant to underline this project.

The concept of *naṣīḥa* also came up in my interviews. According to the muftis, Muslims are not coming only for fatwas, but just as often to seek advice of a not strictly religio-legal nature. I had not seen the concept of *naṣīḥa* dealt with in the scholarly literature before, so I chose to explore the sources, content, and etiquette of such counseling. Based on these findings I have briefly compared fatwa and *naṣīḥa*.

Fatwas, both questions and answers, represent social data, and have been important sources for research on the society and culture of the medieval Muslim world.[3] I took the same approach by using the questions posed as the starting point for defining the issues that challenge Muslim women in Western Europe today. I developed a typology with categories of questions based on the questions that are in fact asked in my materials. In this connection, I found that some important issues of Islamic family law are all but absent from the fatwas: questions of inheritance and *mahr* (the bride-gift). It would be interesting to shed light on the reasons for the silence on these topics, but that falls outside the scope of this book.

I have shown that the fatwas vary in form and linguistic style. The fatwa texts all reflect the muftis' power of definition, but they also exemplify how the fatwa is in various ways adapted to the addressee, who thus also influences the shaping of the text. The means used are education, diplomacy, reprimands, personal opinions, and emotional arguments. The aim is the improvement of the Muslim self of the reader.

My theoretical point of departure was the perspective of recent research on Islamic law that looks at fatwas as an instrument and expression of change in Islamic jurisprudence. I have also drawn on Agrama's analysis of fatwas and authority, and John Bowen's definition of transnational Islam as a global field of reference and debate. Agrama criticizes what he sees as a one-sided focus on fatwas as instruments of change in Islamic jurisprudence and as a bridge between the past and the future. His theory is based on observation of oral fat-

3 Asad 1986, citing a list of references for such research in Lagardère 1995. As an illustration, David S. Powers' article "The Art of the Legal Opinion" demonstrates how different forms of *tawlīj* ("transactions between parents and children") were practiced in 8th-century Medina, were "widespread" in 12th-century al-Andalus, and were employed in 15th-century Morocco. *Tawlīj*, according to Peters, was a way of circumventing the perceived constraints of Islamic inheritance law in order to dispose of one's property as one saw fit (D.S. Powers 1996).

was given face-to-face, but the elements Agrama finds in the oral fatwas, such as the mufti attempting to help people and find solutions, and doing *tarbiyya* or Islamic education, are also found in the written fatwas I have looked at. Based on these fatwas, I analyse the authority of the fatwa into a vertical and a horizontal axis.

When the believer has the freedom to choose, why accept non-liberal fatwas that might even contradict her own interests? Fatwa-giving helps the questioner experience a belonging to the tradition, which is an important link in what Agrama calls the capacity of the fatwa to secure authority. Agrama's theory might also help explain resistance to change, as in his view, what matters is not the creativity of the fatwa, but how it enables a person to progress on the path toward improving the Muslim self—which, in turn, is about the believer's belonging to the tradition. This perspective, I think, should also be considered in questions of reform.

John Bowen describes the development of debates among Muslims in Europe and North America, and the various networks, conferences, and institutions tied to these debates, as a neglected form of transnational Islam. These activities, Bowen says, are an attempt to develop Islamic practice and teachings in accordance with Western norms and values while preserving the tradition from the Muslim world. Seeking for the foremost authority in doctrinal questions becomes a central concern. Agreement is not likely to be reached on who should be considered the chief authority. My analysis of the fatwas shows that the independent reasoning of the muftis is tied to the matter of legitimacy and authority, though it is not necessarily about who the leading authority is. The independent reasoning, of course, signals authority vis-à-vis the questioner (*al-mustaftī*). But just as importantly, if not more so, it is indirectly an argument about legitimacy and authority vis-à-vis other scholars, wherever they might be. The horizontal axis forms part of the global field of debate (across distance in space) and represents continuity with the tradition (a scholarly discourse across distance in time).

One topic that lies outside the scope of this book is the audience's response to the fatwas given, and whether these fatwas figure in conversations and debates on *ḥalāl* and *ḥarām*. We find examples in the scholarly literature that fatwas are indeed discussed.[4] One example is the (in)famous "mortgage fatwa" given by the ECFR in 1999, which allowed Muslims in Europe, on certain conditions, to take out a loan from a bank to buy a house. Many Muslims think that since interest (*ribā*) is forbidden in the Quran (2:275–276), no fatwa may allow

4 See Caeiro 2002, 111–117.

buying a house on an interest-bearing loan. The fatwa has therefore raised lively debate among Muslims both in and outside Europe.[5] We thus see the outline of another layer of "the global field of reference and debate" among Muslims without formal schooling in the Islamic sciences, a result of the democratization of access to knowledge of Islam. A further description and analysis of this layer at the horizontal axis of the fatwa, however, requires further research and not least the gathering of new empirical knowledge.

Of all the topics of the fatwas, marriage-related topics, especially topics connected with entry into marriage, were by far the more numerous. The challenge consists in defining what is considered correct Islamic practice in the encounter with non-Muslim national legislation. By studying the independent reasoning behind the fatwas on this topic, we have gained insight into attitudes to the relationship between *fiqh* and national legislation. We have also gained insight into the view of forced marriage and polygamy, two phenomena that are strongly condemned in the Western context. The texts also showed how muftis in republican France and the multicultural UK are each formed by their national identities, which is reflected in the fatwas they give.

The fatwas I have studied mainly situate themselves within the view of women and gender relations that Ziba Mir-Hosseini describes as *neo-traditionalist*: women and men do not have equal rights, but they have the same worth. This equal worth is reflected in equilibrium within the family and in society, where men's and women's rights and duties counterbalance each other.[6] Because the man has more duties, he also has more rights. Men and women complement each other in the family as a fundamental social institution.[7] Women's participation in society is desirable, but only on the condition that they use the hijab. Gender relations and sexuality must be controlled and regulated, or chaos will ensue.[8] Nevertheless, there is an observable tendency in the fatwas pointing toward gender equality. Mir-Hosseini describes the *equality perspective* as the view that men and women have equal worth, equal rights and equal duties. Equality means that biological sex is not a criterion for determining rights and duties. Gender is a social and human concept, not a part of the divine sphere, nor a matter for the Law-giver (God).[9] The tendency in the fatwas

5 The author's personal experience in conversation with Muslims both in European countries and in Morocco.

6 Mir-Hosseini 2000a, 117.

7 Mir-Hosseini 2000a, 133.

8 Mir-Hosseini 2000a, 89.

9 Mir-Hosseini 2000a, 249–250.

toward equal rights, however, is probably not the outcome of conscious assent to the principles discussed by Mir-Hosseini; rather, it is a by-product, since the purpose of the fatwa is to state the norms for right Islamic practice on the individual and collective level. The tendency toward equal rights is found in the fatwas on *ʿibādāt* (ritual actions). Women's equal rights are advocated where e.g. access to mosques or going on the pilgrimage are concerned.

The tendency toward equal rights is also found in fatwas on entry into marriage, however. Namely, national law is recognized as a means to realizing Islamic objectives, and abiding by national legislation when getting married, therefore, becomes a part of Sharia. This is an interesting concretization of the muftis' demands that Muslims in Europe should follow the law of the land, because it is about marriage and family matters, which are held to have a special place in Islamic identity. As European marriage laws accord equal rights to men and women, recognizing these laws means opening a back door for letting equal rights and equality before the law into Islamic jurisprudence. This is not to say that no objections are stated, but a certain realism with regard to securing rights at the entry into and dissolution of marriage would seem to have won out.

These fatwas, then, may be described as an indirect endorsement of the ideal of equality, which is a part of modern common morality. But are there any connection points between the fatwas and modern common morality? I think it might be important to identify such potential connection points. They could help solve conflicts of values by providing a common moral language for discussing them.

In the fatwas that entailed abiding by national legislations, the muftis used the *maqāṣid al-sharīʿa* as one argument. Can the *maqāṣid al-sharīʿa* serve as a connection point between the fatwas and modern common morality? And is there an understanding of common morality that could serve as a connection point with the fatwa? In an attempt to shed light on these questions, I have chosen to compare concepts referred to by the muftis within the framework of *maqāṣid al-sharīʿa* with the understanding of common morality set out by the Norwegian philosopher Knut Erik Tranøy.

The fatwas have an inner coherence, but also tensions, since they in different ways, directly and indirectly, relate to the two competing sets of norms: complementarity and equal worth versus equality and equal rights. The discrepancy between the two sets of norms seems lesser when the fatwas advocate equality and rights for women, as is the case in fatwas on matters of *ʿibādāt* and on getting married. It is greater when the muftis consider the marital relationship in practice, since their fatwas promote the principle of *qiwāma*, the guardianship of the husband.

Muslims in Western Europe are a relatively new minority. The muftis claim to be living in a new social reality that differs from the Muslim world. They use it to legitimate a new *ijtihād* based on certain concepts and principles of *uṣūl al-fiqh* in their fatwa-giving. Notions of the right to and possibility of new interpretations can contribute to legitimating change. Considered as part of the "discursive tradition" of Islam, fatwa-giving proves to be a discursive field that is both open, in the sense that it is possible for fatwas to change, even women-related ones; but also closed, in the sense that the scholars seek to protect their authority as "guardians of tradition".

I have presented two example interpretations of the theory of *maqāṣid al-sharīʿa*, Yusuf al-Qaradawi's theory and Muhammad Khalid Masud's interpretation of Shatibi, and I have discussed possibilities for and obstacles to reform. Masud's interpretation of the *maqāṣid* theory is being used as an argument for equality before the law. Whether this pro-reform argument will prevail depends not only on its content, but also on who promotes it. As a so-called "new religious intellectual", Masud belongs to a category of actors that stands in opposition to the ulama's claims to authority and monopoly on the interpretation of the sources.[10] The comparison of Qaradawi's and Masud's theories of *maqāṣid* also shows that the derivation of norms, and their acceptance, is not only about the concepts and methods we find in *uṣūl al-fiqh*; at issue are foundational principles of Islam, including views on the relationship between reason and revelation, and the understanding of justice. The debate on women-related questions is thus not only a symptom of Muslim identity politics, it also touches on the very foundations of Islamic belief.

The comparison of Knut Erik Tranøy's theory of common morality with the *maqāṣid al-sharīʿa* theory shows that both are moral theories anchored in universal fundamental values. The fatwas are an interpretation of Islamic common morality grounded in Islam. Tranøy mentions such an Islamic common morality as a phenomenon of countries where Islam is the dominant religion, but I have shown that it also applies in Western Europe, where Muslims live as minorities. I would claim that the theory of *maqāṣid al-sharīʿa* and Tranøy's interpretation of common morality are two different but mutually translatable languages used about one and the same concern, the "good" and the "right". This makes it possible to discuss the foundations for views of what is "right" and "good". Insight into this common moral concern might increase trust between the minority and the majority, and thus help relieve the unease over

10 A discussion of the conflict between the ulama and the new religious intellectuals would take us outside the scope of this book.

multi-religious coexistence in European societies. The scope for such mutual insight and trust, however, may be restricted by currently dominant political discourses in Europe.

References

Abdel-Fadil, Mona. 2011. "The Islam-Online Crisis: A Battle of Wasatiyya vs. Salafi Ideologies?" *CyberOrient* 5 (1). http://www.cyberorient.net/article.do?articleId=6239.

Abel, A. 2010. "Dār Al- Ḥarb." *Encyclopaedia of Islam, Second Edition*. Brill: 2010. http://www.brillonline.nl/subscriber/entry?entry=islam_SIM-1700.

Abu Sulayman, Abdulhamid A. 2003. *Marital Discord: Recapturing the Full Islamic Spirit of Human Dignity*. London/Washington: The International Institute of Islamic Thought.

Abukhalil, Asʿad. 2009. "Revival and Renewal." Ed. John L. Esposito. *The Oxford Encyclopedia of the Islamic World*. Oxford: Oxford University Press.

Adams, C.C. 1968. *Islam and Modernism in Egypt*. New York: Russel & Russel.

Agrama, Hussein Ali. 2010. "Ethics, Tradition, Authority: Toward an Anthropology of the Fatwa." *American Ethnologist* 37 (1) (February): 2–18. doi:10.1111/j.1548–1425.2010.01238.x.

Ahmed, Leila. 1992. *Women and Gender in Islam*. New Haven: Yale University Press.

Ali, Kecia. 2008. "Marriage in Classical Jurisprudence: A Survey of Doctrines." In *The Islamic Marriage Contract: Case Studies in Islamic Family Law*, ed. Asifa Quraishi and Frank Vogel. Cambridge, Massachusetts: Islamic Legal Studies Program, Harvard Law School.

al-Alwani, Taha Jabir. 2003. *Towards a Fiqh for Minorities: Some Basic Reflections*. London: The International Institute of Islamic Thought.

Amin, Qasim. 1992. *The Liberation of Women: A Document in the History of Egyptian Feminism*. Trans. by Samiha Sidhom Peterson. Cairo: The American University in Cairo Press.

Amin, Qasim. 1995. *The New Woman: A Document in the Early Debate on Egyptian Feminism*. Trans. by Samiha Sidhom Peterson. Cairo: The American University in Cairo Press.

Anderson, Michael R. 1996. *Islamic Law and the Colonial Encounter in British India*. Occasional Paper. Grabels: Women Living Under Muslim Laws.

Anderson, Norman. 1976. *Law Reform in the Muslim World*. University of London Legal Series 11. London: University of London, Athlone Press.

Asad, Talal. 1986. *The Idea of an Anthropology of Islam*. Washington, D.C.: Georgetown University, Center for Arab Studies.

Asad, Talal. 2003. *Formations of the Secular: Christianity, Islam, Modernity*. Stanford, California: Stanford University Press.

Attia, Gamal Eldin. 2007. *Towards Realization of the Higher Intents of Islamic Law. Maqāṣid al-Sharīʿah: A Functional Approach*. London: The International Institute of Islamic Thought.

Ayubi, Nazih N. 1995. "Al-Ghazālī, Muḥammad." Ed. John L. Esposito. *Oxford Encyclopedia of the Modern Islamic World*. Oxford: Oxford University Press.

Babès, Leila. 2004. "Norme et autorité religieuse chez les jeunes musulmans de France." In *Les transformations de l'autorité religieuse*, ed. Martine Cohen, Jean Joncheray, and Pierre-Jean Luizard, 199–214. Paris: L'Harmattan.

Badawi, Zaki. 1978. *The Reformers of Egypt*. London: Croom Helm.

Badran, Margot. 2009. "Feminism." Ed. John L. Esposito. *Oxford Encyclopedia of the Modern Islamic World*. Oxford: Oxford University Press.

Bakhtiar, Laleh, trans. 2009. *The Sublime Quran*. Chicago: Kazi Publications.

Bano, Samia. 2007. "Islamic Family Arbitration, Justice and Human Rights in Britain." *Law, Social Justice & Global Development* (1) (December). http://www2.warwick.ac.uk/fac/soc/law/elj/lgd/2007_1/bano.

Baylocq, Cédric. 2012. "The Autonomisation of the Muslim Brotherhood in Europe: *da'wa, Mixité*, and Non-Muslims." In *The Muslim Brotherhood in Europe*, ed. Roel Meijer and Edwin Bakker, 149–168. New York: Columbia University Press.

Becheri, Larabi. 2008. *Al-muslimūn fī ūrūbā bayna al-zawāj al-'urfī wal-zawāj fil-qānūn al-madanī*. Unpublished study. 12 pp.

Bektovic, Safet. 2012. *Islamisk filosofi. Bakgrund, problemstillinger og moderne udforminger*. Fredriksberg: ANIS.

Bernand, M. 2010. "Mu'āmalāt." *Encyclopaedia of Islam, Second Edition*. Brill. http://www.brillonline.nl/subscriber/entry?entry=islam_SIM-5271.

Bin Bayyah, Abdullah. 2007. *Ṣinā't al-fatwā wa-fiqh al-aqalliyyāt*. Jedda: Dār al-minhāj.

Blakar, Rolv Mikkel. 2006. *Språk er makt*. Oslo: Pax.

Bogstad, Therese. 2009. "Mellom juridisk og religiøs diskurs: Argumentasjon om islamsk skilsmisse hos Islamonline.net". MA thesis in the History of Religion. University of Oslo, Department of Culture Studies and Oriental Languages.

Bousquet, G.-H. 2010. "'Ibādāt." *Encyclopaedia of Islam, Second Edition*. Leiden: Brill. http://www.brillonline.nl/subscriber/entry?entry=islam_SIM-3014.

Bowen, John R. 2004. "Beyond Migration: Islam as a Transnational Public Space." *Journal of Ethnic and Migration Studies* 30 (5) (September): 879–894. doi:10.1080/1369183042000245598.

Bowen, John R. 2007. *Why the French Don't Like Headscarves: Islam, the State, and Public Space*. Princeton: Princeton University Press.

Bowen, John R. 2010. *Can Islam Be French? Pluralism and Pragmatism in a Secularist State*. Princeton; Oxford: Princeton University Press.

Brockopp, Jonathan E. 2005. "The Minor Compendium of Ibn Abd Al-Hakam (D. 214/829) and Its Reception in the Early Maliki School." *Islamic Law and Society* 12: 149.

Brooke, Steven. 2012. "The Muslim Brotherhood in Europe and the Middle East: The Evolution of a Relationship." In *The Muslim Brotherhood in Europe*, ed. Roel Meijer and Edwin Bakker, 27–50. New York: Columbia University Press.

Burhanudin, Jajat. 2005. "Aspiring for Islamic Reform: Southeast Asian Requests for *Fatwās* in *al-Manār*." *Islamic Law and Society* 12 (1) (January): 9–26. doi:10.1163/1568519053123858.

Caeiro, Alexandre. 2002. "La normativité islamique à l'épreuve de l'Occident: le cas du Conceil européen de la fatwa et de la recherche". Paris: École des hautes etudes en sciences sociales, DEA.

Caeiro, Alexandre. 2004. "The Social Construction of Sharīʿa: Bank Interest, Home Purchase, and Islamic Norms in the West." *Die Welt Des Islams* 44 (3): 351–375.

Caeiro, Alexandre. 2005. "Religious Authorities or Political Actors? The Muslim Leaders of the French Representative Body of Islam." In *European Muslims and the Secular State*, ed. Jocelyne Cesari and Seán McLoughlin, 71–84. Aldershot: Ashgate Publishing.

Caeiro, Alexandre. 2006. "The Shifting Moral Universes of the Islamic Tradition of Ifta: A Diachronic Study of Four Adab Al-Fatwa Manuals." *The Muslim World* 96 (4): 661–685.

Caeiro, Alexandre. 2010. "The Power of European Fatwas: The Minority Fiqh Project and the Making of an Islamic Counterpublic." *International Journal of Middle East Studies* 42 (3) (August): 435–449.

Caeiro, Alexandre. 2011. "Fatwas for European Muslims: The Minority Fiqh Project and the Integration of Islam in Europe". Ph.D. dissertation, Utrecht: University of Utrecht.

Caeiro, Alexandre, and Mahmoud al-Saify. 2009. "Qaraḍāwī in Europe, Europe in Qaraḍāwī? The Global Mufti's European Politics." In *Global Mufti: The Phenomenon of Yūsuf Al-Qaraḍāwī*, ed. Bettina Gräf and Jakob Skovgaard-Petersen, 109–148. New York: Columbia University Press.

Calder, Norman. 1993. *Studies in Early Muslim Jurisprudence*. Oxford: Clarendon Press.

Calder, Norman. 1996. "Al-Nawawi's Typology of Muftis and Its Significance for a General Theory of Islamic Law." *Islamic Law and Society* 3: 137.

Calder, Norman. 2009a. "SHarīa." *Encyclopaedia of Islam, Second Edition*. Brill.

Calder, Norman. 2009b. "Law: Legal Thought and Jurisprudence." Ed. John L. Esposito. *The Oxford Encyclopedia of the Islamic World*. Oxford: Oxford University Press.

Cavallin, Clemens. 2006. "Forholdet mellom teori og metode." In *Metode i religionsvitenskap*, ed. Siv Ellen Kraft and Richard Natvig, 14–28. Pax forlag A/S.

Chaudhry, Ayesha S. 2013. *Domestic Violence and the Islamic Tradition: Ethics, Law, and the Muslim Discourse on Gender*. New York, NY: Oxford University Press.

Daho, Okacha ben Ahmed. 2006. "L'UOIF et ses structures." In *Qu'est-ce que l'UOIF?*, ed. Lhaj Thami Breze. Paris: l'Archipel.

Darsh, Syed Mutawalli. 1997. *Questions and Answers about Islam*. London: Ta-Ha Publishers Ltd.

Darsh, Syed Mutawalli. n.d. *Muslims in the West: A Fiqh Seminar in France*. n.p.

Deltombe, Thomas. 2005. *L'islam imaginaire: La construction médiatique de l'islamophobie en France, 1975–2005*. Paris: La Découverte.

Dien, Mawil Y. Izzi, and P.E. Walker. 2010. "Wilāya (a.)." *Encyclopaedia of Islam, Second Edition*. Brill. http://www.brillonline.nl/subscriber/entry?entry=islam_COM-1349.

Doniger O'Flaherty, Wendy. 1982. *Women, Androgynes, and Other Mythical Beasts*. Chicago: University of Chicago Press.

Døving, Cora Alexa. 2009. *Integrering: Teori og empiri*. Oslo: Pax forlag A/S.

Dutton, Yasin. 2002. *The Origins of Islamic Law: The Qur'an, the* Muwaṭṭa' *and Madinan* 'Amal. 2nd ed. London: RoutledgeCurzon.

ECFR. 2002a. *Fatwas of European Council for Fatwa and Research*. Cairo: Islamic Inc. Publishing and Distribution.

ECFR. 2002b. *Qarārāt wal-fatāwā*. Ed. al-Majlis al-ūrūbī lil-iftā' wal-buḥūth. Cairo: Dār al-tawzīʿ wal-nashr al-islamiyya.

ECFR. 2013. *Al-qararāt wal-fatāwā al-ṣādira 'an al-majlis al-ūrūbī lil-iftā' wal-buḥūth*. Beirut: Mu'assasat al-rayyān.

Eggen, Nora. 2001. *Islamsk rettskildelære*. Oslo: Department of Public and International Law, Universitety of Oslo.

Eickelman, Dale F. and James Piscatori. 2004. *Muslim Politics*. Princeton and Oxford: Princeton University Press.

Esposito, John L., ed. 2003. *The Oxford Dictionary of Islam*. Oxford: Oxford University Press.

Findley, Carter Vaughn. 2009. "Mecelle." Ed. John L. Esposito. *The Oxford Encyclopedia of the Islamic World*. Oxford: Oxford University Press.

Freeland, Richard, and Martin Lau. 2008. "The Shariʿa and English Law: Identity and Justice for British Muslims." In *The Islamic Marriage Contract: Case Studies in Islamic Family Law*, ed. Asifa Quraishi and Frank Vogel. Cambridge, Massachusetts: Islamic Legal Studies Program, Harvard Law School.

Frégosi, Franck. 2008. *Penser l'islam dans la laïcité: Les musulmans de France et la République*. Paris: Fayard.

Geertz, Clifford. 1993. *The Interpretation of Cultures*. London: Fontana Press.

Geisser, Vincent. 2006. "L'UOIF, la tension clientéliste d'une grande fédération islamique." *Confluences Méditerranée* (57): 83–101.

al-Ghazali, Muhammad. 1989. *Al-sunna al-nabawīya bayna ahl al-fiqh wa-ahl al-hadīth*. Cairo: Dār al-shurūq.

al-Ghazali, Muhammad. 1994. *Les Problèmes de la femme entre les traditions et la modernité*. Beirut: Dar al-Bouraq.

al-Ghazali, Muhammad. 1997. *Fiqh-us-Seerah: Understanding the Life of Prophet Muhammad*. Riyad: International Islamic Federation of Student Organisations.

al-Ghazali, Muhammad. 2009. *The Sunna of the Prophet: The People of Fiqh versus the People of Hadith*. Trans. by Aisha Abdurrahman Bewley. London: Dar al-Taqwa.

Gräf, Bettina. 2008. "IslamOnline.net: Independent, Interactive, Popular." *Arab Media & Society* (4). http://www.arabmediasociety.com/?article=576.

Gräf, Bettina. 2009. "The Concept of *wasaṭiyya* in the Work of Yūsuf Al-Qaraḍāwī." In *Global Mufti: The Phenomenon of Yūsuf Al-Qaraḍāwī*, ed. Bettina Gräf and Jakob Skovgaard-Petersen, 213–238. New York: Columbia University Press.

Gräf, Bettina, and Jakob Skovgaard-Petersen. 2009. "Introduction." In *Global Mufti: The Phenomenon of Yūsuf Al-Qaraḍāwī*, ed. Jakob Skovgaard-Petersen and Bettina Gräf, 109–148. New York: Columbia University Press.

Guergah, Ounis. n.d. *Muḥāḍarāt fil-futyā': mudhakkira li-ṭullāb al-sanat al-thāniya sharī'a wa-'uṣūl al-dīn*. Compendium. n.p.

Guergah, Ounis. 2004. *al-Ḥukm al-zawāj bayna al-'aqd al-'urfī wal-'aqd al-madanī*. Unpublished studie. 8 pp.

Haddad, Yvonne Yazbeck. 1998. "Islam and Gender: Dilemmas in the Changing Arab World." In *Islam, Gender and Social Change*, ed. Yvonne Yazbeck Haddad and John L. Esposito, 3–29. Oxford: Oxford University Press.

Hallaq, Wael B. 1986. "On the Origins of the Controversy about the Existence of Mujtahids and the Gate of Ijtihad." *Studia Islamica* (63): 129–141.

Hallaq, Wael B. 1994. "From *Fatwās* to *Furū'*: Growth and Change in Islamic Substantive Law." *Islamic Law and Society* 1 (1): 29–65.

Hallaq, Wael B. 1997/2003. *A History of Islamic Legal Theories: An Introduction to Sunnī* uṣūl al-fiqh. Cambridge: Cambridge University Press.

Hallaq, Wael B. 2005/2009. *Sharī'a: Theory, Practice, Transformations*. Cambridge: Cambridge University Press.

Hasan, Suhayb, Abdul Hadi al-'Umari, HafeezUllah Khan, SanaUllah Sialkoti, and Shoaib Ahmad Mirpuri. n.d. *A Response to the Unjust, Deceptive and Slanderous Allegations Made against Markazi Jami'at Ahle Hadith UK*. n.p.

Hassan, Said Fares. 2013. *Fiqh al-Aqalliyyāt: History, Development, and Progress*. Palgrave Series in Islamic Theology, Law, and History. New York, NY: Palgrave Macmillan.

Heyd, Uriel. 1969. "Some Aspects of the Ottoman Fetvā." *Bulletin of the School of Oriental and African Studies* 32 (1) (January 1): 35–56. doi:10.2307/613387.

Hirschkind, Charles. 2005. "Civic Virtue and Religious Reason: An Islamic Counter-Public." In *Aural Cultures*, ed. Jim Drobnick, 189–207. Toronto: YYZ Books.

Hoffmann, V. 2010. "Abd Al-Raḥmān, 'Ā'isha." *Encyclopaedia of Islam, Three*. Brill. http://www.brillonline.nl/subscriber/entry?entry=ei3_SIM-0158.

Hourani, Albert. 1987. *Arabic Thought in the Liberal Age 1789–1939*. Cambridge: Cambridge University Press.

Ibn Ashur, Muhammad al-Tahir. 2006. *Ibn Ashur: Treatise on Maqasid al-Shari'ah*. London: The International Institute of Islamic Thought.

Ibn Hazm. n.d. *Jawāmi' al-sīra wa-khamsa rasā'il ukhrā li-Ibn Ḥazm*. www.alwarraq.com.

Ibn Rushd. 2000. *The Distinguished Jurist's Primer (Bidāyat Al-Mujtahid Wa Nihāyat Al-Muqtasid)*. Trans. by Imran Ahsan Khan Nyazee. Vol. 2. 2 vols. Reading: Garnet Publishing.

Ibrahim, Yasir S. 2006. "Rashīd Riḍā and *Maqāṣid Al-Sharī'a*." *Studia Islamica* (102–103): 157–198.

Izzi Dien, Mawil. 2004. *Islamic Law: From Historical Foundations to Contemporary Practice*. The New Edinburgh Islamic Surveys. Edinburgh: Edinburgh University Press.

Johansen, Baber. 1994. "Legal Literature and the Problem of Change: The Case of the Land Rent." In *Islam and Public Law*, ed. Chibli Mallat, 29–47. London: Graham and Trotman.

Johnston, David L. 2014. "Yusuf al-Qaradawi's Purposive Fiqh." In *Maqāṣid al-Sharī'a and Contemporary Reformist Muslim Thought. An Examination*, ed. Adis Duderija, 39–72. New York: Palgrave Macmillan.

Jørgensen, Marianne, and Louise Phillips. 2002. *Discourse Analysis as Theory and Method*. London; Thousand Oaks, Calif.: Sage Publications. http://site.ebrary.com/id/10256893.

Jum'a, Ali. 2005. *Fatāwā al-imām Muhammad 'Abduh*. Cairo?: al-Jama'iyya al-khayriyya al-islāmiyya.

Kadivar, Mohsen. 2013. "Revisiting Women's Rights in Islam: 'Egalitarian Justice' in Lieu of 'deserts-Based Justice.'" In *Gender and Equality in Muslim Family Law: Justice and Ethics in the Islamic Legal Tradition*, ed. Ziba Mir-Hosseini, Kari Vogt, Lena Larsen, and Christian Moe, trans. by Ziba Mir-Hosseini, 213–234. Library of Islamic Law 5. London: I.B. Tauris.

Kamali, Mohammad Hashim. 2002. *Freedom, Equality, and Justice in Islam*. Cambridge: Islamic Texts Society.

Kamali, Mohammad Hashim. 2003. *Principles of Islamic Jurisprudence*. Cambridge: Islamic Texts Society.

Kamali, Mohammad Hashim. 2008. *Maqāṣid al-Sharī'ah Made Simple*. London: The International Institute of Islamic Thought.

Kamali, Mohammad Hashim. 2009. "Law and Ethics in Islam: The Role of the Maqāṣid." In *New Directions in Islamic Thought. Exploring Reform and Muslim Tradition*, ed. Kari Vogt, Lena Larsen, and Christian Moe, 23–46. London: I.B. Tauris.

Karman, Karen-Lise Johansen. 2008. "Rethinking Islamic Jurisprudence for Muslim Minorities: The Politics and the Work of Contemporary Fatwa Councils". PhD dissertation, Aarhus: Aarhus universitet, Det teologiske fakultet.

Katz, Marion Holmes. 2006. "The 'Corruption of the Times' and the Mutability of the Shari'a." *Cardozo Law Review* 28: 171.

Kepel, Gilles. 1987. *Les banlieues de l'islam: Naissance d'une religion en France*. Paris: Éditions du Seuil.

Kepel, Gilles. 1997. *Allah in the West: Islamic Movements in America and Europe*. Oxford: Polity Press.

Kerr, Malcolm H. 1966. *Islamic Reform: The Political and Legal Theories of Muḥammad 'Abduh and Rashīd Riḍā*. Berkeley & Los Angeles: University of California Press.

Khadduri, M. 2010. "Maṣlaḥa." *Encyclopaedia of Islam, Second Edition*. Brill. http://www.brillonline.nl/subscriber/entry?entry=islam_SIM-5019.

Khadduri, Majid. 1984. *The Islamic Conception of Justice*. Baltimore: Johns Hopkins University Press.

Khalafallah, Haifaa. 1999. "Rethinking Islamic Law: Genesis and Evolution in the Islamic Legal Method and Structures. The Case of a 20th Century 'Alim's Journey into His Legal Traditions. Muhammad Al-Ghazali (1917–1996)". Dr. of Philosophy thesis, Washington: Georgetown University.

Khalafallah, Haifaa. 2006. "Muslim Women: Public Authority, Scriptures, and 'Islamic Law.'" In *Beyond the Exotic: Women's Histories in Islamic Societies*, ed. Amira El Azhary Sonbol, 37–52. Cairo: The American University in Cairo Press.

King, Michael, ed. 1995. *God's Law versus State Law: The Construction of an Islamic Identity in Western Europe*. London: Grey Seal Books.

Krämer, Gudrun. 2007. "Justice in Modern Islamic Thought." In *Shari'a: Islamic Law in the Contemporary Context*, ed. Abbas Amanat and Frank Griffel, 20–37. Stanford, California: Stanford University Press.

Kramer, Martin. 1986. *Islam Assembled: The Advent of the Muslim Congresses*. New York: Columbia University Press.

Kuper, Simon. 2009. "Immigrant Muslims in Belleville." *Financial Times*, October 2, sec. Life & Arts.

Laading, Liv. 1986. "Fra harem til kvinnebevegelse: En historisk oversikt over utviklingen i Egypt (1800–1924), med vekt på Qasim Amins diskusjon og nytolkning av kvinnens tradisjonelle status i islam". Mag. art dissertation, Universitety of Oslo.

Lacroix, Stéphane. 2008. "Al-Albani's Revolutionary Approach to Hadith." *ISIM Review* (21): 6–7.

Lacroix, Stéphane. 2011. *Awakening Islam. The Politics of Religious Dissent in Contemporary Saudi Arabia*. Cambridge, Massachusetts: Harvard University Press.

Ladmiral, Yvette. 2006. "Brève histoire de l'UOIF." In *Qu'est-ce que l'UOIF?*, ed. Lhaj Thami Breze. Paris: l'Archipel.

Lagardère, Vincent. 1995. *Histoire et Société en occident musulman au Moyen Âge: Analyse du Mi'yār d'al-Wansarisi*. Madrid: Consejo Superior de Investigaciones Cientificas—Casa de Velàsquez.

Landau, Jacob M. 2009. "Pan-Islam." Ed. John L. Esposito. *The Oxford Encyclopedia of the Islamic World*. Oxford: Oxford University Press.

Laoust, H. 2010. "Ibn Taymiyya, Taḳī Al-Dīn Aḥmad Ibn Taymiyya." *Encyclopaedia of Islam, Second Edition*. Brill. http://www.brillonline.nl/subscriber/entry?entry=islam_SIM-3388.

Larsen, Lena. 1995. "Velkommen til en stor familie … Islam og konversjon i norsk kontekst". Second cycle thesis, Oslo: University of Oslo.

Larsen, Lena. 2010. "Islamic Jurisprudence and Transnational Flows: Exploring the European Council for Fatwa and Research." In *From Transnational Relations to Transnational Laws: Northern European Laws at the Crossroads*, ed. Anne Hellum, Shaheen Sardar Ali, and Anne Griffiths, 139–165. Ashgate.

Larsen, Lena. 2015. "'Men are the Protectors and maintainers of Women …' The Fatwas on Spousal Roles and Rights." In *Men in Charge? Rethinking Authority in Muslim Legal Tradition*, ed. Ziba Mir-Hosseini, Mulki Sharmani and Jana Rumminger, 197–218. London: Oneworld Publications.

Laurence, Jonathan, and Justin Vaisse. 2006. *Integrating Islam: Political and Religious Challenges in Contemporary France*. Washington, D.C.: Brookings Institution Press.

Linant de Bellefonds, Y. 2010. "Kafā'a." *Encyclopaedia of Islam, Second Edition*. Brill. http://www.brillonline.nl/subscriber/entry?entry=islam_SIM-3772.

Maillard, Stanislav. 2006. "L'homme des compromis." In *Qu'est-ce que l'UOIF?*, ed. Lhaj Thami Breze. Paris: l'Archipel.

Mālik ibn Anas. 2001. *Al-Muwaṭṭa'*. Trans. by Aisha Abdurrahman Bewley. Scotland: Medina Press Inverness.

March, Andrew F. 2009. "Sources of Moral Obligation to Non-Muslims in the 'Jurisprudence of Muslim Minorities' (Fiqh al-Aqalliyyat) Discourse." *Islamic Law and Society* 16 (1) (February): 34–94. doi:10.1163/156851908X413757.

al-Marghinani, Burhan al-Din. 1989. *The Hedaya: Commentary on the Islamic Laws*. Trans. by Charles Hamilton. Vol. 1. Karachi: Darul Ishaat Urdu Bazar.

Marzouki, Nadia, and Duncan Mc Donnell. 2016. "Populism and Religion". In *Saving the People: How Populists Hijack Religion*, ed. Nadia Marzouki, Duncan Mc Donnell and Olivier Roy, 1–11. London: Hurst and Company.

Masud, Muhammad Khalid. 1995. *Shatibi's Philosophy of Islamic Law*. Islamabad: Islamic Research Institute/International Islamic University.

Masud, Muhammad Khalid. 2010. "Adab Al-Muftī." *Encyclopaedia of Islam, Three*. Brill. http://www.brillonline.nl/subscriber/entry?entry=ei3_SIM-0354.

Masud, Muhammad Khalid, Brinkley Messick, and David Powers, eds. 1996. *Islamic Legal Interpretation: Muftis and Their Fatwas*. Massachusetts: Harvard University Press.

Mawsuʿa. 2003. *al-Mawsūʿat al-fiqhiyya*. Vol. 40. Kuwait: Wizārat al-awqāf wal-shu'ūn al-islamiyya.

Mayer, Ann E. 1990. "The Sharīʿah: A Methodology or a Body of Substantive Rules." In *Islamic Law and Jurisprudence*, ed. Nicholas Heer. Seattle: University of Washington Press.

Mazid, Nergis. 2002. "Western Mimicry or Cultural Hybridity: Deconstructing Qasim Amin's 'Colonized Voice.'" *American Journal of Islamic Social Sciences* 19 (4): 42–67.

Mir-Hosseini, Ziba. 2000a. *Islam and Gender: The Religious Debate in Contemporary Iran*. London: I.B. Tauris.

Mir-Hosseini, Ziba. 2000b. *Marriage on Trial: A Study of Islamic Family Law*. London: I.B. Tauris.

Mir-Hosseini, Ziba. 2009. "Towards Gender Equality: Muslim Family Laws and the Shariʿah." In *Wanted: Equality and Justice in the Muslim Family*, ed. Zainah Anwar, 23–63. Kuala Lumpur: Musawah/Sisters in Islam.

Mir-Hosseini, Ziba. 2010. "Being From There: Dilemmas of a 'Native Anthropologist.'" In *Conceptualizing Iranian Anthroplogy: Past and Present Perspectives*, ed. Shahnaz R. Nadjmabadi, 180–191. Oxford: Berghahn Books.

Mir-Hosseini, Ziba, Kari Vogt, Lena Larsen, and Christian Moe, eds. 2013. *Gender and Equality in Muslim Family Law: Justice and Ethics in the Islamic Legal Tradition*. Library of Islamic Law 5. London: I.B. Tauris.

Mir-Hosseini, Ziba, Kari Vogt, Lena Larsen, and Christian Moe, eds. 2013b. *Justice through Equality. Building Religious Knowledge for Reform of Muslim Family Laws*. http://www.jus.uio.no/smr/english/about/programmes/oslocoalition/docs/justice-through-equality.pdf

Mir-Hosseini, Ziba, Mulki Al-Sharmani, and Jana Rumminger, eds. 2015. *Men in Charge? Rethinking Authority in Muslim Legal Tradition*. London: Oneworld.

Mitchell, Richard P. 1969. *The Society of the Muslim Brothers*. London: Oxford University Press.

Moosa, Ebrahim. 2014. "On Reading Shāṭibī in Rabat and Tunis." In *Maqāṣid al-Sharīʿa* and *Contemporary Reformist Thought. An Examination*, ed. Adis Duderija, 177–192. New York: Palgrave Macmillan

al-Nawawi, Muhyiddin Abu Zakariya bin Sharaf. "Adāb al-fatwā wal-muftī wal-mustaftī." In *Kitāb majmūʿ: Sharḥ al-muhadhdhab lil-shīrāzī*. Beirut: Dār ahya al-turāth al-ʿarabī.

al-Nawawi, Muhyiddin Abu Zakariya bin Sharaf. *The Etiquettes and Qualifications of Issuing Islamic Judgement, of a Mufti, and the One Seeking His Opinion*. Birmingham: Al-Fadani Publishers and Distributors.

Nettler, Ronald L. 2009. "Ibn Taymīyah." Ed. John L. Esposito. *The Oxford Encyclopedia of the Islamic World*. Oxford: Oxford University Press.

Nielsen, Jørgen S. 1999. *Towards a European Islam*. London: Macmillan Ltd.

Oubrou, Tareq. 2004. "La sharīʿa de minorité: réflexions pour une intégration légale de l'islam." In *Lectures Contemporaines du droit islamique: Europe et monde arabe*, ed. Franck Frégosi, 205–230. Strasbourg: Presses Universitaires de Strasbourg.

Peter, Frank. 2006. "Islamism, Islamic Reformism and the Public Stigmatization of Muslims: A Study of Muslim Discourses in France." *Oriente Moderno* (*Nuova Serie*) 25 (86) (3): 443–460.

Peter, Frank. 2012. "Muslim 'double Talk' and the Ways of the Shariʿa in France." In *The Muslim Brotherhood in Europe*, ed. Roel Meijer and Edwin Bakker, 127–148. New York: Columbia University Press.

Philipp, Thomas. 1978. "Feminism and Nationalist Politics in Egypt." In *Women in the Muslim World*, ed. Lois Beck and Nikki Keddie, 277–294. Cambridge: Harvard University Press.

Poulter, Sebastian. 1990. "The Claim to a Separate Islamic System of Personal Law for British Muslims." In *Islamic Family Law*, ed. Chibli Mallat and Jane Connors, 147–166. London: Graham and Trotman Ltd.

Powers, David. 2002. *Law, Society, and Culture in the Maghrib, 1300–1500*. Cambridge: Cambridge University Press.

Powers, David S. 1996. "The Art of the Legal Opinion: Al-Wansharisi on *Tawlīj*." In *Islamic Legal Interpretation: Muftis and Their Fatwas*, ed. Muhammad Khalid Masud, Brinkley Messick, and David Powers, 98–115. Massachusetts: Harvard University Press.

al-Qaradawi, Yusuf. 1991. *Islamic Awakening between Rejection and Extremism*. Herndon, Virginia: The International Institute of Islamic Thought.

al-Qaradawi, Yusuf. 1995. *Al-fatwā bayna l-inḍibāṭ wal-tasayyub*. Gjentrykk. Amman: Al-maktab al-islāmī.

al-Qaradawi, Yusuf. 2000a. *Al-shaykh al-Ghazālī kamā ʿaraftuhu: raḥlatun niṣf qarn*. Cairo: Dār al-shurūq.

al-Qaradawi, Yusuf. 2000b. *Min hadī al-islām: fatāwā muʿāṣira*. Vol. 1. Beirut: al-Maktaba al-islāmī.

al-Qaradawi, Yusuf. 2001. *Fī fiqh al-aqalliyyāt al-muslima: ḥayāt al-muslimīn wasaṭ al-mujtamaʿāt al-ukhrā*. Cairo: Dār al-shurūq.

al-Qaradawi, Yusuf. 2003a. *The Lawful and the Prohibited in Islam*. London: Al-Birr Foundation.

al-Qaradawi, Yusuf. 2003b. *Min hadī al-islām: fatāwā muʿāṣira*. Vol. 3. Beirut: al-Maktaba al-islāmī.

al-Qaradawi, Yusuf. 2003c. *Fiqh of Muslim Minorities: Contentious Issues and Recommended Solutions*. Cairo: Al-Falah Foundation.

al-Qaradawi, Yusuf. 2004. *Ibn qarya wal-kuttāb*. Vol. 2. Cairo: Dār al-shurūq.

al-Qaradawi, Yusuf. 2006. *Dirāsa fī fiqh maqāṣid al-sharīʿa: bayna al- maqāṣid al-kulliyya al-nuṣūṣ al-juzʾiyya*. Cairo: Dār al-shurūq.

al-Qaradawi, Yusuf. 2009. *Min hadī al-islām: fatāwā muʿāṣira*. Vol. 4. Cairo: Dār al-alam lil-nashr wal-tawzīʿ.

al-Qasimi, Jamal al-Din. 1986. *Al-fatwā fil-islām*. Beirut: Dār al-kutub al-ʿilmiyya.

Quraishi, Asifa, and Frank Vogel, eds. 2008. *The Islamic Marriage Contract: Case Studies in Islamic Family Law*. Cambridge, Massachusetts: Islamic Legal Studies Program, Harvard Law School.

Ramadan, Tariq. 2004. *Western Muslims and the Future of Islam*. Oxford: Oxford University Press.

Ramadan, Tariq. 2009a. *Radical Reform: Islamic Ethics and Liberation*. Oxford: Oxford University Press.

Ramadan, Tariq. 2009b. "A Call for a Moratorium on Corporal Punishment: The Debate in Review." In *New Directions in Islamic Thought. Exploring Reform and Muslim Tradition*, ed. Kari Vogt, Lena Larsen, and Christian Moe, 163–174. London: I.B. Tauris.

al-Raysuni, Ahmad. 2005. *Imam Al-Shatibi's Theory of the Higher Objectives and Intents of Islamic Law*. London: The International Institute of Islamic Thought.

Repstad, Pål. 1993. *Mellom nærhet og distanse: Kvalitative metoder i samfunnsfag*. 2nd ed. Oslo: Universitetsforlaget.

Roald, Anne Sofie. 2001a. *Women in Islam: The Western Experience*. London: Routledge.

Roald, Anne Sofie. 2001b. "The Wise Men: Democratisation and Gender Equalisation in the Islamic Message: Yusuf Al-Qaradawi and Ahmad Al-Kubaisi on the Air." *Encounters* 7 (1). http://dspace.mah.se:8080/handle/2043/12617.

Rohe, Mathias. 2007. *Muslim Minorities and the Law in Europe: Chances and Challenges*. New Delhi: Global Media Publication.

Roy, Olivier. 2007. *Secularism Confronts Islam*. New York: Columbia University Press.

Roy, Olivier. 2016. "The French National Front: From Christian Identity to *Laïcité*". In *Saving the People: How Populists Hijack Religion*, ed. Nadia Marzouki, Duncan Mc Donnell and Olivier Roy, 79–93. London: Hurst and Company.

Sabiq, Sayyid. 1987. *Fiqh al-sunna*. Beirut: Dār al-kitāb al-ʿarabī.

al-Saman, Muhammad Abdullah. 1961. "al-Ḥalāl wal-ḥarām fil-islām." *Majallat al-Azhar* 32 (10) (March): 1151–1152.

Sano, Mustafa Qutub. 2000. *Muʿjam muṣṭalaḥāt ʿuṣūl al-fiqh*. Beirut: Dār al-fikr.

Sarromaa, Sarra. 2009. "Kjønnsdiskurser i endring: om Det Nyes spørrespalte i 1957, 1968 og 1977." *Tidsskrift for ungdomsforskning* 9 (1): 41–64.

Schacht, Joseph. 1960. "Problems of Modern Islamic Legislation." *Studia Islamica* (12): 99–129.

Schacht, Joseph. 1991. *An Introduction to Islamic Law*. Oxford: Clarendon Press.

Schacht, Joseph, and J. Chelhod. 2010. "Raḍāʿ or Riḍāʿ, Also Raḍāʿa." *Encyclopaedia of Islam, Second Edition*. Brill. http://www.brillonline.nl/subscriber/entry?entry=islam COM-0896.

Sedgwick, Mark. 2009. *Muhammad Abduh: A Biography*. Cairo: The American University in Cairo Press.

Sfeir, Antoine, and René Andrau. 2005. *Liberté, égalité, islam: La république face au communautarisme*. Paris: Talandier Éditions.

Shahin, Emad el-Din. 2009. "Salafīyah." Ed. John L. Esposito. *The Oxford Encyclopedia of the Islamic World*. Oxford: Oxford University Press.

Shavit, Uriya. 2015. *Sharīʿa and Muslim Minorities. The* wasaṭī *and* salafī *approaches to* fiqh al-aqalliyāt al-Muslima. Oxford: Oxford University Press.

Sheppard, Gerald T., and Mircea Eliade. 1993. "Canon." *Encyclopedia of Religion*. MacMillan Reference Books.

Skarsaune, Elise. 2006. "Mann og muslim i 'likestillingslandet'. En studie av maskulinitetsforstillinger blant muslimske menn i Oslo." MA thesis in the History of Religion, Oslo: Department of Culture Studies and Oriental Languages, University of Oslo.

Skovgaard-Petersen, Jakob. 1997. *Defining Islam for the Egyptian State: Muftis and Fatwas of the Dār Al-Iftā*. Leiden: Brill.

Sky, Jeanette. 2007. *Kjønn og religion*. Oslo: Pax forlag A/S.

Stowasser, Barbara Freyer. 2009. "Yūsuf Al-Qaraḍāwī on Women." In *Global Mufti: The Phenomenon of Yūsuf Al-Qaraḍāwī*, ed. Bettina Gräf and Jakob Skovgaard-Petersen, 181–212. New York: Columbia University Press.

Stowasser, Barbara Freyer, and Zeinab Abul-Magd. 2008. "Legal Codes and Contemporary Fatawa: Muslim Women and Contesting Paradigms." *Hawwa—Journal of Women in the Middle East and the Islamic World* 6: 32–51.

Svennevig, Jan. 2009. *Språklig samhandling. Innføring i kommunikasjonsteori og diskursanalyse*. Oslo: Cappelen akademisk forlag.

Tallema, Essam. n.d. *Muhammad al-Ghazālī: rabbānī mala' al-dunya wa-shaghal al-nās*. Damaskus: Dar al-qalam.

Tedlock, Barbara. 1991. "From Participant Observation to the Observation of Participation: The Emergence of Narrative Ethnography." *Journal of Anthropological Research* 47 (1): 69–94.

Ternisien, Xavier. 2002. *La France des mosquées*. Paris: Albin Michel.

Ternisien, Xavier. 2005. *Les Frères musulmans*. Paris: Fayard.

Tranøy, Knut Erik. 2001. *Det åpne sinn: Moral og etikk mot et nytt årtusen*. Oslo: Universitetsforlaget.

Tucker, Judith. 1999. *In the House of the Law: Gender and Islamic Law in Ottoman Syria and Palestine*. Cairo: The American University in Cairo Press.

Tucker, Judith. 2008. *Women, Family, and Gender in Islamic Law*. Cambridge: Cambridge University Press.

Turki, Abdel-Magid. 1997. "Le *Muwaṭṭa'* de Mâlik, ouvrage de *fiqh*, entre le *ḥadîth* et le *ra'y*, ou Comment aborder l'étude du mâlikisme kairouanais au IV/Xe siècle." *Studia Islamica* (86): 5–35.

Tyan, E., and J.R. Walsh. 2009. "Fatwā." *Encyclopaedia of Islam, Second Edition*. Brill. http://www.brillonline.nl/subscriber/entry?entry=islam_COM-0219.

Vertovec, Steven. 1996. "Multiculturalism, Culturalism and Public Incorporation." *Ethnic and Racial Studies* 19 (1): 49–69.

Vikør, Knut S. 2005. *Between God and the Sultan: A History of Islamic Law*. London: Hurst & Co.

Vogt, Kari. 1995. *Kommet for å bli: islam i Vest-Europa*. Oslo: J.W. Cappelens Forlag AS.

Vogt, Kari. 2005. *Islam: tradisjon, fundamentalisme og reform*. Oslo: J.W. Cappelens Forlag AS.

Vogt, Kari, Lena Larsen, and Christian Moe, eds. 2009. *New Directions in Islamic Thought: Exploring Reform and Tradition*. London: I.B. Tauris.

Wadel, Cato. 1991. *Feltarbeid i egen kultur*. Flekkefjord: Seek A/S.

Warraich, Sohail Akbar, and Cassandra Balchin. 2006. *Recognising the Un-Recognised: Inter-Country Cases and Muslim Marriages & Divorces in Britain*. London: Women Living Under Muslim Laws.

Watt, Montgomery. 1979. *Islamic Philosophy and Theology*. Edinburgh: Edinburgh University Press.

Wehr, Hans. 1976. *A Dictionary of Modern Written Arabic*. Ed. J. Milton Cowan. 3rd ed. Wiesbaden: Harrassowitz.

Welchman, Lynn. 2007. *Women and Muslim Family Laws in Arab States: A Comparative Overview of Textual Development and Advocacy*. Amsterdam: Amsterdam University Press.

Witt-Brattström, Ebba. 2009. "Krigen mot kvinnene." *Klassekampens bokmagasin*, November 14.

Zaman, Muhammad Qasim. 2002. *The Ulama in Contemporary Islam: Custodians of Change*. Princeton: Princeton University Press.

Zaman, Muhammad Qasim. 2009. "The Ulama and Contestations on Religious Authority" in *Islam and Modernity. Key Issues and Debates*, ed. Muhammad Khalid Masud, Armando Salvatore and Martin van Bruinessen, 206–236. Edinburgh: Edinburgh University Press.

Zaman, Muhammad Qasim. 2012. *Modern Islamic Thought in a Radical Age: Religious Authority and Internal Criticism*. Cambridge; New York: Cambridge University Press.

Zomeño, Amalia. 2008. "The Stories in the Fatwas and the Fatwas in History." In *Narratives of Truth in Islamic Law*, ed. Baudouin Dupret, Barbara Drieskens, and Annelies Moors, 25–50. London: I.B. Tauris.

Zorgati, Ragnhild Johnsrud. 2007. "Beyond Boundaries: Islamic and Christian Texts Dealing with Conversion and Mixed Marriages in Medieval Iberia". Ph.D. dissertation, Oslo: Faculty of Humanities, University of Oslo.

Zuhur, Sherifa. 1992. *Revealing Reveiling: Islamist Gender Ideology in Contemporary Egypt*. SUNY Series in Middle Eastern Studies. Albany, NY: State University of New York Press.

Index of Quranic Verses Cited

General Index

If you have any questions regarding this title, please contact:

Koninklijke Brill BV
Plantijnstraat 2
2321 JC Leiden
Email: info@brill.com

Batch number: 10703823